ADOBE
FLASH
CS4 REVEALED

JIM SHUMAN

ADOBE
FLASH
CS4 REVEALED

JIM SHUMAN

DELMAR
CENGAGE Learning™

Australia • Brazil • Japan • Korea • Mexico • Singapore • Spain • United Kingdom • United States

DELMAR
CENGAGE Learning™

Adobe Flash CS4 Revealed

Jim Shuman

Vice President, Career and Professional Editorial:
Dave Garza

Director of Learning Solutions: Sandy Clark

Senior Acquisitions Editor: Jim Gish

Managing Editor: Larry Main

Product Managers: Jane Hosie-Bounar,
Nicole Calisi

Editorial Assistant: Sarah Timm

Vice President Marketing, Career and
Professional: Jennifer McAvey

Executive Marketing Manager:
Deborah S. Yarnell

Marketing Manager: Erin Brennan

Marketing Coordinator: Jonathan Sheehan

Production Director: Wendy Troeger

Senior Content Project Manager:
Kathryn B. Kucharek

Developmental Editor: Pam Conrad

Technical Editor: Sasha Vodnik

Art Directors: Bruce Bond, Joy Kocsis

Cover Design: Lisa Kuhn, Curio Press, LLC

Cover Art: Lisa Kuhn, Curio Press, LLC

Text Designer: Ann Small

Proofreader: Wendy Benedetto

Indexer: Alexandra Nickerson

Technology Project Manager:
Christopher Catalina

Production Technology Analyst:
Tom Stover

For product information and technology
assistance, contact us at
**Cengage Learning Customer & Sales Support,
1-800-354-9706**

For permission to use material from this text or
product, submit all requests online at
www.cengage.com/permissions
Further permissions questions can be e-mailed to
permissionrequest@cengage.com

Adobe® Photoshop®, Adobe® InDesign®, Adobe®
Illustrator®, Adobe® Flash®, Adobe® Dreamweaver®,
Adobe® Fireworks® and Adobe® Creative Suite® are trademarks or registered trademarks of Adobe Systems, Inc. in
the United States and/or other countries. Third party
products, services, company names, logos, design, titles,
words, or phrases within these materials may be trademarks of their respective owners.

Library of Congress Control Number: 2008938853

Hardcover edition:
ISBN-13: 978-1-4354-8259-3
ISBN-10: 1-4354-8259-X

Soft cover edition:
ISBN-13: 978-1-4354-4194-1
ISBN-10: 1-4354-4194-X

Delmar
5 Maxwell Drive
Clifton Park, NY 12065-2919
USA

Cengage Learning is a leading provider of customized learning solutions with office locations around the globe, including Singapore, the United Kingdom, Australia, Mexico,
Brazil, and Japan. Locate your local office at:
international.cengage.com/region

Cengage Learning products are represented in
Canada by Nelson Education, Ltd.

To learn more about Delmar, visit
www.cengage.com/delmar

Purchase any of our products at your local college
store or at our preferred online store
www.ichapters.com

Notice to the Reader

Printed in the United States of America
3 4 5 6 7 13 12 11 10

Revealed Series Vision

The Revealed Series is your guide to today's hottest multimedia applications. These comprehensive books teach the skills behind the application, showing you how to apply smart design principles to multimedia products such as dynamic graphics, animation, websites, software authoring tools, and digital video.

A team of design professionals including multimedia instructors, students, authors, and editors worked together to create this series. We recognized the unique learning environment of the multimedia classroom and created a series that:

- Gives you comprehensive step-by-step instructions

- Offers in-depth explanation of the "Why" behind a skill

- Includes creative projects for additional practice

- Explains concepts clearly using full-color visuals

It was our goal to create a book that speaks directly to the multimedia and design community—one of the most rapidly growing computer fields today. We think we've done just that, with a sophisticated and instructive book design.

—The Revealed Series

Author's Vision

Writing a textbook on a web application and animation program is quite challenging. How do you take such a feature-rich program like Adobe Flash CS4 and put it in a context that helps users learn? My goal is to provide a comprehensive, yet manageable, introduction to Adobe Flash CS4—just enough conceptual information to provide the needed context—and then move right into working with the application. My thought is that you'll get so caught up in the hands-on activities and compelling projects that you'll be pleasantly surprised at the level of Flash skills and knowledge you've acquired at the end of each chapter.

What a joy it has been to be a part of such a creative and energetic publishing team. The Revealed Series is a great format for teaching and learning Flash, and the Revealed Series team took the ball and ran with it. I would like to thank Nicole Pinard and Jim Gish, who provided the vision for the project, and Jane Hosie-Bounar for her management expertise, and everyone at Delmar and Cengage Learning for their professional guidance. A special thanks to Pam Conrad for her hard work, editorial expertise, and constant encouragement. I also want to give a heartfelt thanks to my wife, Barbara, for her patience and support. This book is dedicated to my loving mother, Roberta Gray Shuman.

—Jim Shuman

SERIES & AUTHOR VISION

v

Introduction to Adobe Flash CS4

Welcome to *Adobe Flash CS4—Revealed*. This book offers creative projects, concise instructions, and complete coverage of basic to advanced Adobe Flash CS4 skills, helping you to create and publish Flash animations. Use this book both while you learn and as your own reference guide.

This text is organized into 12 chapters. In these chapters, you will learn many skills to create interesting graphics-rich movies that include sound, animation, and interactivity. In addition, you will learn how to publish your own Flash movies.

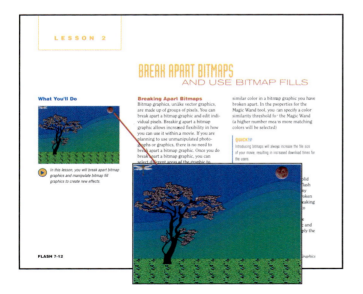

What You'll Do

A What You'll Do figure begins every lesson. This figure gives you an at-a-glance look at what you'll do in the chapter, either by showing you a page or pages from the current project or a tool you'll be using.

Comprehensive Conceptual Lessons

Before jumping into instructions, in-depth conceptual information tells you "why" skills are applied. This book provides the "how" and "why" through the use of professional examples. Also included in the text are tips and sidebars to help you work more efficiently and creatively, or to teach you a bit about the history or design philosophy behind the skill you are using.

Step-by-Step Instructions

This book combines in-depth conceptual information with concise steps to help you learn Flash CS4. Each set of steps guides you through a lesson where you will create, modify, or enhance a Flash CS4 file. Step references to large colorful images and quick step summaries round out the lessons. The Data Files for the steps are provided on the CD at the back of this book.

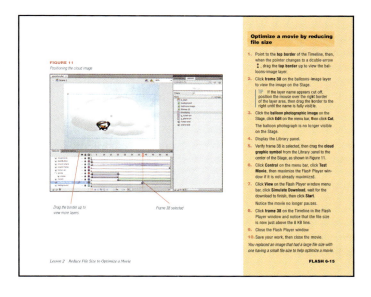

Projects

This book contains a variety of end-of-chapter materials for additional practice and reinforcement. The Skills Review contains hands-on practice exercises that mirror the progressive nature of the lesson material. The chapter concludes with four projects: two Project Builders, one Design Project, and one Portfolio Project. The Project Builders and the Design Project require you to apply the skills you've learned in the chapter. Portfolio Projects encourage students to solve challenges based on the content explored in the chapter and then add the completed projects to their portfolios.

What Instructor Resources Are Available with This Book?

The Instructor Resources CD-ROM is Delmar's way of putting the resources and information needed to teach and learn effectively into your hands. All the resources are available for both Macintosh and Windows operating systems.

Instructor's Manual

Available as an electronic file, the Instructor's Manual includes chapter overviews and detailed lecture topics for each chapter, with teaching tips. The Instructor's Manual is available on the Instructor Resources CD-ROM.

PowerPoint Presentations

Each chapter has a corresponding PowerPoint presentation that you can use in lectures, distribute to your students, or customize to suit your course.

Data Files for Students

To complete most of the chapters in this book, your students will need Data Files. The Data Files are available on the CD at the back of this text book. Instruct students to use the Data Files List at the end of this book. This list gives instructions on organizing files.

Solutions to Exercises

Solution Files are Data Files completed with comprehensive sample answers. Use these files to evaluate your students' work. Or distribute them electronically so students can verify their work. Sample solutions to all lessons and end-of-chapter material are provided.

Test Bank and Test Engine

ExamView is a powerful testing software package that allows instructors to create and administer printed and computer (LAN-based) exams. ExamView includes hundreds of questions that correspond to the topics covered in this text, enabling students to generate detailed study guides that include page references for further review. The computer-based and LAN-based/online testing component allows students to take exams using the EV Player, and also saves the instructor time by grading each exam automatically.

CHAPTER 3 | **WORKING WITH SYMBOLS AND INTERACTIVITY**

CHAPTER 4 CREATING ANIMATIONS

CHAPTER 11   USING ADVANCED ACTIONSCRIPT

CONTENTS

Intended Audience

This book is designed for the beginner or intermediate user who wants to learn how to use Adobe Flash CS4. The book is designed to provide basic and in-depth material that not only educates, but encourages you to explore the nuances of this exciting program.

Approach

The book allows you to work at your own pace through step-by-step tutorials. A concept is presented and the process is explained, followed by the actual steps. To learn the most from the use of the text, you should adopt the following habits:

- Proceed slowly: Accuracy and comprehension are more important than speed.

- Understand what is happening with each step before you continue to the next step.

- After finishing a process, ask yourself: Can I do the process on my own? If the answer is no, review the steps.

Icons, Buttons, and Pointers

Symbols for icons, buttons, and pointers are shown each time they are used.

Fonts

Data Files contain a variety of commonly used fonts, but there is no guarantee that these fonts will be available on your computer. Each font is identified in cases where fonts other than Arial or Times New Roman are used. If any of the fonts in use are not available on your computer, you can make a substitution, realizing that the results may vary from those in the book.

Windows and Macintosh

Adobe Flash CS4 works virtually the same on Windows and Macintosh operating systems. In those cases where there is a difference, the abbreviations (Win) and (Mac) are used.

Windows System Requirements

Adobe Flash CS4 requires the following:

- Microsoft® Windows® XP with Service Pack 2 (Service Pack 3 recommended) or Windows Vista™ Home Premium, Business, Ultimate, or Enterprise with Service Pack 1 (certified for 32-bit editions)

- 1GHz or faster processor

- 3.5GB of available hard-disk space (additional free space required during installation)

- 1GB of RAM

- 1024 × 768 monitor resolution with 16-bit video card

- DVD-ROM drive

- QuickTime 7.1.2 software required for multimedia features

Macintosh System Requirements

Adobe Flash CS4 requires the following:

- PowerPC® G4 or multicore Intel® processor

- Mac OS X v.10.4.11-10.5.4

- 1GB of RAM

- 1024 × 768 display (1,280 × 800 recommended) with 16-bit video card

- DVD-ROM drive

- 4GB of available hard-disk space for installation (additional free space required during installation)

- QuickTime 7.1.2 software required for multimedia features

Data Files

To complete the lessons in this book, you need the Data Files on the CD located on the inside back cover. Your instructor will tell you where to store the files as you work, such as to your hard drive, a network server, or a USB storage device. When referring to the Data Files for this book, the instructions in the lessons will mention "the drive and folder where your Data Files are stored."

Projects

Several projects are presented at the end of each chapter that allow students to apply the skills they have learned in the unit. Two projects, Ultimate Tours and the Portfolio, build from chapter to chapter. You will need to contact your instructor if you plan to work on these without having completed the previous chapter's project.

Creating a Portfolio

The Portfolio Project and Project Builders allow students to use their creativity to come up with original Flash animations and screen designs. You might suggest that students create a portfolio in which they can store their original work.

INDEX

INDEX

INDEX

INDEX

Flash CS4 Art Credits

Chapter	Art credit for opening pages
Chapter 1	© Dimitri Vervitsiotis/Digital Vision/Getty Images
Chapter 2	© Veer
Chapter 3	© Barbara Peacock/Photodisc/Getty Images
Chapter 4	© Stuart Westmorland/Digital Vision/Getty Images
Chapter 5	© Nick Norman/National Geographic Image Collection/Getty Images
Chapter 6	© Philip and Karen Smith/Digital Vision/Getty Images
Chapter 7	© Georgette Douwma/Photodisc/Getty Images
Chapter 8	© Veer
Chapter 9	© Jeff Rotman/Digital Vision/Getty Images
Chapter 10	© Paul Souders/Photodisc/Getty Images
Chapter 11	© Plush Studios/Digital Vision/Getty Images
Chapter 12	© David Tipling/Digital Vision/Getty Images
Data Files/Glossary/Index	© David Newham/Alamy

ART CREDITS

chapter

1

GETTING STARTED WITH
ADOBE FLASH CS4

1. Understand the Adobe Flash CS4 workspace

2. Open a document and play a movie

3. Create and save a movie

4. Work with the Timeline

5. Distribute an Adobe Flash movie

6. Plan an application or a website

GETTING STARTED WITH
ADOBE FLASH CS4

Introduction

Adobe Flash CS4 Professional is a development tool that allows you to create compelling interactive experiences, often by using animation. You can use Flash to create entire websites, including e-commerce, entertainment, education, and personal use sites. In addition, Flash is an excellent program for developing animations that are used in websites, such as product demonstrations, banner ads, online tutorials, and electronic greeting cards. Also, Flash can be used to create applications, such as games and simulations, that can be delivered over the web and on DVDs. These applications can even be scaled to be displayed on mobile devices, such as cell phones. While it is known as a tool for creating complex animations for the web, Flash also has excellent drawing tools and tools for creating interactive controls, such as navigation buttons and menus. Furthermore, Flash provides the ability to incorporate sounds and video easily into an application.

Flash has become the standard for both professional and casual applications as well as for web developers. Flash is popular because the program is optimized for the web. Web developers need to provide high-impact experiences for the user, which means making sites come alive and turning them from static

text and pictures to dynamic, interactive experiences. The problem has been that incorporating high-quality graphics and motion into a website can dramatically increase the download time and frustrate viewers as they wait for an image to appear or for an animation to play. Flash directly addresses this problem by allowing developers to use vector images, which reduce the size of graphic files. Vector images appeal to designers because they are scalable, which means they can be resized and reshaped without distortion. For example, using a vector graphic, you can easily have an object, such as an airplane, become smaller as it moves across the screen without having to create the plane in different sizes.

In addition, Flash provides for streaming content over the Internet. Instead of waiting for the entire contents of a web page to load, the viewer sees a continuous display of images. Another reason Flash has become a standard is that it is made by Adobe. Adobe makes other programs, such as Dreamweaver, Fireworks, Photoshop, and Illustrator. Together these products can be used to create compelling interactive websites and applications. This chapter provides an overview of Flash and presents concepts that are covered in more detail in later chapters.

Tools You'll Use

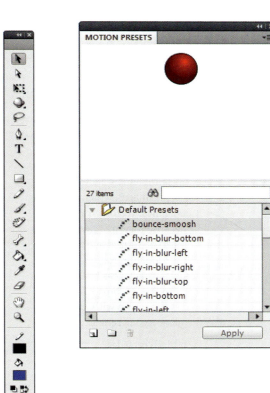

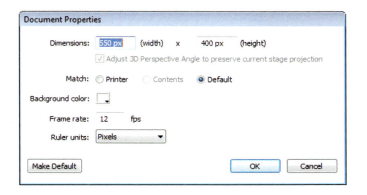

UNDERSTAND THE
ADOBE FLASH CS4 WORKSPACE

What You'll Do

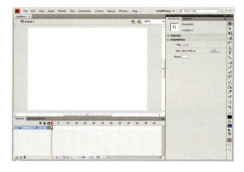

 In this lesson, you will learn about the development workspace in Adobe Flash and how to change Flash settings to customize your workspace.

Organizing the Flash Workspace

As a designer, one of the most important things for you to do is to organize your workspace—that is, to decide what to have displayed on the screen and how to arrange the various tools and panels. Because **Flash** is a powerful program with many tools, your workspace may become cluttered. Fortunately, it is easy to customize the workspace to display only the tools needed at any particular time.

The development process in Flash operates according to a movie metaphor: objects placed on the Stage also appear in frames on a Timeline. As you work in Flash, you create a movie by arranging objects (such as graphics and text) on the Stage, and then animating the objects using the Timeline. You can play the movie on the Stage as you are working on it by using the movie controls (start, stop, rewind, and so on). When done the movie can be incorporated into a website or as part of an application, such as a game.

When you start Flash, three basic parts of the workspace are displayed: a menu bar that organizes commands within menus, a Stage where objects are placed, and a Timeline used to organize and control the objects on the Stage. In addition, one or more panels may be displayed. Panels, such as the Tools panel, are used when working with objects and features of the movie. Figure 1 shows a typical Flash workspace.

Stage

The **Stage** contains all of the objects (such as drawings, photos, clip art, and text) that are part of the movie that will be seen by your viewers. It shows how the objects behave within the movie and how they interact with each other. You can resize the Stage and change the background color applied to it. You can draw objects directly on the Stage or drag them from the Library panel to the Stage. You can also import objects developed in another program directly to the Stage. You can specify the size of the Stage (in pixels), which will be the size of the area within your browser window that displays the movie. The gray area surrounding the Stage is the Pasteboard. You can place objects on the Pasteboard as you are creating a movie. However, neither the Pasteboard nor the objects on it will appear when the movie is played in a browser or the Flash Player.

Timeline (Frames and Layers)

The **Timeline** is used to organize and control the movie's contents by specifying when each object appears on the Stage. The Timeline is critical to the creation of movies because a movie is merely a series of still images that appear over time. The images are contained within **frames**, which are segments of the Timeline. Frames in a Flash movie are similar to frames in a motion picture. When a Flash movie is played, a playhead moves from frame to frame on the Timeline, causing the contents of each frame to appear on the Stage in a linear sequence.

The Timeline indicates where you are at any time within the movie and allows you to insert, delete, select, copy, and move frames. It shows the animation in your movie and the layers that contain objects. **Layers** help to organize the objects on the Stage. You can draw and edit objects on one layer without affecting objects on other layers. Layers are a way to stack objects so they can overlap and give a 3D appearance on the Stage.

Panels

Panels are used to view, organize, and modify objects and features in a movie. The most commonly used panels are the Tools panel, the Properties panel (also called the Property inspector), and the Library panel.

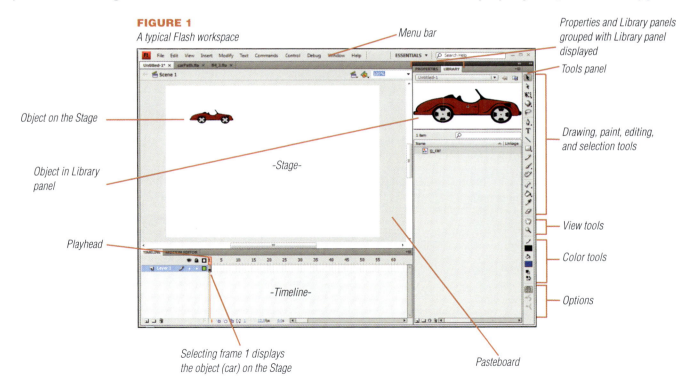

FIGURE 1
A typical Flash workspace

Properties and Library panels grouped with Library panel displayed

Tools panel

Object on the Stage

Object in Library panel

Drawing, paint, editing, and selection tools

-Stage-

Playhead

View tools

Color tools

-Timeline-

Options

Selecting frame 1 displays the object (car) on the Stage

Pasteboard

For example, the Properties panel is used to change the properties of an object, such as the fill color of a circle. The Properties panel is context sensitive, so that if you are working with text it displays the appropriate options, such as font and font size.

You can control which panels are displayed individually or you can choose to display panel sets. Panel sets are groups of the most commonly used panels. For example, the Properties and the Library panels are often grouped together to make a panel set. You use the Window menu on the menu bar to display and hide panels.

Tools Panel
The **Tools panel** contains a set of tools used to draw and edit graphics and text. It is divided into four sections.

The **Tools** section includes draw, paint, text, and selection tools, which are used to create lines, shapes, illustrations, and text. The selection tools are used to select objects so that they can be modified in several ways.

The **Views** section includes the Zoom tool and the Hand tool, which are used to zoom in on and out of parts of the Stage and to pan the Stage window, respectively.

The **Colors** section includes tools and icons used to change the stroke (border of an object) and fill (area inside an object) colors.

The **Options** section includes options for selected tools, such as allowing you to choose the size of the brush when using the Brush tool.

Although several panels open automatically when you start Flash, you may choose to display them only when they are needed. This keeps your workspace from becoming too cluttered. Panels are floating windows, meaning that you can move them around the workspace. This allows you to group (dock) panels together as a way to organize them in the workspace. In addition, you can control how a panel is displayed. That is, you can expand a panel to show all of its features or collapse it to show only the title bar. Collapsing panels reduces the clutter on your workspace, provides a larger area for the Stage, and still provides easy access to often used panels.

If you choose to rearrange panels, first decide if you want a panel to be grouped (docked) with another panel, stacked above or below another panel, a floating panel, or simply a stand-alone panel. An example of each of these is shown in Figure 2.

Arranging panels can be a bit tricky. It's easy to start moving panels around and find that the workspace is cluttered with panels arranged in unintended ways. While you cannot use the Flash Undo feature on the Edit menu to undo a panel move, you can always close a panel or choose the Reset Essentials option from the Workspace command on the Windows

FIGURE 2
Arranging panels

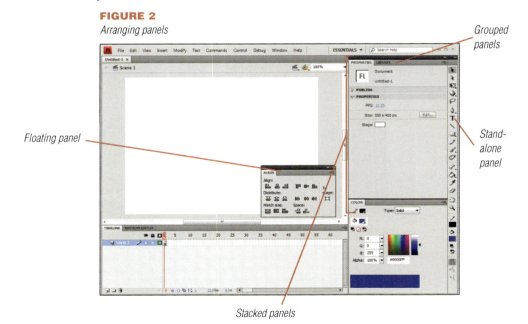

Floating panel

Grouped panels

Stand-alone panel

Stacked panels

menu. This command displays the default panel arrangement, which is a good starting position when working with Flash.

The key to rearranging panels is the blue drop zone that appears when a panel is being moved. Refer to Figure 3. The drop zone is the area to which the panel can move and is indicated by either a blue line or a rectangle with a blue border. A single blue line indicates the position for stacking a panel above or below another panel. A rectangle with a blue border indicates the position for grouping panels. If you move a panel without using a drop zone, the panel becomes a floating panel and is neither grouped nor stacked with other panels. To move a panel, you drag the panel by its tab until the desired blue drop zone appears, then you release the mouse button. (*Note*: Dragging a panel by its tab moves only that panel. To move a panel set you must drag the group by its title bar.)

Figure 3 shows the Library panel being grouped with the Properties panel. The process is to drag the Library panel tab adjacent to the Properties panel tab. Notice the rectangle with the blue border that surrounds the Properties panel. This indicates the drop zone for the Library panel which groups them together. Figure 4 shows the Library panel after being ungrouped and placed as a floating panel.

FIGURE 3
Grouping the Library panel

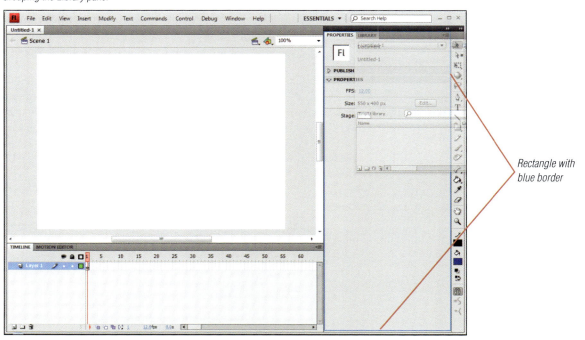

Rectangle with blue border

In addition to moving panels, you can collapse them so that only the title bar appears, and then you can expand them to display the entire panel. The Collapse to Icons button is located in the upper-right corner of each panel, as shown in Figure 4. The Collapse to Icons button is a toggle button, which means it changes or toggles between two states. When clicked, the Collapse to Icons button changes to the Expand Panels button. Finally, if you want to close a panel, you can use the Close option from the drop down menu on the panel title bar, as shown in Figure 4 or you can deselect a panel option on the Windows menu.

Regardless of how you decide to customize your development workspace, the Stage and the menu bar are always displayed. Usually, you display the Timeline, Tools panel, Library panel, Properties panel, and one or more other panels.

Other changes that you can make to the workspace are to change the size of the Stage, move the Stage around the Pasteboard, and change the size of the Timeline panel. To increase the size of the Stage so that the objects on the Stage can be more easily edited, you can change the magnification setting using commands on the View menu or by using the View tools on the Tools panel. The Hand tool on the Tools panel and the scroll bars at the bottom and right of the Stage can be used to reposition the Stage. The Timeline can be resized by dragging the top border. The more complex your Flash movie, the more layers that are used in the Timeline. Increasing the size of the Timeline allows you to view several layers at one time.

FIGURE 4

Ungrouping the Library panel

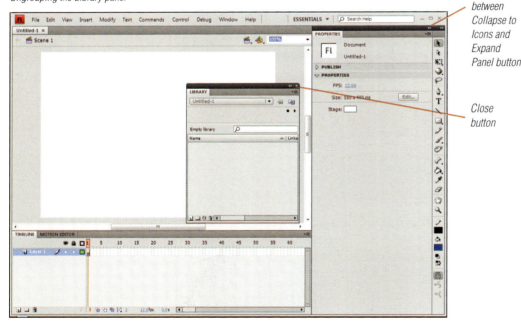

Toggle between Collapse to Icons and Expand Panel button

Close button

QUICKTIP

When working with panels, you can collapse, move, and close them as suits your working style. Settings for an object are not lost if you close or collapse a panel. If, at any time the panels have become confusing, simply return to the Essentials workspace and open panels as needed.

Getting Started with Adobe Flash CS4

FIGURE 5

The Flash Welcome screen

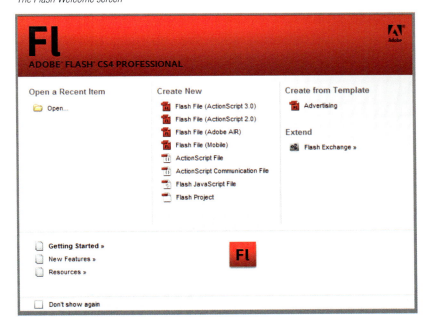

Start Adobe Flash and work with panels

1. Start the Adobe Flash CS4 program **Fl** .

   The Adobe Flash CS4 Welcome screen appears, as shown in Figure 5. This screen allows you to open a recent document or create a new Flash file.

2. Click **Flash File (ActionScript 3.0)** under Create New.

3. Click **Window** on the menu bar, point to **Workspace**, then click **Reset 'Essentials'**.

   TIP As you are rearranging your workspace, you can always select the Reset 'Essentials' option on the Window Workspace submenu to display the default workspace.

4. Click **Window** on the menu bar, then note the panels with check marks. The check marks identify which panels are open.

   TIP The Properties and Library panels may be grouped depending upon the configuration of your Essentials workspace. If so, only the panel that is active (the tab that is selected) will have a check mark.

5. With the Windows menu still open, click **Hide Panels**.

6. Click **Window** on the menu bar, then click **Timeline**.

7. Click **Window** on the menu bar, then click **Tools**.

8. Click **Window** on the menu bar, then click **Library**.

9. Click **Window** on the menu bar, then click **Properties**.

   At this point the Library and Properties panels should be grouped.

10. Click the **Library panel tab** to display the panel.

11. Click the **Properties panel tab** to display the panel.

(continued)

12. Click the **Library panel tab**, then drag the **panel** to the Stage as a floating panel.

13. Click the **Collapse to Icons button** on the Library panel title bar.

14. Click the **Expand Panels button** on the Library panel title bar.

15. Click the **Library panel tab**, drag the **panel** to the right of the Properties panel tab, then when a rectangle with a blue border appears, release the mouse button to group the panels, as shown in Figure 6.

    Note: If the panels do not appear as shown in Figure 6, repeat the step making sure there is a rectangle with a blue border before releasing the mouse button.

16. Click the **Collapse to Icons button** in the upper-right corner of the grouped panels, as shown in Figure 6.

17. Click the **Expand Panels button** delete icon to display the grouped panels.

18. Click **Window** on the menu bar, point to **Workspace**, then click **Reset 'Essentials'**.

    The Essentials workspace appears.

You started Flash and configured the workspace by hiding, moving, and displaying selected panels.

Change the Stage view and display of the Timeline

1. Click **View** on the menu bar, point to **Magnification**, then click **50%**.

2. Click the **Hand tool** 🖑 on the Tools panel, click the middle of the Stage, then drag the **Stage** around the Pasteboard.

(continued)

FIGURE 6
Library panel grouped with the Properties panel

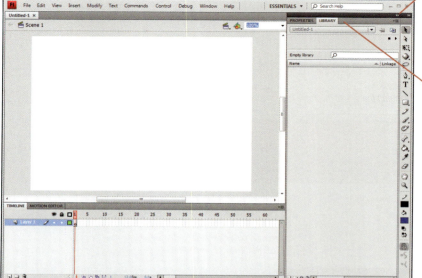

Use to toggle between Collapse to Icons and Expand Panel button

Grouped panels

Note: If your panels do not group, continue to drag the Library panel tab making sure the rectangle with a blue border appears before releasing the mouse button

Understanding your workspace

Organizing the Flash workspace is like organizing your desktop. You may work more efficiently if you have many of the most commonly used items in view and ready to use. Alternately, you may work better if your workspace is relatively uncluttered, giving you more free "desk space." Fortunately, Flash makes it easy for you to decide which items to display and how they are arranged while you work. For example, to toggle the Main toolbar, click Window on the menu bar, point to Toolbars, then click Main. You should become familiar with quickly opening, collapsing, expanding, and closing the various windows, toolbars, and panels in Flash, and experimenting with different layouts and screen resolutions to find the workspace that works best for you.

FIGURE 7

Changing the size of the Timeline panel

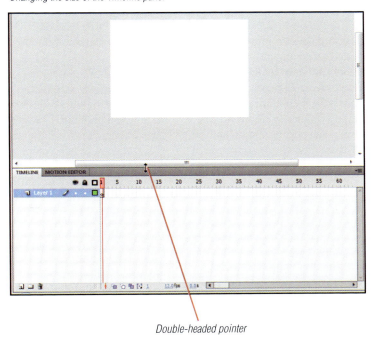

Double-headed pointer

3. Move the pointer to the top of the Timeline title bar, when the pointer changes to a double-headed pointer ↕ , click and drag up to increase the size of the Timeline, as shown in Figure 7.

   Increasing the size of the Timeline panel allows you to view more layers as you add them to the Timeline.

4. Point to the top of the Timeline title bar, when the pointer changes to a double-headed pointer ↕ , click and drag the **title bar** down to decrease the size of the Timeline.

5. Double-click the word **TIMELINE** to collapse the Timeline.

6. Double-click the word **TIMELINE** again to expand the Timeline.

7. Click **View** on the menu bar, point to **Magnification**, then click **100%**.

8. Click **ESSENTIALS** on the menu bar, then click **Reset 'Essentials'**.

   This resets the workspace to the Essentials template.

9. Click the **Selection tool** ▶ on the Tools panel.

10. Click **File** on the menu bar, then click **Save**.

11. Navigate to the drive and folder where your Data Files are stored, type **workspace** for the filename, then click **Save**.

12. Click **File** on the menu bar, then click **Close**.

You used a View command to change the magnification of the Stage; you used the Hand tool to move the Stage around the workspace; you resized, collapsed, and expanded the Timeline panel; then you saved the document.

OPEN A DOCUMENT
AND PLAY A MOVIE

What You'll Do

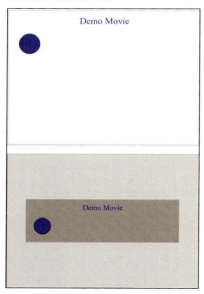

 In this lesson, you will open a Flash document (movie); preview, test, and save the movie; then change the movie's document settings.

Opening a Movie in Flash

Flash files are called documents (or movies, interchangeably) and have an .fla file extension. If you have created a movie in Flash and saved it with the name mymovie, the filename will be mymovie.fla. Files with the .fla file extension can only be opened and edited using Flash. After they are opened, you can edit and resave them.

In order for Flash movies to be viewed on computers that do not have the Flash program installed, the movies must be changed to the Flash Player (.swf) file format. Files using the .swf file format are created from Flash movies using the Publish command. Flash .swf movies can be played in a browser without the Flash program, but the Flash Player must be installed on the computer. Flash Players are pre-installed on almost all computers. For those that do not have the player, it can be downloaded free from the Adobe website, *www.adobe.com*. Because .swf files cannot be edited in the Flash program, you should preview the Flash .fla files on the Stage and test them before you publish them as .swf files. Be sure to keep the original .fla file so that you can make changes if needed at a later date.

Previewing a Movie

After creating a new Flash movie or opening a previously saved movie, you can preview it within the workspace in several ways. When you preview a movie, you play the frames by directing the playhead to move through the Timeline, and you watch the movement on the Stage.

Control Menu Commands (and Keyboard Shortcuts)

Figure 8 shows the Control menu commands, which resemble common DVD-type options:

- Play ([Enter] (Win) or [return] (Mac)) begins playing the movie frame by frame, from the location of the playhead to the end of the movie. For example, if the playhead is on frame 5 and the last frame is frame 40, choosing the Play command will play frames 5–40 of the movie.

When a movie starts, the Play command changes to a Stop command. You can also stop the movie by pressing [Enter] (Win) or [return] (Mac).

- Rewind ([Shift][,] (Win)) or [option] ⌘ [R] (Mac) moves the playhead to frame 1.
- Step Forward One Frame (.) moves the playhead forward one frame at a time.
- Step Backward One Frame (,) moves the playhead backward one frame at a time.

You can turn on the Loop Playback setting to allow the movie to continue playing repeatedly. A check mark next to the Loop Playback command on the Control menu indicates that the feature is active. To turn off this feature, click the Loop Playback command.

Controller

You can also preview a movie using the Controller. To display the Controller, click the Controller option on the Toolbars command of the Window menu.

The decision of which controls to use (the Control menu, keyboard shortcuts, or the Controller) is a matter of personal preference.

Testing a Movie

When you play a movie within workspace, some interactive fu (such as buttons that are used to jump from one part of the movie to another) do not work. To preview the full functionality of a movie you need to play it using a Flash Player. You can use the Test Movie command on the Control menu to test the movie using a Flash Player.

You can drag the playhead along the Timeline to play frames and display their contents on the Stage. This process, called "scrubbing," provides a quick way to view parts of the movie.

FIGURE 8
Control menu commands

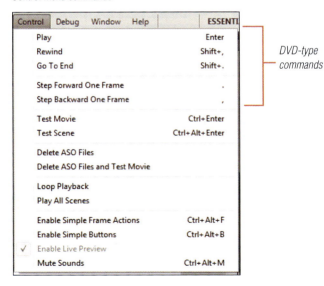

DVD-type commands

Test a movie

1. Click **Control** on the menu bar, then click **Test Movie**.
   The Flash Player window opens, as shown in Figure 11 and the movie starts playing automatically.

2. Click **Control** on the menu bar of the Flash Player window (Win) or application menu bar (Mac), then review the available commands.

3. Click **File** on the menu bar of the Flash Player window (Win) or application menu bar (Mac), then click **Close** to close the Flash Player window.

4. Use your file management program to navigate to the drive and folder where you saved the demomovie.fla file and notice the demomovie.swf file that was created when you tested the movie in the Flash Player window.

   > TIP   When you test a movie, Flash automatically creates a file that has an .swf extension in the folder where your movie is stored and then plays the movie in the Flash Player.

5. Return to the Flash program.

You tested a movie in the Flash Player window and viewed the .swf file created as a result of testing the movie.

FIGURE 11
Flash Player window

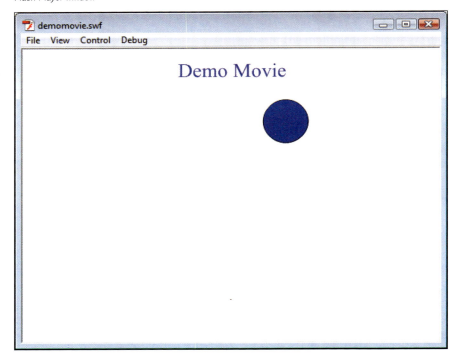

FIGURE 12

Document Properties dialog box

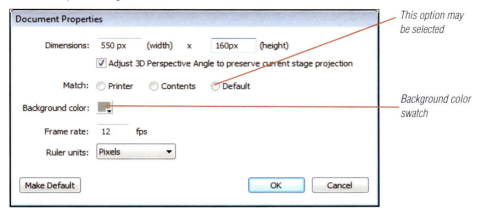

This option may be selected

Background color swatch

FIGURE 13

Completed changes to document properties

This value might differ

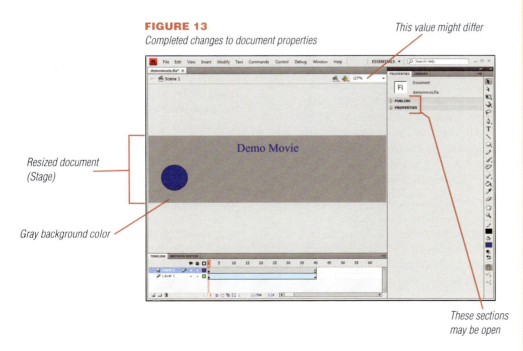

Resized document (Stage)

Gray background color

Demo Movie

These sections may be open

Change the Document Properties

1. Click **Modify** on the menu bar, then click **Document** to display the Document Properties dialog box.

2. Double-click the number in the **height text box**, then type **160**.

3. Click the **Background color swatch**, then click the **middle gray (#999999) color swatch** in the far-left column of the color palette.

   Note: The Color Swatch palette allows you to click a color to choose it or to enter a number that represents the color.

4. Review the remaining default values shown in Figure 12, then click **OK**.

5. Click **View** on the menu bar, point to **Magnification**, then click **Fit in Window** if it is not already selected. Your screen should resemble Figure 13.

6. Click **File** on the menu bar, then click **Save As**.

7. Navigate to the drive and folder where your Data Files are stored, type **demomovie banner** for the filename, then click **Save** (Win) or **Save As** (Mac).

8. Click **File** on the menu bar, then click **Close**.

You set the document properties including the size of the Stage and background color, then set the magnification and saved the document.

CREATE AND SAVE
A MOVIE

What You'll Do

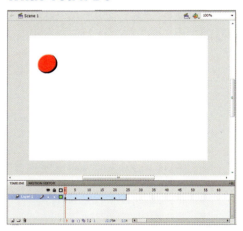

In this lesson, you will create a Flash movie that will include a simple animation, you will add animation effects, and then save the movie.

Creating a Flash Movie

Flash movies are created by placing objects (graphics, text, sounds, photos, and so on) on the Stage, editing these objects (for example, changing their brightness), animating the objects, and adding interactivity with buttons and menus. You can create graphic objects in Flash using the drawing tools, or you can create them in another program, such as Adobe Fireworks, Illustrator, or Photoshop, and then import them into a Flash movie. In addition, you can acquire clip art and stock photographs and import them into a movie. When objects are placed on the Stage, they are automatically placed on a layer and in the currently selected frame of the Timeline.

Figure 14 shows a movie that has an oval object created in Flash. Notice that the playhead is on frame 1 of the movie. The object placed on the Stage appears in frame 1 and appears on the Stage when the playhead is on frame 1. The dot in frame 1

on the Timeline indicates that this frame is a keyframe. The concept of keyframes is critical to understanding how Flash works. A **keyframe** indicates that there is a change in the movie, such as the start or end of an animation, or the playing of a sound. A keyframe is automatically designated in frame 1 of every layer. In addition, you can designate any frame to be a keyframe.

The circle object in Figure 14 was created using the Oval tool. To create an oval or a rectangle, you select the desired tool and then drag the pointer over an area on the Stage. *Note:* Flash groups the Oval and Rectangle tools, along with three other drawing tools, using one button on the Tools panel. To display a menu of these tools, click and hold the rectangle (or oval) button on the Tools panel to display the menu and then click the tool you want to use. If you want to draw a perfect circle or square, press and hold [Shift] after the tool is selected, and then drag the pointer.

If you make a mistake, you can click Edit on the menu bar, and then click Undo. To make changes to an object, such as resizing or changing its color, or to animate an object, you must first select it. You can use the Selection tool to select an entire object or group of objects. You drag the Selection tool pointer around the entire object to make a **marquee**. An object that has been selected displays a dot pattern or a blue border.

Creating an Animation

Figure 15 shows another movie that has 12 frames, as specified in the Timeline. The blue background color on the Timeline indicates a motion animation that starts in frame 1 and ends in frame 12. The dotted line indicates the path the object will follow during the animation. In this case, the object will move from left to right across the Stage. The movement of the object is caused by having the object in different places on the Stage in different frames of the movie. In this case, frame 6 will display the object midway through the animation. A basic motion animation requires two keyframes. The first keyframe sets the starting position of the object, and the second keyframe sets the ending position of the object. The number of frames between the two keyframes determines the length of the animation. For example, if the starting keyframe is frame 1 and the ending

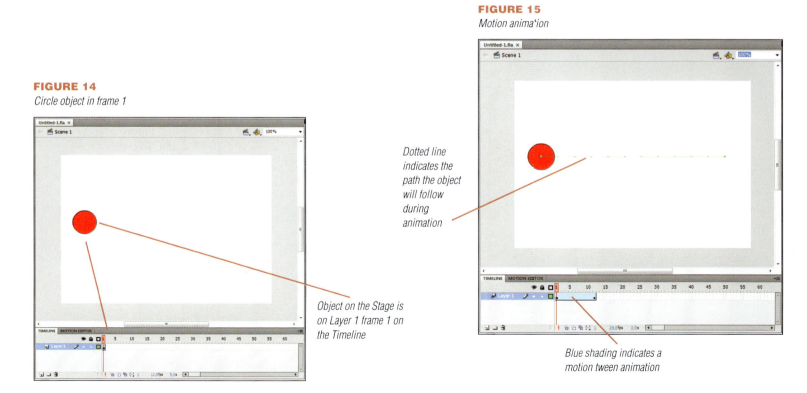

FIGURE 15
Motion animation

Dotted line indicates the path the object will follow during animation

FIGURE 14
Circle object in frame 1

Object on the Stage is on Layer 1 frame 1 on the Timeline

Blue shading indicates a motion tween animation

keyframe is frame 12, the object will be animated for 12 frames. As an object is being animated, Flash automatically fills in the frames between them, with a process called **motion tweening**.

The Motion Tween Animation Process

Having an object move around the screen is one of the most common types of animations. Flash provides a process called motion tween that makes it relatively simple to move objects. The process is to select an object on the Stage, then select the Motion Tween command from the Insert menu. If the object is not a symbol, a dialog box opens asking if you want to change the object into a symbol. Creating a symbol allows you to reuse the object for this and other movies, as well as to apply a motion tween. Only symbols can be motion tweened. The final step in the animation process is to select the ending frame for the animation and drag the object to another location on the Stage.

Two important things happen during the animation process. First, the Timeline shows the **tween span** (also called motion span), that is the number of frames in the motion tween. The tween span can be identified on the Timeline by a blue color, which in this case extends for 12 frames. A tween span is equal to one second in duration. The number of frames in a tween span varies and is determined by the number of frames per second setting. In this example, we set the number of frames per second to 12, so the number of frames in a tween for this movie is 12 frames. You can use the Document option from the Modify menu to change the frames per second. You can increase or decrease the length of the animation by pointing to either end of the span and dragging it to a new frame. Second, a dotted line, as shown in Figure 16, called the **motion path**, represents the path

FIGURE 16
Line showing the motion path

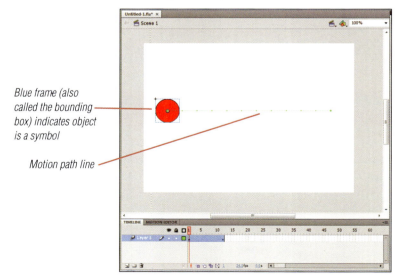

Blue frame (also called the bounding box) indicates object is a symbol

Motion path line

the object takes from the beginning frame to the ending frame. This path can be reshaped to cause the object to travel in a non-linear way. Reshaping a path can be done by using the Selection tool on the Tools panel.

Motion Presets

Flash provides several preconfigured motion tweens that you can apply to an object on the Stage. These allow you to bounce an object across the Stage, fly-in an object from off the Stage, cause an object to pulsate and to spiral in place, as well as many other types of object animations. Figure 17 shows the Motion Presets panel where you choose a preset and apply it to an object. You can preview each preset before applying it and you can easily change to a different preset, if desired.

Adding Effects to an Object

In addition to animating the location of an object (or objects), you can also animate an object's appearance. Objects have proper-ties such as color, brightness, and size. You can alter an object's properties as it is being animated using the motion tween process. For example, you could give the appearance of the object fading in by changing its transparency (alpha setting) or having it grow larger by altering its size over the course of the animation. Another useful effect is applying filters, such as drop shad-ows or bevels. All of these changes can be made using the Properties panel after selecting the object.

FIGURE 17

Motion Presets panel

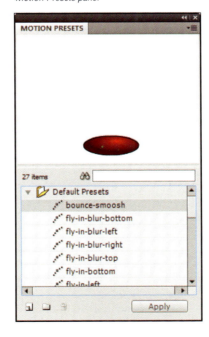

Create objects using drawing tools

1. Click **File** on the menu bar, then click **New**.
2. Click **OK** in the New Document window to choose Flash File (ActionScript 3.0) as the new document to create, then save the movie as **tween**.
3. Click **View** on the menu bar, point to **Magnification**, then click **100%**.
4. Click and hold the **Rectangle tool** ▭ (or the Oval tool if it is displayed) on the Tools panel to display the list of tools, as shown in Figure 18, then click the **Oval tool** ◯.
5. Verify that the Object Drawing option ◯ in the Options area of the Tools panel is deselected, as shown in Figure 18.
6. Click the **Fill Color tool color swatch** on the Tools panel, then, if necessary, click the **red color swatch** in the left column of the color palette.
7. Click the **Stroke Color tool color swatch** on the Tools panel, then, if necessary, click the **black color swatch** in the left column of the color palette.
8. Press and hold **[Shift]**, drag the **pointer** on the left side of the Stage to draw the circle, as shown in Figure 19, then release the mouse button.

   Pressing and holding [Shift] creates a circle.
9. Click the **Selection tool** ▸ on the Tools panel, then drag a **marquee** around the object to select it, as shown in Figure 20, then release the mouse button

   The object appears covered with a dot pattern.

You created an object using the Oval tool and then selected the object using the Selection tool.

FIGURE 18
Drawing tools menu

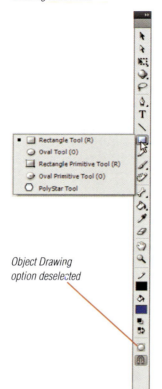

Object Drawing
option deselected

FIGURE 19
Drawing a circle

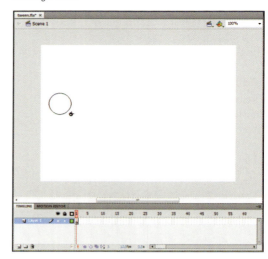

FIGURE 20
Creating a marquee selection

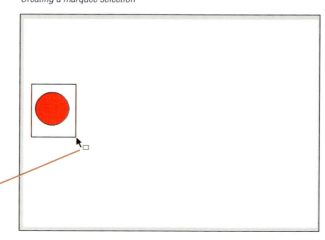

Use the Selection tool to
draw a marquee, which
selects the entire object

FIGURE 21

The circle on the right side of the Stage

Indicates the
active frame,
which is
frame 12

FIGURE 22

Pointing to the end of the tween span

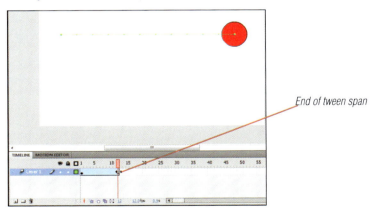

End of tween span

Create a motion tween animation

1. Click **Insert** on the menu bar, then click **Motion Tween**, which opens the Convert selection to symbol for tween dialog box.

2. Click **OK**.

   A blue border surrounds the object indicating that the object is selected. In this case the play-head automatically moved to frame 12, the last frame in the tween span. *Note:* Depending on the frames per second setting, your playhead may be on another frame.

3. Click and then drag the **circle** to the right side of the Stage, as shown in Figure 21.

4. Press **[Enter]**(Win) or **[return]**(Mac) to play the movie.

   The playhead moves through frames 1–12 on the Timeline, and the circle moves across the Stage.

5. Click **frame 6** on Layer 1 on the Timeline.

   Notice that the object is halfway across the screen. This is the result of the tweening process in which the frames between 1 and 12 are filled in with the object in the correct location for each frame.

6. Verify the Selection tool ![cursor] is selected, point to the end of the tween span until the pointer changes to a double-headed arrow ↔, as shown in Figure 22.

7. Click and drag the **tween span** to frame 48.

8. Press **[Enter]**(Win) or **[return]**(Mac) to play the movie.

   Notice it now takes longer (4 seconds, not 1 second) to complete the animation. Also notice that a diamond symbol appears in

   (continued)

frame 48 indicating that a keyframe has been placed in that frame. The diamond symbol indicates a change in the animation. In this case it indicates the end of the animation.

9. Click **frame 24** and notice that the object is still halfway across the screen.

10. Click **File** on the menu bar, then click **Save**.

You created a motion tween animation and changed the length of the tween span.

Reshaping the Motion Path

1. Click **File** on the menu bar, click **Save As**, then save the document with the filename **tween-effects.fla**.

2. Verify the Selection tool ▲ is selected.

3. Click **frame 1** to select it.

   Note: When you see the direction to click a frame, click the frame on the layer not the number on the Timeline.

4. Point to just below the middle of the path until the pointer changes to a pointer with an arc ↳ , as shown in Figure 23.

5. Click and drag the **path** to reshape the path, as shown in Figure 24.

6. Play the movie.

   Note: When you see the direction to play the movie, press [Enter] (Win) or [return] (Mac).

7. Test the movie.

   Note: When you see the direction to test the movie, click Control on the menu bar, then click Test Movie.

8. View the movie, then close the Flash Player window.

(continued)

FIGURE 23
Using the Selection tool to reshape a motion path

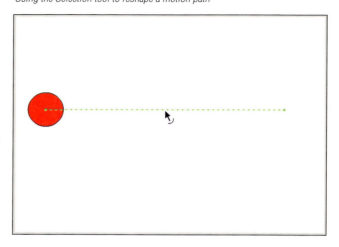

FIGURE 24
Reshaping the motion path

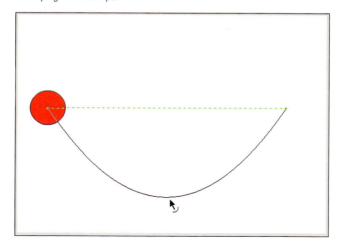

You used the Selection tool to reshape a motion path and the Undo command to undo the reshape.

Changing the transparency of an object

1. Click the **Properties panel tab** to display the Properties panel, as shown in Figure 25.

   Note: If the Properties panel is not open, click Window on the menu bar, then click Properties.

2. Verify frame 1 is selected, then click the **object** on the Stage to select it.

   Note: To verify the object is selected, review the available settings in the Properties panel. Make sure POSITION AND SIZE is one of the options.

3. Click **COLOR EFFECT** on the Properties panel, click the **Style list arrow**, then click **Alpha**.

4. Drag the **Alpha slider** △ to **0**.

   This causes the object to become transparent.

5. Click **frame 48** on the layer to select it.

6. Click **the middle of the bounding box** on the Stage to select the object and check that the object's properties are displayed in the Properties panel.

   Note: To verify the object is selected, review the available settings in the Properties panel. Make sure POSITION AND SIZE is one of the options.

   (continued)

FIGURE 25

The Properties panel displayed

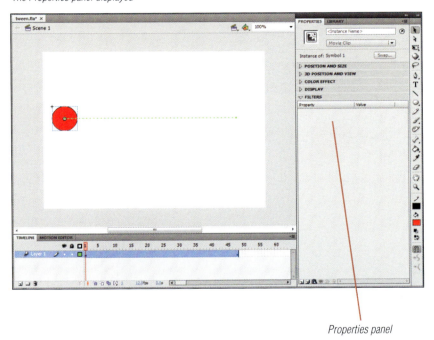

Properties panel

7. Drag the **Alpha slider** to **100**.

8. Play the movie.

9. Test the movie.

10. View the movie, then close the Flash Player window.

You used the Color Effect option on the Properties panel to change the transparency of an object.

Resize an object

1. Click **frame 1** select it.

2. Click the **object** to select it.

3. Click **POSITION AND SIZE** on the Properties panel if this section is not already open.

4. Review the width (W) and height (H) of the object.

The width and height are the dimensions of the bounding box around the circle.

5. Click **frame 48** to select it, then click the **object** to select it.

6. Point to the number for the width and when the pointer changes into a double-headed arrow, drag the **pointer** right to increase the width so that the circle grows in size to 80, as shown in Figure 26.

Hint: You can also double-click a value in the Properties panel and type the new value.

7. Play the movie.

8. Test the movie.

9. View the movie, then close the Flash Player window.

(continued)

FIGURE 26
Resizing the circle

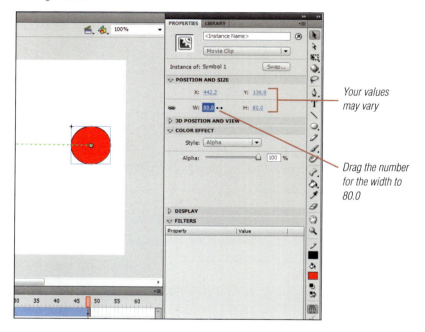

Your values may vary

Drag the number for the width to 80.0

FIGURE 27

The Add filter icon

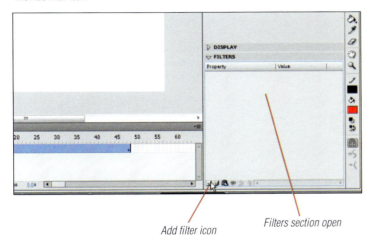

Add filter icon   Filters section open

10. Click **frame 1** to select it, then click the **object** to select it.

11. Drag the **Alpha slider** 🏠 to **100**.

You used the Position and Size option on the Properties panel to change the size of an object.

Add a filter to an object

1. Verify the object is selected by viewing the Properties panel and verifying the object's properties are displayed.

2. Click **FILTERS** on the Properties panel to display the Filters section if it is not already displayed.

3. Click the **Add filter icon** 🔲 at the bottom of the Filters section, as shown in Figure 27.

4. Click **Drop Shadow**, point to the number for the angle, when the pointer changes to a double-headed arrow 🔄 , drag the 🔄 **pointer** right to change the number of degrees to **100**.

5. Play the movie.

6. Click **frame 1** to select it, then click the **object** to select it.

7. Click the **Delete Filter icon** 🗑 at the bottom of the Filters section to remove the drop shadow filter.

8. Click the **Add filter icon** 🔲 at the bottom of the panel.

(continued)

9. Click **Bevel**, test the movie, then close the Flash Player window.

10. Point to the number for the Filter distance and when the pointer changes into a double-headed arrow ↔ , drag the ↔ **pointer** right to increase the setting to **35**.

You used the Filters option in the Properties panel to add and delete filters.

Add a motion preset

1. Verify the playhead is on frame 1 and the object is selected.

2. Click **Window** on the menu bar, then click **Motion Presets**.

3. Drag the **Motion Presets panel** so that it does not obscure the Stage.

4. Click the **list arrow** for the Default Presets, then click **bounce-smoosh** and watch the animation in the preview widow, as shown in Figure 28.

5. Click **Apply**.

   A dialog box opens asking if you want to replace the current motion object with the new selection. You can only apply one motion tween or motion preset to an object at any one time.

6. Click **Yes**.

   The bevel filter is deleted and a new path is displayed.

7. Play the movie, then test the movie.

   Notice the object disappears from the Stage.

   (continued)

FIGURE 28
The Motion Presets panel

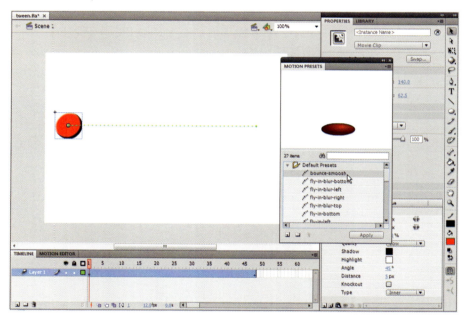

FIGURE 33
Drawing a square

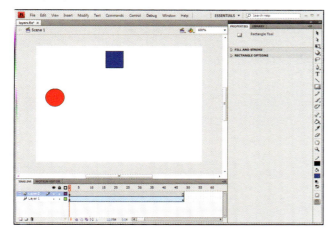

FIGURE 34
Positioning the square at the bottom of the Stage

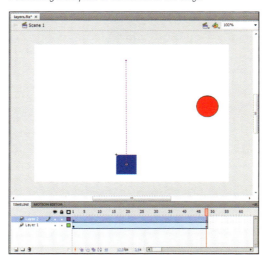

Add a layer

1. Open tween.fla and save it as **layers.fla**.
2. Click **frame 1** on Layer 1.
3. Click **Insert** on the menu bar, point to **Timeline**, then click **Layer**.

   A new layer—Layer 2—appears at the top of the Timeline.

You added a layer to the Timeline.

Create a second animation

1. Click **frame 1** on Layer 2.
2. Select the **Rectangle tool** on the Tools panel.
3. Click the **Fill Color tool color swatch** on the Tools panel, then click the **blue color swatch** in the left column of the color palette.
4. Press and hold [**Shift**], then draw a square resembling the dimensions and position of the square, as shown in Figure 33.
5. Click the **Selection tool** on the Tools panel, then drag a **marquee** around the square to select the object.
6. Click **Insert** on the menu bar, click **Motion Tween**, then click **OK** in the Convert selection to symbol for tween dialog box.
7. Click **frame 48** on Layer 2, then drag the **square** to the bottom of the Stage, as shown in Figure 34.
8. Play the movie.

   The square appears on top if the two objects intersect.

You drew an object and used it to create a second animation.

Work with layers and view Timeline features

1. Click **Layer 2** on the Timeline, then drag it below Layer 1, as shown in Figure 35.

   Layer 2 is now the bottom layer.

2. Play the movie and notice how the square appears beneath the circle if the objects intersect.

3. Click **Layer 2** on the Timeline, then drag it above Layer 1.

4. Play the movie and notice how the square appears above the circle if they intersect.

5. Click the **Frame View icon** 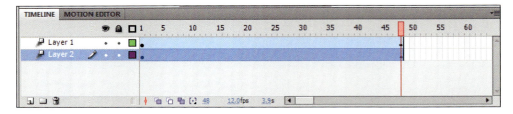 on the right corner of the Timeline title bar, as shown in Figure 36, to display the menu.

6. Click **Tiny** to display more frames.

   Notice how more frames appear on the Timeline, but each frame is smaller.

7. Click the **Frame View icon** ▾≡ , then click **Short**.

8. Click the **Frame View icon** ▾≡ , click **Preview**, then note the object thumbnails that appear on the Timeline.

9. Click the **Frame View icon** ▾≡ , then click **Normal**.

You changed the order of the layers, the display of frames, and the way the Timeline is viewed.

FIGURE 35
Changing the stacking order of layers

FIGURE 36
Changing the view of the Timeline

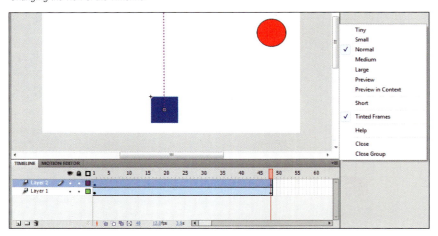

Getting Started with Adobe Flash CS4

FIGURE 37

Changing the frame rate

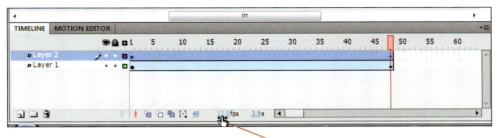

Pointer changes to double-
headed arrow

FIGURE 38

Displaying the Properties option

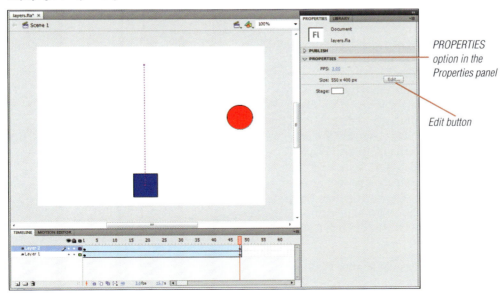

PROPERTIES
option in the
Properties panel

Edit button

1. Point to the **Frame Rate (fps)** on the bottom of the Timeline so the pointer changes to a double-headed arrow in Figure 37.

2. Drag the **pointer** to change the frame rate to 3.

   TIP   Alternately, you can double-click the frame rate number, then type a new number.

3. Play the movie and notice that the speed of the movie changes.

4. Click a blank area of the Stage, then verify the Properties panel is the active panel. If not, click **Window, Properties**.

5. If the PROPERTIES options are not displayed, click **PROPERTIES** on the Properties panel to display the options, as shown in Figure 38.

   The Properties panel provides information about the Stage, including size and background color.

6. Click the **Edit button** in the PROPERTIES section of the Properties panel to display the Document Properties dialog box.

   TIP   Another way to open the Document Properties dialog box is using the Modify menu.

7. Change the frame rate to **18**, click **OK**, then play the movie.

8. Change the frame rate to **12** using the Properties panel.

9. Click **frame 20** on the Timeline and notice the position of the objects on the Stage.

10. Drag the **playhead** left and right to display specific frames.

11. Save your work.

You changed the frame rate of the movie and used the playhead to display the contents of frames.

DISTRIBUTE AN ADOBE
FLASH MOVIE

What You'll Do

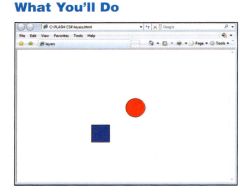

 In this lesson, you will prepare a movie for distribution in various formats.

Distributing Movies

When you develop Flash movies, the program saves them in a file format (.fla) that only users who have the Flash program installed on their computers can view. Usually, Flash movies are viewed on the web as part of a website or directly from a viewer's computer using the Flash Player. Flash files (.fla) cannot be viewed on the web using a web browser. They must be converted into a Flash Player file (.swf) so that the web browser knows the type of file to play (.swf) and the program needed to play the file (Flash Player). In addition, the HTML code needs to be created that instructs the web browser to play the swf file. Fortunately, Flash generates both the swf and HTML files when you use the publish feature of Flash.

The process for publishing a Flash movie is to create and save a movie and then click the Publish command on the File menu. You can specify various settings, such as dimensions for the window in which the movie plays in the browser, before publishing the movie. Publishing a movie creates two files: an HTML file and a Flash Player (.swf) file. Both the HTML and swf files retain the same name as the Flash movie file, but with different file extensions:

- .html—the HTML document
- .swf—the Flash Player file

For example, publishing a movie named layers.fla generates two files–layers.html and layers.swf. The HTML document contains the code that the browser interprets to display the movie on the web. The code also specifies which Flash Player movie the browser should play. Sample HTML code referencing a Flash Player movie is shown in Figure 39. If you are familiar with HTML code, you will recognize this as a complete HTML document. Even if you are not familiar with HTML code, you might recognize the code, as seen in Figure 39, that the browser uses to display the Flash movie. For example, the movie source is set to layers.swf; the background color is set to white (#ffffff is the code for white), and the display dimensions (determined by the size of the Stage) are set to 550 × 400.

Flash provides several other ways to distribute your movies that may or may not involve delivery on the web. You can create a standalone movie called a **projector**. Projector files, such as Windows .exe files, maintain the movie's interactivity. Alternately, you can create self-running movies, such as QuickTime .mov files, that are not interactive.

You can play projector and non-interactive files directly from a computer, or you can incorporate them into an application, such as a game, that is downloaded or delivered on a CD or DVD. In addition, Flash provides features for creating movies specifically for mobile devices, such as cell phones.

FIGURE 39

Sample HTML code

```
</head>
<body bgcolor="#ffffff">
<!--url's used in the movie-->
<!--text used in the movie-->
<!-- saved from url=(0013)about:internet -->
<script language="JavaScript" type="text/javascript">
        AC_FL_RunContent(
                'codebase',
'http://download.macromedia.com/pub/shockwave/cabs/flash/swflash.cab#version=10,0,0,0',
                'width', '550',
                'height', '400',
                'src', 'layers',
                'quality', 'high',
                'pluginspage', 'http://www.adobe.com/go/getflashplayer',
                'align', 'middle',
                'play', 'true',
                'loop', 'true',
                'scale', 'showall',
                'wmode', 'window',
                'devicefont', 'false',
                'id', 'layers',
                'bgcolor', '#ffffff',
                'name', 'layers',
                'menu', 'true',
                'allowFullScreen', 'false',
                'allowScriptAccess','sameDomain',
                'movie', 'layers',
                'salign', ''
                ); //end AC code
</script>
<noscript>
        <object classid="clsid:d27cdb6e-ae6d-11cf-96b8-444553540000"
codebase="http://download.macromedia.com/pub/shockwave/cabs/flash/swflash.cab#version=10,0,0,0" width="550"
height="400" id="layers" align="middle">
        <param name="allowScriptAccess" value="sameDomain" />
        <param name="allowFullScreen" value="false" />
        <param name="movie" value="layers.swf" /><param name="quality" value="high" /><param name="bgcolor"
value="#ffffff" />        <embed src="layers.swf" quality="high" bgcolor="#ffffff" width="550" height="400"
name="layers" align="middle" allowScriptAccess="sameDomain" allowFullScreen="false" type="application/x-
shockwave-flash" pluginspage="http://www.adobe.com/go/getflashplayer" />
        </object>
</noscript>
</body>
</html>
```

Publish a movie for distribution on the web

1. Verify layers.fla is open.

2. Click **File** on the menu bar, then click **Publish**.

   The files layers.html and layers.swf are automatically generated and saved in the same folder as the Flash document.

3. Use your file management program to navigate to the drive and folder where you save your work.

4. Notice the three files that begin with "layers," as shown in Figure 40.

   Layers.fla, the Flash movie; layers.html, the HTML document; layers.swf, the Flash Player file.

5. Double-click **layers.html** to play the movie in the browser.

   Note: Depending on your browser, browser settings and version, you may need to complete additional steps to view the layers.html document.

   TIP Click the browser button on the taskbar if the movie does not open automatically in your browser.

   Notice the animation takes up only a portion of the browser window, as shown in Figure 41. This is because the Stage size is set to 550 x 440, which is smaller than the browser window.

6. Close the browser.

You used the Publish command to create an HTML document (.html) and a Flash Player file (.swf), then you displayed the HTML document in a web browser.

FIGURE 40
The three layers files after publishing the movie

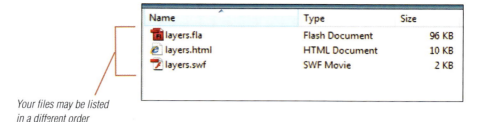

Your files may be listed in a different order

FIGURE 41
The animation played in a browser window

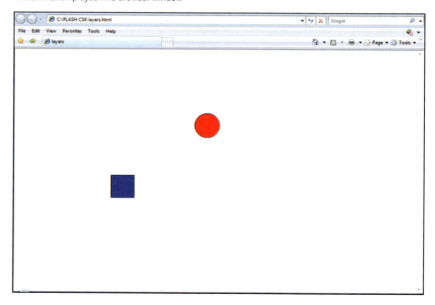

FIGURE 42

Publish Settings dialog box with the Formats tab selected

1. Return to Flash, click **File** on the menu bar, then click **Publish Settings** to open the Publish Settings dialog box.

2. Verify the Formats tab is selected, as shown in Figure 42.

   Notice the various file formats (and their file names) that can be generated automatically when you publish a Flash document.

3. Click the **Windows Projector (.exe)** (Win) or **Macintosh Projector** (Mac) **check box**.

4. Click **Publish**, then click **OK**.

5. Use your file management program to navigate to the drive and folder where you save your work.

6. Double-click **layers.exe** (Win), or **layers** (Mac), then notice that the application plays in the Flash Player window.

   In this case, the Flash Player window is sized to the dimensions of the Stage.

   Note: You must have the Flash Player installed to view the movie.

7. Close the Flash Player window.

8. Close layers.fla in Flash, saving your changes if prompted.

You created and displayed a stand-alone projector file.

PLAN AN APPLICATION OR A
WEBSITE

What You'll Do

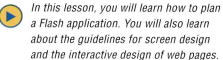

In this lesson, you will learn how to plan a Flash application. You will also learn about the guidelines for screen design and the interactive design of web pages.

Planning an Application or a Website

Flash can be used to develop animations that are part of a product, such as a game or educational tutorial, and delivered via the internet, a CD, a DVD, or a mobile device. You can use Flash to create enhancements to web pages, such as animated logos and interactive navigation buttons. You can also use Flash to create entire websites. No matter what the application, the first step is planning. Often, the temptation is to jump right into the program and start developing movies. The problem is that this invariably results in a more time-consuming process at best; and wasted effort, resources, and money at worst. The larger and more complex the project is, the more critical the planning process becomes. Planning an application or an entire website should involve the following steps:

Step 1: Stating the Purpose (Goals). "What, specifically, do we want to accomplish?"

Determining the goals is a critical step in planning because goals guide the development process, keep the team members on track, and provide a way to evaluate the application or website, both during and after its development.

Step 2: Identifying the Target Audience. "Who will use our application or website?"

Understanding the potential viewers helps in developing an application or a website that can address their needs. For example, children respond to exploration and surprise, so having a dog wag its tail when the mouse pointer rolls over it might appeal to this audience.

Step 3: Determining the Treatment. "What is the look and feel?"

The treatment is how the application or website will be presented to the user, including the tone, approach, and emphasis.

Tone. Will the application or website be humorous, serious, light, heavy, formal, or informal? The tone of a site can often be used to make a statement—projecting a progressive, high-tech, well-funded corporate image, for instance.

Approach. How much direction will be provided to the user? An interactive game might focus on exploration such as when the user points to an object on the screen and the object becomes animated. While an informational website might provide lots of direction and include lists of options in the form of drop-down menus.

Emphasis. How much emphasis will be placed on the various multimedia elements? For example, a company may want to develop an informational application or website that shows the features of its new product line, including video demonstrations and sound narrations of how each product works. The budget might not allow for the expense of creating the videos, so the emphasis would shift to still pictures with text descriptions.

Step 4: Developing the Specifications and Storyboard. "What precisely does the application or website include and how does it work?"

The specifications state what will be included in each screen, including the arrangement of each element and the functionality of each object (for example, what happens when you click the button labeled Skip Intro). Specifications should include the following:

Playback System. The choice of what configuration to target for playback is critical, especially Internet connection speed, browser versions, screen resolution, screen size especially when targeting mobile devices, and plug-ins.

Elements to Include. The specifications should include details about the various elements that are to be included in the site. What are the dimensions for the animations, and what is the frame rate? What are the sizes of the various objects such as photos, buttons, and so on? What fonts, font sizes, and font formatting will be used? Should video or sound be included?

Functionality. The specifications should include the way the program reacts to an action by the user, such as a mouse click. For example, clicking a door (object) might cause a doorbell to ring (sound), the door

Rich media content and accessibility
Flash provides the tools that allow you to create compelling applications and websites by incorporating rich media content, such as animations, sound, and video. Generally, incorporating rich media enhances the user's experience. However, accessibility becomes an issue for those persons who have visual, hearing, or mobility impairments, or have a cognitive disability. Designers need to utilize techniques that help ensure accessibility, such as providing consistency in navigation and layout, labeling graphics, captioning audio content throughout the applications and website, and providing keyboard access.

to open (an animation), an "exit the program" message to appear (text), or an entirely new screen to be displayed.

The **user interface** involves designing the appearance of objects (how each object is arranged on the screen) and the interactivity (how the user navigates through the site).

A **flowchart** is a visual representation of how the contents in an application or a website are organized and how various screens are linked. It provides a guide for the developer and helps to identify problems with the navigation scheme before work begins. Figure 43 shows a simple flowchart illustrating the site organization and links.

A **storyboard** shows the layout of the various screens. It describes the contents and illustrates how text, graphics, animation, and other screen elements will be positioned. It also indicates the navigation process, such as menus and buttons. Figure 44 shows a storyboard. The exact content (such as a specific photo) does not have to be decided, but it is important to show where text, graphics, photos, buttons, and other elements, will be placed. Thus, the storyboard includes placeholders for the various elements.

Using Screen Design Guidelines

The following screen design guidelines are used by application and web developers.

The implementation of these guidelines is affected by the goals of the application or website, the intended audience, and the content.

Balance in screen design refers to the distribution of optical weight in the layout. Optical weight is the ability of an object to attract the viewer's eye, as determined by the object's size, shape, color, and so on. Figure 44 shows a fairly well-balanced layout, especially if the logo has as much optical weight as the text description. In general, a balanced design is more appealing to a viewer. However, for a game application or entertainment site, a balanced layout may not be desired.

FIGURE 43

Sample Flowchart

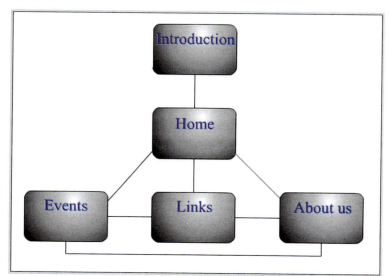

FIGURE 44

Sample Storyboard

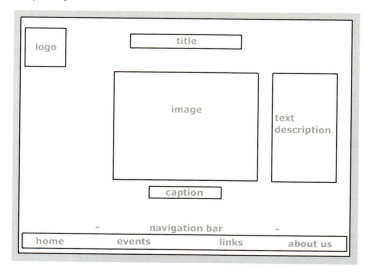

Unity helps the screen objects reinforce each other. **Intra-screen** unity has to do with how the various screen objects relate and how they all fit in. For example, a children's game might only use cartoon characterizations of animals for all the objects—including navigation buttons and sound control buttons, as well as the on-screen characters. **Inter-screen** unity refers to the design that viewers encounter as they navigate from one screen to another, and it provides consistency throughout the application. For example, all navigation buttons are located in the same place on each screen.

Movement refers to the way the viewer's eyes move through the objects on the screen. Different types of objects and various animation techniques can be used to draw the viewer to a location on the screen.

For example, a photo of a waterfall may cause the viewer's eyes to follow the flow of the water down, especially if the waterfall is animated. The designer could then place an object, such as a logo or link, below the waterfall.

Using Interactive Design Guidelines

In addition to screen design guidelines, interactive guidelines determine the interactivity of the application. The following guidelines are not absolute rules but are affected by the goals of the application, the intended audience, and the content:

- Make it simple, easy to understand, and easy to use so that viewers do not have to spend time learning what the application is about and what they need to do.

- Build in consistency in the navigation scheme. Help the users know where they are in the application and help them avoid getting lost.
- Provide feedback. Users need to know when an action, such as clicking a button, has been completed. Changing its color or shape, or adding a sound can indicate this.
- Give the user control. Allow the user to skip long introductions; provide controls for starting, stopping, and rewinding animations, video, and audio; and provide controls for adjusting audio.

Project management

Developing websites or any extensive application, such as a game, involves project management. A project plan needs to be developed that provides the project scope and identifies the milestones, including analyzing, designing, building, testing, and launching. Personnel and resource needs are identified, budgets built, tasks assigned, and schedules developed. Successful projects are a team effort relying on the close collaboration of designers, developers, project managers, graphic artists, programmers, testers, and others. Adobe provides various product suites, such as their Creative Suite 4 (CS4) Web Collection series, that include programs such as Flash, Dreamweaver, Fireworks, Photoshop, and Illustrator. These are the primary tools needed to develop interactive applications and websites. These programs are designed for easy integration. So, a graphic artist can use Photoshop to develop an image that can easily be imported into Flash and used by an animator. In addition, other tools in the suites, such as Adobe Bridge and Adobe Version Cue, help ensure efficient workflow when working in a team environment.

The Flash Workflow Process

After the planning process, you are ready to start work on the Flash documents. The following steps can be used as guidelines in a general workflow process suggested by Adobe.

Step 1: Create and/or acquire the elements to be used in the application. The elements include text, photos, drawings, video, and audio. The elements become the raw material for the graphics, animations, menus, buttons, and content that populate the application and provide the interactivity. You can use the various Flash drawing and text tools to create your own images and text content; or, you can use another program, such as Adobe Photoshop, to develop the elements, and then import them into Flash. Alternately, you can acquire stock clip art and photographs. You can produce video and audio content in-house and import it into Flash or you can acquire these elements from a third party.

Step 2: Arrange the elements and create the animations. Arrange the elements (objects) on the Stage and on the Timeline to define when and how they appear in your application. Once the elements are available, you can create the various animations called for in the specifications.

Step 3: Apply special effects. Flash provides innumerable special effects that can be applied to the various media elements and animations. These include graphic and text filters, such as drop shadows, blurs, glows, and bevels. In addition, there are effects for sounds and animations such as fade-ins and fade-outs, acceleration and deceleration, and morphing.

Step 4: Create the interactivity. Flash provides a scripting feature, ActionScript, which allows you to develop programming code to control how the media elements behave, including how various objects respond to user interactions, such as clicking buttons and rolling over images.

Step 5: Test and publish the application. Testing should be done throughout the development process, including using the Test Movie feature in the Control menu to test the movie using the Flash Player and to publish the movie in order to test it in a browser.

Using the Flash Help feature

Flash provides a comprehensive Help feature that can be very useful when first learning the program. You access the Help feature from the Help menu. The Help feature is organized by categories, including Using Flash CS4 Professional, which have several topics such as Workspace and Managing documents. In addition, the Help feature has a Help Search feature. You use the Help Search feature to search for topics using keywords, such as Timeline. Searching by keywords accesses the Flash Community Help feature, which displays links to content relevant to the search terms. Other resources not affiliated with Adobe are available through the web. You may find some by searching the web for Flash resources.

FIGURE 45

The Flash Help categories

FIGURE 46

The Flash Help Search feature

Search term

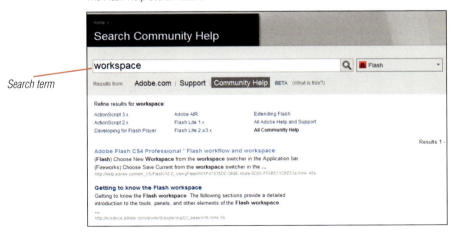

1. Start a new Flash document.

2. Click **Help** on the menu bar, then click **Flash Help**.

   Note: If you see a page not found message, be sure you are connected to the Internet.

3. Click the **Expand button** ⊞ next to Workspace to expand the category, as shown in Figure 45.

4. Click **The Timeline**, then click **About the Timeline**.

5. Read through the text in About the Timeline.

6. Scroll to display the top of the Help window.

7. Click in the **Search text box**, then type **workspace**.

8. Press **[Enter]** (Win) or **[return]** (Mac) to access the Community Help site.

9. Study the various links provided on the site.

   Note: Figure 46 shows the results of one search for workspace. New links are added regularly because this is community-based help. Therefore, your results may differ.

10. Close the Community Help site and the Flash Help site, then exit the Flash program.

You used the Flash Help feature to access information on the Timeline and the workspace.

Start Flash, open a movie, set the magnification and make changes to the workspace.

1. Start Flash, open fl1_2.fla, then save it as **skillsdemo1**. This movie has two layers. Layer 1 contains the heading and the line at the top of the Stage. Layer 2 contains an animation that runs for 75 frames.
2. Change the magnification to 50% using the View menu. (*Hint:* Click View, point to Magnification, then click 50%.)
3. Change the magnification to Fit in Window.
4. Change the Timeline view to Small. (*Hint:* Click the Frame View icon in the upper-right corner of the Timeline title bar.)
5. Hide all panels.
6. Display the Tools panel, Timeline panel, Properties panel, and the Library panel.
7. Group the Library and Properties panels if they are not already grouped.
8. Drag the Library panel from the Properties panel and position it on the Stage.
9. Collapse the Library panel.
10. Close the Library panel to remove it from the screen.
11. Reset the Essentials workspace.

Play and test a movie.

1. Drag the playhead to view the contents of each frame. Use the commands on the Control menu to play and rewind the movie.
2. Press [Enter] (Win) or [return] (Mac) to play and stop the movie.

3. Use the Controller to rewind, play, stop, and start the movie.
4. Test the movie in the Flash Player window, then close the Flash Player window.

Change the document size and background color.

1. Use the Properties panel to display the Document Properties dialog box.
2. Change the document height to 380.
3. Change the background color to a medium gray color (#999999).
4. Close the Document Properties dialog box.
5. Play the movie.

Create an object, create a motion tween animation, and apply effects.

1. Insert a new layer above Layer 2, then select frame 1 of the new layer.
2. Draw a green ball in the middle of the left side of the Stage, approximately the same size as the red ball. (*Hint:* The green gradient color can be used to draw the ball. Several gradient colors are found in the bottom row of the color palette when you click on the Fill Color tool in the Tools panel.)
3. Use the Selection tool to draw a marquee around the green ball to select it, then create a motion tween to animate the green ball so that it moves across the screen from left to right.

4. Use the Selection tool to reshape the motion path to an arc by dragging the middle of the path downward.
5. Play the movie.
6. Use the Undo command to undo the reshape. (*Note:* You may need to use the Undo feature twice.)
7. Use the Selection tool to select frame 75 of the new layer, click the green ball if it is not already selected to select it, then use the Properties panel to change the transparency (alpha) from 100% to 20%. (*Hint:* If the Properties panel COLOR EFFECT option is not displayed, make sure the Properties panel is open and click the green ball to make sure it is selected.)
8. Play the movie, then rewind it.
9. Click frame 75 on Layer 3 and click the green ball to select it.
10. Use the Properties panel to increase the width of the ball to 80.
11. Play the movie.
12. Select frame 1 on Layer 3 and click the green ball to select it.
13. Use the Filters option in the Properties panel to add a drop shadow.
14. Play the movie.
15. Select frame 1 on Layer 2 and click the red ball to select it.
16. Open the Motion Presets panel and add a bounce-smoosh preset.
17. Play the movie.
18. Save the movie.

Change the frame rate and change the view of the Timeline.

1. Change the frame rate to 8 frames per second, play the movie, then change the frame rate to 12.
2. Change the view of the Timeline to display more frames.
3. Change the view of the Timeline to display a preview of the object thumbnails.
4. Change the view of the Timeline to display the Small view.
5. Click frame 1 on Layer 1, use the playhead to display each frame, then compare your screens to Figure 47.
6. Save the movie.

Publish a movie.

1. Click File on the menu bar, then click Publish.
2. Open your browser, then open skillsdemo1.html.
3. View the movie, then close your browser.

Create a projector file.

1. Display the Publish Settings dialog box.
2. Select the appropriate projector setting for your operating system.
3. Publish the movie, then close the Publish Settings dialog box.
4. Use your file management program to navigate to the drive and folder where yousave your work, then open the skills-demo1 projector file.

5. View the movie, then close the Flash Player window.

6. Save and close the Flash document.
7. Exit Flash.

FIGURE 47
Completed Skills Review

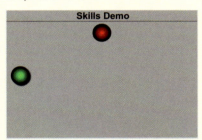

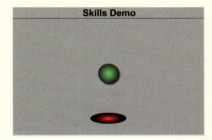

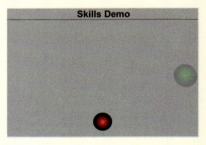

A friend cannot decide whether to sign up for a class in Flash or Dreamweaver. You help her decide by showing her what you already know about Flash. Since you think she'd enjoy a class in Flash, you decide to show her how easy it is to create a simple animation. You decide to animate three objects. The first object is placed on the center of the Stage and pulsates throughout the movie. The second object enters the Stage from the left side and moves across the middle of the Stage and off the right side of the Stage. The third object enters the Stage from the right side and moves across the middle of the Stage and off the left side of the Stage. The motion paths for the two objects that move across the Stage are reshaped so they go above and below the pulsating object in the middle of the Stage.

1. Open a Flash document, then save it as **demonstration**.
2. Change the view to 50%.
3. Use the tools on the Tools panel to create a circle (or object of your choice) and color of your choice on the middle of the Stage.
4. Draw a marquee around the object to select it and apply a pulse motion preset.
5. Insert a new layer, then select frame 1 on the layer.
6. Create a simple shape or design, and place it off the left side of the Stage and halfway down the Stage.

7. Select the object and insert a motion tween that moves the object directly across the screen and off the right side of the Stage.
8. Reshape the motion path so that the object goes in an arc below the center pulsating object.
9. Insert a new layer, then select frame 1 on the layer.
10. Create an object and place it off the right side of the Stage and halfway down the Stage.

11. Draw a marquee to select the object and insert a motion tween that moves the object directly across the screen and off the left side of the Stage.
12. Reshape the motion path so that the object goes in an arc above the center pulsating object.
13. Play the movie.
14. Add a background color.
15. Play the movie and test it.
16. Save the movie, then compare your movie to the sample provided in Figure 48.

FIGURE 48
Sample completed Project Builder 1

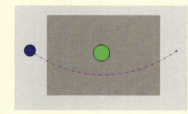 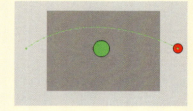

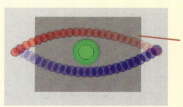

This figure shows the animated objects with outlines of their positions during the animations. Your completed project will not show these outlines.

You've been asked to develop a simple movie about recycling for a day care center. For this project, you will add two animations to an existing movie. You will show three objects that appear on the screen at different times, and then move each object to a recycle bin at different times. You can create the objects using any of the Tools on the Tools panel.

1. Open fl1_3.fla, then save it as **recycle**.
2. Play the movie and study the Timeline to familiarize yourself with the movie's current settings. Currently, there are no animations.
3. Insert a new layer above Layer 2, then draw a small object in the upper-left corner of the Stage.
4. Create a motion tween that moves the object to the recycle bin. (*Hint:* Be sure to select frame 40 on the new layer before creating the motion tween animation.)
5. Reshape the path so that the object moves in an arc to the recycle bin. (*Note:* At this time, the object will appear outside the recycle bin when it is placed in the bin.)
6. Insert a new layer above the top layer, draw a small object in the upper-center of the Stage, then create a motion tween that moves the object to the recycle bin.
7. Insert a new layer above the top layer, draw a small object in the upper-right corner of the Stage, then create a motion tween that moves the object to the recycle bin.
8. Reshape the path so that the object moves in an arc to the recycle bin.
9. Move Layer 1 to the top of all the layers.
10. Play the movie and compare your movie to the sample provided in Figure 49.
11. Save the movie.

FIGURE 49
Sample completed Project Builder 2

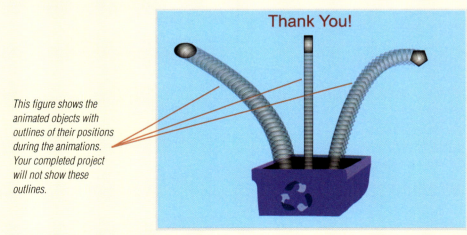

This figure shows the animated objects with outlines of their positions during the animations. Your completed project will not show these outlines.

DESIGN PROJECT

Figure 50 shows the home page of a website. Study the figure and answer the following questions. For each question, indicate how you determined your answer.

1. Connect to the Internet, then go to *www. argosycruises.com*.

2. Open a document in a word processor or open a new Flash document, save the file as **dpc1**, then answer the following questions. (*Hint*: Use the Flash Text tool if you open a Flash document.)
   - Whose website is this?
   - What is the goal(s) of the site?
   - Who is the target audience?
   - What treatment (look and feel) is used?
   - What are the design layout guidelines being used (balance, movement, etc.)?
   - How can animation enhance this page?
   - Do you think this is an effective design for the company, its products, and its target audience? Why, or why not?
   - What suggestions would you make to improve the design, and why?

FIGURE 50
Design Project

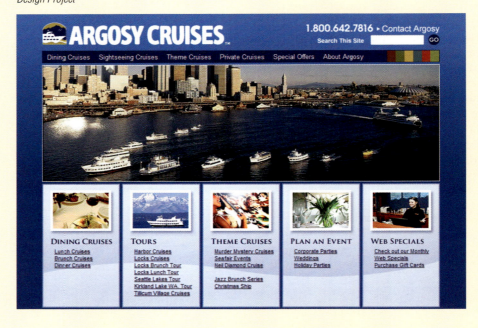

There are numerous companies in the business of developing websites for others. Many of these companies use Flash as one of their primary development tools. These companies promote themselves through their own websites and usually provide online portfolios with samples of their work. Log onto the Internet, then use your favorite search engine and keywords such as Flash developers and Flash animators to locate three of these companies, and generate the following information for each one. A sample website is shown in Figure 51.

1. Company name:
2. Contact information (address, phone, and so on):
3. Website URL:
4. Company mission:
5. Services provided:
6. Sample list of clients:
7. Describe three ways the company seems to have used Flash in its website. Were these effective? Why, or why not?
8. Describe three applications of Flash that the company includes in its portfolio (or showcases or samples). Were these effective? Why, or why not?

9. Would you want to work for this company? Why, or why not?
10. Would you recommend this company to another company that was looking to enhance its website? Why, or why not?

FIGURE 51
Sample website for Portfolio Project

DRAWING OBJECTS IN
ADOBE FLASH

1. Use the Flash drawing tools

2. Select objects and apply colors

3. Work with drawn objects

4. Work with text and text objects

5. Work with layers and objects

2 DRAWING OBJECTS IN
ADOBE FLASH

Introduction

Computers can display graphics in either a bitmap or a vector format. The difference between these formats is in how they describe an image. Bitmap graphics represent the image as an array of dots, called **pixels**, which are arranged within a grid. Each pixel in an image has an exact position on the screen and a precise color. To make a change in a bitmap graphic, you modify the pixels. When you enlarge a bitmap graphic, the number of pixels remains the same, resulting in jagged edges that decrease the quality of the image. Vector graphics represent the image using lines and curves, which you can resize without losing image quality. Also, the file size of a vector image is generally smaller than the file size of a bitmap image, which makes vector images particularly useful for a website. However, vector graphics are not as effective as bitmap graphics for representing photo-realistic images. One of the most compelling features of Flash is the ability to create and manipulate vector graphics.

Images (objects) created using Flash drawing tools have a stroke (border line), a fill, or both. In addition, the stroke of an object can be segmented into smaller lines. You can modify the size, shape, rotation, and color of each stroke, fill, and segment.

Flash provides two drawing modes, called models. In the Merge Drawing Model, when you draw two shapes and one overlaps the other, a change in the top object may affect the object beneath it. For example, if you draw a circle on top of a rectangle and then move the circle off the rectangle, the portion of the rectangle covered by the circle is removed. The Object Drawing Model allows you to overlap shapes which are then kept separate, so that changes in one object do not affect another object. Another way to avoid having changes in one object affect another is to place them on separate layers on the Timeline as you did in Chapter 1.

Tools You'll Use

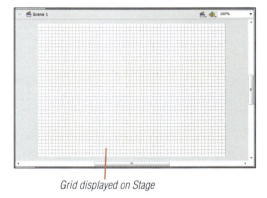

Grid displayed on Stage

USE THE
FLASH DRAWING TOOLS

What You'll Do

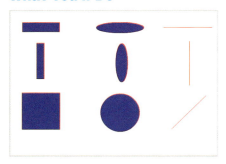

In this lesson, you will use several drawing tools to create various vector graphics.

Using Flash Drawing and Editing Tools

When you point to a tool on the Tools panel, its name appears next to the tool. Figure 1 identifies the tools described in the following paragraphs. Several of the tools have options that modify their use. These options are available in the Options area of the Tools panel when the tool is selected.

Selection—Used to select an object or parts of an object, such as the stroke or fill; and to reshape objects. The options for the Selection tool are Snap to Objects (aligns objects), Smooth (smoothes lines), and Straighten (straightens lines).

Subselection—Used to select, drag, and reshape an object. Vector graphics are composed of lines and curves (each of which is a segment) connected by **anchor points**. Selecting an object with this tool displays the anchor points and allows you to use them to edit the object.

Free Transform—Used to rotate, scale, skew, and distort objects.

Gradient Transform—Used to transform a gradient fill by adjusting the size, direction, or center of the fill.

The Free and Gradient Transform tools are grouped within one icon on the Tools panel.

3D Rotation—Used to create 3D effects by rotating movie clips in 3D space on the Stage.

3D Translation—Used to create 3D effects by moving movie clips in 3D space on the Stage.

The 3D Rotation and the 3D Translation tools are grouped within one icon on the Tools panel.

Lasso—Used to select objects or parts of objects. The Polygon Mode option allows you to draw straight lines when selecting an object.

Pen—Used to draw lines and curves by creating a series of dots, known as anchor points, that are automatically connected. Other tools used to add, delete, and convert the anchor points created by the Pen tool are grouped with the Pen tool. To see the menu containing these tools, hold down the Pen tool until the menu opens.

Text—Used to create and edit text.

Line—Used to draw straight lines. You can draw vertical, horizontal, and 45° diagonal lines by pressing and holding [Shift] while drawing the line.

Rectangle—Used to draw rectangular shapes. Press and hold [Shift] to draw a perfect square.

Oval—Used to draw oval shapes. Press and hold [Shift] to draw a perfect circle.

Primitive Rectangle and Oval—Used to draw objects with properties, such as corner radius or inner radius, that can be changed using the Properties panel.

PolyStar—Used to draw polygons and stars.

The Rectangle, Oval, Primitive and PolyStar tools are grouped within one tool on the Tools panel.

Pencil—Used to draw freehand lines and shapes. The Pencil Mode option displays a menu with the following commands: Straighten (draws straight lines), Smooth (draws smooth curved lines), and Ink (draws freehand with no modification).

Brush—Used to draw (paint) with brush-like strokes. Options allow you to set the size and shape of the brush, and to determine the area to be painted, such as inside or behind an object.

Spray Brush—Used to spray colors and patterns onto objects. Dots are the default pattern for the spray. However, you can use a symbol, such as a flag, to create the pattern.

The Brush and Spray Brush tools are grouped together.

Deco—Used to turn graphic shapes into geometric patterns or create kaleidoscopic-like effects.

Bone—Used to animate a set of objects, such as arms and legs, using a series of linked objects to create character animations.

Bind—Used to adjust the relationships between individual bones.

Paint Bucket—Used to fill enclosed areas of a drawing with color. Options allow you to fill areas that have gaps and to make adjustments in a gradient fill.

Ink Bottle—Used to apply line colors and thickness to the stroke of an object.

The Paint Bucket and Ink Bottle are grouped together.

Eyedropper—Used to select stroke, fill, and text attributes so they can be copied from one object to another.

Eraser—Used to erase lines and fills. Options allow you to choose what part of the object to erase, as well as the size and shape of the eraser.

FIGURE 1
Flash tools

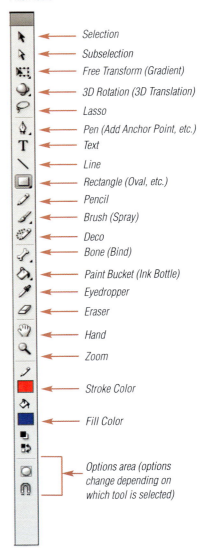

Selection
Subselection
Free Transform (Gradient)
3D Rotation (3D Translation)
Lasso
Pen (Add Anchor Point, etc.)
Text
Line
Rectangle (Oval, etc.)
Pencil
Brush (Spray)
Deco
Bone (Bind)
Paint Bucket (Ink Bottle)
Eyedropper
Eraser
Hand
Zoom
Stroke Color
Fill Color
Options area (options change depending on which tool is selected)

Hand—Used to move the Stage around the Pasteboard by dragging the Stage.

Zoom—Used to change the magnification of an area of the Stage. Clicking an area of the Stage zooms in and holding down [Alt] (Win) or [option] ⌘ (Mac) and clicking zooms out.

Stroke Color—Used to set the stroke color of drawn objects.

Fill Color—Used to set the fill color of drawn objects.

Options—Used to select an option for a tool, such as the type of rectangle (object drawn) or size of the brush when using the Brush tool.

Working with Grouped Tools

To display a list of grouped tools, you click the tool and hold the mouse button until the menu opens. For example, if you want to select the Oval tool and the Rectangle tool is displayed, you click and hold the Rectangle tool. Then, when the menu opens, you click the Oval tool option. You know a tool is a grouped tool if you see an arrow in the lower-right corner of the tool icon.

Working with Tool Options

Some tools have additional options that allow you to modify their use. For example, the brush tool has options to set the brush size and to set where the brush fill will be applied. If additional options for a tool are available, they appear at the bottom of the Tools panel in the Options area when the tool is selected. If the option has a menu associated with it, then the option icon will have an arrow in the lower-right corner. Click and hold the option until the menu opens.

Tools for Creating Vector Graphics

The Oval, Rectangle, Pencil, Brush, Line, and Pen tools are used to create vector objects.

Positioning Objects on the Stage

Flash provides several ways to position objects on the Stage including rulers, gridlines, and guides. The Rulers, Grid, and Guides commands, which are found on the View menu, are used to turn on and off these features. Figure 2 shows ruler lines being used to position an object.

FIGURE 2

Using rulers to position an object

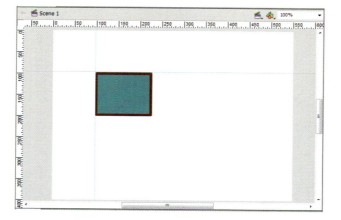

After displaying the rulers, you can drag the lines from the top ruler or the left side ruler to the Stage. To remove a ruler line, you drag the ruler line up to the top ruler or across to the left ruler. You can specify the unit of measure for the rulers.

Figure 3 shows the gridlines displayed and being used to position an object. You can modify the grid size and color. In addition to using rulers and guides to help place objects, you can create a new layer as a Guide layer that you use to position objects on the Stage. When you turn gridlines and guides on, they appear on the Stage. However, they do not appear in the Flash movie when you test or publish it.

Other methods for positioning objects include the align options found on the Align command of the Modify menu, as shown in Figure 4, and the options on the Align panel.

FIGURE 3
Using gridlines to position an object

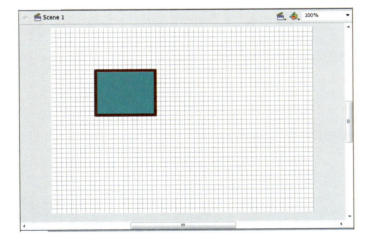

FIGURE 4
The Align command option from the Modify menu

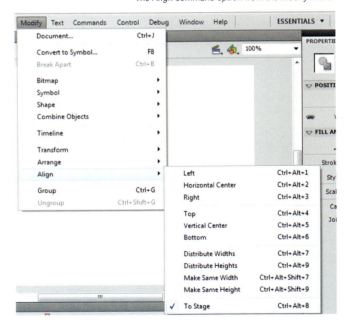

Show gridlines and check settings

1. Open **fl2_1.fla** from the drive and folder where your Data Files are stored, then save it as **tools**.

2. Click **Window** on the menu bar, point to **Workspace**, then click **Reset 'Essentials'**.

3. Click **View** on the menu bar, point to **Magnification**, then click **Fit in Window**.

4. Click the **Stroke Color tool color swatch** on the Tools panel, then click the **red color swatch** in the left column of the Color palette.

5. Click the **Fill Color tool color swatch** on the Tools panel, then click the **blue color swatch** in the left column of the Color palette.

6. Click **View** on the menu bar, point to **Grid**, then click **Show Grid** to display the gridlines.

   A gray grid appears on the Stage.

7. Point to each tool on the Tools panel, then read its name.

8. Click the **Text tool** T, then click **CHARACTER** to open the area if it is not open already.

   Notice the options in the Properties panel including the CHARACTER area, as shown in Figure 5. The Properties panel options change depending on the tool selected. For the Text tool the properties include the character family and the paragraph family.

You opened a document, saved it, set up the workspace, changed the stroke and fill colors, displayed the grid, viewed tool names on the Tools panel, and then viewed the Text tool options in the Properties panel.

FIGURE 5

Tool name on the Tools panel

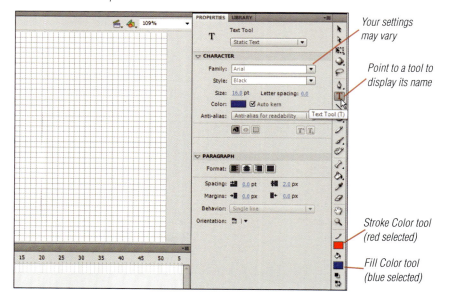

Your settings may vary

Point to a tool to display its name

Stroke Color tool (red selected)

Fill Color tool (blue selected)

Drawing Objects in Adobe Flash

FIGURE 6
Objects created with drawing tools

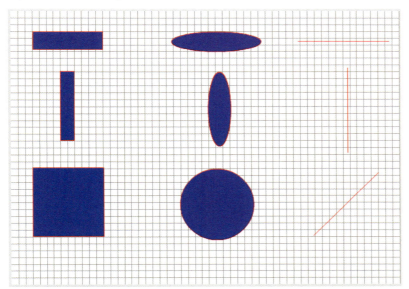

1. Click the **Rectangle tool** 🔲 on the Tools panel.

   Note: If the Rectangle tool is not displayed, click and hold the Oval tool to display the group of tools.

2. Verify that the Object Drawing option 🔘 in the Options area of the Tools panel is deselected.

   | TIP When the Object Drawing option is deselected, the object is drawn so that its stroke and fill can be selected separately.

3. Using Figure 6 as a guide, draw the three rectangle shapes.

   | TIP Use the grid to approximate shape sizes and hold down [Shift] to draw a square. To undo an action, click the Undo command on the Edit menu.

   Notice the blue color for the fill and the red color for the strokes (border lines).

4. Click and hold down the **Rectangle tool** 🔲 on the Tools panel, then click the **Oval tool** 🔘 .

5. Using Figure 6 as a guide, draw the three oval shapes.

   | TIP Hold down [Shift] to draw a perfect circle.

6. Click the **Line tool** ＼ , then, using Figure 6 as a guide, draw the three lines.

   | TIP Hold down [Shift] to draw a straight line.

You used the Rectangle, Oval, and Line tools to draw objects on the Stage.

Use the Pen, Pencil, and Brush tools

1. Click **Insert** on the menu bar, point to **Timeline**, then click **Layer**.

   A new layer—Layer 2—appears above Layer 1.

2. Click **frame 5** on Layer 2.

3. Click **Insert** on the menu bar, point to **Timeline**, then click **Keyframe**.

   Since the objects were drawn in frame 1 on Layer 1, they are no longer visible when you insert a keyframe in frame 5 on Layer 2. A keyframe allows you to draw in any location on the Stage on the specified frame.

4. Click the **Zoom tool** 🔍 on the Tools panel, click near the upper-left quadrant of the Stage to zoom in, then scroll as needed to see more of the grid.

5. Click the **Pen tool** ✏️. on the Tools panel, position it in the upper-left quadrant of the Stage, as shown in Figure 7, then click to set an anchor point.

6. Using Figure 8 as a guide, click the remaining anchor points to finish drawing an arrow.

   | TIP   To close an object, be sure to re-click the first anchor point as your last action.

7. Click the **Paint Bucket tool** 🪣 , then click inside the arrow.

8. Click **View** on the menu bar, point to **Magnification**, then click **Fit in Window**.

9. Insert a **new layer**, Layer 3, then insert a **keyframe** in frame 10.

10. Click the **Pencil tool** ✏️ on the Tools panel.

11. Click **Pencil Mode** in the Options area of the Tools panel, then click the **Smooth option** ⟨, as shown in Figure 9.

(continued)

FIGURE 7
Positioning the Pen tool on the Stage

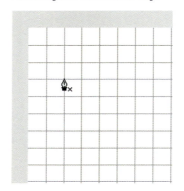

FIGURE 8
Setting anchor points to draw an arrow

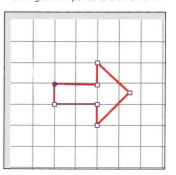

FIGURE 9
Pencil tool options

Click the Pencil Mode Smooth icon to display the 3 options (Note: The Straighten icon might be displayed instead of the Smooth icon.)

Drawing Objects in Adobe Flash

FIGURE 10
Images drawn using drawing tools

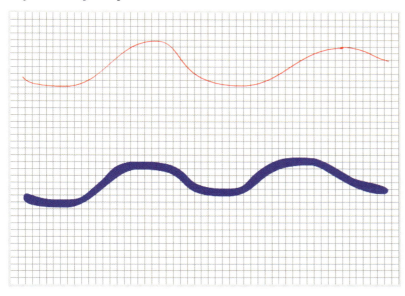

FIGURE 11
The dot pattern indicating the object is selected

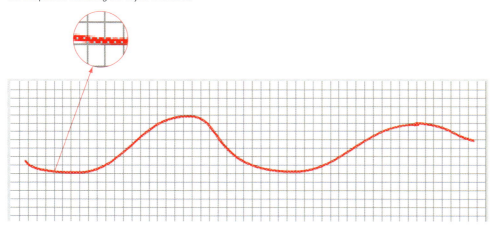

12. Draw the top image, as shown in Figure 10.

13. Click the **Brush tool** ✏ on the Tools panel.

14. Click the **Brush Size Icon** •. in the Options area of the Tools panel, then click the fifth option from the top.

15. Draw the bottom image, as shown in Figure 10.

Notice the Pencil tool displays the stroke color and the Brush tool displays the fill color.

You added a layer, inserted a keyframe, then used the Pen tool to draw an arrow; you selected the Smooth option for the Pencil tool and drew an object; you selected a brush size for the Brush tool and drew an object.

Modify an object using tool options

1. Click the **Selection tool** ↖ on the Tools panel, then drag a **marquee** around the top object to select it.

   The line displays a dot pattern, as shown in Figure 11, indicating that it is selected.

2. Click the **Pencil Mode Smooth icon** ⌇. in the Options area of the Tools panel three times. The line becomes smoother.

3. Use the stroke slider △ in the FILL AND STROKE area of the Properties panel to change the stroke size to **20**.

4. Click the **Style list arrow** in the FILL AND STROKE area, then click **Dotted**.

5. Repeat step 4 and change the line style to **Hairline**.

(continued)

6. Click **View** on the menu bar, point to **Grid**, then click **Show Grid** to remove the gridlines.

7. Save your work.

You smoothed objects using the tool options.

Use the Spray tool with a symbol

1. Click **Insert** on the menu bar, point to **Timeline**, then click **Layer**.

2. Click **frame 15** on Layer 4.

3. Click **Insert** on the menu bar, point to **Timeline**, then click **Keyframe**.

4. Click and hold the **Brush tool** on the Tools panel, then click the **Spray Brush tool**.

5. Display the Properties panel if it is not already displayed, then click the **Edit button** in the SYMBOL area of the Properties panel, as shown in Figure 12.

   Note: If the Properties panel does not display the options for the Spray Brush tool, click the Selection tool, then click the Spray Brush tool.

6. Click **Flag** in the Swap Symbol dialog box, then click **OK**.

7. Click the **Random scaling check box** to select it, then click to deselect the **Rotate symbol check box** and the **Random rotation check box** if they are checked.

8. Display the Brush section of the Properties panel, then set the width and height to **9 px**.

(continued)

FIGURE 12
The properties for the Spray Brush tool

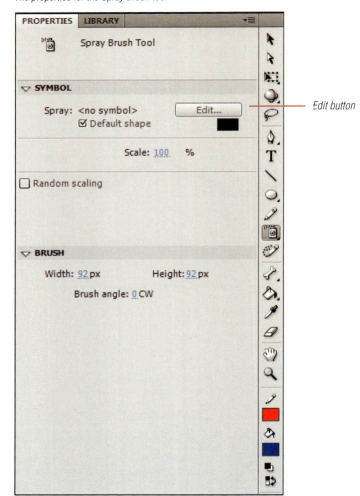

Edit button

FIGURE 13

A design created using the Spray Brush tool

9. Click the **Spray Brush tool** 🖌 in the Tools panel, then slowly draw the **U** in USA, as shown in Figure 13.

10. Click the **Selection tool** ↖ in the Tools panel, click the **Spray Brush tool** 🖌, then draw the **S** in USA.

11. Click the **Selection tool** ↖ in the Tools panel, click the **Spray Brush tool** 🖌, then draw the **A** in USA.

Hint: If you need to redo the drawing use the Selection tool to draw a marquee around the drawing, then delete the selection.

12. Save your work.

You specified a symbol as a pattern and used the Spray Brush tool to complete a drawing.

SELECT OBJECTS
AND APPLY COLORS

What You'll Do

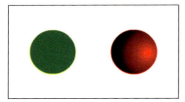

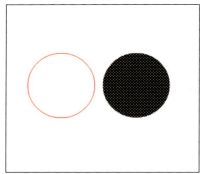

 In this lesson, you will use several techniques to select objects, change the color of strokes and fills, and create a gradient fill.

Selecting Objects

Before you can edit a drawing, you must first select the object, or the part of the object, on which you want to work. Objects are made up of a stroke(s) and a fill. Strokes can have several segments. For example, a rectangle will have four stroke segments, one for each side of the object. These can be selected separately or as a whole. Flash highlights objects that have been selected, as shown in Figure 14. When the stroke of an object is selected, a colored line appears. When the fill of an object is selected, a dot pattern appears; and when objects are grouped, a bounding box appears.

Using the Selection Tool

You can use the Selection tool to select part or all of an object, and to select multiple objects. To select only the fill, click just the fill; to select only the stroke, click just the stroke. To select both the fill and the stroke, double-click the object or draw a marquee around it. To select part of an object, drag a marquee that defines the area you wish to select, as shown in Figure 14. To select multiple objects or combinations of strokes

and fills, press and hold [Shift], then click each item. To deselect an item(s), click a blank area of the Stage.

Using the Lasso Tool

The Lasso tool provides more flexibility than the Selection tool when selecting an object(s) or parts of an object on the Stage. You can use the tool in a freehand manner to draw any shape that then selects the object(s) within the shape. Alternately, you can use the Polygon Mode option to draw straight lines and connect them to form a shape that will select any object(s) within the shape.

Drawing Model Modes

Flash provides two drawing modes, called models. In the Merge Drawing Model mode, the stroke and fill of an object are separate. Thus, as you draw an object such as a circle, the stroke and fill can be selected individually as described earlier. When using the Object Drawing Model mode, the stroke and fill are combined and cannot be selected individually. However, you can use the Break Apart option from the Modify menu to separate the stroke and fill so that they can be selected individually. In addition, you can turn off either the stroke or fill when drawing an object in either mode. You can toggle between the two modes by clicking the Object Drawing option in the Options area of the Tools panel.

Working with Colors

Flash allows you to change the color of the stroke and fill of an object. Figure 15 shows the Colors area of the Tools panel. To change a color, you click the color swatch of the Stroke Color tool or the color swatch of the Fill Color tool, and then select a color swatch on the Color palette. The Color palette, as shown in Figure 16, allows you to select a color from the palette or type in a six-character code that represents the values of three colors (red, green, blue), referred to as

RGB. When these characters are combined in various ways, they can represent virtually any color. The values are in a hexadecimal format (base 16), so they include letters and digits (A–F + 0–9 = 16 options), and they are preceded by a pound sign (#). The first two characters represent the value for red, the next two for green, and the last two for blue. For example, #000000 represents black (lack of color); #FFFFFF represents white; and #FFCC66 represents a shade of gold. You do not have to memorize the codes. There are reference manuals with the codes, and many programs allow you to set the values visually by selecting a color from a palette. You can also use the Properties panel to change the stroke and fill colors.

You can set the desired colors before drawing an object, or you can change a

color of a previously drawn object. You can use the Ink Bottle tool to change the stroke color, and you can use the Paint Bucket tool to change the fill color.

Working with Gradients

A gradient is a color fill that makes a gradual transition from one color to another. Gradients can be very useful for creating a 3D effect, drawing attention to an object, and generally enhancing the appearance of an object. You can apply a gradient fill by using the Paint Bucket tool. The position of the Paint Bucket tool over the object is important because it determines the direction of the gradient fill. The Color palette can be used to create and alter custom gradients.

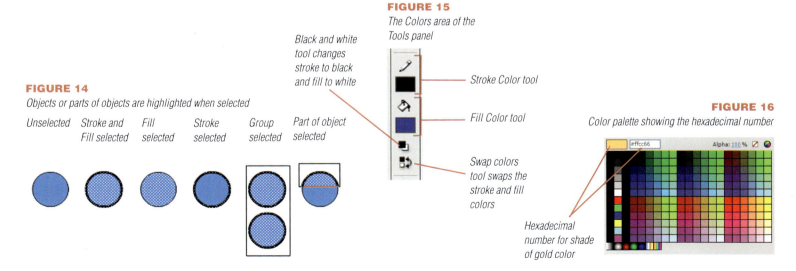

FIGURE 15

The Colors area of the Tools panel

Black and white tool changes stroke to black and fill to white

Stroke Color tool

Fill Color tool

Swap colors tool swaps the stroke and fill colors

FIGURE 14

Objects or parts of objects are highlighted when selected

Unselected | Stroke and Fill selected | Fill selected | Stroke selected | Group selected | Part of object selected

FIGURE 16

Color palette showing the hexadecimal number

Hexadecimal number for shade of gold color

#ffcc66   Alpha: 100 %

Select a drawing using the Selection tool

1. Click **frame 1** on the Timeline.

    TIP The options available to you in the Properties panel differ depending on whether you click a frame number on the Timeline or a frame within a layer.

2. Click the **Selection tool** on the Tools panel if it is not already selected, then drag a **marquee** around the circle to select the entire object (both the stroke and the fill).

3. Click anywhere on the Stage to deselect the object.

4. Click inside the circle to select the fill only, then click outside the circle to deselect it.

5. Click the stroke of the circle to select it, as shown in Figure 17, then deselect it.

6. Double-click the **circle** to select it, press and hold **[Shift]**, double-click the **square** to select both objects, then deselect both objects.

7. Click the right border of the square to select it, as shown in Figure 18, then deselect it.

    Objects, such as rectangles, have border segments that can be selected individually.

8. Drag a **marquee** around the square, circle, and diagonal line to select all three objects.

9. Click a blank area of the Stage to deselect the objects.

10. Click inside the oval in row 2 to select the fill, then drag it outside the stroke, as shown in Figure 19.

11. Look at the Properties panel.

    Notice the stroke color is none and the fill color is blue. This is because only the object's

    (continued)

FIGURE 17

Using the Selection tool to select the stroke of the circle

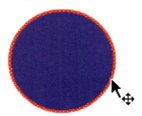

FIGURE 18

Using the Selection tool to select a segment of the stroke of the square

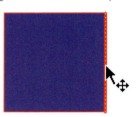

FIGURE 19

Separating the stroke and fill of an object

FIGURE 20
Circles drawn with the Oval tool

FIGURE 21

Changing the stroke color

fill is selected. You can use the Properties panel to verify what you have selected when working with the Selection tool.

12. Click **Edit** on the menu bar, then click **Undo Move**.

You used the Selection tool to select the stroke and fill of an object, and to select multiple objects.

Change fill and stroke colors

1. Click **Layer 4**, click **Insert** on the menu bar, point to **Timeline**, then click **Layer**.

2. Click **frame 20** of the new layer, click **Insert** on the menu bar, point to **Timeline**, then click **Keyframe**.

3. Select the **Oval tool** on the Tools panel, then draw two circles similar to those shown in Figure 20.

4. Click the **Fill Color tool color swatch** on the Tools panel, then click the **yellow color swatch** in the left column of the Color palette.

5. Click the **Paint Bucket tool** on the Tools panel, then click the fill of the right circle.

6. Click the **Stroke Color tool color swatch** on the Tools panel, then click the **yellow color swatch** in the left column of the color palette.

7. Click and hold the **Paint Bucket tool** on the Tools panel, click the **Ink Bottle tool** , point to the red stroke line of the left circle, as shown in Figure 21, then click to change the stroke color to yellow.

You used the Paint Bucket and Ink Bottle tools to change the fill and stroke colors of an object.

Create a gradient and make changes to the gradient

1. Click the **Fill Color tool color swatch** on the Tools panel, then click the **red gradient color swatch** in the bottom row of the Color palette, as shown in Figure 22.

2. Click and hold the **Ink Bottle tool** on the Tools panel, click the **Paint Bucket tool**, then click the **yellow circle**.

3. Click different parts of the right circle to view how the gradient changes.

4. Click the right side of the circle, as shown in Figure 23.

5. Click and hold the **Free Transform tool** on the Tools panel, then click the **Gradient Transform tool**.

6. Click the **gradient-filled circle**.

7. Drag each of the four handles shown in Figure 24 to determine the effect of each handle on the gradient, then click the **Stage** to deselect the circle.

8. Click the **Selection tool** on the Tools panel, then click inside the left circle.

9. Click the **Fill Color tool color swatch** in the FILL AND STROKE area of the Properties panel, click the **Hex Edit text box**, type **#006637** (two zeros), then press **[Enter]** (Win) or **[return]** (Mac).

   The Fill color swatch and the fill color for the circle change to a shade of green.

10. Save your work.

You applied a gradient fill, you used the Gradient Transform tool to alter the gradient, and you applied a new color using its Hexadecimal number.

FIGURE 22
Selecting the red gradient

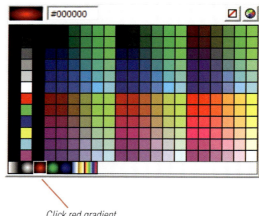

```
#000000
```

Click red gradient color swatch to select it

FIGURE 23
Clicking the right side of the circle

FIGURE 24
Gradient Transform handles

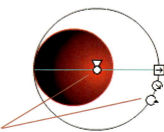

Handles are used to adjust the gradient effect

FIGURE 25
Circle drawn using the Object Drawing Model mode

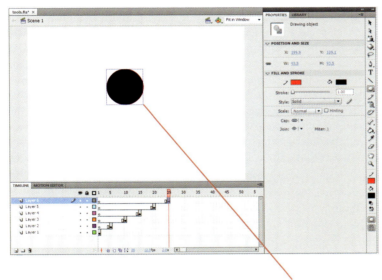

Blue outline indicates
the object is selected

1. Insert a **new layer**, then insert a **keyframe** on frame 25.
2. Select the **Oval tool** , click the **Stroke Color tool color swatch**, then click the **red swatch**.
3. Click the **Fill Color tool color swatch**, then click the **black swatch**.
4. Click the **Object Drawing option** in the Options area of the Tools panel to change the mode to Object Drawing Model.
5. Draw a **circle** as shown in Figure 25.

    Notice that when you use Object Drawing Model mode, objects are automatically selected, and the stroke and fill areas are combined.
6. Click the **Selection tool** on the Tools panel, then click a blank area of the Stage to deselect the object.
7. Click once on the **circle**, then drag the circle around the Stage.

    The entire object is selected, including the stroke and fill areas.
8. Click **Modify** on the menu bar, then click **Break Apart**.

    Breaking apart an object drawn in Object Drawing Model mode allows you to select the strokes and fills individually.
9. Click a blank area of the Stage, click the fill area of the circle, drag to the right, then save your work.

    Notice the fill moves but the stroke stays.

You used the Object Drawing Model mode to draw an object, deselect it, and then break it apart to display and then separate the stroke and fill.

WORK WITH DRAWN OBJECTS

What You'll Do

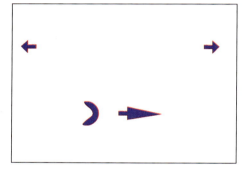

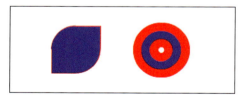

 In this lesson, you will copy, move, and transform (resize, rotate, and reshape) objects.

Copying and Moving Objects

To copy an object, select it, and then click the Copy command on the Edit menu. To paste the object, click the Paste command on the Edit menu. You can copy an object to another layer by selecting the frame on the layer prior to pasting the object. You can copy and paste more than one object by selecting all the objects before using the Copy or Paste commands.

You move an object by selecting it and dragging it to a new location. You can position an object more precisely by selecting it and then pressing the arrow keys, which move the selection up, down, left, and right in small increments. In addition, you can change the X and Y coordinates in the Properties panel to position an object exactly on the Stage.

Transforming Objects

You use the Free Transform tool and the Transform panel to resize, rotate, skew, and reshape objects. After selecting an object, you click the Free Transform tool to display eight square-shaped handles used to transform the object, and a circle-shaped transformation point located at the center of the object. The transformation point is the point around which the object can be rotated. You can also change its location.

Resizing an Object

You enlarge or reduce the size of an object using the Scale option, which is available when the Free Transform tool is selected. The process is to select the object and click the Free Transform tool, and then click the Scale option in the Options area of the Tools panel. Eight handles appear around the selected object. You drag the corner handles to resize the object without changing its proportions. That is, if the object starts out as a square, dragging a corner handle will change the size of the object, but it will still be a square. On the other hand, if you drag one of the middle handles, the object will be reshaped as taller, shorter, wider, or narrower. In addition, you can change the Width and Height settings in the Properties panel to resize an object in increments of one-tenth of one pixel.

Drawing Objects in Adobe Flash

Rotating and Skewing an Object

You use the Rotate and Skew option of the Free Transform tool to rotate an object and to skew it. The process is to select the object, click the Free Transform tool, and then click the Rotate and Skew option in the Options area of the Tools panel. Eight square-shaped handles appear around the object. You drag the corner handles to rotate the object, or you drag the middle handles to skew the object, as shown in Figure 26. The Transform panel can be used to rotate and skew an object in a more precise way; select the object, display the Transform panel (available via the Window menu), enter the desired rotation or skew in degrees, and then press [Enter] (Win) or [return] (Mac).

Distorting an Object

You can use the Distort and Envelope options to reshape an object by dragging its handles. The Distort option allows you to reshape an object by dragging one corner without affecting the other corners of the object. The Envelope option provides more than eight handles to allow more precise distortions. These options are accessed through the Transform command on the Modify menu.

Reshaping a Segment of an Object

You use the Subselection tool to reshape a segment of an object. You click an edge of the object to display handles that can be dragged to reshape the object.

You use the Selection tool to reshape objects. When you point to the edge of an object, the pointer displays an arc symbol. Using the Arc pointer, you drag the edge of the object you want to reshape, as shown in Figure 27. If the Selection tool points to a corner of an object, the pointer changes to an L-shape. You drag the pointer to reshape the corner of the object.

Flipping an Object

You use a Flip option on the Transform menu to flip an object either horizontally or vertically. You select the object, click the Transform command on the Modify menu, and then choose Flip Vertical or Flip Horizontal. Other Transform options allow you to rotate and scale the selected object. The Remove Transform command allows you to restore an object to its original state.

FIGURE 26

Using handles to manipulate an object

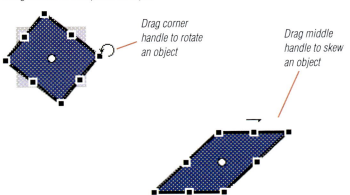

Drag corner handle to rotate an object

Drag middle handle to skew an object

FIGURE 27

Using the Selection tool to distort an object

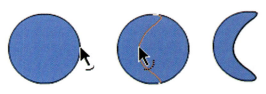

Copy and move an object

1. Click **frame 5** on the Timeline.

2. Click the **Selection tool** ![selection tool icon] on the Tools panel, then draw a **marquee** around the arrow object to select it.

3. Click **Edit** on the menu bar, click **Copy**, click **Edit** on the menu bar, then click **Paste in Center**.

4. Drag the newly copied **arrow** to the upper-right corner of the Stage, as shown in Figure 28.

5. Verify the right arrow object is selected on the Stage, press the **down arrow key [↓]** on the keyboard to move the object in approximately one-pixel increments, and notice how the Y coordinate in the Properties panel changes.

6. Press the **right arrow key [→]** on the keyboard to move the object in one-pixel increments, and notice how the X coordinate in the Properties panel changes.

7. Select the **number** in the X coordinate box in the Properties panel, type **450**, as shown in Figure 29, then press **[Enter]** (Win) or **[return]** (Mac).

8. Point to the **Y coordinate**, when the pointer changes to a double-headed arrow ![pointer icon] drag the ![pointer icon] **pointer** to change the setting to **30**.

9. Select the **left arrow object**, then set the X and Y coordinates to **36** and **30**, respectively.

10. Click a blank area of the Stage to deselect the object.

You used the Selection tool to select an object, then you copied and moved the object.

FIGURE 28
Moving the copied object

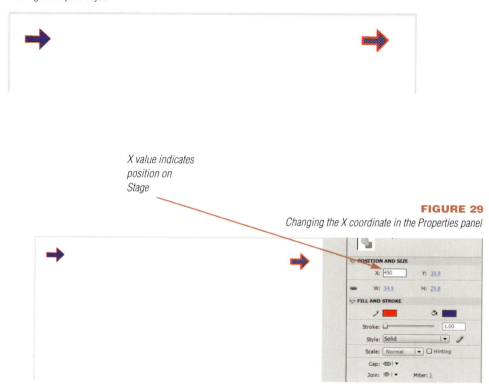

X value indicates
position on
Stage

FIGURE 29
Changing the X coordinate in the Properties panel

X and Y coordinates

The Stage dimensions are made up of pixels (dots) matching the Stage size. So, a Stage size of 550×400 would be 550 pixels wide and 400 pixels high. Each pixel has a location on the Stage designated as the X (across) and Y (down) coordinates. The location of any object is determined by its position from the upper-left corner of the Stage, which is 0,0. So, an object having coordinates of 450,30 would be positioned at 450 pixels across and 30 pixels down the Stage. The registration point of an object is used to align it with the coordinates. The registration point is initially set at the upper-left corner of an object.

FIGURE 30

Resizing an object using the corner handles

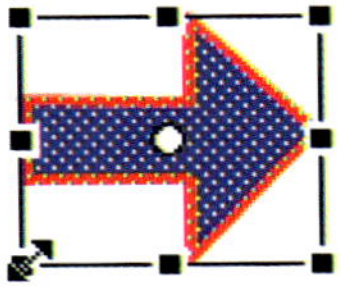

FIGURE 31

Reshaping an object using the middle handles

Transform options

Different transform options, such as rotate, skew, and scale, can be accessed through the Options area on the Tools panel when the Free Transform tool is selected, the Transform command on the Modify menu, and the Transform panel via the Transform command on the Window menu.

Resize and reshape an object

1. Draw a **marquee** around the arrow object on the right side of the Stage to select the object.

2. Select the **Free Transform tool** on the Tools panel.

   Note: You may need to click and hold the Gradient tool to display the Free Transform tool.

3. Select the **Scale option** in the Options area of the Tools panel.

4. Drag each **corner handle** toward and then away from the center of the object, as shown in Figure 30.

   As you drag a corner handle, the object's size is changed, but its proportions remain the same.

5. Click **Edit** on the menu bar, then click **Undo Scale**.

6. Repeat Step 5 until the arrow returns to its original size.

   > TIP The object is its original size when the option Undo Scale is no longer available on the Edit menu.

7. Verify the arrow is still selected and the handles are displayed, then select the **Scale option**.

8. Drag each **middle handle** toward and then away from the center of the object, as shown in Figure 31.

   As you drag the middle handles, the object's size and proportions change.

9. Click **Edit** on the menu bar, then click **Undo Scale** as needed to return the arrow to its original size.

You used the Free Transform tool and the Scale option to display an object's handles, and you used the handles to resize and reshape the object.

Rotate, skew, and flip an object

1. Verify that the Free Transform tool and the right arrow are selected (handles displayed), then click the **Rotate and Skew option** in the Options area of the Tools panel.

2. Click the **upper-right corner handle**, then rotate the object clockwise.

3. Click the **upper-middle handle**, then drag it to the right.

   The arrow slants down and to the right.

4. Click **Edit** on the menu bar, click the **Undo Skew** command, then repeat, selecting the Undo Rotate command, until the arrow is in its original shape and orientation.

5. Click the **Selection tool** on the Tools panel, verify that the right arrow is selected, click **Window** on the menu bar, then click **Transform**.

6. Click the **Rotate text box**, type **45**, then press **[Enter]** (Win) or **[return]** (Mac).

   The arrow rotates 45°, as shown in Figure 32.

7. Click **Edit** on the menu bar, then click **Undo Transform**.

8. Close the Transform panel.

9. Draw a **marquee** around the arrow in the upper-left corner of the Stage to select the object.

10. Click **Modify** on the menu bar, point to **Transform**, then click **Flip Horizontal**.

11. Save your work.

You used options on the Tools panel and the Transform panel, as well as commands on the Modify menu to rotate, skew, and flip an object.

FIGURE 32
Using the Transform panel to rotate an object

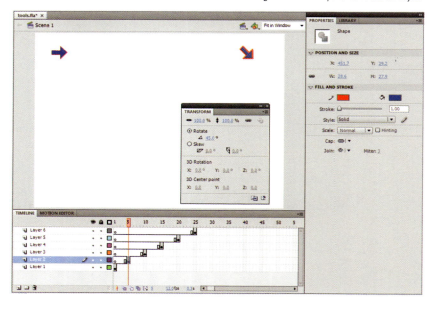

Drawing Objects in Adobe Flash

FIGURE 33

Using the Subselection tool to select an object

Click the tip of the
object to display
the handles

FIGURE 34

Using the Subselection tool to drag a handle to reshape the object

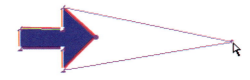

FIGURE 35

Using the Selection tool to drag an edge to reshape the object

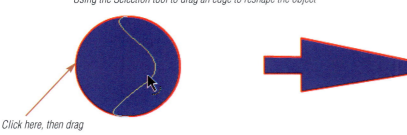

Click here, then drag

Use the Zoom, Subselection, and Selection tools

1. Select the **arrow** in the upper-right corner of the Stage, click **Edit** on the menu bar, click **Copy**, click **Edit** on the menu bar, then click **Paste in Center**.

2. Click the **Zoom tool** 🔍 on the Tools panel, then click the middle of the copied object to enlarge the view.

3. Click the **Subselection tool** ⟨ on the Tools panel, then click the **tip of the arrow** to display the handles, as shown in Figure 33.

    TIP   The handles allow you to change any segment of the object.

4. Click the **handle** at the tip of the arrow, then drag it, as shown in Figure 34.

5. Select the **Oval tool** ⬭ on the Tools panel, then deselect the **Object Drawing option** ⬭ in the Options area of the Tools panel.

6. Verify the Fill color is set to blue, then draw a **circle** to the left of the arrow you just modified.

7. Click the **Selection tool** ⟨ on the Tools panel, then point to the left edge of the circle until the Arc pointer ⟨ is displayed.

8. Drag the ⟨ **pointer** to the position shown in Figure 35.

9. Click **View** on the menu bar, point to **Magnification**, then click **100%**.

10. Save your work.

You used the Zoom tool to change the view, and you used the Subselection and Selection tools to reshape objects.

Use the Primitive Rectangle and Oval tools

1. Insert a **new layer** above Layer 6, click **frame 30** on Layer 7, then insert a **Keyframe**.

2. Click and hold down the **Oval tool** (or the Rectangle tool if it is displayed) to display the menu.

3. Click the **Rectangle Primitive tool**, then click the **Reset button** in the Properties panel RECTANGLE OPTIONS area to clear all of the settings.

4. Hold down **[Shift]**, point to the middle of the Stage, then draw the **square** shown in Figure 36.

5. Click the **Selection tool** in the Tools panel, then drag **the upper-right corner handle** toward the center of the object.
   As you drag the corner, the radius of each of the four corners is changed.

6. Click the **Reset button** in the Properties panel to clear the setting.

7. Slowly drag the **slider** in the RECTANGLE OPTIONS area to the right until the radius changes to 100, then slowly drag the **slider** to the left until the radius changes to –100.

8. Click the **Reset Button** on the Properties panel to clear the radius settings.

9. Click the **Lock corner radius icon** in the Properties panel RECTANGLE OPTIONS area to unlock the individual controls.

10. Type **-60** in the upper-left corner radius text box, then type **-60** in the upper-right corner text box, as shown in Figure 37.

(continued)

FIGURE 36
Drawing an object with the Rectangle Primitive tool

The corner handles can be dragged to change the radius of the corners; in addition, the Properties panel can be used to make changes to the object

FIGURE 37
Setting the corner radius of two corners

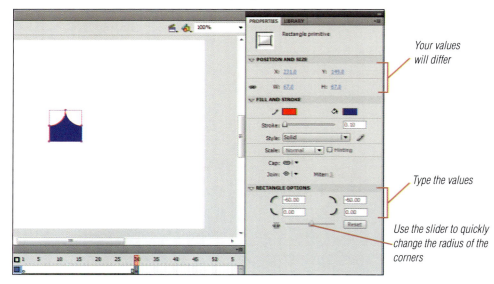

Your values will differ

Type the values

Use the slider to quickly change the radius of the corners

Drawing Objects in Adobe Flash

FIGURE 38
Drawing an object with the Oval Primitive tool

FIGURE 39
Setting the stroke value to 12

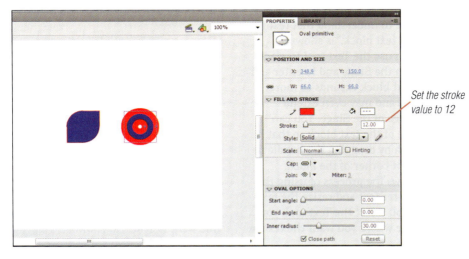

Set the stroke value to 12

11. Click the **Reset button** in the Properties panel to clear the radius settings.
12. Click the **Lock corner radius icon** ⊜ to unlock the individual controls.
13. Set the upper-left corner radius to **60** and the lower-right corner to **60**.
14. Click a blank area of the Stage to deselect the object.
15. Click and hold the **Rectangle Primitive tool** ▢ , click the **Oval Primitive tool** ◌ on the Tools panel, then hold down **[Shift]** and draw the **circle** shown in Figure 38.

    TIP   Remember some tools are grouped. Click and hold a grouped tool, such as the Oval tool, to see the menu of tools in the group.

16. Click the **Reset button** in the Properties panel OVAL OPTIONS area to clear any settings.
17. Drag the **Start angle slider** ◌ and the **End angle slider** ◌ to view their effect on the circle, then drag each **slider** back to 0.
18. Click the **Reset button** to clear the settings.
19. Drag the **Inner radius slider** ◌ to see the effect on the circle, then set the inner radius to **30**.
20. Display the FILL AND STROKE area of the Properties panel, then set the Stroke value to **12**, as shown in Figure 39.
21. Save your work.

You used the Primitive tools to create objects and the Properties panel to alter them.

Enter text and change text attributes

1. Click **Layer 7**, insert a **new layer**, then insert a **keyframe** in frame 35 of the new layer.

2. Click the **Text tool** T on the Tools panel, click the left-center of the Stage, then type **We have great events each year including a Rally**!

3. Click the **I-Beam pointer** I before the word "Rally," as shown in Figure 44, then type **Car** followed by a space.

4. Verify that the Properties panel is displayed, then drag the I-Beam pointer I across the text to select all the text.

5. Make the following changes in the CHARAC-TER area of the Properties panel: Family: **Arial**; Style: **Black** (Win) or **Bold** (Mac); Size:**16**; Color: **#990000**, then click the **text box**.

   Your Properties panel should resemble Figure 45.

6. Verify the text block is selected, position the **text pointer** ⊹ over the circle handle until the pointer changes to a double arrow ↔, then drag the **handle** to just before the word each, as shown in Figure 46.

7. Select the text using the **I-Beam pointer** I, then click the **Align center icon** ▣ in the PARAGRAPH area of the Properties panel.

8. Click the **Selection tool** ▸ on the Tools panel, click the **text object**, then drag the **object** to the lower-middle of the Stage.

   TIP   The Selection tool is used to select the text block, and the Text tool is used to select and edit the text within the text block.

You entered text and changed the font, type size, and text color; you also resized the text block and changed the text alignment.

FIGURE 44
Using the Text tool to enter text

We have great events each year including a |Rally!|

FIGURE 45
Changes in the CHARACTER area of the Properties panel

FIGURE 46
Resizing the text block

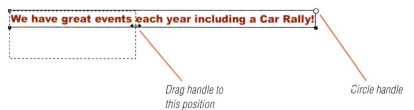

We have great events each year including a Car Rally!

Drag handle to this position

Circle handle

Drawing Objects in Adobe Flash

FIGURE 47
The Filters options in the Properties panel

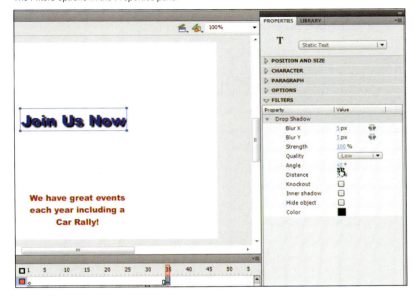

Using filters

You can apply special effects, such as drop shadows, to text using options in the FILTERS area of the Properties panel. The process is to select the desired text, display the FILTERS area of the Properties panel, choose the desired effect, and make any adjustments, such as changing the angle of a drop shadow. You can copy and paste a filter from one object to another using the clipboard icon in the FILTERS area of the Properties panel.

Add a Filter effect to text

1. Click the **Text tool** T on the Tools panel, click the center of the Stage, then type **Join Us Now**. *Hint:* If the text box does not appear, double-click the Stage.

2. Drag the **I-Beam pointer** I across the text to select it, then use the Properties panel to change the Font size to **30** and the Text (fill) color to **#003399**.

3. Click **CHARACTER** on the Properties panel to close the CHARACTER area, then close all areas in the Properties panel except for the FILTERS area.

4. Click the **Selection tool** on the Tools panel, then verify the text block is selected.

5. Click the **Add filter icon** at the bottom of the FILTERS area, then click **Drop Shadow**.

6. Point to the **Angle value** in the FILTERS area of the Properties panel, as shown in Figure 47.

7. When the pointer changes to a double-headed arrow, drag the pointer to the right to view the effect on the shadow, then set the Angle to **50**.

8. Click the **Distance value**, when the pointer changes to a double-headed arrow, drag the pointer to the right and notice the changes in the drop shadow.

9. Set the Distance to **6**.

10. Use the **Selection tool** to select the text position and position it as needed to match the placement shown in Figure 47, then save your work.

You used the Filter panel to create a drop shadow and then made changes to it.

Skew text and align objects

1. Click the **Text tool** T to select it, click the pointer near the top middle of the Stage twice, then type **Classic Car Club**.

2. Click **CHARACTER** in the Properties panel to display the CHARACTER area.

   The attributes of the new text reflect the most recent settings entered in the Properties panel.

3. Drag the **I-Beam pointer** I to select the text, then use the CHARACTER area of the Properties panel to change the font size to **40** and the fill color to **#990000**.

4. Click the **Selection tool** on the Tools panel to select the text box, then select the **Free Transform tool** on the Tools panel.

5. Click the **Rotate and Skew option** in the Options area of the Tools panel.

6. Drag the top middle handle to the right, as shown in Figure 48, to skew the text.

7. Click the **Selection tool** on the Tools panel.

8. Drag a **marquee** around all of the objects on the Stage to select them.

9. Click **Modify** on the menu bar, point to **Align**, verify To Stage has a check mark next to it, then click **Horizontal Center**.

   Note: If the Modify menu closes before you select Horizontal Center, repeat step 9.

10. Click a blank area of the Stage to deselect the objects.

You entered a heading, changed the font size and color, and skewed text using the Free Transform tool, then you aligned the objects on the Stage.

FIGURE 48
Skewing the text

FIGURE 49

Reshaping a letter

Drag this handle; notice the lines are drawn
from the anchor points on either side of the
anchor point being dragged

FIGURE 50

Applying a gradient fill to each letter

Reshape and apply a gradient to text

1. Click the **Selection tool** , click the **Classic Car Club text block** to select it, click **Modify** on the menu bar, then click **Break Apart**.

   The letters are now individual text blocks.

2. Click **Modify** on the menu bar, then click **Break Apart**.

   The letters are filled with a dot pattern, indicating that they can now be edited.

3. Click the **Zoom tool** on the Tools panel, then click the **"C"** in Classic.

4. Click the **Subselection tool** on the Tools panel, then click the edge of the letter **"C"** to display the object's segment handles.

5. Drag a lower handle on the "C" in Classic, as shown in Figure 49.

6. Click the **Selection tool** , then click a blank area of the Stage to deselect the objects.

7. Click **View** on the menu bar, point to **Magnification**, then click **Fit in Window**.

8. Click the **Fill Color tool color swatch** on the Tools panel, then click the **red gradient color swatch** in the bottom row of the Color palette.

9. Click the **Paint Bucket tool** on the Tools panel, then click the top of each letter to change the fill to a red gradient, as shown in Figure 50.

10. Use the status bar to change the movie frame rate to **3**, click **Control** on the menu bar, click **Test Movie**, watch the movie, then close the Flash Player window.

11. Save your work, then close the movie.

You broke apart a text block, reshaped text, and added a gradient to the text.

WORK WITH LAYERS
AND OBJECTS

What You'll Do

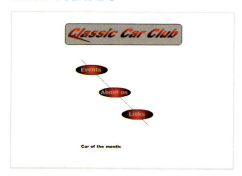

 In this lesson, you will create, rename, reorder, delete, hide, and lock layers. You will also display objects as outlines on layers, use a Guide layer, distribute text to layers, and create a Folder layer.

Learning About Layers

Flash uses two types of spatial organization. First, there is the position of objects on the Stage, and then there is the stacking order of objects that overlap. An example of overlapping objects is text placed on a banner. Layers are used on the Timeline as a way to organize objects. Placing objects on their own layer makes them easier to work with, especially when reshaping them, repositioning them on the Stage, or rearranging their order in relation to other objects. In addition, layers are useful for organizing other elements such as sounds, animations, and ActionScript.

There are five types of layers, as shown in the Layer Properties dialog box displayed in Figure 51 and discussed next.

Normal—The default layer type. All objects on these layers appear in the movie.

Mask—A layer that hides and reveals portions of another layer.

Masked—A layer that contains the objects that are hidden and revealed by a Mask layer.

Folder—A layer that can contain other layers.

Guide (Standard and Motion)—A Standard Guide layer serves as a reference point for positioning objects on the Stage. A Motion Guide layer is used to create a path for animated objects to follow.

Motion Guide, Mask, and Masked layer types are covered in a later chapter.

Working with Layers

The Layer Properties dialog box, accessed through the Timeline command on the Modify menu, allows you to specify the type of layer. It also allows you to name, show (and hide), and lock them. Naming a layer provides a clue to the objects on the layer. For example, naming a layer Logo might indicate that the object on the layer is the company's logo. Hiding a layer(s) may reduce the clutter on the Stage and make it easier to work with selected objects from the layer(s) that are not hidden. Locking a layer(s) prevents the objects from being accidentally edited. Other options in the Layer Properties dialog box allow you to view layers as outlines and change the outline color.

Outlines can be used to help you determine which objects are on a layer. When you turn on this feature, each layer has a colored box that corresponds with the color of the objects on its layer. Icons on the Layers area of the Timeline, as shown in Figure 52, correspond to features in the Layer Properties dialog box.

FIGURE 51
The Layer Properties dialog box

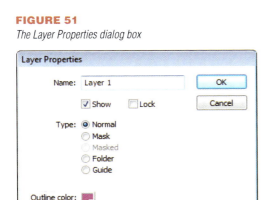

Show or Hide All Layers

FIGURE 52
The Layers area of the Timeline

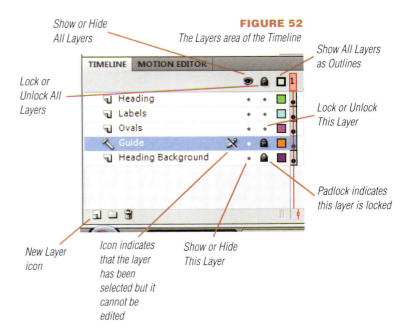

Show All Layers as Outlines

Lock or Unlock All Layers

Lock or Unlock This Layer

New Layer icon

Icon indicates that the layer has been selected but it cannot be edited

Show or Hide This Layer

Padlock indicates this layer is locked

Using a Guide Layer

Guide layers are useful in aligning objects on the Stage. Figure 53 shows a Guide layer that has been used to align three buttons along a diagonal path. The buttons are on one layer and the diagonal line is on another layer, the Guide layer. The process is to insert a new layer above the layer containing the objects to be aligned, you use the Layer Properties command from the Timeline option on the Modify menu to display the Layer Properties dialog box, select Guide as the layer type, and then draw a path that will be used as the guide to align the objects. You then verify the Snap to Guides option from the Snapping command on the View menu is turned on, and drag the desired objects to the Guide line. Objects have a transformation point that is used when snapping to a guide. By default, this point is at the center of the object. Figure 54 shows the process.

A Guide layer used to align objects on the Stage

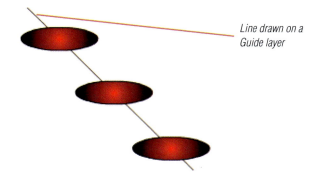

Line drawn on a
Guide layer

The transformation point of an object

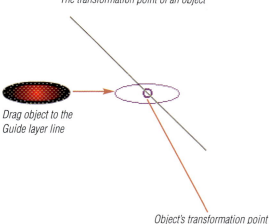

Drag object to the
Guide layer line

Object's transformation point

Distributing Text to Layers

Text blocks are made up of one or more characters. When you break apart a text block, each character becomes an object that can be edited independently of the other characters. You use the Distribute to Layers command from the Timeline option on the Modify menu, which causes each character to automatically be placed on its own layer. Figure 55 shows the seven layers created after the text block containing 55 Chevy has been broken apart and distributed to layers.

Using Folder Layers

As movies become larger and more complex, the number of layers increases. Flash allows you to organize layers by creating folders and grouping other layers in the folders. Figure 56 shows a Folder layer —Layer 4—with seven layers in it. The process is to select the layer that is to become a Folder layer, then use the Layer Properties dialog box to specify a Folder layer. To place other layers in the Folder layer, you drag them from the Timeline to the Folder layer. You click the Folder layer triangle next to Layer 4 to open and close the folder.

FIGURE 55
Distributing text to layers

FIGURE 56
A Folder layer

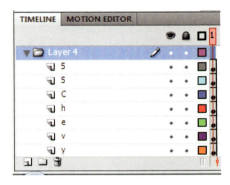

Create and reorder layers

1. Open fl2_2.fla from the drive and folder where your Data Files are stored, then save it as **layers2.fla**.

2. Click the **Selection tool** , click **View** on the menu bar, point to **Magnification**, then click **Fit in Window**.

3. Click the **New Layer icon** on the bottom of the Timeline (below the layer names) to insert a new layer, Layer 2.

4. Click **Frame 1** of Layer 2.

5. Select the **Rectangle tool** on the Tools panel, then set each corner radius to **10** in the RECTANGLE OPTIONS area of the Properties panel, and set the Stroke to **2** in the FILL AND STROKE area.

6. Click the **Fill Color tool color swatch** on the Tools panel, click the **Hex Edit text box**, type **#999999**, then press **[Enter]** (Win) or **[return]** (Mac).

7. Click the **Stroke Color tool color swatch** on the Tools panel, click the **Hex Edit text box**, type **#000000**, then press **[Enter]** (Win) or **[return]** (Mac).

8. Draw the **rectangle** shown in Figure 57 so it covers the text heading.

9. Drag **Layer 1** above Layer 2 on the Timeline, as shown in Figure 58.

10. Click the **Selection tool** on the Tools panel.

11. Click a blank area of the Stage to deselect the objects.

You added a layer, drew an object on the layer, and reordered layers.

FIGURE 57
Drawing a rectangle with a rounded corner

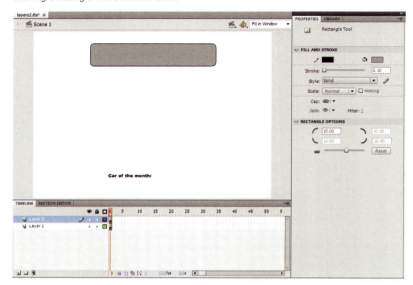

FIGURE 58
Dragging Layer 1 above Layer 2

Drag Layer 1 above Layer 2

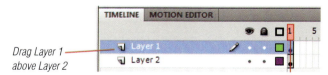

FIGURE 59
Renaming layers

Your outline colors
may vary

The amount of
text you see
may vary

Timeline icon

FIGURE 60
Expanding the layer name area of the Timeline

Drag the
Timeline icon

1. Double-click **Layer 1** on the Timeline, type **Heading** in the Layer Name text box, then press **[Enter]** (Win) or **[return]** (Mac).

2. Rename Layer 2 as **Heading Background.**

3. Point to the **Timeline icon** ▦ below the layer names, as shown in Figure 59.

4. When the pointer changes to a double arrow ⊣⊢, drag the **icon** to the right to display all the layer names, as shown in Figure 60.

5. Click the **Heading layer**, then click the **Delete icon** 🗑 on the bottom of the Timeline.

6. Click **Edit** on the menu bar, then click **Undo Delete Layer**.

7. Click **Heading Background** to display both layers.

You renamed layers to associate them with objects on the layers, then deleted and restored a layer.

Hide, lock, and display layer outlines

1. Click the **Show or Hide All Layers icon** 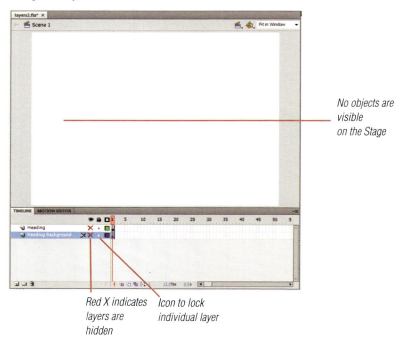 to hide all layers, then compare your image to Figure 61.

2. Click the **Show or Hide All Layers icon** to show all the layers.

3. Click the **Heading Background layer**, then click the **Show or Hide This Layer icon** twice to hide and then show the layer.

4. Click the **Lock or Unlock All Layers icon** to lock all layers.

5. With the layers locked, try to select and edit an object.

6. Click the **Lock or Unlock All Layers icon** again to unlock the layers.

7. Click the **Heading Background layer**, then click the **Lock or Unlock This Layer** to lock the layer.

8. Click the **Show All Layers as Outlines icon** to display the outlines of all objects.

   Notice the outlines are color-coded. For example, the two text objects are identified by their color (green) as being on the Heading layer (green).

9. Click the **Show All Layers as Outlines icon** to turn off this feature.

You hid and showed layers, you locked and unlocked layers, and you displayed the outlines of objects on a layer.

FIGURE 61
Hiding all the layers

No objects are visible on the Stage

Red X indicates layers are hidden

Icon to lock individual layer

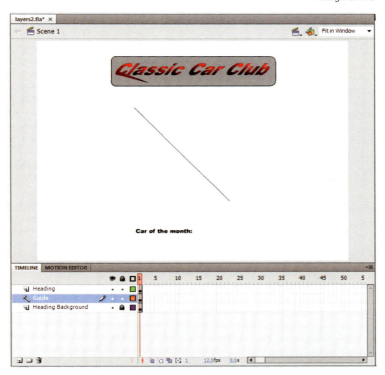

FIGURE 62

A diagonal line

Create a guide for a Guide layer

1. Click the **Heading Background layer**, then click the **New Layer icon** on the bottom of the Timeline to add a new layer, Layer 3.

2. Rename the layer **Guide**.

3. Verify that the Guide layer is selected.

4. Click **Modify** on the menu bar, point to **Timeline**, then click **Layer Properties** to display the Layer Properties dialog box.

5. Click the **Guide option button** in the Type area, then click **OK**.

   A symbol appears next to the word Guide indicating that this is a Guide layer.

6. Click **frame 1** of the Guide layer.

7. Click the **Line tool** on the Tools panel, press and hold **[Shift]**, then draw the diagonal line, as shown in Figure 62.

8. Click the **Lock or Unlock This Layer icon** on the Guide layer to lock it.

You created a guide for a Guide layer and drew a guide line.

Add objects to a Guide layer

1. Add a new layer on the Timeline above the Guide layer, name it **Ovals**, then click **frame 1** of the Ovals layer.

2. Click the **Fill Color tool color swatch** 🎨 on the Tools panel, then click the **red gradient color swatch** in the bottom row of the Color palette.

3. Select the **Oval tool** ⬭ on the Tools panel, then verify that the **Object Drawing option** ⬭ in the Options area of the Tools panel is deselected.

4. Draw the **oval**, as shown in Figure 63.

5. Click the **Selection tool** ▸ on the Tools panel, then draw a **marquee** around the oval object to select it.

   | TIP Make sure the entire object (stroke and fill) is selected.

6. Point to the center of the oval, click, then slowly drag it to the Guide layer line, as shown in Figure 64.

7. With the oval object selected, click **Edit** on the menu bar, then click **Copy**.

8. Click **Edit** on the menu bar, click **Paste in Center**, then align the copied object to the Guide layer line beneath the first oval.

9. Click **Edit** on the menu bar, click **Paste in Center**, then align the copied object to the bottom of the Guide layer line.

   | TIP When objects are pasted in the center of the Stage, one object may cover up another object. Move them as needed.

You created a Guide layer and used it to align objects on the Stage.

FIGURE 63
An oval object

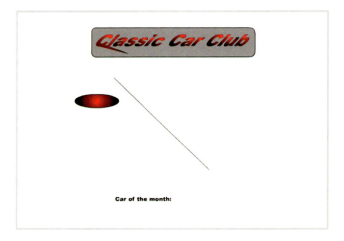

FIGURE 64
Dragging an object to the Guide layer line

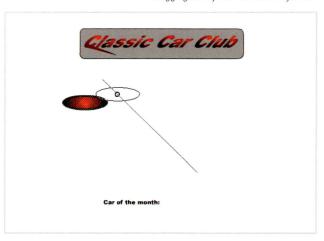

FIGURE 65
Adding text to the oval objects

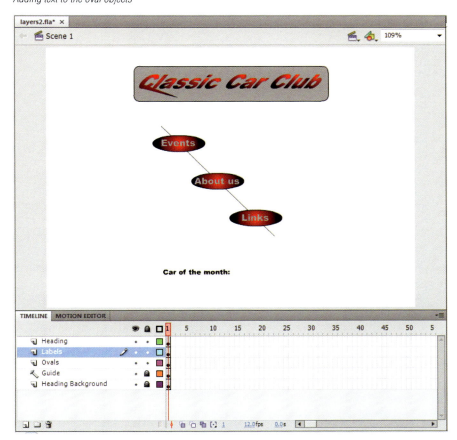

Adding text on top of an object

1. Insert a **new layer** on the Timeline above the Ovals layer, then name it **Labels**.

2. Click **frame 1** of the Labels layer.

3. Click the **Text tool** T on the Tools panel, click the **top oval**, then type **Events**.

4. Drag the **I-Beam pointer** I across Events to select the text, then, using the Properties panel set the font to **Arial**, the style to **Black** (Win) or **Bold** (Mac), the font size to **14**, and the fill color to **#999999**.

5. Click the **Selection tool** on the Tools panel, click the **text box** to select it, then drag the **text box** to center it on the oval, as shown in Figure 65.

   | TIP You can use the arrow keys on the keyboard to nudge the text into place.

6. Repeat Steps 3 through 5, typing **About us** and **Links** text blocks.

7. Test the movie, then close the Flash Player window.

8. Save and then close the document.

9. Exit Flash.

You used the Text tool to create text blocks that were placed on objects.

Use the Flash drawing tools.

1. Start Flash, open fl2_3.fla, then save it as **skillsdemo2**. Refer to Figure 66 as you complete these steps. (*Note:* Figure 66 shows the objects after changes have been made to them. For example, in step 5 you draw a rectangle in the middle of the Stage. Then, in a later step you rotate the rectangle 45 degrees.)

2. Set the view to Fit in Window, then display the Grid.

3. Set the stroke color to black (Hex: **#000000**) and the fill color to blue (Hex: **#0000FF**).

4. Use the Oval tool to draw an oval on the left side of the Stage, then draw a circle beneath the oval. (*Hint:* Use the Undo command as needed.)

5. Use the Rectangle tool to draw a rectangle in the middle of the Stage, then draw a square beneath the rectangle.

6. Use the Line tool to draw a horizontal line on the right side of the Stage, then draw a vertical line beneath the horizontal line and a diagonal line beneath the vertical line.

7. Use the Pen tool to draw an arrow-shaped object above the rectangle. (*Hint:* Use the Zoom tool to enlarge the area of the Stage.)

8. Use the Paint Bucket tool to fill the arrow with the blue color. (*Hint:* If the arrow does not fill, be sure you closed the arrow shape by clicking the first anchor point as your last action.)

9. Use the Pencil tool to draw a freehand line above the oval, then select the line and use the Smooth option to smooth out the line.

10. Use the Rectangle Primitive tool to draw a rectangle below the square and then use the Selection tool to drag a corner to round all the corners.

11. Save your work.

Select objects and apply colors.

1. Use the Selection tool to select the stroke of the circle, then deselect the stroke.

2. Use the Selection tool to select the fill of the circle, then deselect the fill.

3. Use the Ink Bottle tool to change the stroke color of the circle to red (Hex: **#FF0000**).

4. Use the Paint Bucket tool to change the fill color of the square to a red gradient.

5. Change the fill color of the oval to a blue gradient.

6. Save your work.

Work with drawn objects.

1. Copy and paste the arrow object.

2. Move the copied arrow to another location on the Stage.

3. Use the Properties panel to set the height of each arrow to 30.

4. Flip the copied arrow horizontally.

5. Rotate the rectangle to a 45° angle.

6. Skew the square to the right.

7. Copy one of the arrows and use the Subselection tool to reshape it, then delete it.

8. Use the Selection tool to reshape the circle to a crescent shape.

9. Save your work.

Work with text and text objects.

1. Enter the following text in a text block at the top of the Stage: **Gateway to the Pacific**.

2. Select the text, then change the text to font: **Tahoma**, size: **24**, color: **red**.

3. Use the Align option on the Modify menu to horizontally center the text block.

4. Use the up and down arrow keys on the keyboard to align the text block with a gridline.

5. Skew the text block to the right.

6. Save your work.

Work with layers.

1. Insert a layer into the document.

2. Change the name on the new layer to **Heading Bkgnd**.

3. Use the Rectangle Primitive tool to draw a rounded corner rectangle with a blue color that covers the words Gateway to the Pacific.

4. Switch the order of the layers.

5. Lock all layers.

6. Unlock all layers.

7. Hide the Heading Bkgnd layer.

8. Show the Heading Bkgnd layer.

9. Show all layers as outlines.

10. Turn on, then turn off the view of the outlines.

11. Create a new layer as a Guide layer, draw a guildeline on the new layer, lock the layer, then snap the arrows to the guideline.

12. Add a layer and use the Text tool to type **Seattle** below the heading.

13. Save your work.

Use the Merge Drawing Model mode.

1. Insert a new layer and name it **MergeDraw**.
2. Select the Rectangle tool and verify that the Object Drawing option is deselected.
3. Draw a square in the upper-right of the Stage, then use the Oval tool to draw a circle with a different color that covers approximately half of the square.
4. Verify the stroke and fill of the circle are selected, then using the Selection tool drag the circle off the square. (*Note:* Depending on the size of the circle and where you drew it to overlap the square, your results may vary from what is shown in Figure 66.)

Use the Object Drawing Model mode.

1. Insert a new layer and name it **ObjectDraw**.
2. Select the Rectangle tool and verify that the Object Drawing option is selected.
3. Draw a square with a blue fill color, then use the Oval tool to draw a circle with a different color that covers approximately half of the square.
4. Use the Selection tool to drag the circle off the square. (*Note:* Depending on the size of the circle and where you drew it to overlap the square, your results may vary from what is shown in Figure 66.)
5. Select the Rectangle tool and click the Object Drawing option to deselect it, then repeat step 3 and step 4. Notice how the dragging the circle off the square has a different effect when the Object Drawing option is turned off.

6. Save your work, then compare your image to the example shown in Figure 66.

Use the Spray tool with a symbol.

1. Add a new layer to the Timeline, then add a Keyframe to Frame 5 of the new layer.
2. Name the layer Aces Wild.
3. Select the Spray Brush tool.
4. Click the Edit button in the Symbol section of the Properties panel. (*Note:* If the Properties panel does not display the options for the Spray Brush tool, click the Selection tool, then click the Spray Brush tool.)
5. Select the Ace symbol.
6. Set the Scale width and height to 60.
7. Turn on Rotate symbol and turn off the other options.
8. Set the Brush width and height to 8 px.
9. Draw the W as shown in Figure 66.
10. Click the Selection tool on the Tools panel, then select the Spray Brush tool.
11. Draw the i.
12. Click the Selection tool, select the Spray Brush tool, then draw the n to complete a drawing similar to the one shown in Figure 66. (*Hint:* If you need to redo the drawing, use the Selection tool to draw a marquee around the drawing, then delete the selection.)
13. Test the movie, then save and close the document. (*Note:* If the movie displays too quickly, adjust the frame rate.)
14. Exit Flash.

FIGURE 66
Completed Skills Review

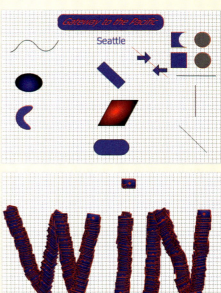

Drawing Objects in Adobe Flash

A local travel company, Ultimate Tours, has asked you to design several sample home pages for its new website. The goal of the website is to inform potential customers of its services. The company specializes in exotic treks, tours, and cruises. Thus, while its target audience spans a wide age range, they are all looking for something out of the ordinary.

1. Open a new Flash document and save it as **ultimatetours2**. Refer to Figure 67 as you complete this project.
2. Set the document properties, including the size (your choice) and background color.
3. Create the following on separate layers and name the layers:
   - A text heading; select a font size and font color. Skew the heading, break it apart, then reshape one or more of the characters.
   - A subheading with a different font size and color.
   - At least three objects.
4. Use one or more of the align features (gridlines, rulers, Align command on the Modify menu, arrow keys) to align the objects on the Stage.
5. On another layer, add text to the objects.
6. Lock all layers.
7. Compare your image to the example shown in Figure 67.
8. Save your work.
9. Test the movie, close the Flash Player window, then close the movie.

FIGURE 67
Sample completed Project Builder 1

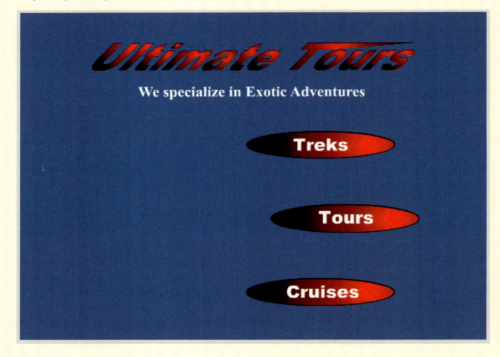

You have been asked to create several sample designs for the home page of a new organization called The Jazz Club. The club is being organized to bring together music enthusiasts for social events and charitable fundraising activities. The club members plan to sponsor weekly jam sessions and a show once a month. Because the club is just getting started, the organizers are looking to you for help in developing a website.

1. Plan the site by specifying the goal, target audience, treatment ("look and feel"), and elements you want to include (text, graphics, sound, and so on).
2. Sketch out a storyboard that shows the layout of the objects on the various screens and how they are linked together. Be creative in your design.
3. Open a new Flash document and save it as **thejazzclub2**.
4. Set the document properties, including the size and background color, if desired.
5. Display the gridlines and rulers and use them to help align objects on the Stage.
6. Create a heading with a background, text objects, and drawings to be used as links to the categories of information provided on the website. (*Note:* Some of the characters are individual text blocks [e.g. the S in Sessions] allowing you to move the text block without moving the other characters.)

(*Hint:* Use the Oval, Line, and Brush tools to create the notes. After selecting the Brush tool, experiment with the different Brush tool shapes found in the Options area at the bottom of the Tools panel.)

7. Hide the gridlines and rulers.
8. Save your work, then compare your image to the example shown in Figure 68.

FIGURE 68
Sample completed Project Builder 2

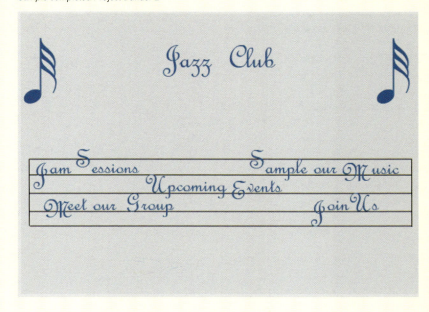

Figure 69 shows the home page of a website. Study the figure and complete the following. For each question indicate how you determined your answer.

1. Connect to the Internet, then go to *www.nps.org*.
2. Open a document in a word processor or open a new Flash document, save the file as **dpc2**, then answer the following questions. (*Hint*: Use the Text tool in Flash.)
   - Whose website is this?
   - What is the goal(s) of the site?
   - Who is the target audience?
   - What is the treatment ("look and feel") that is used?
   - What are the design layout guidelines being used (balance, movement, and so on)?
   - What may be animated on this home page?
   - Do you think this is an effective design for the company, its products, and its target audience? Why or why not?
   - What suggestions would you make to improve the design and why?

FIGURE 69
Design Project

You have decided to create a personal portfolio of your work that you can use when you begin your job search. The portfolio will be a website done completely in Flash.

1. Research what should be included in a portfolio.
2. Plan the site by specifying the goal, target audience, treatment ("look and feel"), and elements you want to include (text, graphics, sound, and so on).
3. Sketch a storyboard that shows the layout of the objects on the various screens and how they are linked together. Be creative in your design.
4. Design the home page to include personal data, contact information, previous employment, education, and samples of your work.
5. Open a new Flash document and save it as **portfolio2**.
6. Set the document properties, including the size and background color, if desired.
7. Display the gridlines and rulers and use them to help align objects on the Stage.
8. Add a border the size of the Stage. (*Hint*: Use the Rectangle tool and set the fill color to none.)

9. Create a heading with its own background, then create other text objects and drawings to be used as links to the categories of information provided on the website. (*Hint*: In the example shown here, the Tahoma font is used. You can replace this font with Impact or any other appropriate font on your computer.)

FIGURE 70
Sample Completed Portfolio Project

10. Hide the gridlines and rulers.
11. Save your work, then compare your image to the example shown in Figure 70.

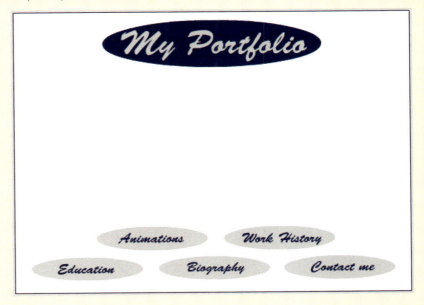

WORKING WITH SYMBOLS
AND INTERACTIVITY

1. Create symbols and instances

2. Work with libraries

3. Create buttons

4. Assign actions to frames and buttons

5. Importing graphics

WORKING WITH SYMBOLS
AND INTERACTIVITY

Introduction

An important benefit of Flash is its ability to create movies with small file sizes. This allows the movies to be delivered from the web more quickly. One way to keep the file size small is to create reusable graphics, buttons, and movie clips. Flash allows you to create a graphic (drawing) and then make unlimited copies, which you can use throughout the current movie and in other movies. Flash calls the original drawing a **symbol** and the copied drawings **instances**. Flash stores symbols in the Library panel—each time you need a copy of the symbol, you can open the Library panel and drag the symbol to the Stage, which creates an instance (copy) of the symbol. Using instances reduces the movie file size because Flash stores only the symbol's information (size, shape, color), but Flash does not save the instance in the Flash movie. Rather, a link is established between the symbol and an instance so that the instance has the same properties (such as color and shape) as the symbol.

What is especially valuable about this process is that you can change the properties for each instance. For example, if your website is to contain drawings of cars that are similar, you can create just one drawing, convert it to a symbol, insert as many instances of the car as needed, and then change an individual instance as desired.

There are three categories of symbols: graphic, button, and movie clip. A graphic symbol is useful because you can reuse a single image and make changes in each instance of the image. A button symbol is useful because you can create buttons for interactivity, such as starting or stopping a movie. A movie clip symbol is useful for creating complex animations because you can create a movie within a movie. Symbols can be created from objects you draw using the Flash drawing tools. In addition, you can import graphics into a Flash document that can then be converted into symbols.

Tools You'll Use

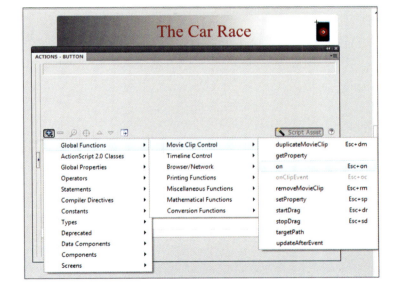

CREATE SYMBOLS
AND INSTANCES

What You'll Do

In this lesson, you will create graphic symbols, turn them into instances, and then edit the instances.

Creating a Graphic Symbol

You can use the New Symbol command on the Insert menu to create and then draw a symbol. You can also draw an object and then use the Convert to Symbol command on the Modify menu to convert the object to a symbol. The Convert to Symbol dialog box, shown in Figure 1, allows you to name the symbol and specify the type of symbol you want to create (Movie Clip, Button, or Graphic). When naming a symbol, it's a good idea to use a naming convention that allows you to quickly identify the type of symbol and to group like symbols together. For example, you could identify all graphic symbols by naming them g_*name* and all buttons as b_*name*. In Figure 1, the drawing on the Stage is being converted into a graphic symbol, which will be named g_ball.

After you complete the Convert to Symbol dialog box, Flash places the symbol in the Library panel, as shown in Figure 2. In Figure 2, an icon identifying the symbol as a graphic symbol and the symbol name are listed in the Library panel, along with a preview of the selected symbol. To create an

instance of the symbol, you simply drag a symbol from the Library panel to the Stage. To edit a symbol, you select it from the Library panel or you use the Edit Symbols command on the Edit menu. This displays the symbol in an edit window, where changes can be made to it. When you edit a symbol, the changes are reflected in all instances of that symbol in your movie. For example, you can draw a car, convert the car to a symbol, and then create several instances of the car. You can uniformly change the size of all the cars by double-clicking the car symbol in the Library panel to open the edit window, and then rescaling it to the desired size.

Working with Instances

You can have as many instances as needed in your movie, and you can edit each one to make it somewhat different from the others. You can rotate, skew (slant), and resize graphic and button instances. In addition, you can change the color, brightness, and transparency. However, there are some limitations. An instance is a single object with no segments or parts, such as a stroke and a fill. You cannot select a part of an instance. Therefore, any changes to the color of the instance are made to the entire object. Of course, you can use layers to stack other objects on top of an instance to change its appearance. In addition, you can use the Break Apart command on the Modify menu to break the link between an instance and a symbol. Once the link is broken, you can make any changes to the object, such as changing its stroke and fill color. However, because the link is broken,

the object is no longer an instance; if you make any changes to the original symbol, then the object is not affected.

The process for creating an instance is to open the Library panel and drag the desired symbol to the Stage. Once the symbol is on the Stage, you select the instance by using the Selection tool to drag a marquee around it. A blue border indicates that the object is selected. Then, you can use the Free Transform tool options (such as Rotate and Skew, or Scale) to modify the

entire image, or you can use the Break Apart command to break apart the instance and edit individual strokes and fills.

QUICKTIP

You need to be careful when editing an instance. Use the Selection tool to drag a marquee around the instance, or click the object once to select it. Do not double-click the instance when it is on the Stage; otherwise, you will open an edit window that is used to edit the symbol, not the instance.

FIGURE 1

Using the Convert to Symbol dialog box to convert an object to a symbol

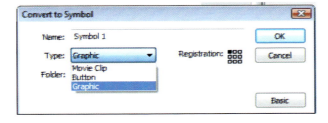

FIGURE 2

A graphic symbol in the Library panel

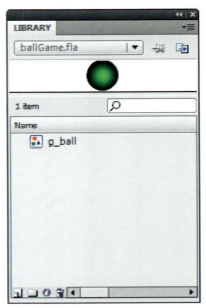

Create a symbol

1. Open fl3_1.fla from the drive and folder where your Data Files are stored, then save it as **coolCar**. This document has one object, a car, that was created using the Flash drawing tools.

2. Verify the Properties panel, the Library panel, and the Tools panel are displayed.

3. Set the magnification to **100%**.

4. Click the **Selection tool** on the Tools panel, then drag a **marquee** around the car to select it.

5. Click **Modify** on the menu bar, then click **Convert to Symbol**.

6. Type **g_car** in the Name text box.

7. Click the **Type list arrow** to display the symbol types, as shown in Figure 3.

8. Click **Graphic**, then click **OK**.

9. Click the **Library panel tab**, then study the Library panel, as shown in Figure 4, and notice it displays the symbol (red car) in the Item Preview window, an icon indicating that this is a graphic symbol, and the name of the symbol (g_car).

   The symbol is contained in the library, and the car on the Stage is now an instance of the symbol.

You opened a file with an object, converted the object to a symbol, and displayed the symbol in the Library panel.

FIGURE 3
Options in the Convert to Symbol dialog box

FIGURE 4
Newly created symbol in the Library panel

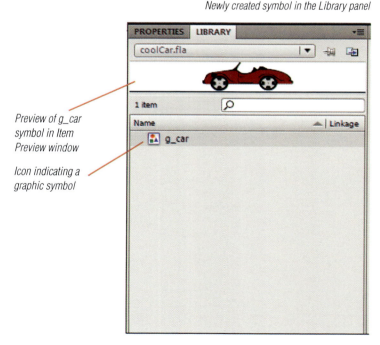

Preview of g_car symbol in Item Preview window

Icon indicating a graphic symbol

FIGURE 5
Creating an instance

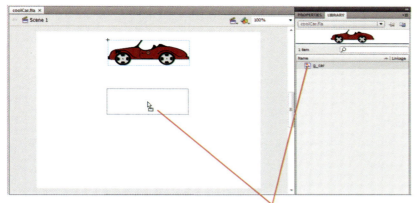

Drag the symbol from the Library
panel to below the original
instance to create a second
instance of the symbol

This area may
not be open

FIGURE 6
The alpha set to 50%

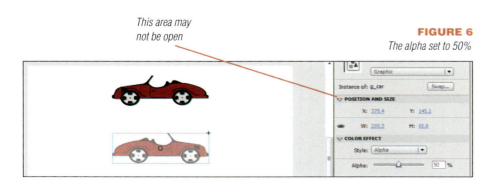

Create and edit an instance

1. Point to the **car image** in the Item Preview
   window of the Library panel, then drag the
   image to the Stage beneath the first car, as
   shown in Figure 5.

   TIP You can also drag the name of the
   symbol from the Library panel to the Stage.
   Both cars on the Stage are instances of the
   graphic symbol in the Library panel.

2. Verify the bottom car is selected, click
   Modify on the menu bar, point to **Transform**,
   then click **Flip Horizontal**.

3. Display the Properties panel, then display
   the COLOR EFFECT area if it is not
   already showing.

4. Click the **Style list arrow**, then click **Alpha**.

5. Drag the **Alpha slider** to 50%.

   Notice how the transparency changes.
   Figure 6 shows the transparency set to 50%.

6. Click a blank area of the Stage to deselect
   the object.

   Changing the alpha setting gives the car
   a more transparent look.

*You created an instance of a symbol and edited the
instance on the Stage.*

Edit a symbol in the edit window

1. Display the Library panel, double-click the **g_car symbol icon** in the Library panel to display the edit window, then compare your screen to Figure 7.

The g_car symbol appears in the edit window, indicating that you are editing the g_car symbol.

TIP You can also edit a symbol by clicking Edit on the menu bar, then clicking Edit Symbols.

2. Click a blank area of the window to deselect the car.

3. Verify the Selection tool is selected, then click the **light gray hubcap** inside the front wheel to select it.

4. Press and hold **[Shift]**, then click the **hubcap** inside the back wheel so both hubcap fills are selected.

5. Set the **Fill Color** to the **blue gradient color swatch** in the bottom row of the color palette, deselect the image, then compare your image to Figure 8.

6. Click **Scene 1** at the top left of the edit window to exit the edit window and return to the main Timeline and main Stage.

Changes you make to the symbol affect every instance of the symbol on the Stage. The hubcap fill becomes a blue gradient in the Library panel and on the Stage.

You edited a symbol in the edit window that affected all instances of the symbol.

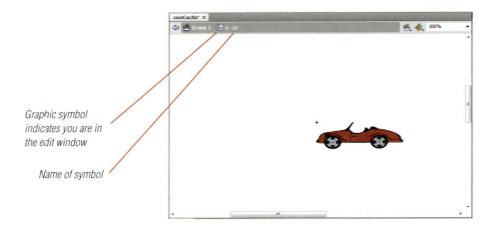

FIGURE 7
Edit window

Graphic symbol indicates you are in the edit window

Name of symbol

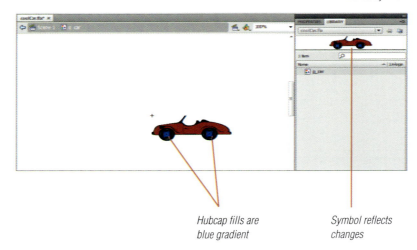

FIGURE 8
Edited symbol

Hubcap fills are blue gradient

Symbol reflects changes

FIGURE 9

The car with the maroon body selected

FIGURE 10

Changing the symbol affects only the one instance of the symbol

Instance of the
symbol

Object that is no
longer an instance
of the symbol

Break apart an instance

1. Drag a **marquee** around the bottom car to select it if it is not selected.

2. Click **Modify** on the menu bar, then click **Break Apart**.

   The object is no longer linked to the symbol, and its parts (strokes and fills) can now be edited.

3. Click a blank area of the Stage to deselect the object.

4. Click the **blue front hubcap**, press and hold **[Shift]**, then click the **blue back hubcap** so both hubcaps are selected.

5. Set the **Fill Color** to the **light gray color swatch (#999999)** in the left column of the color palette.

6. Double-click the **g_car symbol icon** in the Library panel to display the edit window.

7. Click the **maroon front body** of the car to select it, press and hold **[Shift]**, then click the **maroon back body** of the car, as shown in Figure 9.

8. Set the **Fill Color** to the **red gradient color swatch** in the bottom row of the color palette.

9. Click **Scene 1** at the top left of the edit window, then compare your image to Figure 10.

   The body color of the car in the original instance is a different color, but the body color of the car to which you applied the Break Apart command remains unchanged.

10. Save your work.

You used the Break Apart command to break the link of the instance to its symbol, you edited the object, and then you edited the symbol.

WORK WITH
LIBRARIES

What You'll Do

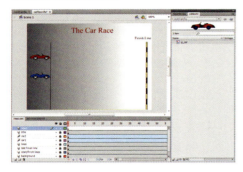

 In this lesson, you will use the Library panel to organize the symbols in a movie.

Understanding the Library

The library in a Flash document contains the symbols and other items such as imported graphics, movie clips, and sounds. The Library panel provides a way to view and organize the items, and allows you to change the item name, display item properties, and add and delete items. Figure 11 shows the Library panel for a document. Refer to this figure as you read the following descriptions of the parts of the library.

Title tab—Identifies this as the Library panel.

List box—The list box below the title tab can be used to select an open document and display the Library panel associated with that open document. This allows you to use the items from one movie in another movie. For example, you may have developed a drawing in one Flash movie and need to use it in the movie you are working on. With both documents open, you simply use the list box to display the library with the desired drawing, and then drag it to the Stage of the current movie. This will automatically place the drawing in the library for the current movie. In addition to the movie libraries, you can create permanent libraries that are available whenever you start Flash. Flash also has sample libraries that contain buttons and other objects. The permanent and sample libraries are accessed through the Common Libraries command on the Window menu. All assets in all of these libraries are available for use in any movie.

Options menu—Shown in Figure 12; provides access to several features used to edit symbols (such as renaming symbols) and organize symbols (such as creating a new folder).

Item Preview window—Displays the selected item. If the item is animated or a sound file, a control button appears, allowing you to preview the animation or play the sound.

Toggle Sorting Order icon—Allows you to reorder the list of folders and items within folders.

Name text box—Lists the folder and item names. Each item type has a different icon associated with it. Clicking an item name or icon displays the item in the Item Preview window.

New Symbol icon—Displays the Create New Symbol dialog box, allowing you to create a new symbol.

New Folder icon—Allows you to create a new folder.

Properties icon—Displays the Properties dialog box for the selected item.

Delete Item icon—Deletes the selected item or folder.

To make changes to an item, you can double-click the item icon in the Library panel to display the edit window.

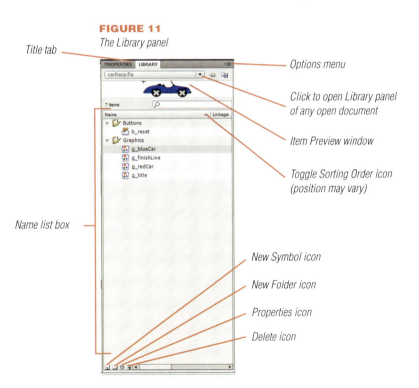

FIGURE 11
The Library panel

Title tab

Options menu

Click to open Library panel of any open document

Item Preview window

Toggle Sorting Order icon (position may vary)

Name list box

New Symbol icon

New Folder icon

Properties icon

Delete icon

FIGURE 12
The Options menu

New Symbol...
New Folder
New Font...
New Video...

Rename
Delete
Duplicate...
Move to...

Edit
Edit with...
Edit with Soundbooth
Play
Update...

Properties...
Component Definition...
Shared Library Properties...

Select Unused Items

Expand Folder
Collapse Folder
Expand All Folders
Collapse All Folders

Help

Close
Close Group

Create folders in the Library panel

1. Open fl3_2.fla, then save it as **carRace**.

2. Verify the Properties panel, the Library panel, and the **Tools panel** are displayed.

3. Set the magnification to **100%**.

   This movie has eight layers containing various objects such as text blocks, lines, and a background. Two layers contain animations of cars.

4. Test the movie, then close the Flash Player window.

5. Click the **Show or Hide All Layers icon** 👁 on the Timeline to hide all of the layers.

6. Click the **Show or Hide This Layer icon** ⋅ for each layer to show the contents of each layer.

   Note: The reset layer shows an empty Stage. This is because the word Reset is located in frame 65 at the end of the movie and does not appear in frame 1.

7. Click each item in the Library panel to display it in the Item Preview window. Notice that there is one button symbol (b_reset) and five graphic symbols.

   Note: The g_finishLine graphic will look like a black line because the preview window is small.

8. Click the **New Folder icon** 🗔 in the Library panel, as shown in Figure 13.

9. Type **Graphics** in the Name text box, then press **[Enter]** (Win) or **[return]** (Mac).

(continued)

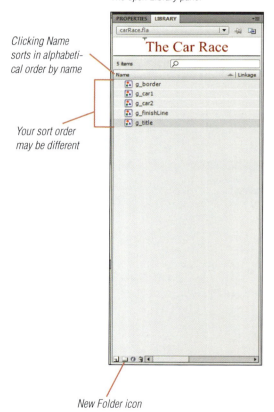

FIGURE 13
The open Library panel

Clicking Name sorts in alphabetical order by name

Your sort order may be different

New Folder icon

FIGURE 14
The Library panel with the folders added

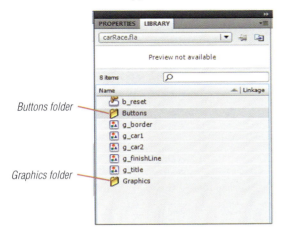

Buttons folder

Graphics folder

FIGURE 15
The Library panel after moving the symbols to the folders

Your folders might be expanded

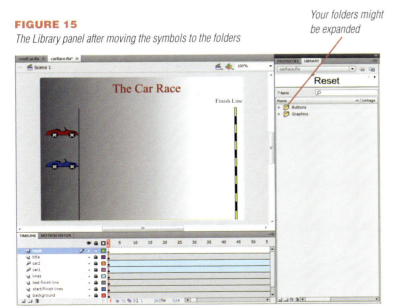

10. Click the **New Folder icon** [icon] on the Library panel.

11. Type **Buttons** in the Name text box, then press [**Enter**] (Win) or [**return**] (Mac).

Your Library panel should resemble Figure 14.

You opened a Flash movie and created folders in the Library panel.

Organize items within Library panel folders

1. Click **Name** on the Name list box title bar and notice how the items are sorted.

2. Repeat step 1 and notice how the items are sorted.

3. Drag the **g_title symbol** in the Library panel to the Graphics folder.

4. Drag the other graphic symbols to the Graphics folder.

5. Drag the **b_reset symbol** to the Buttons folder, then compare your Library panel to Figure 15.

6. Click the **Graphics folder expand list arrow** [arrow] to open it and display the graphic symbols.

7. Click the **Buttons folder expand list arrow** [arrow] to open it and display the button symbol.

8. Click the **Graphics folder collapse list arrow** [arrow] to close the folder.

9. Click the **Buttons folder collapse list arrow** [arrow] to close the folder.

Note: To remove an item from a folder, drag the item down to a blank area of the Library panel.

You organized the symbols within the folders and opened and closed the folders.

Display the properties of symbols, rename symbols, and delete a symbol

1. Click the **expand list arrow** ▶ for the Graphics folder to display the symbols.

2. Click the **g_car1 symbol**, then click the **Properties icon** ⓘ at the bottom of the Library panel to display the Symbol Properties dialog box.

3. Type **g_redCar** in the Name text box, as shown in Figure 16, then click **OK**.

4. Repeat Steps 2 and 3 renaming the g_car2 symbol to **g_blueCar**.

   > TIP Double-click the name to rename it without opening the Symbol Properties dialog box.

5. Click **g_border** in the Library panel to select it.

6. Click the **Delete icon** 🗑 at the bottom of the Library panel.

   > TIP You can also select an item and press [Delete], or you can use the Options menu in the Library panel to remove an item from the library. The Undo command in the Edit menu can be used to undelete an item.

You used the Library panel to display the properties of symbols, rename symbols, and delete a symbol.

FIGURE 16
Renaming a symbol

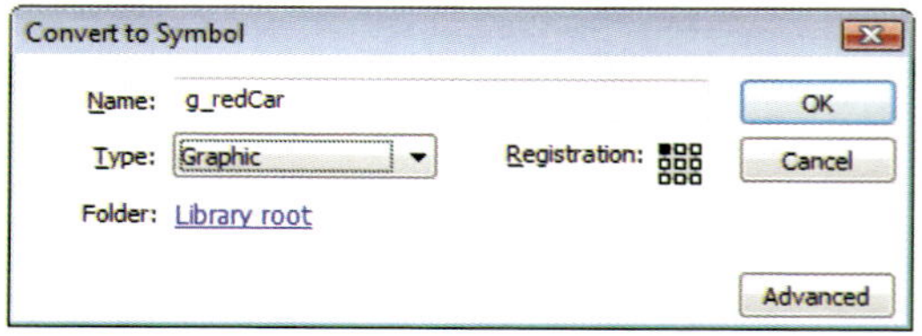

FIGURE 17

The carRace.fla document and the coolCar.fla Library panel

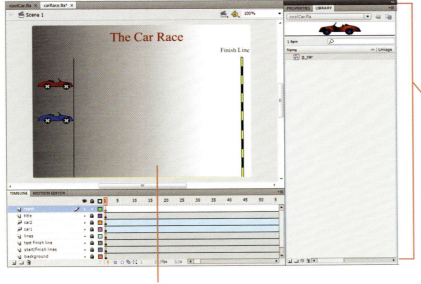

*The Library
panel for the
coolCar.fla
document*

The carRace.fla document

Use multiple Library panels

1. Click the **Library panel list arrow** near the top of the Library panel to display a list of open documents.

2. Click **coolCar.fla**, then click **g_car**.

    The Library panel for the coolCar document is displayed. However, the carRace document remains open, as shown in Figure 17.

3. Click **frame 1** on the reset layer, then drag the **car** from the Library panel to the center of the Stage.

    The reset layer is the only unlocked layer. Objects cannot be placed on locked layers.

4. Click the **Library panel list arrow** to display the open documents.

5. Click **carRace.fla** to view the carRace document's Library panel.

    Notice the g_car symbol is automatically added to the Library panel of the carRace document.

6. Click the **g_car symbol** in the Library panel.

7. Click the **Delete icon** 🗑 at the bottom of the Library panel.

    You deleted the g_car symbol from the carRace library but it still exists in the coolCar library. The car was also deleted from the Stage.

8. Save your work.

9. Click the **coolCar.fla tab** at the top of the workspace to display the document.

10. Close the coolCar document and save the document if asked.

You used the Library panel to display the contents of another library and added an object from that library to the current document.

CREATE
BUTTONS

What You'll Do

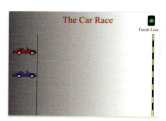

 In this lesson, you will create a button, edit the four button states, and test a button.

Understanding Buttons

Button symbols are used to provide inter-activity. When you click a button, an action occurs, such as starting an animation or jumping to another frame on the Timeline. Any object, including Flash drawings, text blocks, and imported graphic images, can be made into buttons. Unlike graphic sym-bols, buttons have four states: Up, Over, Down, and Hit. These states correspond to the use of the mouse and recognize that the user requires feedback when the mouse is pointing to a button and when the but-ton has been clicked. This is often shown by a change in the button (such as a differ-ent color or different shape). An example of a button with different colors for the four different states is shown in Figure 18. These four states are explained in the fol-lowing paragraphs.

Up—Represents how the button appears when the mouse pointer is not over it.

Over—Represents how the button appears when the mouse pointer is over it.

Down—Represents how the button appears after the user clicks the mouse.

Hit—Defines the area of the screen that will respond to the click. In most cases, you will want the Hit state to be the same or similar to the Up state in location and size.

When you create a button symbol, Flash automatically creates a new Timeline. The Timeline has only four frames, one for each button state. The Timeline does not play; it merely reacts to the mouse pointer by displaying the appropriate button state and performing an action, such as jumping to a specific frame on the main Timeline.

The process for creating and previewing buttons is as follows:

Create a button symbol—Draw an object or select an object that has already been created and placed on the Stage. Use the Convert to Symbol command on the Modify menu to convert the object to a button symbol and to enter a name for the button.

Edit the button symbol—Select the button and choose the Edit Symbols command on the Edit menu or double-click the button symbol in the Library panel. This displays the button Timeline, shown in Figure 19, which allows you to work with the four button states. The Up state is the original button symbol. Flash automatically places it in frame 1. You need to determine how the original object will change for the other states. To change the button for the Over state, click frame 2 and insert a keyframe. This automatically places a copy of the

button that is in frame 1 into frame 2. Then, alter the button's appearance for the Over state by, for instance, changing the fill color. Use the same process for the Down state. For the Hit state, you insert a keyframe on frame 4 and then specify the area on the screen that will respond to the pointer. If you do not specify a hit area, the image for the Up state is used for the hit area. You add a keyframe to the Hit frame only if you are going to specify the hit area.

Return to the main Timeline—Once you've finished editing a button, you

choose the Edit Document command on the Edit menu, or click Scene 1 above the edit window, to return to the main Timeline.

Preview the button—By default, Flash disables buttons so that you can manipulate them on the Stage. You can preview a button by choosing the Enable Simple Buttons command on the Control menu. You can also choose the Test Movie command on the Control menu to play the movie and test the buttons.

FIGURE 18

The four button states

Up   Over   Down   Hit

FIGURE 19

The button Timeline

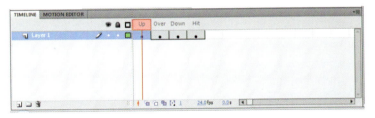

Create a button

1. Insert a new layer above the top layer in the Timeline, then name the layer **signal**.

2. Select the **Rectangle Primitive tool**, click the **Stroke Color tool** on the Tools panel, then click the **No Stroke icon** in the upper-right corner of the color palette.

3. Set the **Fill Color** to the **red gradient Color swatch** in the bottom row of the color palette.

4. Display the Properties panel, click the **Reset button** in the RECTANGLE OPTIONS area, then set the corner radius to **5**.

5. Draw the **rectangle** shown in Figure 20.

6. Click the **Zoom tool** on the Tools panel, then click the **rectangle** to enlarge it.

7. Select the **Gradient Transform tool** on the Tools panel, then click the **rectangle**.

   You may need to click and hold the Free Transform tool first.

8. Drag the **diagonal arrow** toward the center of the rectangle as shown in Figure 21 to make the red area more round.

9. Click the **Selection tool** on the Tools panel, then drag a **marquee** around the rectangle to select it.

10. Click **Modify** on the menu bar, then click **Convert to Symbol**.

11. Type **b_signal** in the Name text box, click the **Type list arrow**, click **Button**, then click **OK**.

12. Display the Library panel, drag the **b_signal symbol** to the Buttons folder.

You created a button symbol on the Stage and dragged it to the Buttons folder in the Library panel.

FIGURE 20
The rectangle object

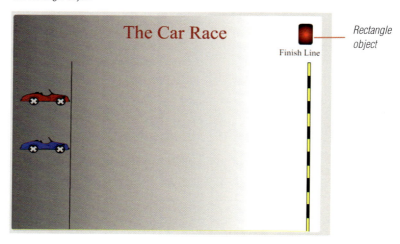

Rectangle object

FIGURE 21
Adjusting the gradient

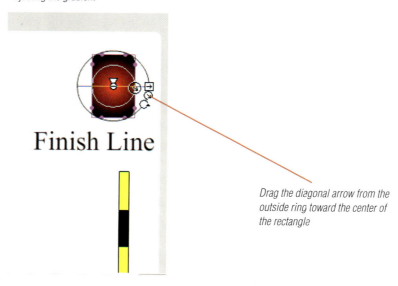

Drag the diagonal arrow from the outside ring toward the center of the rectangle

FIGURE 22
Specifying the hit area

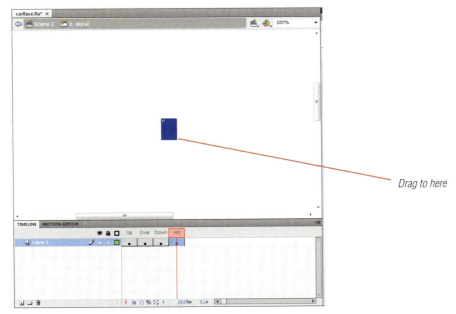

Drag to here

1. Open the Buttons folder, right-click (Win) or control-click (Mac) **b_signal** in the Library panel, then click **Edit**.

   Flash displays the edit window showing the Timeline with four button states.

2. Click the blank **Over frame** on Layer 1, then insert a keyframe.

   TIP   The [F6] key inserts a keyframe in the selected frame (Win).

3. Set the **Fill Color** to the **gray gradient color swatch** on the bottom of the color palette.

4. Insert a **keyframe** in the Down frame on Layer 1.

5. Set the **Fill Color** to the **green gradient color swatch** on the bottom of the color palette.

6. Insert a **keyframe** in the Hit frame on Layer 1.

7. Select the **Rectangle tool** on the Tools panel, set the **Fill Color** to the **blue color swatch** in the left column of the color palette.

8. Draw a **rectangle** slightly larger than the button, as shown in Figure 22, then release the mouse button.

   TIP   The Hit area will not be visible on the Stage.

9. Click **Scene 1** above the edit window to return to the main Timeline.

You edited a button by changing the color of its Over and Down states, and you specified the Hit area.

Test a button

1. Click the **Selection tool** , then click a blank area of the Stage.

2. Click **Control** on the menu bar, then click **Enable Simple Buttons**.

   This command allows you to test buttons on the Stage without viewing the movie in the Flash Player window.

3. Point to the **signal button** on the Stage, then compare your image to Figure 23.

   The pointer changes to a hand , indicating that the object is clickable, and the button changes to a gray gradient, the color you selected for the Over State.

4. Press and hold the **mouse button**, then notice that the button changes to a green gradient, the color you selected for the Down state, as shown in Figure 24.

   (continued)

FIGURE 23
The button's Over state

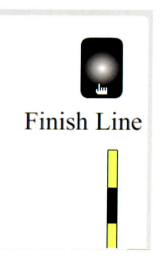

FIGURE 24
The button's Down state

The button Hit area

All buttons have an area that responds to the mouse pointer, including rolling over the button and clicking it. This hit area is usually the same size and shape as the button itself. However, you can specify any area of the button to be the hit area. For example, you could have a button symbol that looks like a target with just the bulls-eye center being the hit area.

Working with Symbols and Interactivity

FIGURE 25
The button's Up state

Finish Line

FIGURE 26
View options from the View list

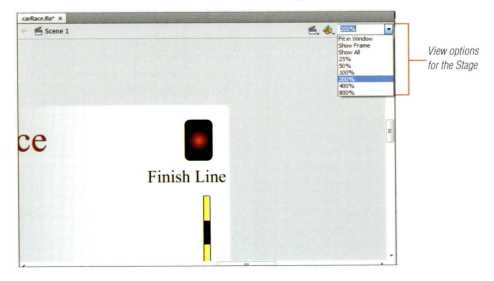

*View options
for the Stage*

5. Release the mouse and notice that the button changes to a gray gradient, the color you selected for the Over state.

6. Move the mouse away from the signal button, and notice that the button returns to a red gradient, the Up state color, as shown in Figure 25.

7. Click **Control** on the menu bar, then click **Enable Simple Buttons** to turn off the command.

8. Click the **View list arrow** above the Stage, as shown in Figure 26, then click **Fit in Window**.

   This shortcut allows you to change the magnification view without using the Magnification command on the View menu or the Zoom tool in the Tools panel.

9. Save your work.

You used the mouse to test a button and view the button states.

ASSIGN ACTIONS
TO FRAMES AND BUTTONS

What You'll Do

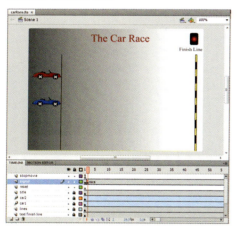

In this lesson, you will use ActionScripts to assign actions to frames and buttons.

Understanding Actions

In a basic movie, Flash plays the frames sequentially, repeating the movie without stopping for user input. However, you may often want to provide users with the ability to interact with the movie by allowing them to perform actions, such as starting and stopping the movie or jumping to a specific frame in the movie. One way to provide user interaction is to assign an action to the Down state of a button. Then, whenever the user clicks the button, the action occurs. Flash provides a scripting language, called ActionScript, that allows you to add actions to buttons and frames within a movie. For example, you can place a stop action in a frame that pauses the movie, and then you can assign a play action to a button that starts the movie when the user clicks the button.

Analyzing ActionScript

ActionScript is a powerful scripting language that allows those with even limited programming experience to create complex actions. For example, you can create order

forms that capture user input or volume controls that display when sounds are played. A basic ActionScript involves an event (such as a mouse click) that causes some action to occur by triggering the script. The following is an example of a basic ActionScript:

```
on (release) {
    gotoAndPlay(10);
}
```

In this example, the event is a mouse click (indicated by the word release) that causes the movie's playback head to go to frame 10 and play the frame. This is a simple example of ActionScript code and is easy to follow. Other ActionScript code can be quite complex and may require programming expertise to understand.

ActionScript 2.0 and 3.0

Adobe has identified two types of Flash CS4 users, designers and developers. Designers focus more on the visual features of a Flash movie, including the user interface design, drawing objects, and acquiring and editing additional assets (such as sound clips). Whereas, developers focus more on the programming aspects of a Flash movie, including creation of complex animations and writing the code that specifies how the movie responds to user interactions. In many cases, designers and developers work together to create sophisticated Flash applications. In other cases, designers work without the benefit of a developer's programming expertise. In order to accommodate the varying needs of these two types of uses, Flash CS4 provides two versions of ActionScript, 2.0 and 3.0,

called AS2 and AS3. ActionScript 3.0 is used by developers because it provides a programming environment that is more familiar to them and can be used to create movies that download more quickly. However, the differences between AS2 and AS3 are transparent to designers who do not have programming expertise. AS2 allows the new Flash user to create compelling applications while not having to have a background in programming. At the same time it provides an introduction to ActionScript that can be the basis for learning ActionScript 3.0. ActionScript 2.0 will be used in this chapter. You can

specify ActionScript 2.0 when creating a new document or you can use the Flash section of the Publish Settings command found on the File menu to specify AS2.

An advantage of using AS2 is a feature called Script Assist, which provides an easy way to use ActionScript without having to learn the scripting language. The Script Assist feature within the Actions panel allows you to assign basic actions to frames and objects, such as buttons. Figure 27 shows the Actions panel displaying an ActionScript indicating that when the user clicks the selected object (a button, in this example, b_signal), the movie goes to frame 2.

FIGURE 27

The Actions panel displaying an ActionScript

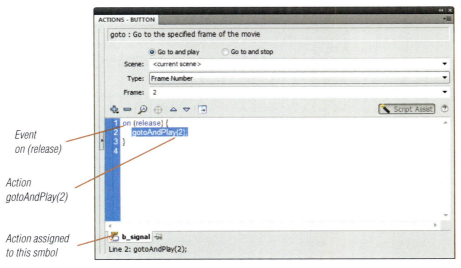

*Event
on (release)*

*Action
gotoAndPlay(2)*

*Action assigned
to this smbol*

The process for assigning actions to buttons, shown in Figure 28, is as follows:

- Select the button on the Stage that you want to assign an action to.
- Display the Actions panel, using the Window menu.
- Select the Script Assist button to display the Script Assist panel within the ActionScript panel.
- Click the Add a new item to the script icon to display a list of Action categories.
- Select the appropriate category from a drop-down list. Flash provides several Action categories. The Timeline Control category within the Global Functions menu allows you to create scripts for controlling movies and navigating within movies. You can use these

actions to start and stop movies, jump to specific frames, and respond to user mouse movements and keystrokes.

- Select the desired action, such as goto.
- Specify the event that triggers the action, such as on (release). This step in the process is not shown in Figure 28.

Button actions respond to one or more mouse events, including:

Release—With the pointer inside the button Hit area, the user presses and releases (clicks) the mouse button. This is the default event.

Key Press—With the button displayed, the user presses a predetermined key on the keyboard.

Roll Over—The user moves the pointer into the button Hit area.

Drag Over—The user holds down the mouse button, moves the pointer out of the button Hit area, and then back into the Hit area.

Using Frame Actions—In addition to assigning actions to buttons, you can assign actions to frames. Actions assigned to frames are executed when the playhead reaches the frame. A common frame action is stop, which is often assigned to the first and last frame of a layer on the Timeline.

FIGURE 28
The process for assigning actions to buttons

3. Click the Add a new item to the script icon

Hide/Display arrow; click at any time and as needed to hide or display the Toolbox pane

1. Select the button

2. Click the Script Assist button to toggle between on (seen here) and off

4. Select the Actions category and the action

Understanding the Actions panel—The Actions panel has two panes. The left pane (also called the Toolbox pane) uses folders to display the Action categories. The right pane, called the Script pane, is used with the Script Assist feature and it displays the ActionScript code as the code is being generated. When using the Script Assist feature, it is best to close the left pane. This is done by clicking the Hide/Display arrow as shown in Figure 29. The lower-left corner of the Script pane displays the symbol name or the frame to which the action(s) will apply. Always verify that the desired symbol or frame is displayed.

Using Frame Labels—Buttons are often used to move the playhead to a specific location on the Timeline. For example, clicking a Start button might cause the playhead to jump from frame 1 to frame 10 to start an animation. In addition to referencing frame numbers, like 10, you can reference frame labels in the ActionScript code. Frame labels have an advantage over frame numbers, especially in large and complex applications, because adding or deleting frames will not disrupt the navigation to a frame reference you already have in actions, since the label remains attached to the frame even if the frame moves. The process is to select a frame and use the Properties panel to specify a name. Then use the name in the ActionScript code instead of the frame number. Figure 30 shows the Timeline with a frame label and the Actions panel with the code that references the label.

FIGURE 29

The Actions panel

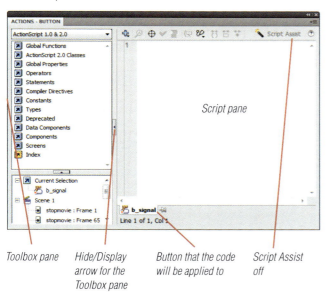

Toolbox pane   Hide/Display arrow for the Toolbox pane   Button that the code will be applied to   Script Assist off

FIGURE 30

The Timeline with a frame label

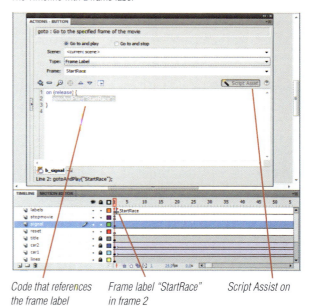

Code that references the frame label   Frame label "StartRace" in frame 2   Script Assist on

Assign a stop action to frames

1. Click **Control** on the menu bar, then click **Test Movie**.

   The movie plays and continues to loop.

2. Close the Flash Player window.

3. Insert a **new layer**, name it **stopmovie**, then click **frame 1** on the layer to select the frame.

4. Click **Window** on the menu bar, then click **Actions** to display the Actions panel.

5. Study the Actions panel. If the Toolbox pane is displayed as shown in Figure 31, then click the **Hide/Display arrow** to hide the pane.

6. Click the **Script Assist button** to turn on the Script Assist feature.

7. Verify stopmovie:1 (indicating the layer and frame to which the action will be applied) is displayed in the lower-left corner of the Script pane.

8. Click the **Add a new item to the script button** ⊕ to display the Script categories, point to **Global Functions**, point to **Timeline Control**, then click **stop**, as shown in Figure 32.

9. Move the Actions panel as needed to see the Timeline, then click **frame 65** on the stopmovie layer.

10. Insert a **keyframe** in frame 65 on the stopmovie layer, then repeat Step 8. Compare your screen to Figure 33. Test the movie.

    The movie does not play because there is a stop action assigned to frame 1.

11. Close the Flash Player window.

You inserted a layer and assigned a stop action to the first and last frames on the layer.

FIGURE 31
The Actions panel Toolbox pane

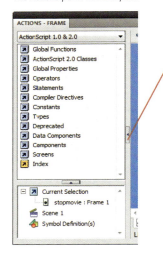

Hide/Display arrow for the Toolbox pane

FIGURE 32
Assigning an action to frame 1 on the stopmovie layer

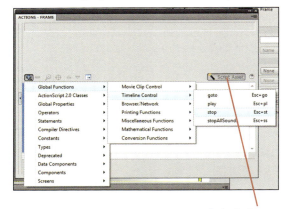

Script Assist on

FIGURE 33
Script for the stopmovie layer

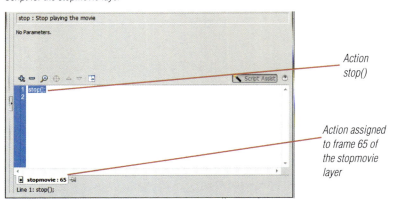

Action stop()

Action assigned to frame 65 of the stopmovie layer

Working with Symbols and Interactivity

FIGURE 34
Assigning an event and an action to a button

Button selected

Action assigned
to the button
named b_signal

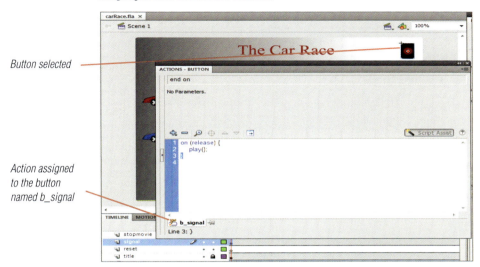

1. Click **frame 1** on the Signal layer.

2. Move the **Actions panel** to view the signal button on the Stage (if necessary).

   TIP You can collapse the Actions panel to view more of the Stage, then expand the Actions panel when needed. Alternately, you can drag the bottom of the Actions panel up to make the panel smaller.

3. Click the **Selection tool** ▶ on the Tools panel, then click the **button** on the Stage.

4. Verify b_signal is displayed in the lower left of the Actions panel.

   This ensures that the actions specified in the Actions panel will apply to the b_signal button.

5. Click ⊕ to display the Script categories, point to **Global Functions**, point to **Timeline Control**, then click **play**.

   Release is the default event, as shown in Figure 34.

6. Click **Control** on the menu bar, then click **Test Movie**.

7. Click the **signal button** to play the animation.

8. Close the Flash Player window.

You used the Actions panel to assign a play action to a button.

Assign a goto frame action to a button

1. Click **Control** on the menu bar, then click **Test Movie**.

2. Click the **signal button**.

   The movie plays and stops, and the word Reset, which is actually a button, appears.

3. Click the **Reset button** and notice nothing happens because it does not have an action assigned to it.

4. Close the Flash Player window.

5. Click **frame 65** on the reset layer to display the Reset button on the Stage.

   Note: You many need to move the Actions panel to view the Reset button on the Stage.

6. Click the **Reset button** on the Stage to select it.

7. Verify b_reset is displayed in the lower left of the Actions panel.

8. Verify Script Assist is active, click ⊈, point to **Global Functions**, point to **Timeline Control**, click **goto**, then verify Frame 1 is specified, as shown in Figure 35.

9. Click **Control** on the menu bar, then click **Test Movie**.

10. Click the **signal button** to start the movie, then when the movie stops, click the **Reset button**.

11. Close the Flash Player window.

You used the Actions panel to assign an action to a button.

FIGURE 35
Assigning a goto action to a button

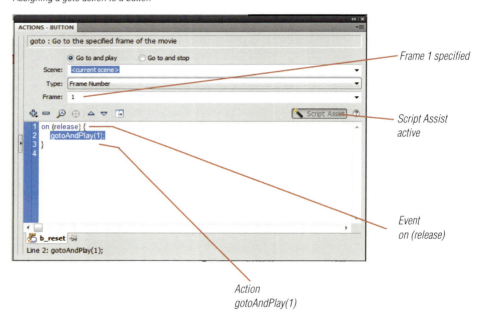

Frame 1 specified

Script Assist active

Event on (release)

Action gotoAndPlay(1)

FIGURE 36
Assigning a keypress action to a button

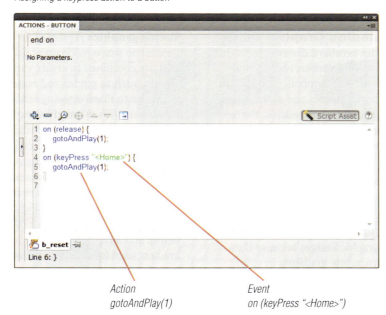

Action
gotoAndPlay(1)

Event
on (keyPress "<Home>")

1. Click the **right curly bracket** (}) in the Actions panel to highlight the bracket in Step 3 of the ActionScript.

2. Click ⊞ in the Script Assist window, point to **Global Functions**, point to **Movie Clip Control**, then click **on**.

   The Script Assist window displays several event options. Release is selected.

3. Click the **Release check box** to deselect the option.

4. Click the **Key Press check box** to select it, then press the [**Home**] **key** on the keyboard.

   > TIP If your keyboard does not have a [Home] key, use [fn]+[←] (Mac) or one of the function keys (Win) to complete the steps.

5. Click ⊞ in the Script Assist window, point to **Global Functions**, point to **Timeline Control**, then click **goto**.

   The ActionScript now indicates that pressing the [Home] key will cause the playhead to go to frame 1, as shown in Figure 36.

   The Reset button can now be activated by clicking it or by pressing the [Home] key.

6. Click **File** on the menu bar, point to **Publish Preview**, then click **Default – (HTML)**.

   The movie opens in your default browser.

   Note: If a warning message opens, follow the messages to allow blocked content.

7. Click the **signal button** to start the movie, then when the movie stops, press the [**Home**] **key**.

8. Close the browser window.

9. Close the Actions panel, then save and close the movie.

You added an event that triggers a goto frame action.

Importing graphics

1. Start a new Flash document, then save it as **sailing.fla**.

2. Click **File** on the menu bar, point to **Import**, then click **Import to Library**.

3. Navigate to the folder where your Data Files are stored, click **islandview.jpg**, then click **Open** (Win) or **Import to Library** (Mac).

   Islandview.jpg is a digital photo that was edited in Photoshop and saved as a .jpg file.

4. Display the Library panel and notice the icon used for bitmap graphics.

5. Drag the **islandview icon** to the Stage, then lock the layer.

6. Click **File** on the menu bar, point to **Import**, then click **Import to Library**.

7. Navigate to the folder where your Data Files are stored, then click **sailboat.ai**.

   This graphic was created using Adobe Illustrator and is made up of several layers.

8. Click **Open** (Win) or **Import to Library** (Mac).

   A dialog box appears asking you to choose the layers to import. All layers are selected by default.

9. Click **OK**.

   The graphic is added to the Library panel as a symbol.

10. Add a new layer to the Timeline, click **frame 1** on the layer, then drag the **sailboat icon** to the Stage, as shown in Figure 39.

(continued)

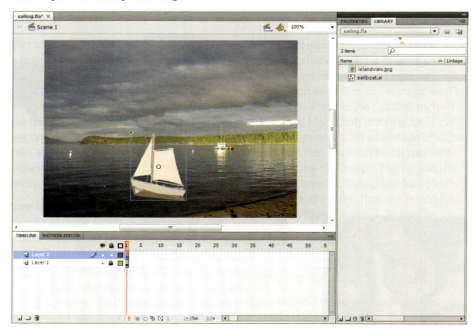

FIGURE 39
Positioning the sailboat image on the Stage

Working with Symbols and Interactivity

FIGURE 40
Changing the color of the sail

FIGURE 41
Rotating and skewing the sailboat image

11. Click **Modify** on the menu bar, click **Break apart**, then repeat this step until the dotted pattern that indicates the image is no longer a symbol appears.

12. Click the **Selection tool** , then click a blank area of the Pasteboard.

13. Click the **left sail**, then change the color to a rainbow pattern, as shown in Figure 40.

    Hint: The rainbow color is found at the bottom of the palette for the Fill Color tool.

14. Use the **Selection tool** to drag a **marquee** around the entire sailboat to select it, then convert the image to a graphic symbol named **sailboat**.

15. Change the width of the boat to **60** on the Properties panel.

16. Click the **Zoom tool** on the Tools panel, click the **sailboat** twice, then scroll as needed to view both sailboats.

    Notice how the bitmap photograph becomes distorted, while the vector sailboat does not.

17. Change the magnification to **Fit in Window**.

18. Use the **Free Transform tool** to rotate and skew the sailboat slightly to the left as shown in Figure 41.

19. Test the movie, close the Flash Player window, then save your work and exit Flash.

You imported bitmap and vector graphics, and edited the vector graphic.

Create a symbol.

1. Start Flash, open fl3_3.fla, then save it as **skillsdemo3**. This document consists of a single object that was created using the Flash drawing tools.

2. Use the Selection tool to drag a marquee around the ball to select it.

3. Convert the ball to a graphic symbol with the name g_beachball.

4. Double-click the g_beachball symbol on the Library panel to open the edit window, change the fill color to a rainbow gradient, add a text block that sits on top of the ball with the words **BEACH BALL** (see Figure 42), change the font color to white, then click Scene 1 to return to the main Timeline.

5. With the ball selected, create a motion tween animation that moves the ball from the left edge of the Stage to the right edge of the Stage.

6. Use the Selection tool to drag the middle of the motion path up to near the middle of the Stage to create an arc.

7. Select the last frame of the animation on the Timeline and set Rotate to 1 time in the Rotation area of the Properties panel.

8. Play the movie.
   The ball should move across the Stage in an arc and spin at the same time.

9. Lock the beachball-spin layer.

Create and edit an instance.

1. Insert a new layer and name it **redBall**.

2. Click frame 1 on the redBall layer, then drag the g_beachball symbol from the Library panel so it is on top of the ball on the Stage.

3. Use the arrow keys to align the ball so that it covers the ball on the Stage.

4. With the ball selected, break apart the object.

5. Change the fill color of the ball to a red gradient and change the text to **RED BALL**.

6. Insert a new layer and name it **greenBall**.

7. Click frame 12 on the greenBall layer, then insert a keyframe.

8. Drag the g_beachball symbol from the Library panel so it is on top of the ball that is near the middle of the Stage.
   (*Note:* Align only the balls, not the text.)

9. With the ball selected, break apart the object and change the fill color of the ball to a green gradient and the text to **GREEN BALL**.

10. Move the beachball-spin layer to above the other layers.

11. Insert a new layer and name it **title**.

12. Click frame 1 on the title layer, create a text block at the top middle of the Stage with the words **Beachball Spin** using Arial as the font, blue as the color, and 20 as the font size.

13. Insert a new layer above the title layer and name it **titlebkgnd**.

14. Draw a primitive rectangle with a corner radius of 10, a medium gray fill (#999999) and no stroke that covers the Beachball Spin title text.

15. Verify the rectangle is selected, convert it to a graphic symbol, then name it **g_bkgnd**.

16. Move the title layer so it is above the title-bkgnd layer.

17. Play the movie, then save your work.

Create a folder in the Library panel.

1. Click the New Folder button at the bottom of the Library panel to create a new folder.

2. Name the folder **Graphics**.

3. Move the two graphic symbols to the Graphics folder.

4. Expand the Graphics folder.

5. Save your work.

Work with the Library panel.

1. Rename the g_bkgnd symbol to **g_title-bkgnd** in the Library panel.

2. Collapse and expand the folder.

3. Save your work.

Create a button.

1. Insert a new layer above the title layer and name it **startButton**.

2. Drag the g_title-bkgnd symbol from the Library panel to the bottom center of the Stage.

3. Create a text block with the word **Start** formatted with white, bold, 22-pt Arial, then position the text block on top of the g_title-bkgnd object. Center the text block on top of the g_title-bkgnd object.

4. Select the rectangle and the text. (*Hint*: Drag a marquee around both objects or click the Selection tool, press and hold [Shift], then click each object.)

5. Convert the selected objects to a button symbol and name it **b_start**.
6. Create a new folder named **Buttons** in the Library panel and move the b_start button symbol to the folder.
7. Display the edit window for the b_start button.
8. Insert a keyframe in the Over frame.
9. Select the text and change the color to gray.
10. Insert a keyframe in the Down frame.
11. Select the text and change the color to blue.
12. Insert a keyframe in the Hit frame.
13. Draw a rectangular object that covers the button area for the Hit state.
14. Click Scene 1 to exit the edit window and return to the main Timeline.
15. Save your work.

Test a button.

1. Turn on Enable Simple Buttons.
2. Point to the button and notice the color change.
3. Click the button and notice the other color change.

Stop a movie.

1. Insert a new layer and name it **stopmovie**.
2. Insert a keyframe in frame 24 on the new layer.
3. With frame 24 selected, display the Actions panel.
4. Assign a stop action to the frame.
5. Click frame 1 on the stopmovie layer.
6. Assign a stop action to frame 1.
7. Save your work.

Assign a goto action to a button.

1. Click Control on the menu bar, then click Enable Simple Buttons to turn off this feature.
2. Use the Selection tool to select the Start button on the Stage.
3. Use Script Assist in the Actions panel to assign an event and a goto action to the button. (*Hint*: Refer to the section on assigning a goto action as needed.)
4. Test the movie.

FIGURE 42
Completed Skills Review

Import a graphic.

1. Import BeachScene.jpg from the drive and folder where your Data Files are stored to the Library panel.
2. Insert a new layer and name the layer **background**.
3. Select frame 1 on the background layer, then drag the BeachScene image to the Stage.
4. Move the background layer to the bottom of the Timeline.
5. Test the movie.
6. Save your work, then compare your image to Figure 42.
7. Exit Flash.

The Ultimate Tours travel company has asked you to design a sample navigation scheme for its website. The company wants to see how its home page will link with one of its main categories (Treks). Figure 43 shows a sample home page and Treks screen. Using the figures or the home page you created in Chapter 2 as a guide, you will add a Treks screen and link it to the home page. (*Hint*: Assume that all of the drawings on the home page are on frame 1, unless noted.)

1. Open ultimatetours2.fla (the file you created in Chapter 2 Project Builder 1), then save it as **ultimatetours3**.
2. Insert a layer above the Subheading layer and name it **logo**.
3. Import the UTLogo.jpg file from the drive and folder where your Data Files are stored to the Library panel.
4. Select frame 1 on the logo layer and drag the logo image to the upper-left corner of the Stage.
5. Select the logo and convert it to a graphic symbol with the name **g_utlogo**.
6. Lock the **logo layer**.
7. Select the layer that the Ultimate Tours text block is on, then insert a keyframe on a frame at least five frames farther along the Timeline.
8. Insert a new layer, name it **treks headings**, insert a keyframe on the last frame of the movie, then create the Treks screen shown in Figure 43, except for the home graphic. (*Note:* The underline was created using the Line tool.)
9. Convert the Treks graphic on the home page to a button symbol named **b_treks**, then edit the symbol so that different colors appear for the different states.
10. Assign a goto action that jumps the playhead to the Treks screen when the Treks button is clicked. (*Hint:* You need to use ActionScript 2.0 to complete the steps that follow. You can set the ActionScript version by selecting Publish Settings from the File menu, clicking the Flash tab and specifying ActionScript 2.0.)
11. Insert a new layer and name it **stopmovie**. Add stop actions that cause the movie to stop after displaying the home page and after displaying the Treks page. Make sure there is a keyframe in the last frame of the stopmovie layer.
12. Insert a new layer and name it **homeButton**, insert a keyframe on the last frame of the movie, then draw the home button image with the Home text.
13. Convert the image to a button symbol named **b_home**, then edit the symbol so that different colors appear for the different states. Assign a goto action for the button that jumps the movie to frame 1.
14. Select the last frame of the movie on the **logo layer** and insert a keyframe. (*Note:* You do this so that the logo appears on the home page and on the Treks page.)
15. Test the movie.
16. Save your work, then compare your web pages to the samples shown in Figure 43.

FIGURE 43

Sample completed Project Builder 1

Home page

Treks page

Convert to a button symbol

Convert to a button symbol

You have been asked to assist the International Student Association (ISA). The association sponsors a series of monthly events, each focusing on a different culture from around the world. The events are led by a guest speaker who makes a presentation, followed by a discussion. The events are free and they are open to everyone. ISA would like you to design a Flash movie that will be used with its website. The movie starts by providing information about the series, and then provides a link to the upcoming event.

1. Open a new Flash ActionScript 2.0 document and save it as **isa3**.
2. Create an initial Information screen with general information about the association's series.
3. Assign an action to frame 1 that stops the movie.
4. Create two more screens: a next event screen that presents information about the next event and a series screen that lists the series (all nine events for the school year—September through May).
5. Add a button on the general information screen that jumps the movie to the next event screen, and add a second button on the information screen that jumps the movie to the series screen.
6. On the next event and series screens, add a Return button that jumps the movie back to the general information screen.
7. On the next event screen, create a second button that jumps the movie to the series screen.
8. On the series screen, create a second button that jumps the movie to the event screen.
9. For each button you create, specify different colors for each state of each button.
10. Add an action that stops the movie on the next event screen, and another action that stops the movie on the series screen. (*Hint:* Place the stop actions on the same layer as the stop action created in step 3.)
11. Test the movie.
12. Save your work, then compare your movie to the sample shown in Figure 44.

FIGURE 44

Sample completed Project Builder 2

Sample general information screen

Sample next event screen

Sample series screen

DESIGN PROJECT

Figure 45 shows the home page of a website. Study the figure and complete the following questions. For each question, indicate how you determined your answer.

1. Connect to the Internet and go to *www.zoo.org*. Notice that this website has images that change as you visit the website.
2. Open a document in a word processor or open a new Flash document, save the file as **dpc3**, then answer the following questions. (*Hint*: Use the Text tool in Flash.)
   - Whose website is this?
   - What is the goal(s) of the site?
   - Who is the target audience?
   - What treatment ("look and feel") is used?
   - What are the design layout guidelines being used (balance, movement, and so on)?
   - What may be animated in this home page?
   - Do you think this is an effective design for the company, its products, and its target audience? Why or why not?
   - What suggestions would you make to improve the design, and why?

FIGURE 45
Design Project

This is a continuation of the Chapter 2 Portfolio Project, which is the development of a personal portfolio. The home page has several categories, including the following:

- Personal data
- Contact information
- Previous employment
- Education
- Samples of your work

In this project, you will create a button that will be used to link the home page of your portfolio to the animations page. Next, you will create another button to start the animation.

1. Open portfolio2.fla (the file you created in Portfolio Project, Chapter 2), then save it as **portfolio3**. (*Hint*: When you open the file, you may receive a warning message that the font is missing. You can replace this font with the default, or with any other appropriate font on your computer.)

2. Unlock the layers as needed.

3. Insert a new layer, name it **sampleAnimations**, then insert a keyframe on frame 2.

4. Create a Sample Animations screen that has a text block with an oval background and the words **Sample Animations** at the top of the Stage, then add another text block and oval background with the word **Tweened**. (*Note*: This screen will have several animation samples added to it later.)

5. Insert a new layer, name it **home button**, then insert a keyframe on frame 2.

6. Add another text block with an oval background that says **Home** at the bottom of the Stage.

7. Insert a new layer, name it **tweened Animation**, then insert a keyframe on frame 3.

8. Create an animation(s) of your choice using objects you draw or import, or objects from the Library panel of another document. (*Note*: To create a motion tween animation when starting in a frame other than frame 1, you need to specify the ending frame of the animation by inserting a keyframe before repositioning the object on the Stage.) (*Hint*: To create more than one animation that plays at the same time, put each animation on its own layer.)

9. Insert a new layer, name it **animationHeading**, then insert a keyframe on frame 3.

10. Add a heading to the screen used for the animation(s).

11. On the Sample Animations screen, convert the Tweened and Home text blocks into button symbols, then edit each symbol so that different colors appear for the different states. For the Tweened button, assign an action that jumps to the frame that plays an animation. For the Home button, assign an action to the Home button that jumps to the frame that displays My Portfolio. (*Hint*: You need to use ActionScript 2.0. You can set the ActionsScript version by selecting Publish Settings from the File menu, clicking the Flash tab and specifying ActionScript 2.0.)

12. Change the Animations graphic on the home page to a button, then edit the symbol so that different colors appear for the different states. Assign an action to the Animations button that jumps to the Sample Animations screen.

13. Insert a new layer, then name it **stopmovie**. Insert keyframes and assign stop actions to the appropriate frames.

14. Test the movie.

15. Save your work, then compare your movie to the sample shown in Figure 46.

FIGURE 46
Sample completed Portfolio Project

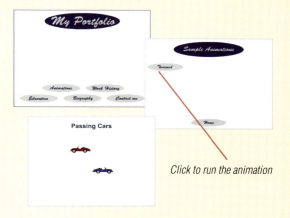

Click to run the animation

chapter

4

CREATING ANIMATIONS

1. Create motion tween animations

2. Create classic tween animations

3. Create frame-by-frame animations

4. Create shape tween animations

5. Create movie clips

6. Animate text

4 CREATING ANIMATIONS

Introduction

Animation can be an important part of your application or website, whether the focus is on e-commerce (attracts attention and provides product demonstrations), education (simulates complex processes such as DNA replication), or entertainment (provides interactive games).

How Does Animation Work?

The perception of motion in an animation is actually an illusion. Animation is like a motion picture in that it is made up of a series of still images. Research has found that our eye captures and holds an image for one-tenth of a second before processing another image. By retaining each impression for one-tenth of a second, we perceive a series of rapidly displayed still images as a single, moving image. This phenomenon is known as persistence of vision and provides the basis for the frame rate in animations. Frame rates of 10–12 frames-per-second (fps) generally provide

an acceptably smooth computer-based animation. Lower frame rates result in a jerky image, while higher frame rates may result in a blurred image. Flash uses a default frame rate of 12 fps.

Flash Animation

Creating animation is one of the most powerful features of Flash, yet developing basic animations is a simple process. Flash allows you to create animations that can move and rotate an object around the Stage, and change its size, shape, or color. You can also use the animation features in Flash to create special effects, such as an object zooming or fading in and out. You can combine animation effects so that an object changes shape and color as it moves across the Stage. Animations are created by changing the content of successive frames. Flash provides two animation methods: frame-by-frame animation and tweened animation. Tweened animations can be motion, classic, or shape tweens.

Tools You'll Use

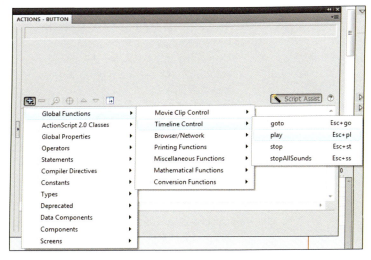

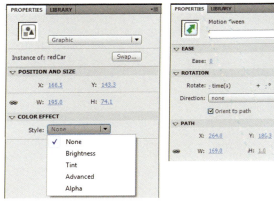

CREATE MOTION TWEEN
ANIMATIONS

What You'll Do

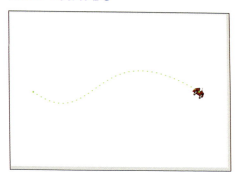

In this lesson, you will create and edit motion tween animations.

Understanding Motion Tween Animations

An animation implies some sort of movement in an object. However, the concept of animation is quite a bit more broad. Objects have specific properties such as position, size, color, and shape. Any change in a property of an object over time (i.e., across frames in the Timeline) can be considered an animation. So, having an object start at the left of the screen in frame 1 and then having it move across the screen and end up at the right side in frame 10 would be a change in the position property of the object. Each of the in-between frames (2-9) would show the position of the object as it moves across the screen. In a motion tween animation, you specify the position of the object in the beginning and ending frames and Flash fills in the in-between frames, a process known as tweening. Fortunately, you can change several properties with one motion tween. For example, you could have a car move

across the screen and, at the same time, you could have the size of the car change to give the impression of the car moving away from the viewer. Motion tweens are new to Flash CS4.

The process for creating a motion tween animation is to select the frame and layer where the animation will start. If necessary, insert a keyframe (by default, frame 1 of each layer has a keyframe). Select the object on the Stage, then select the Motion Tween command from the Insert menu. If the object is not already a symbol, you will be asked if you want to convert it to a symbol. You must convert the object to a symbol if prompted, because only symbols can have a motion tween applied. Then you select the ending frame and make any changes to the object, such as moving it to another location or resizing it. When you create a motion tween, a tween span appears on the Timeline.

Tween Spans

Figure 1 shows a motion tween animation of a car that starts in frame 1 and ends in frame 30. The Onion Skin feature is enabled so that outlines of the car are displayed for each frame of the animation in the figure. Notice a blue highlight appears on the Timeline for the frames of the animation. The blue highlighted area is called the tween or motion span. By default the number of frames in a tween span is equal to the number of frames in one second of the movie. So, if the frame rate is 12 frames per second, then the span is 12 frames. You can increase or decrease the number of frames in the span by dragging the end of the span. In addition, you can move the span to a different location on the Timeline, and you can copy the span to have it apply to another object.

Motion Path

The animation shown in Figure 2 includes a position change (from frame 1 to frame 30); a motion path showing the position change is displayed on the Stage. Each symbol on the path corresponds to a frame on the Timeline and indicates the location of the object (in this example, the car) when the frame is played. A motion path can be altered by dragging a point on the path

FIGURE 1

Sample motion tween animation

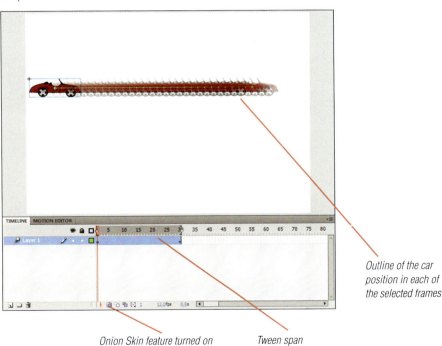

Outline of the car position in each of the selected frames

Onion Skin feature turned on   *Tween span*

using the Selection and Subselection tools or by manipulating Bezier handles as shown in Figure 3. Entire paths can be moved around the Stage and reshaped using the Free Transform tool.

Property Keyframes

A keyframe indicates a change in a Flash movie, such as the start or ending of an animation. Motion tween animations use property keyframes that are specific to each property such as a position keyframe, color keyframe, or rotation keyframe. In most cases these are automatically placed on the Timeline as the motion tween animation is created.

Keep in mind:

- Only one object on the Stage can be animated in each tween span.
- You can have multiple motion tween animations playing at the same time, if they are on different layers.
- A motion tween is, in essence, an object animation because while several changes can be made in the object's properties, only one object is animated for each motion tween.
- The types of objects that can be tweened include graphic, button, and movie clip symbols, as well as text fields.
- You can remove a motion tween animation by clicking the tween span on the Timeline and choosing Remove Tween from the Insert menu.

FIGURE 2
The motion path

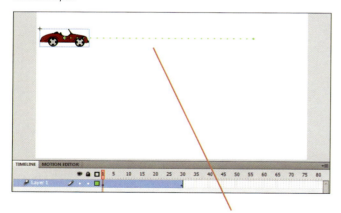

Motion path with symbols corresponding to a frame in the Timeline and showing the location of the car when the frame is played

FIGURE 3
Bezier handles used to alter the path

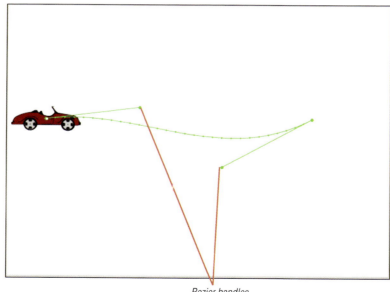

Bezier handles

FIGURE 4
Positioning the car object

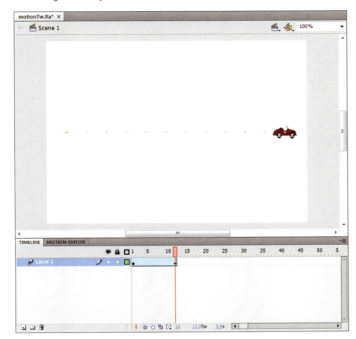

FIGURE 5
Change the end of the tween span

Drag pointer
to here

Create a motion tween animation

1. Open **fl4_1.fla** from the drive and folder where your Data Files are stored, then save it as **motionTw**.

   This document has one drawn object—a car that has been converted to a symbol.

2. Click the **Selection tool** ▸ on the Tools panel, then click the **car** to select it.

3. Click **Insert** on the menu bar, then click **Motion Tween**.

   Notice the tween span appears on the Timeline. The number of frames in the span equals the frames per second for the movie.

4. Verify the playhead is on the last frame of the tween span, then drag the **car** to the right side of the Stage, as shown in Figure 4.

   A motion path appears on the Stage with dots indicating the position of the object for each frame. A diamond symbol appears in frame 12. This is a position keyframe automatically inserted at the end of the motion path. This assumes the document frame rate is set to 12.

   Note: To see the diamond symbol more clearly, move the playhead.

5. Point to the end of the tween span, when the pointer changes to a double arrow ↔, drag the **tween span** to frame 40, as shown in Figure 5.

6. Click **frame 1** on the Timeline, then press the **period key** to move the playhead one frame at a time and notice the position of the car for each frame.

7. Play the movie, then save your work.

You created a motion tween animation, extended the length of the animation, and viewed the position of the animated object in each frame of the animation.

Edit a motion path

1. Click the **Selection tool** ▶ on the Tools panel, then click a blank area of the Stage.

2. Click **frame 1** on Layer 1.

3. Point to the middle of the motion path, as shown in Figure 6.

4. When the pointer changes to a pointer with an arc ▶, drag the ▶ **pointer** down, as shown in Figure 7.

(continued)

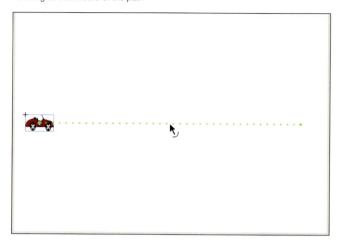

FIGURE 6
Pointing to the middle of the path

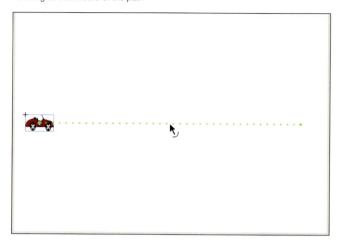

FIGURE 7
Dragging the motion path down

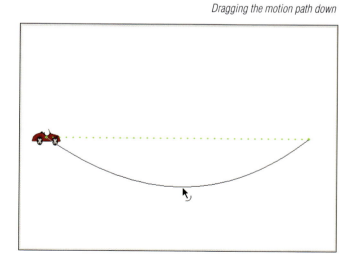

Creating Animations

FIGURE 8

FIGURE 8

Displaying the Bezier handles

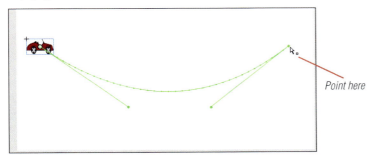

Point here

Drag pointer
to here

FIGURE 9

Using the handles to alter the shape of the path

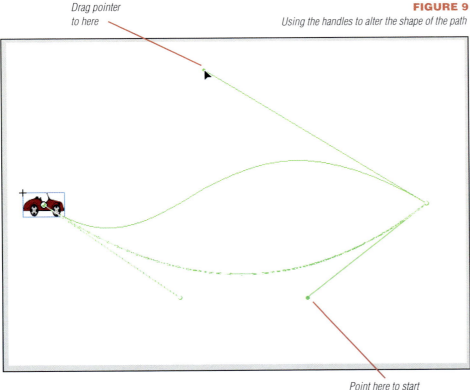

Point here to start

5. Play the movie, then click **frame 1** on Layer 1.

6. Click the **Subselection tool** on the Tools panel, point to the end of the motion path, when the pointer changes into an arrow with a small square , click the end of path to display Bezier handles, as shown in Figure 8.

7. Point to the **lower right handle**, when the pointer changes into a delta symbol , drag the handle up and toward the center of the Stage to form a horizontal S shape, as shown in Figure 9.

8. Play the movie, then save your work.

You edited a motion path by using the Selection tool to drag the path and by using the Subselection tool to display and reposition Bezier handles.

Change the ease value of an animation

1. Play the movie and notice that the car moves at a constant speed.

2. Display the **Properties panel**, then click **frame 1** on Layer 1.

3. Point to the **Ease value**, when the pointer changes to a hand with a double arrow 👆, drag the 👆 **pointer** to the right to set the value at **100**, as shown in Figure 10.

4. Play the movie.

   The car starts moving fast and slows down near the end of the animation. Notice the word "out" is displayed next to the ease value in the Properties panel indicating that the object will ease out, slow down, at the end of the animation.

5. Click **frame 1** on Layer 1.

6. Point to the **Ease value** in the Properties panel, then drag the 👆 **pointer** to the left to set the value to **–100**.

7. Play the movie.

   The car starts moving slowly and speeds up near the end of the animation. Notice the word "in" is displayed next to the ease value in the Properties panel. Also, notice the dots are grouped closer together at the beginning of the motion path indicating that the object does not move very far in that section of the path.

8. Set the ease value to **0**.

9. Save your work.

You changed the ease out and ease in values of the animation.

FIGURE 10
Changing the ease value

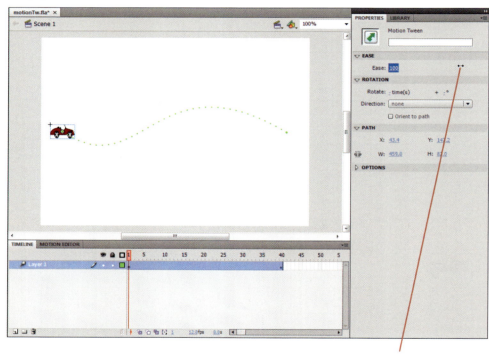

Drag the pointer to the right

FIGURE 11
Changing the width of the object

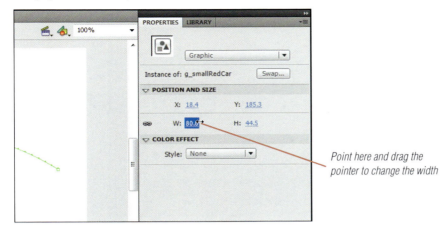

Point here and drag the
pointer to change the width

FIGURE 12
Using the Free Transform tool to skew the object

Point to the middle handle and
drag the pointer to the right

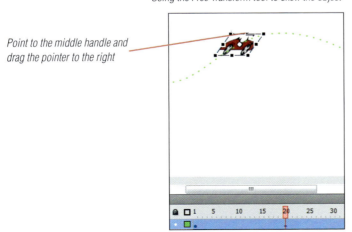

Resize and reshape an object

1. Click **frame 1** on Layer 1.

2. Click the **Selection tool** , then click the **car**.

3. Point to the **width (W:)** value in the Properties panel, when the pointer changes to a hand with a double arrow , drag the **pointer** to the right to set the value to **80**, as shown in Figure 11.

4. Play the movie.

5. Click **frame 40** on Layer 1, then click the **car**.

6. Point to the **width (W:)** value in the Properties panel, when the pointer changes to a hand with a double arrow , drag the **pointer** to the left to set the value to **30**.

7. Play the movie.

   The car starts out large and ends up small.

8. Click **frame 20** on Layer 1.

9. Click the **Free Transform tool** in the Tools panel, then verify the Rotate and Skew option is selected.

10. Point to the **top middle handle**, when the pointer changes to a double line , drag the **pointer** to the right to skew the object, as shown in Figure 12.

   A skew keyframe appears in frame 20.

11. Play the movie, use the Undo command on the Edit menu to undo the skew, then save the movie.

   Note: You may have to click the Undo command more than one time to undo the skew.

   The skew keyframe is removed from frame 20.

You resized and skewed a motion tween object.

Create a color effect

1. Click the **Selection tool** ▸ in the Tools panel.

2. Click **frame 40** on Layer 1.

3. Click the **car** to select it.

4. Click the **Style list arrow** in the COLOR EFFECTS area of the Properties panel.

5. Click **Alpha**, then drag the **slider** ⌂ to set the value to **0%**, as shown in Figure 13.

6. Play the movie.

   Notice the car slowly becomes transparent.

7. Reset the Alpha to **100%**.

8. Click **frame 40** on Layer 1.

9. Click the **car** to select it.

10. Click the **Style list arrow** in the COLOR EFFECT area of the Properties panel.

11. Click **Advanced**, then set the x R + value for Red to **100**, as shown in Figure 14.

12. Play the movie.

   Notice the car slowly changes to a shade of red. Because the car is a symbol, it is one part (not a composite of pieces). As a result changes made to the color value affect the entire car.

13. Set the x R + value back to **0**, then save your work.

You changed the alpha and advanced color option for an object.

FIGURE 13
Setting the Alpha (transparency) value

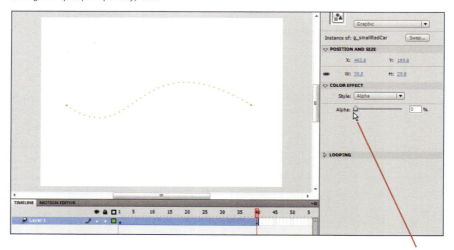

Drag the slider to the left

FIGURE 14
Changing a color value for the object

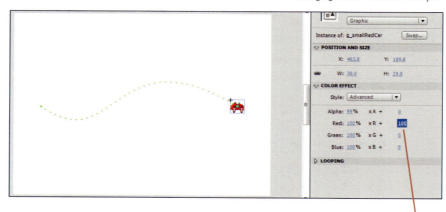

Setting the red value

FIGURE 15

Aligning the car to the path

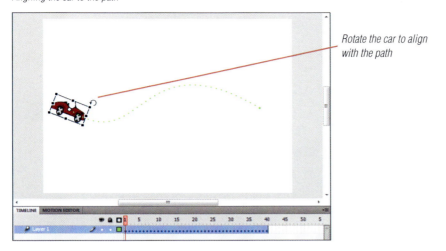

Rotate the car to align
with the path

FIGURE 16

Aligning the car to the end of the motion path

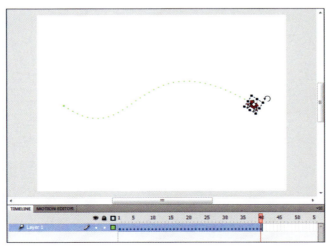

Orient an object to a path

1. Play the movie.

   Notice the car follows the path but it is not oriented to the path.

2. Click **frame 1** on Layer 1.

3. Click the **Orient to path check box** in the ROTATION area of the Properties panel.

4. Click the **Free Transform tool** ⊞ on the Tools panel, then verify the Rotate and Skew option ↻ near the bottom of the Tools panel is selected.

5. Point to the upper-right corner of the car, when the pointer changes into a circular arrow ↻ , rotate the front of the car so that it aligns with the path, as shown in Figure 15.

6. Click **frame 40** on Layer 1, then rotate the back of the car so that it aligns with the path, as shown in Figure 16.

7. Play the movie.

   The car is oriented to the path.

   Notice the diamond symbol in each Layer 1 frame. These are rotation keyframes that indicate the object will change in each frame as it rotates to stay oriented to the path.

8. Save your work, then close the document.

You oriented an object to a motion path and aligned the object with the path in the first and last frames of the motion tween.

Copy a motion path

1. Open fl4_2.fla, save it as **tweenEdits**, then play the movie.

2. Insert a **new layer** and name it **biker2**, then click **frame 1** on the biker2 layer.

3. Verify the Selection tool ▶ is selected, drag the **g_biker symbol** from the Library panel to the Stage, as shown in Figure 17.

4. Click any frame on the tween span on the biker layer.

5. Click **Edit** on the menu bar, point to **Timeline**, then click **Copy Motion**.

6. Click the new instance of the biker, click **Edit** on the menu bar, point to **Timeline**, then click **Paste Motion**.

7. Play the movie, then hide the biker layer.

8. Click **frame 1** on the biker2 layer, click the **Free Transform tool** ▦ on the Tools panel, then click the **path** to select it, as shown in Figure 18.

(continued)

FIGURE 17
Dragging the biker symbol to the Stage

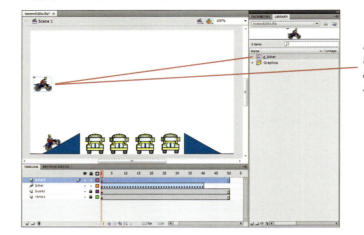

Drag g_biker symbol from the Library panel and position it on the Stage

FIGURE 18
Selecting the path with the Free Transform tool

Click the path to select it and display the handles

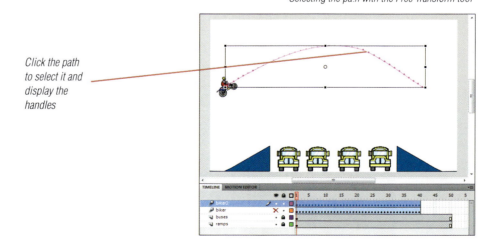

FIGURE 19

Positioning the path

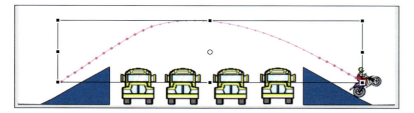

FIGURE 20

Aligning the biker to the path

9. Click **Modify** on the menu bar, point to **Transform**, then click **Flip Horizontal**.

10. Use the arrow keys on the keyboard to position the path, as shown in Figure 19.

11. Click the **biker object**, click **Modify** on the menu bar, point to **Transform**, then click **Flip Horizontal**.

12. Use the Free Transform tool and the arrow keys to align the biker, as shown in Figure 20.

13. Play the movie, then save your work.

You copied a motion path to another object.

Rotate an object

1. Click **frame 1** on the biker2 layer, then display the Properties panel.

2. Point to the **Rotate times value** in the ROTATION area of the Properties panel, when the pointer changes to a hand with a double arrow 🖐, drag the 🖐 **pointer** to the right to set the count to **1**, as shown in Figure 21.

3. Verify the Direction is set to **CW (Clockwise)**, then play the movie.

   The biker object rotates one time in a clockwise direction. Look at the Timeline. Notice some of the keyframes have been removed from the motion tween span. This is because, as the biker rotates, he is no longer oriented to the path. Motion tweens do not allow an object to be rotated and oriented to a path simultaneously since orienting an object to a path rotates the object in each frame along the path. You can use a classic tween to rotate and orient an object to a path at the same time. The remaining keyframes at the beginning and ending of the tween span were used to align the original biker to the ramp.

4. Click **frame 1** on the biker2 layer, set the rotation count to **2**, click the **Direction list arrow**, click **CCW** (Counter Clockwise), then play the movie.

5. Click **Orient to path** to select it.

   The rotate value is automatically set to no times (indicated by a -), as shown in Figure 22.

6. Play the movie, then save your work.

You caused an object to rotate by setting the rotate value and specifying a rotation direction.

FIGURE 21
Changing the rotate value

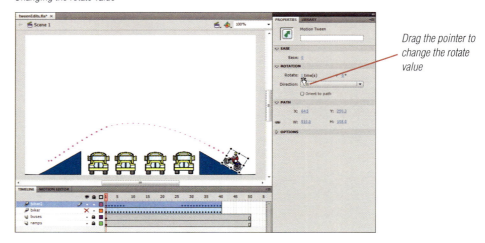

Drag the pointer to change the rotate value

FIGURE 22
The Properties panel showing that the rotate value is set to no times

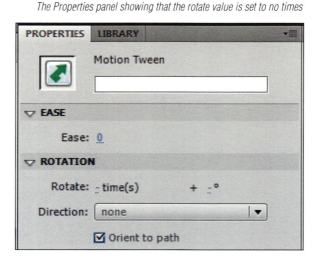

FIGURE 23
Timeline showing the motion tween removed

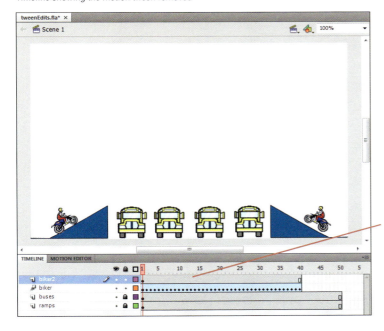

Removal of motion tween in the biker2 layer removes the blue highlight in the Timeline

Remove a motion tween

1. Unhide the **biker layer**, then play the movie.

2. Click anywhere on the tween span on the biker2 layer to select the path.

3. Click **Insert** on the menu bar, then click **Remove Tween**.

4. Click a blank area of the Stage, then notice that the blue highlight on the biker2 layer is gone, as shown in Figure 23.

5. Play the movie and notice that the biker on the biker2 layer is visible but it does not move.

6. Use the Undo command in the Edit menu to undo the Remove Tween process.

   Note: You may need to select the Undo command more than one time.

7. Click **biker2** on the Timeline to select the layer.

8. Click the **Delete icon** 🗑 at the bottom of the Timeline to delete the biker2 layer that includes the motion tween.

9. Test the movie, then close the Flash Player window.

10. Save your work.

You removed an object's motion tween, undid the action, then deleted a layer containing a motion tween and undid the action.

Work with multiple motion tweens

1. Click **frame 40** on the biker layer, then click the **biker** on the Stage.

2. Lock the **biker layer**, then add a **new layer** above the biker layer and name it **bikeOffStage**.

3. Click **frame 40** on the bikeOffStage layer.

4. Click **Insert** on the menu bar, point to **Timeline**, then click **Keyframe**.

5. Drag an instance of the **g_biker symbol** from the Library panel so it is on top of the biker on the Stage, as shown in Figure 24.

6. Use the the Free Transform tool [icon] and the arrow keys on the keyboard to align the two biker objects.

7. Click **frame 41** on the **bikeOffStage** layer, then insert a **keyframe**.

8. Use the **arrow keys** on the keyboard and the **Free Transform tool** [icon] to align the biker with the bottom of the ramp, as shown in Figure 25.

(continued)

FIGURE 24
Placing an instance of the g_biker symbol on top of the object on the Stage

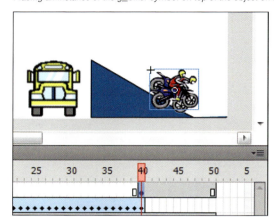

FIGURE 25
Aligning the biker with the ramp

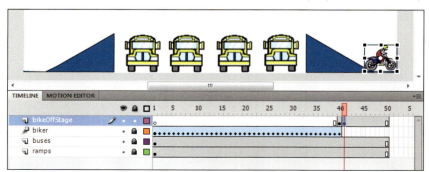

Creating Animations

FIGURE 26
Dragging the biker object off the Stage

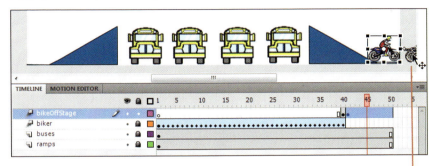

Drag the object off
the Stage

9. Click the **Selection tool** , then click
   the **biker**.

10. Click the **View list arrow**, then click **100%**.

11. Click **Insert** on the menu bar, then click
    Motion Tween.

12. Click **frame 45** on the bikeOffStage layer,
    then drag the **biker** off the Stage, as shown
    in Figure 26.

13. Test the movie, close the Flash Player
    window, save your work, then close the
    document.

You created a second motion tween for the movie.

CREATE CLASSIC TWEEN
ANIMATIONS

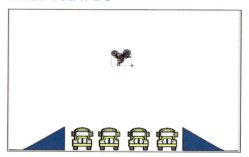

 In this lesson, you will create a motion guide and attach an animation to it.

Understanding Classic Tweens

Classic tweens are similar to motion tweens in that you can create animations that change the properties of an object over time. Motion tweens are easier to use and allow the greatest degree of control over tweened animations. Classic tweens are a bit more complex to create, however, they provide certain capabilities that some developers desire. For example, with a motion tween, you can alter the ease value so that an object starts out fast and ends slow, but with a classic tween, you can alter the ease value so that an object starts out fast, slows down, and then speeds up again. You can do this because a motion tween consists of one object over the tween span, but a classic tween can have more than one instance of the object over the tween span. The process for creating a classic tween animation that moves an object is to select the starting frame and, if necessary, insert a keyframe. Next, insert a keyframe at the ending frame, and click anywhere on the layer between the keyframes. Then select classic tween from the Insert menu, select the ending

frame, and move the object to the position you want it to be in the ending frame. While all prior versions of Flash used classic tweening only, you now have a choice between classic tweens and motion tweens.

Understanding Motion Guides

When you use motion tweening to generate an animation that moves an object, a motion path that shows the movement is automatically created on the Stage. When you use classic tweening, the object moves in a straight line from the beginning location to the ending location on the Stage. There is no path displayed. You can draw a path, called a **motion guide**, that can be used to alter the path of a classic tween animation as shown in Figure 27. A motion guide is drawn on the motion guide layer with the classic tween animation placed on its own layer beneath the motion guide layer, as shown in Figure 28. The process for creating a motion guide and attaching it to a classic tween animation is:

- Create a classic tween animation.
- Insert a new layer above the classic tween animation layer and change the

layer properties to a Guide layer. Drag the classic tween animation layer to the guide layer so that it indents, as shown in Figure 28. This indicates that the classic tween animation layer is associated with the motion guide layer.

- Draw a path using the Pen, Pencil, Line, Circle, Rectangle, or Brush tools.
- Attach the object to the path by clicking the first keyframe of the layer that contains the animation, and then dragging the object by its transformation point to the beginning of the path. Select the end keyframe and then repeat the steps to attach the object to the end of the path.

Depending on the type of object you are animating and the path, you may need to orient the object to the path.

The advantages of using a motion guide are that you can have an object move along any path, including a path that intersects itself, and you can easily change the shape of the path, allowing you to experiment with different motions. A consideration when using a motion guide is that, in some instances, orienting the object along the path may result in an unnatural-looking animation. You can fix this by stepping through the animation one frame at a time until you reach the frame where the object is positioned poorly. You can then insert a keyframe and adjust the object as desired.

Transformation Point and Registration Point

Each symbol has a transformation point in the form of a circle (O) that is used to orient the object when it is being animated. For example, when you rotate a symbol, the transformation point is the pivot point around which the object rotates. The transformation point is also the point that snaps to a motion guide, as shown in Figure 27. When attaching an object to a path, you can drag the transformation point to the path. The default position for a transformation point is the center of the object. You can reposition the transformation point while in the symbol edit mode by dragging the transformation point to a different location in the object. Objects also have a registration point (+) that is used to position the object on the Stage using ActionScript code. The transformation and registration points can overlap—this is displayed as a plus sign within a circle ⊕.

FIGURE 27

A motion guide with an object (motorbike) attached

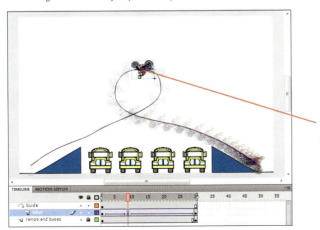

Transformation point ⊕

FIGURE 28

A motion guide layer

Motion guide layer containing the path

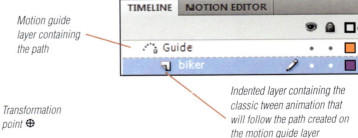

Indented layer containing the classic tween animation that will follow the path created on the motion guide layer

Create a classic tween animation

1. Open fl4_3.fla, then save it as **cTween**.

2. Insert a **new layer**, then name it **biker**.

3. Click **frame 1** on the biker layer, then drag the **biker symbol** from the Library panel to the Stage, as shown in Figure 29.

4. Click **frame 30** on the biker layer, click **Insert** on the menu bar, point to **Timeline**, then click **Keyframe**.

5. Drag the **biker** to the position shown in Figure 30.

6. Click **frame 2** on the biker layer, click **Insert** on the menu bar, then click **Classic Tween**.

   An arrow appears on the Timeline indicating that this is a classic tween.

7. Play the movie.

You created an animation using a classic tween.

Add a motion guide and orient the object to the guide

1. Insert a **new layer**, then name it **Guide**.

2. Click **Modify** on the menu bar, point to **Timeline**, then click **Layer Properties**.

3. Click the **Guide option button**, click **OK**, then drag the **biker layer** up to the Guide layer, as shown in Figure 31.

   The biker layer indents below the Guide layer.

4. Click **frame 1** on the Guide layer, click the **Pencil tool** 🖊 on the Tools panel, then set the stroke color to **black**.

(continued)

FIGURE 29
Dragging the biker symbol to the Stage

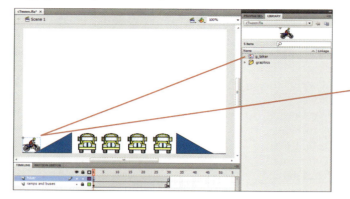

Drag g_biker symbol from the Library panel and position it on the Stage

FIGURE 30
Repositioning the biker

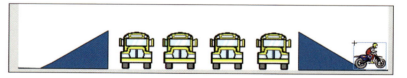

FIGURE 31
Dragging the biker layer up to the Guide layer

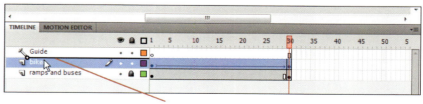

Drag biker layer up to but not above the Guide layer

Creating Animations

FIGURE 32

Drawing a guide path on a Guide layer

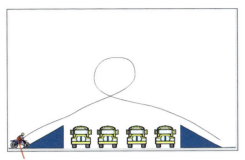

Point to the
middle of the
biker object

FIGURE 33

Aligning the object with the guide path

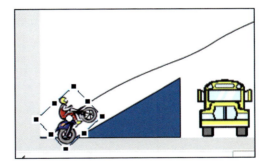

FIGURE 34

Aligning the object with the end of the guide path

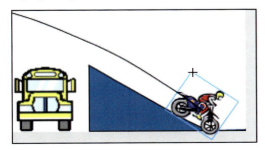

Lesson 2   Create Classic Tween Animations

5. Point to the middle of the biker, then draw a line with a loop similar to the one shown in Figure 32.

6. Click **frame 30** on the biker layer, click the **Selection tool**, then drag the **biker** so that it snaps to the end of the line.

   Hint: Use the Zoom tool to zoom in on the biker to make it easier to see you have placed the transformation point on the path.

7. Play the movie.

8. Click **frame 1** on the biker layer, then click the **biker** to select the object.

9. Click the **Free Transform tool** on the Tools panel, then rotate the **biker**, as shown in Figure 33.

10. Click **frame 30** on the biker layer, then rotate the **biker**, as shown in Figure 34.

11. Click the **Selection tool**, then click **frame 1** on the biker layer.

12. Display the Properties panel, then click the **Orient to path check box**.

13. Play the movie.

14. Click **frame 1** on the biker layer, then set the Ease value in the Properties panel to **100**.

15. Insert a **keyframe** on the frame on the biker layer that displays the highest point in the animation, then set the ease value to **100**.

16. Test the movie, save your work, then close the document.

You added a motion guide, oriented the animated object to the guide, and set an ease value.

CREATE FRAME-BY-FRAME
ANIMATIONS

What You'll Do

In this lesson, you will create frame-by-frame animations.

Understanding Frame-by-Frame Animations

A frame-by-frame animation (also called a frame animation) is created by specifying the object that is to appear in each frame of a sequence of frames. Figure 35 shows three images that are variations of a cartoon character. In this example, the head and body remain the same, but the arms and legs change to represent a walking motion. If these individual images are placed into succeeding frames (with keyframes), an animation is created.

Frame-by-frame animations are useful when you want to change individual parts of an image. The images in Figure 35 are simple—only three images are needed for the animation. However, depending on the complexity of the image and the desired movements, the time needed to display each change can be substantial. When creating a frame-by-frame animation, you need to consider the following points:

- The number of different images. The more images there are, the more effort is needed to create them. However, the greater the number of images, the less change you need to make in each image and the more realistic the movement in the animation may seem.
- The number of frames in which each image will appear. Changing the number of frames in which the object appears may change the effect of the animation. If each image appears in only one frame, the animation may appear rather jerky, since the frames change very rapidly. However, in some cases, you may want to give the impression of a rapid change in an object, such as rapidly blinking colors. If so, you could make changes in the color of an object from one frame to another.
- The movie frame rate. Frame rates below 10 may appear jerky, while those above 30 may appear blurred. The frame rate is easy to change, and you should experiment with different rates until you get the desired effect.

Keyframes are critical to the development of frame animations because they signify a change in the object. Because frame animations are created by changing the object, each frame in a frame animation may need to be a keyframe. The exception is when you want an object displayed in several frames before it changes.

Creating a Frame-by-Frame Animation

To create a frame animation, select the frame on the layer where you want the animation to begin, insert a keyframe, and then place the object on the Stage. Next, select the frame where you want the change to occur, insert a keyframe, and then change the object. You can also add a new object in place of the original one. Figure 36 shows the first three frames of an animation in which three different objects are placed one on top of the other in succeeding frames. In the figure, the movement is shown as shadows. These shadows are visible because the Onion Skin feature is turned on. In this movie, the objects stay in place during the animation. However, a frame animation can also involve movement of the object around the Stage.

Using the Onion Skin Feature

Normally, Flash displays one frame of an animation sequence at a time on the Stage. Turning on the Onion Skin feature allows you to view an outline of the object(s) in any number of frames. This can help in positioning animated objects on the Stage.

FIGURE 35
Three images used in an animation

FIGURE 36
A frame-by-frame animation of 3 figures appearing to walk in place

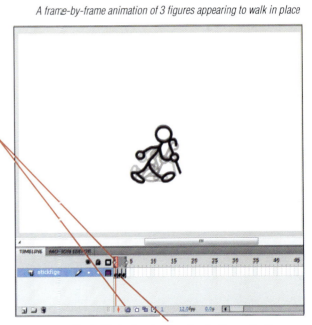

Onion Skin feature is turned on so that all of the objects in frames 1-3 are viewable even though the playhead is on frame 1

The 3 objects placed on top of each other on the Stage, each in its own frame on the Timeline

Create an in-place frame-by-frame animation

1. Open fl4_4.fla, then save it as **frameAn**.

2. Insert a **new layer**, name it **stickfigs**, click **frame 1** of the stickfigs layer, then drag **stickfig1** from the Library panel to the center of the Stage so it touches the white walkway.

3. Click **frame 2** of the stickfigs layer to select it, click **Insert** on the menu bar, point to **Timeline**, then click **Keyframe**.

4. Drag **stickfig2** so it is on top of stickfig1, as shown in Figure 37, use the arrow keys on the keyboard to align the heads, then click a blank area of the Stage to deselect stickfig2.

5. Select **stickfig1** by clicking the foot that points up, as shown in Figure 38, then press **[Delete]**.

6. Click **frame 3** on Layer 1 to select it, insert a **keyframe**, drag **stickfig3** so it is on top of stickfig2, then use the **arrow keys** on the keyboard to align the heads.

7. Click a blank area of the Stage to deselect stickfig3.

8. Select **stickfig2** by clicking the foot that points down, as shown in Figure 39, then press **[Delete]**.

9. Play the movie.

You created a frame-by-frame animation.

FIGURE 37
Dragging stickfig2 on top of stickfig1

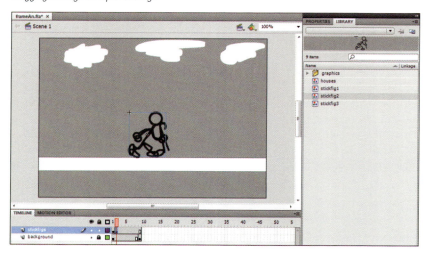

FIGURE 38
Selecting stickfig1

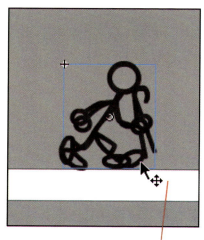

Click foot that points up

FIGURE 39
Selecting stickfig2

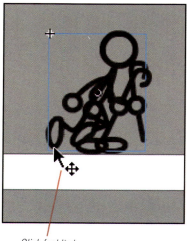

Click foot that points down

FIGURE 40

Moving the houses layer to below the stickfigs layer

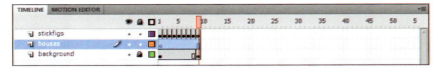

FIGURE 41

Positioning the houses symbol on the Stage

FIGURE 42

Repositioning the houses object

Copy frames and add a moving background

1. Click **frame 1** of the stickfigs layer, hold down **[Shift]**, then click **frame 3**.

2. Click **Edit** on the menu bar, point to **Timeline**, then click **Copy Frames**.

3. Click **frame 4** of the stickfigs layer, click **Edit** on the menu bar, point to **Timeline**, then click **Paste Frames**.

4. Click **frame 7**, then repeat step 3.

5. Click **frame 10** of the stickfigs layer, hold down **[Shift]**, then click **frame 13**.

6. Click **Edit** on the menu bar, point to **Timeline**, then click **Remove Frames**.

7. Insert a **new layer**, name the layer **houses**, then drag the **houses layer** below the stickfigs layer, as shown in Figure 40.

8. Click **frame 1** of the houses layer, then drag the **houses symbol** from the Library panel to the Stage, position the house, as shown in Figure 41.

9. Play the movie.

10. Click **frame 1** of the houses layer, click **Insert** on the menu bar, then click **Motion Tween**.

11. Click **frame 9** on the houses layer, then drag the **houses object** to the left, as shown in Figure 42.

12. Test the movie, close the Flash Player window, save your work, then close the document.

You copied frames and added a motion tween to a movie with an in-place frame-by-frame animation.

Create a frame-by-frame animation of a moving object

1. Open fl4_5.fla, then save it as **frameM**.

    This document has a background layer that contains a row of houses and clouds.

2. Insert a **new layer**, then name it **stickfigs**.

3. Click **View** on the menu bar, point to **Magnification**, then click **50%**.

4. Click **frame 5** on the stickfigs layer, then insert a **keyframe**.

5. Drag **stickfig1** from the Library panel to the left edge of the Stage, as shown in Figure 43.

6. Click **frame 6** on the stickfigs layer, then click **Insert** on the menu bar, point to **Timeline**, then click **Blank Keyframe**.

    A blank keyframe keeps the object in the previous frame from appearing in the current frame.

7. Click the **Edit Multiple Frames button** on the Timeline status bar to turn it on.

    This allows you to view the contents of more than one frame at a time.

8. Drag **stickfig2** to the right of stickfig1, as shown in Figure 44.

9. Click **frame 7** on the stickfigs layer, then insert a **Blank Keyframe**.

10. Drag **stickfig3** to the right of stickfig2, as shown in Figure 45.

(continued)

FIGURE 43
Positioning stickfig1 on the Stage

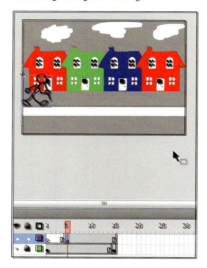

FIGURE 44
Positioning stickfig2 on the Stage

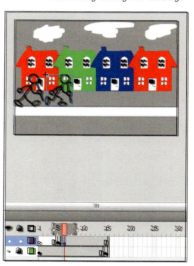

FIGURE 45
Positioning stickfig3 on the Stage

FIGURE 46

FIGURE 46

Adding stickfig3 as the final object

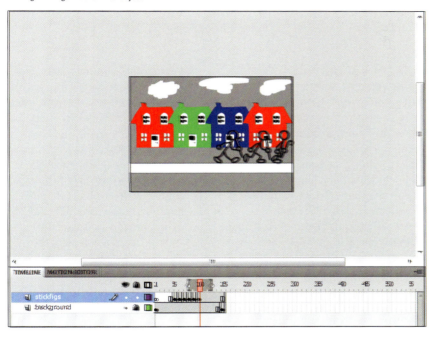

11. Click **frame 8** on the stickfigs layer, insert a **Blank Keyframe**, then drag **stickfig1** from the Library panel to the right of stickfig3.

12. Click **frame 9** on the stickfigs layer, insert a **Blank Keyframe**, then drag **stickfig2** to the right of stickfig1.

13. Click **frame 10** on the stickfigs layer, insert a **Blank Keyframe**, then drag **stickfig3** to the right of stickfig2.

    Your screen should resemble Figure 46.

14. Click **frame 11** on the stickfigs layer, then insert a **Blank Keyframe**.

15. Click the **Edit Multiple Frames button** on the Timeline status bar to turn it off.

16. Test the movie, then close the Flash Player window.

17. Change the frame rate to **6** fps.

18. Test the movie, then close the Flash Player window.

19. Save the movie, then close the document.

You created a frame-by-frame animation that causes objects to appear to move across the screen.

CREATE SHAPE TWEEN
ANIMATIONS

What You'll Do

 In this lesson, you will create a shape tween animation and specify shape hints.

Shape Tweening

In previous lessons, you learned that you can use motion tweening to change the shape of an object. You accomplish this by selecting the Free Transform tool and then dragging the handles to resize and skew the object. While this is easy and allows you to include motion along with the change in shape, there are two drawbacks. First, you are limited in the type of changes (resizing and skewing) that can be made to the shape of an object. Second, you must work with the same object throughout the animation. When you use **shape tweening**, however, you can have an animation change the shape of an object to any form you desire, and you can include two objects in the animation with two different shapes. As with motion tweening, you can use shape tweening to change other properties of an object, such as the color, location, and size.

Using Shape Tweening to Create a Morphing Effect

Morphing involves changing one object into another, sometimes unrelated, object.

For example, you could turn a robot into a man, or turn a football into a basketball. The viewer sees the transformation as a series of incremental changes. In Flash, the first object appears on the Stage and changes into the second object as the movie plays. The number of frames included from the beginning to the end of this shape tween animation determines how quickly the morphing effect takes place. The first frame in the animation displays the first object and the last frame displays the second object. The in-between frames display the different shapes that are created as the first object changes into the second object.

When working with shape tweening, you need to keep the following points in mind:

- Shape tweening can be applied only to editable graphics. To apply shape tweening to instances, groups, symbols, text blocks, or bitmaps, you must break apart the object to make it editable. To do this, you use the Break Apart command on the Modify menu. When you break apart an instance of a symbol, it is no longer linked to the original symbol.

- You can shape tween more than one object at a time as long as all the objects are on the same layer. However, if the shapes are complex and/or if they involve movement in which the objects cross paths, the results may be unpredictable.
- You can use shape tweening to move an object in a straight line, but other options, such as rotating an object, are not available.
- You can use the settings in the Properties panel to set options (such as the ease value, which causes acceleration or deceleration) for a shape tween.
- Shape hints can be used to control more complex shape changes.

Properties Panel Options

Figure 47 shows the Properties panel options for a shape tween. The options allow you to adjust several aspects of the animation, as described in the following:

- Adjust the rate of change between frames to create a more natural appearance during the transition by setting an ease value. Setting the value between -1 and -100 will begin the shape tween gradually and accelerate it toward the end of the animation. Setting the value between 1 and 100 will begin the shape tween rapidly and decelerate it toward the end of the animation. By default, the rate of change is set to 0, which causes a constant rate of change between frames.
- Choose a blend option. The Distributive option creates an animation in which the in-between shapes are smoother and more irregular. The Angular option preserves the corners and straight lines and works only with objects that have these features. If the objects do not have corners, Flash defaults to the Distributive option.

Shape Hints

You can use shape hints to control the shape's transition appearance during animation. Shape hints allow you to specify a location on the beginning object that corresponds to a location on the ending object. Figure 48 shows two shape animations of the same objects, one using shape hints and the other not using shape hints. The figure also shows how the object being reshaped appears in one of the in-between frames. Notice that with the shape hints, the object in the in-between frame is more recognizable.

FIGURE 47
The Properties panel options for a shape tween

FIGURE 48
Two shape animations with and without shape hints

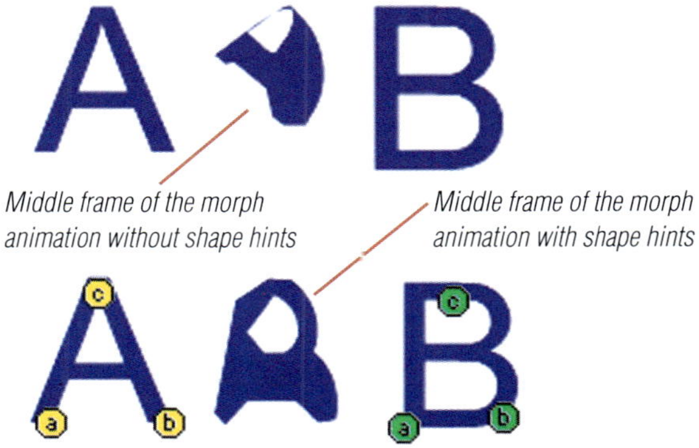

Middle frame of the morph animation without shape hints

Middle frame of the morph animation with shape hints

Create a shape tween animation

1. Open fl4_6.fla, then save it as **antiqueCar**.

2. Set the view to **Fit in Window**.

   | TIP This chapter assumes you always set the magnification to Fit in Window.

3. Click **frame 30** on the shape layer, then insert a **keyframe**.

4. Click the **Selection tool** on the Tools panel, then click a blank area of the pasteboard to deselect the car.

5. Point to the right side of the top of the car, then use the arc pointer to drag the **car top** to create the shape shown in Figure 49.

6. Click anywhere on the shape layer between frames 1 and 30.

7. Click **Insert** on the menu bar, then click **Shape Tween**.

8. Click **frame 1** on the shape layer, then play the movie.

9. Click **frame 30** on the shape layer.

10. Click the **Selection tool** on the Tools panel, then drag a **marquee** around the car to select it if it is not already selected.

11. Drag the **car** to the right side of the Stage.

12. Play the movie, then save and close it.

You created a shape tween animation, causing an object to change shape as it moves over several frames.

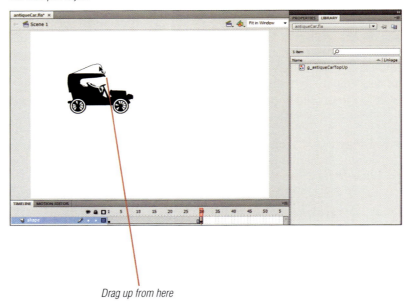

FIGURE 49
The reshaped object

Drag up from here

FIGURE 50

Positioning the car instance on the Stage

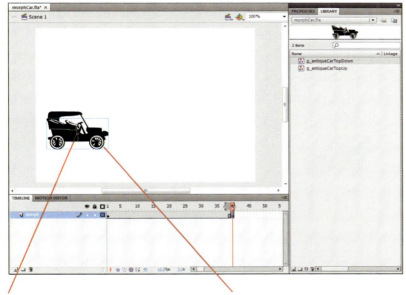

Transformation point appears when the mouse is released

Line up both cars so it appears that there is only one car; use the spokes on the wheels to help you know when the two objects are aligned

Create a morphing effect

1. Open fl4_7.fla, then save it as **morphCar**.

2. Click **frame 40** on the morph layer.

3. Click **Insert** on the menu bar, point to **Timeline**, then click **Blank Keyframe**.

   TIP Inserting a blank keyframe prevents the object in the preceding keyframe from automatically being inserted into the blank keyframe.

4. Click the **Edit Multiple Frames button** on the Timeline.

   Turning on the Edit Multiple Frames feature allows you to align the two objects to be morphed.

5. Display the Library panel.

6. Drag the **g_antiqueCarTopDown graphic** symbol from the Library panel directly on top of the car on the Stage, as shown in Figure 50.

   TIP Use the arrow keys to move the object in small increments as needed.

7. Make sure the **g_antiqueCarTopDown** object is selected, click **Modify** on the menu bar, then click **Break Apart**.

8. Click the **Edit Multiple Frames button** to turn off the feature.

9. Click anywhere between frames 1 and 40 on the morph layer, click **Insert** on the menu bar, then click **Shape Tween**.

10. Click **frame 1** on the Timeline, then play the movie.

    The first car morphs into the second car.

11. Save the movie.

You created a morphing effect, causing one object to change into another.

Adjust the rate of change in a shape tween animation

1. Click **frame 40** on the morph layer.

2. Click the **Selection tool** on the Tools panel, then drag a **marquee** around the car to select it (if necessary).

3. Drag the **car** to the right side of the Stage.

4. Click **frame 1** on the morph layer.

5. Set the ease value on the Properties panel to **−100**, as shown in Figure 51.

6. Click the **Stage**, then play the movie.

   The car starts out slow and speeds up as the morphing process is completed.

7. Repeat Steps 4 and 5, but change the ease value to **100**.

8. Click **frame 1** on the Timeline, then play the movie.

   The car starts out fast and slows down as the morphing process is completed.

9. Save your work, then close the movie.

You added motion to a shape tween animation and changed the ease value.

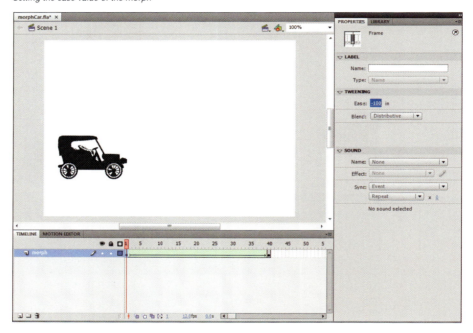

FIGURE 51

Setting the ease value of the morph

FIGURE 52
Positioning a shape hint

FIGURE 53
Adding shape hints

FIGURE 54
Matching shape hints

Use shape hints

1. Open fl4_8.fla, then save it as **shapeHints**.

2. Play the movie and notice how the L morphs into a Z.

3. Click **frame 15** on the Timeline, the midpoint of the animation, then notice the shape.

4. Click **frame 1** on the hints layer to display the first object.

5. Make sure the object is selected, click **Modify** on the menu bar, point to **Shape**, then click **Add Shape Hint**.

6. Drag the **Shape Hint icon** to the location shown in Figure 52.

7. Repeat Steps 5 and 6 to set a second and third Shape Hint icon, as shown in Figure 53.

8. Click **frame 30** on the hints layer.

   The shape hints are stacked on top of each other.

9. Drag the **Shape Hint icons** to match Figure 54.

10. Click **frame 15** on the hints layer, then notice how the object is more recognizable now that the shape hints have been added.

11. Click **frame 1** on the Timeline, then play the movie.

12. Save your work, then close the movie.

You added shape hints to a morph animation.

CREATE MOVIE
CLIPS

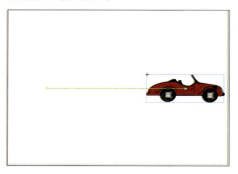

 In this lesson, you will create, edit, and animate a movie clip.

Understanding Movie Clip Symbols

Until now you have been working with two kinds of symbols, graphic and button. A third type is a **movie clip symbol**, which provides a way to create more complex types of animations. A movie clip is essentially a movie within a movie. Each movie clip has its own Timeline, which is independent of the main Timeline. This allows you to nest a movie clip that is running one animation within another animation or in a scene on the main Timeline. Because a movie clip retains its own Timeline, when you insert an instance of the movie clip symbol into a Flash document, the movie clip continues in an endless loop even if the main Timeline stops.

The wheels on a car rotating while the car is moving across the screen is an example of a movie clip with an animation that is nested in another animation. To create the animated movie clip, a drawing of a wheel separate from the car is converted into a movie clip symbol. Then the movie clip symbol is opened in the edit window, which includes a Timeline that is unique to the movie clip. In the edit window, an animation is created that causes the wheel to rotate. After exiting the edit window and returning to the main Timeline, an instance of the movie clip symbol is placed on each wheel of the car. Finally, the car, including the wheels, is animated on the main Timeline. As the car is moving across the screen, the wheels are rotating according to their own Timeline. This process is shown in Figure 55.

In addition to allowing you to create more complex animations, movie clips help to organize the different reusable pieces of a movie and provide for smaller movie file sizes. This is because only one movie clip symbol needs to be stored in the Library panel while an unlimited number of instances of the symbol can be used in the Flash document. An animated movie clip can be viewed in the edit window that is displayed when you double-click on the movie clip symbol in the Library panel; and it can be viewed when you test or publish the movie that contains the movie clip. It is important to note that an animated movie clip cannot be viewed simply by playing the movie on the main Timeline.

In this lesson, you will learn how to create a movie clip symbol from a drawn object, edit the movie clip to create an animation, and nest the movie clip in another animation.

FIGURE 55

The process of nesting a movie clip within an animation

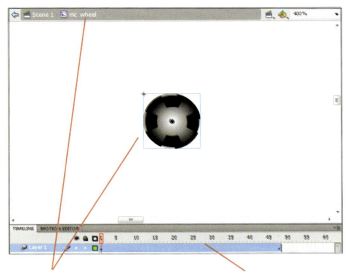
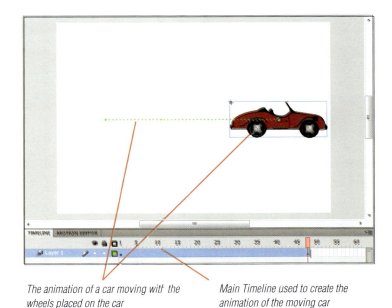

The movie clip of a wheel that has been animated to rotate shown in the edit window

Timeline in the edit window used to create the animation of the rotating wheel

The animation of a car moving with the wheels placed on the car

Main Timeline used to create the animation of the moving car

Break apart a graphic symbol and select parts of the object to separate from the graphic

1. Open fl4_9.fla, then save it as **mClip**.

   This document has one graphic symbol—a car that has been placed on the Stage.

2. Click the **Selection tool** ⊾ on the Tools panel, then click the **car** to select it.

3. Click **Modify** on the menu bar, then click **Break Apart**.

4. Click a blank area of the Stage to deselect the object.

5. Click the **Zoom tool** 🔍 on the Tools panel, then click the **front wheel** two times to zoom in on the wheel.

6. Click the **Selection tool** ⊾ on the Tools panel.

7. Click the **gray hubcap**, hold down **[Shift]**, then click the rest of the wheel, as shown in Figure 56.

   Hint: There are several small parts to the wheel, so click until a dot pattern covers the entire wheel, but do not select the tire. Use the Undo command if you select the tire.

8. Drag the **selected area** down below the car, as shown in Figure 57.

9. Compare your selected wheel to Figure 57, if your wheel does not match the figure, use the Undo command to move the wheel back to its original position, and repeat step 7.

You broke apart a graphic symbol and selected parts of the object to separate from the graphic.

FIGURE 56
Selecting the wheel

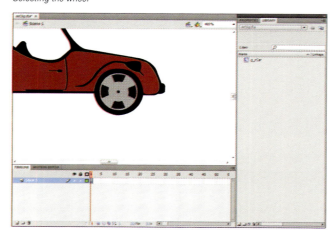

FIGURE 57
Separating the wheel from the car

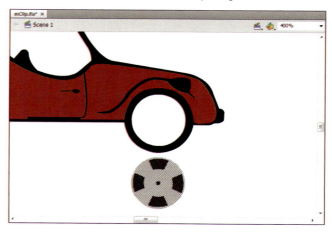

Creating Animations

FIGURE 58

Selecting the gray area of the wheel

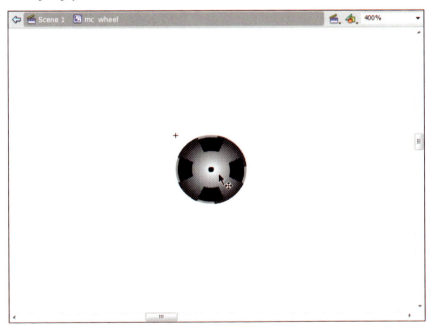

1. Verify the wheel is selected, click **Modify** on the menu bar, then click **Convert to Symbol**.

2. Type **mc_wheel** for the name, select **Movie Clip** for the Type, then click **OK**.

   The mc_wheel movie clip appears in the Library panel.

3. Double-click the **mc_wheel icon** in the Library panel to display the edit window.

4. Click the **Zoom tool** 🔍 on the Tools panel, then click the **wheel** twice to zoom in on the wheel.

   The movie clip has been broken apart as indicated by the dot pattern.

5. Click the **Selection tool** ▸ , click a blank area of the Stage to deselect the object, then click the **gray area** of the wheel to select it, as shown in Figure 58.

6. Click the **Fill color tool color swatch** on the Tools panel, then click the **gray gradient color swatch** in the bottom row of the palette.

You created a movie clip symbol and edited it to change the color of the object.

Animate a movie clip

1. Use the Selection tool 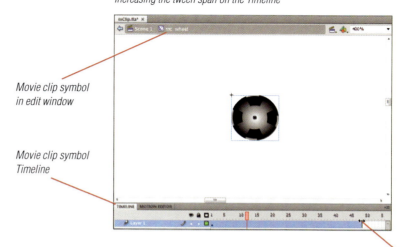 to drag a marquee around the entire wheel to select it.

2. Click **Insert** on the menu bar, click **Motion Tween**, then click **OK** for the Convert selection to symbol for tween dialog box.

3. Point to the end of the tween span on Layer 1 of the Timeline, when the pointer changes to a double-headed arrow ↔ , drag the span to **frame 48**, as shown in Figure 59.

4. Click **frame 1** on Layer 1.

5. Display the Properties panel.

6. Change the rotate value to **4** times and verify the Direction is **CW (Clockwise)**, as shown in Figure 60.
   Hint: If you don't see the Rotate option, click the Selection tool, then drag a marquee around the object.

7. Verify the frame rate in the Timeline status bar is **12**, test the movie, then close the Flash Player window.

8. Click **Scene 1** near the top left side of the edit widow to exit the edit window.

9. Drag the **wheel** on the Stage and position it so it is on top of the front wheel of the car.

10. Click **View** on the menu bar, point to **Magnification**, then click **Fit in Window**.

11. Drag the **mc_wheel movie clip** from the Library panel and position it using the arrow keys as needed so it is on the back wheel.
    Hint: Use the Zoom tool as needed to zoom in on the wheel.

(continued)

FIGURE 59
Increasing the tween span on the Timeline

Movie clip symbol in edit window

Movie clip symbol Timeline

Drag the tween span to frame 48

FIGURE 60
Changing the rotate value

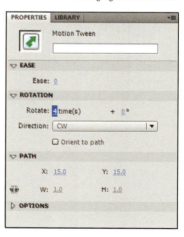

FIGURE 61
Repositioning the car

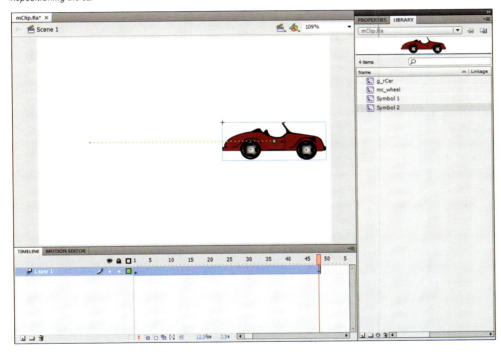

12. Test the movie and notice how the wheels turn, then close the Flash Player window.

13. Use the Selection tool ▶ to drag a marquee around the car to select it and the wheels.

14. Click **Insert** on the menu bar, click **Motion Tween**, then click **OK**.

15. Drag the tween span on Layer 1 to **frame 48**.

16. Click **frame 48** on Layer 1, then drag the **car** to the right side of the Stage, as shown in Figure 61.

17. Test the movie, then close the Flash Player window.

18. Save your work, then close the document.

You edited a movie clip to create an animation, then nested the movie clip in an animation on the main Timeline.

ANIMATE TEXT

What You'll Do

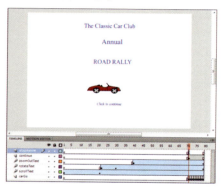

 In this lesson, you will animate text by scrolling, rotating, zooming, and resizing it.

Animating Text

You can motion tween text block objects just as you do graphic objects. You can resize, rotate, reposition, and change their colors. Figure 62 shows three examples of animated text with the Onion Skin feature turned on. When the movie starts, each of the following occurs one after the other:

- The Classic Car Club text block scrolls in from the left side to the top center of the Stage. This is done by creating the text block, positioning it off the Stage, and creating a motion-tweened animation that moves it to the Stage.
- The Annual text block appears and rotates five times. This occurs after you create the Annual text block, position it in the middle of the Stage under the heading, and use the Properties panel to specify a clockwise rotation that repeats five times.
- The ROAD RALLY text block slowly zooms out and appears in the middle of the Stage. This occurs after you create the text block and use the Free Transform tool handles to resize it to a small block at the beginning of the animation. Then, you resize the text block to a larger size at the end of the animation.

Once you create a motion animation using a text block, the text block becomes a symbol and you are unable to edit individual characters within the text block. You can, however, edit the symbol as a whole.

FIGURE 62
Three examples of animated text

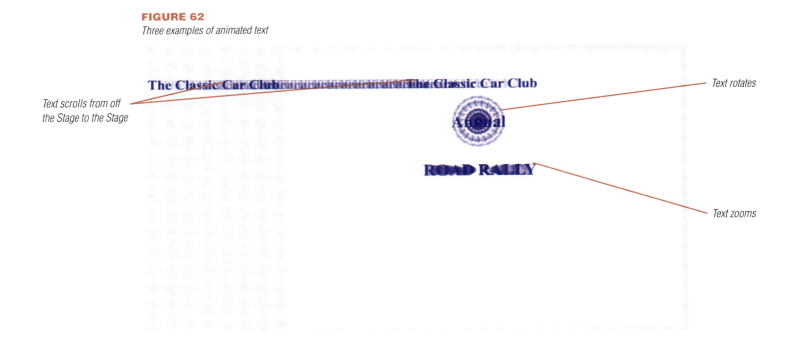

Text scrolls from off
the Stage to the Stage

Text rotates

Text zooms

Select, copy, and paste frames

1. Open fl4_10.fla, then save the movie as **textAn**.

   This document has a frame-by-frame animation of a car where the front end rotates up and down, and then the car moves off the screen.

2. Play the movie, then click **frame 1** on the Timeline.

3. Press the **period [.] key** to move through the animation one frame at a time and notice the changes to the object in each frame.

4. Change the view to **Fit in Window**.

5. Click **frame 9** on the carGo layer, press and hold **[Shift]**, then click **frame 1** to select all the frames, as shown in Figure 63.

6. Click **Edit** on the menu bar, point to **Timeline**, then click **Cut Frames**.

7. Click the **Frame View icon** ▾☰ near the upper right of the Timeline, then click **Small**.

8. Click **frame 71** on the carGo layer.

9. Click **Edit** on the menu bar, point to **Timeline**, then click **Paste Frames**.

10. Click **frame 1** on the carGo layer.

11. Point to the **vertical line** on the Timeline until the ┿ appears, then drag it to the left until frame 80 appears on the Timeline, as shown in Figure 64 (if necessary).

12. Change the view to **100%**.

13. Play the movie, then save your work.

You selected frames and moved them from one location on the Timeline to another location on the Timeline.

FIGURE 63

Selecting a range of frames

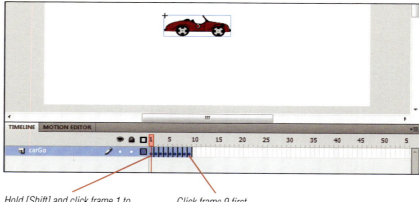

Hold [Shift] and click frame 1 to select the range of frames

Click frame 9 first

FIGURE 64

Expanding the view of the Timeline

Drag the pointer to the left

FIGURE 65
Positioning the Text tool pointer outside the Stage

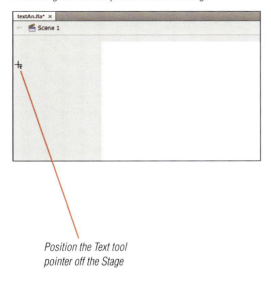

Position the Text tool
pointer off the Stage

FIGURE 66
Positioning the text block

This will be the position of the text
block at the end of the animation

Create animated text

1. Insert a **new layer**, then name it **scrollText**.

2. Click **frame 1** on the scrollText layer.

3. Click the **Text tool** T on the Tools panel,
    click the ⊥ᴛ **pointer** outside the Stage in the
    upper-left corner of the pasteboard, as shown
    in Figure 65, then click to display a text box.

    > TIP   You may need to scroll the Stage to
    > make room for the text box.

4. Click the **Family list arrow** in the Properties
    panel, then click **Times New Roman** if it is
    not already selected.

5. Change the Character size to **20**.

6. Click the **Text (fill) color swatch** ▮ ,
    then click the **blue color swatch** on the left
    column of the color palette.

7. Type **The Classic Car Club**.

8. Click the **Selection tool** ▸ , click **Insert**
    on the menu bar, then click **Motion Tween**.

9. Click **frame 20** on the scrollText layer, then
    insert a **keyframe**.

10. Drag the **text block** horizontally to the top
    center of the Stage, as shown in Figure 66.

11. Click **frame 1** on the Timeline, then play
    the movie.

    The text moves to center Stage from
    offstage left.

*You created a text block object and applied a
motion tween animation to it.*

Create rotating text

1. Insert a **new layer**, then name it **rotateText**.

2. Insert a **keyframe** in frame 21 on the rotateText layer.

3. Click the **Text tool** T on the Tools panel, position the pointer beneath the "a" in "Classic," then click to display a blank text box.

4. Change the Character size in the Properties panel to **24**, type **Annual**, then compare your image to Figure 67.

5. Click the **Selection tool** ▶ on the Tools panel, verify Annual is selected, click **Insert** on the menu bar, then click **Motion Tween**.

6. Set the Rotate value in the Properties panel to **2** times with a **CW** (clockwise) direction.

   TIP You may need to click the frame in the Timeline to have the rotate setting appear.

7. Point to the end of the tween span (frame 79) until the pointer changes to ↔ , then drag the ↔ **pointer** to frame 30, as shown in Figure 68.

8. Click **frame 79** on the rotateText layer, then insert a **keyframe**.

9. Click **frame 1** on the Timeline, then play the movie.

   The Annual text rotates clockwise two times.

You inserted a new layer, created a rotating text block, applied a motion tween to text, and used the Properties panel to rotate the text box.

FIGURE 67
Positioning the Annual text block

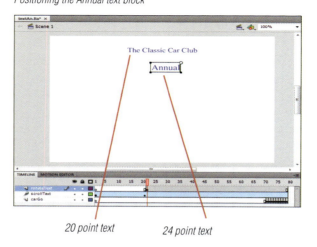

20 point text   24 point text

FIGURE 68
Resizing the tween span from frame 79 to frame 30

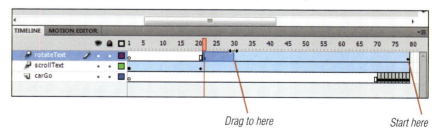

Drag to here   Start here

FIGURE 69

Using the Text tool to type ROAD RALLY

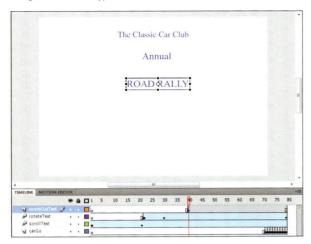

FIGURE 70

Resizing the Text block

Resize and fade in text

1. Insert a **new layer**, name it **zoomOutText**, then insert a **keyframe** in frame 40 on the layer.

2. Click the **Text tool** **T** , position the pointer beneath the Annual text box, aligning it with the "h" in "The," then type **ROAD RALLY**, as shown in Figure 69.

3. Click the **Selection tool** , click **frame 40** on the zoomOutText layer, click **Insert** on the menu bar, then click **Motion Tween**.

4. Click **frame 40** on the zoomOutText layer, click the **Free Transform tool** , then click the **Scale button** in the Options area of the Tools panel.

5. Drag the upper-left corner handle inward to resize the text block, as shown in Figure 70.

6. Click **frame 79** on the ZoomOutText layer, verify the Scale option in the Options area of the Tools panel is selected, then drag the upper-left corner handle outward to resize the text block to its original size.

7. Test the movie, then close the Flash Player window.

You created a motion animation that caused a text block to zoom out.

Make a text block into a button

1. Insert a **new layer**, then name it **continue**.

2. Insert a **keyframe** in frame 71 on the continue layer.

3. Click the **Text tool** T on the Tools panel, position the **Text tool pointer** ⊤ beneath the back wheel of the car, then type **Click to continue**.

4. Drag the **pointer** over the text to select it, change the character size in the Properties panel to **12**, click the **Selection tool** ↖ on the Tools panel, then compare your image to Figure 71.

5. Verify that the text box is selected, click **Modify** on the menu bar, click **Convert to Symbol**, type **b_continue** in the Name text box, set the Type to **Button**, then click **OK**.

6. Double-click the **text block** to edit the button.

7. Insert a **keyframe** in the Over frame, set the fill color to the **black color swatch** in the left column of the color palette.

8. Insert a **keyframe** in the Down frame, set the fill color to the **bright green color swatch** in the left column of the color palette.

9. Insert a **keyframe** in the Hit frame, select the **Rectangle tool** ▭ on the Tools panel, then draw a **rectangle** that covers the text block, as shown in Figure 72.

10. Click **Scene 1** at the top left of the edit window to return to the main Timeline.

You made the text block into a button.

FIGURE 71
Adding a button

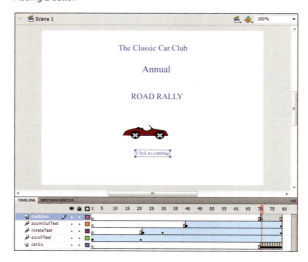

FIGURE 72
The rectangle that defines the hit area

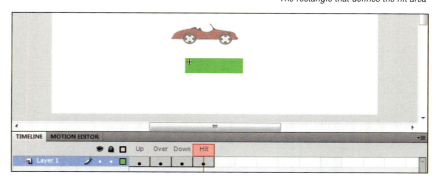

FIGURE 73

Adding a play action

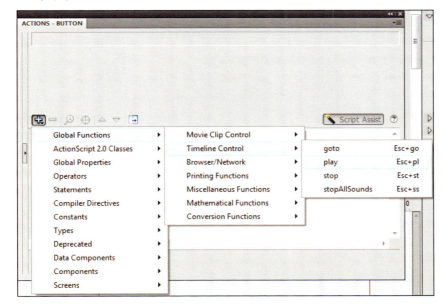

1. Display the Actions panel.

2. Click the **Selection tool** ▶ on the Tools panel, then click the **Click to continue button** on the Stage.

3. Verify the Script Assist button is turned on, then verify the button symbol and b_continue are displayed in the lower-left corner of the Actions panel.

   Note: You need to have ActionScript 2.0 active. You can check your ActionScript version by choosing Publish Settings on the Edit menu, then selecting the Flash tab.

4. Click the **Add a new item to the script button** ⊕ in the Script Assist window, point to **Global Functions**, point to **Timeline Control**, then click **play**, as shown in Figure 73.

5. Insert a **new layer**, name it **stopmovie**, then insert a **keyframe** in frame 71 on that layer.

6. Verify that stopmovie:71 is displayed in the lower-left corner of the Actions panel.

7. Click the **Add a new item to the script button** ⊕ in the Script Assist window, point to **Global Functions**, point to **Timeline Control**, then click **stop**.

8. Click **Control** on the menu bar, click **Test Movie**, then click the **Click to continue button** when it appears.

   The movie plays the animated text blocks, then plays the animated car when you click the Click to continue button.

9. Close the Flash Player movie window, save and close the movie, then exit Flash.

You inserted a play button and added a play action to it, then inserted a stop action on another layer.

Create a motion tween animation.

1. Start Flash, open fl4_11.fla, then save it as **skillsdemo4**.
2. Insert a keyframe in frame 20 on the ballAn layer.
3. Display the Library panel, then drag the g_vball graphic symbol to the lower-left corner of the Stage.
4. Click frame 20 on the ballAn layer, then insert a motion tween.
5. Point to the end of frame 20, when the pointer changes to a double-headed arrow, drag the pointer to frame 40 to set the tween span from frames 20 to 40.
6. With frame 40 selected, drag the object to the lower-right corner of the Stage.
7. Change the view of the Timeline to Small so more frames are in view.
8. Insert a blank keyframe in frame 41.
9. Play the movie, then save your work.

Edit a motion tween.

1. Click frame 20, use the Selection tool to alter the motion path to form an arc, then play the movie.
2. Use the Subsection tool to display the Bezier handles, use them to form a curved path, then play the movie.
3. Select frame 20, use the Properties panel to change the ease value to **100**, then play the movie.
4. Select frame 20, change the ease value to **-100**, then play the movie.

5. Select frame 40, select the object, use the Properties panel to change the width of the object to **30**, then play the movie. (*Hint:* Verify the Lock width and height values together chain is unbroken. This will ensure that when one value is changed, the other value changes proportionally.)
6. Select frame 35, select the object, use the Free transform tool to skew the object, then play the movie.
7. Select frame 40, select the object, use the Properties panel to change the alpha setting to **0**, then play the movie.
8. Change the alpha setting back to **100**.
9. Select frame 40, select the object, then use the Advanced Style option in the COLOR EFFECT area of the Properties panel to create a red color.
10. Lock the ballAn layer.
11. Play the movie, then save your work.

Create a classic tween.

1. Insert a new layer and name it **v-ball**.
2. Insert a keyframe in frame 76 on the v-ball layer.
3. Insert a keyframe in frame 41 on the v-ball layer.
4. Drag an instance of the g_vball symbol from the Library panel to the lower-left corner of the Stage.
5. Insert a keyframe in frame 50 on the v-ball layer and drag the ball to the lower-right corner of the Stage.

6. Click on any frame between 41 and 50 on the v-ball layer and insert a Classic tween.
7. Insert a blank keyframe at frame 51 on the v-ball layer.
8. Play the movie, then save your work.

Create a motion guide.

1. Insert a new layer above the v-ball layer and name it **path**.
2. Insert a keyframe in frame 76 on the path layer.
3. Change the path layer to a Guide layer.
4. Insert a keyframe at frame 41 on the path layer.
5. Select the pencil tool, point to the middle of the ball and draw a path with a loop.
6. Insert a keyframe in frame 50 on the path layer.
7. Drag the v-ball layer up to the path layer so that it indents below the path layer.
8. Click frame 41 on the v-ball layer and attach the ball to the path.
9. Click frame 50 on the v-ball layer and attach the ball to the path.
10. Click frame 41 on the v-ball layer and use the Properties panel to orient the ball to the path.
11. Lock the v-ball and path layers.
12. Hide the path layer.
13. Play the movie, then save the movie.

Create a frame animation.

1. Insert a new layer and name it **corner-ball**.
2. Insert a keyframe in frame 76 on the corner-ball layer.

3. Insert a keyframe in frame 51 on the corner-ball layer, then drag the g_vball graphic from the Library panel to the lower-left corner of the Stage.

4. Insert a blank keyframe in frame 55 on the corner-ball layer, then drag g_vball graphic from the Library panel to the upper-left corner of the Stage.

5. Insert a blank keyframe in frame 59 on the corner-ball layer, then drag the g_vball graphic from the Library panel to the upper-right corner of the Stage.

6. Insert a blank keyframe in the frame 63 on the corner-ball layer, then drag the g_vball graphic from the Library panel to the lower-right corner of the Stage.

7. Insert a blank keyframe in frame 66 on the corner-ball layer.

8. Lock the corner-ball layer.

9. Change the movie frame rate to 3 frames per second, then play the movie.

10. Change the movie frame rate to 12 frames per second, play the movie, then save your work.

Create a movie clip.

1. Insert a new layer and name it **spin-ball**.

2. Insert a keyframe at frame 76 on the spin-ball layer.

3. Insert a keyframe at frame 51 on the spin-ball layer.

4. Drag an instance of the g_vball symbol from the Library panel to the center of the Stage.

5. Select the ball and convert it to a movie clip with the name **mc_ball**.

6. Display the edit window for the mc_ball movie clip.

7. Create a motion tween that rotates the ball 6 times counterclockwise in 12 frames.

8. Exit the edit window.

9. Insert a blank keyframe in frame 66 of the spin-ball layer.

10. Lock the spin-ball layer.

11. Test the movie, close the Flash Player window, then save your work.

Animate text.

1. Insert a new layer above the spin-ball layer and name it **heading**.

2. Insert a keyframe in frame 76 on the heading layer.

3. Click frame 1 on the heading layer.

4. Use the Text tool to type **Having fun with a** in a location off the top-left of the Stage.

5. Change the text to Arial, 20 point, light gray (#CCCCCC), and boldface.

6. Select frame 1 on the heading layer and insert a motion tween.

7. Click frame 10 on the heading layer, insert a keyframe, then use the Selection tool to drag the text to the top-center of the Stage.

8. Play the movie and save your work.

9. Lock the heading layer.

10. Insert a new layer and name it **zoom**.

11. Insert a keyframe in frame 76 on the zoom layer.

12. Insert a keyframe in frame 11 on the zoom layer.

13. Use the Text tool to type **Volleyball** below the heading, then center it as needed.

14. Select frame 11 on the zoom layer and create a motion tween.

15. Insert a keyframe in frame 20 on the zoom layer.

16. Click frame 11 on the zoom layer and select the text block.

17. Use the Free Transform tool to resize the text block to approximately one-fourth its original size.

18. Select frame 20 on the zoom layer, and resize the text block to approximately the size shown in Figure 74.

19. Lock the zoom layer.

20. Test the movie, close the Flash Player window, save your work.

Morph text.

1. Insert a new layer above the heading layer and name it **morph**.

2. Insert a keyframe in frame 66 on the morph layer.

3. Drag the g_vball symbol to the center of the Stage.

4. Use the Properties panel to resize the width to **60** px. (*Hint*: Verify the Lock width and height values together chain is unbroken. This will ensure that when one value is changed, the other value changes proportionally.)

5. Break apart the object.
6. Insert a blank keyframe in frame 76 on the morph layer.
7. Turn on the Edit Multiple Frames feature.
8. Drag the g_vball symbol to the Stage and use the Properties panel to resize the width to **60** px. *(Hint:* Verify the Lock width and height values together chain is unbroken.

This will ensure that when one value is changed, the other value changes proportionally).
9. Center the football on top of the volleyball.
10. Break apart the football object.
11. Turn off the Edit Multiple Frames feature.
12. Click frame 66 on the morph layer and insert a shape tween.

13. Test the movie, then close the Flash Player window.
14. Add shape hints to the volleyball and the football.
15. Lock the morph layer.
16. Test the movie, close the Flash Player window, then save your work.
17. Exit Flash.

FIGURE 74
Completed Skills Review

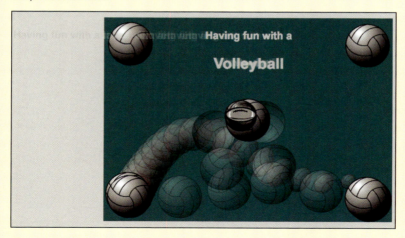

The Ultimate Tours travel company has asked you to design several sample animations for its website. Figure 75 shows a sample home page and the Cruises screen. Using these (or one of the home pages you created in Chapter 3) as a guide, complete the following:

(Tip: If you need to insert frames, select the frame where the inserted frame is to go and press [F5] (Win) or use the Timeline command from the Insert menu (Win) (Mac). To insert several frames, select a range of frames and press [F5] (Win), or use the Timeline command from the Insert menu (Win) (Mac). To move the contents of a frame, you can select the frames you want to move, then use the Cut and Paste commands from the Edit menu to move the contents.)

1. Open ultimatetours3.fla (the file you created in Chapter 3 Project Builder 1) and save it as **ultimatetours4**.

2. Animate the heading Ultimate Tours on the home page so that it zooms out from a transparent text block.

3. Have the logo appear next.

4. After the heading and logo appear, make the subheading We Specialize in Exotic Adventures appear.

5. Make each of the buttons (Treks, Tours, Cruises) scroll from the bottom of the Stage to its position on the Stage. Stagger the buttons so they scroll onto the Stage one after the other.

6. Assign a stop action after the home page appears.

7. Add a new layer, name it **cruises headings**, then add the text blocks shown in Figure 75 (Featured Cruises, Panama Canal, Caribbean, Galapagos).

8. Insert keyframes in the ending frames for the Ultimate Tours title, logo, and home button so that they appear on the cruises screen.

9. Import the graphic file ship.gif from the drive and folder where your Data Files are stored to the Library panel, then rename the graphic file **g_ship**. (*Hint*: To import a graphic to the Library panel, click File on the menu bar, point to Import, then click Import to Library. Navigate to the drive and folder where your Data Files are stored, then select the desired file and click Open (Win) or Import to Library (Mac).)

10. Create a motion tween animation that moves the ship across the screen, then alter the motion path to cause a dip in it, similar to the path shown in Figure 75.

11. Orient the boat to the motion path.

12. Assign a goto action to the Cruises button so it jumps to the frame that has the Cruises screen.

13. Test the movie, then compare your movie to the example shown in Figure 75.

FIGURE 75

Sample completed Project Builder 1

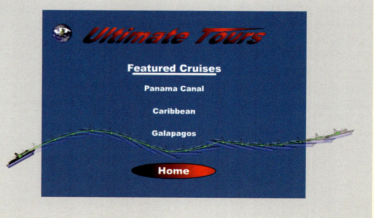

You have been asked to demonstrate some of the animation features of Flash. You have decided to create a movie clip that includes a frame-by-frame animation and then use the movie clip in a motion tween animation. Figure 76 shows the stick figure that will walk across the screen and jump up at each line on the sidewalk. The movement across the screen is a motion tween. The jumping up is a movie clip.

To complete this project, do the following:

1. Start a new Flash document and name it **jumper4**.
2. Add a background color, sidewalk with lines, and houses or other graphics of your choice, adding layers as needed and naming them appropriately. (*Note:* You can open a previous movie that used the stick figures, such as frameAn, then with your movie open, click the list arrow under the Library panel tab. This displays a list of all open documents. Click the name of the file that has the stick figures to display its Library panel. Then drag the symbols you need to the Stage of your movie. This will place the objects in the jumper4 Library panel.)
3. Create a new movie clip. (*Note:* You can create a new movie clip by selecting New Symbol from the Insert menu, then you can drag objects from the Library panel to the movie clip edit window.)
4. Edit the clip to create a frame-by-frame animation of the stick figures walking in place. In the movie clip, place the stick figures one after the other, but have one of the stick figures in the sequence placed above the others to create a jumping effect. You will use each stick figure two times in the sequence.
5. Exit the edit window and place the movie clip on the Stage, then create a motion tween that moves the movie clip from the left side to the right side of the Stage.
6. Test the movie. (*Note:* Movie clips do not play from the Stage, you must use the Test Movie command.)
7. Close the Flash Player movie, then save the movie.

FIGURE 76
Sample completed Project Builder 2

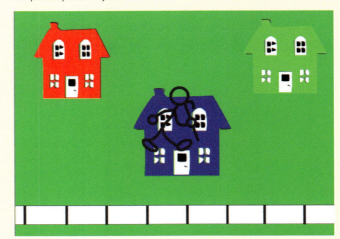

DESIGN PROJECT

Figure 77 shows a website for kids. Study the figure and complete the following. For each question, indicate how you determined your answer.

1. Connect to the Internet, then go to *www.smokeybear.com/kids*.
2. Open a document in a word processor or open a new Flash document, save the file as **dpc4**, then answer the following questions. (*Hint*: Use the Text tool in Flash.)
   - What seems to be the purpose of this site?
   - Who would be the target audience?
   - How might a frame animation be used in this site?
   - How might a motion tween animation be used?
   - How might a motion guide be used?
   - How might motion animation effects be used?
   - How might the text be animated?

FIGURE 77
Design Project

This is a continuation of the Portfolio Project in Chapter 3, which is the development of a personal portfolio. The home page has several categories, including the following:

- Personal data
- Contact information
- Previous employment
- Education
- Samples of your work

In this project, you will create several buttons for the sample animations screen and link them to the animations.

1. Open portfolio3.fla (the file you created in Portfolio Project, Chapter 3) and save it as **portfolio4**. (*Hint*: When you open the file, you may receive a missing font message, meaning a font used in this document is not available on your computer. You can choose a substitute font or use a default font. If you have to use a default font or if you substitute a font, the resulting text may not look as intended.)

2. Display the Sample Animation screen and change the heading to Sample Animations.

3. Add layers and create buttons with labels, as shown in Figure 78, for the tweened animation, frame-by-frame animation, motion path animation, and animated text.

4. Create a tween animation or use the passing cars animation from Chapter 3, and link it to the appropriate button on the Sample Animations screen by assigning a go to action to the button.

5. Create a frame-by-frame animation, and link it to the appropriate button on the Sample Animations screen.

6. Create a motion path animation, and link it to the appropriate button on the Sample Animations screen.

FIGURE 78
Sample completed Portfolio Project

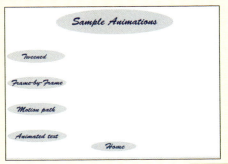

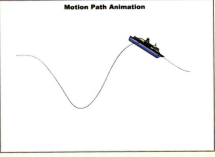

7. Create several text animations, using scrolling, rotating, and zooming; then link them to the appropriate button on the Sample Animations screen.

8. Add a layer and create a Home button that links the Sample Animations screen to the Home screen.

9. Create frame actions that cause the movie to return to the Sample Animations screen after each animation has been played.

10. Test the movie.

11. Save your work, then compare sample pages from your movie to the example shown for two of the screens in Figure 78.

CREATING SPECIAL EFFECTS

1. Create a mask effect

2. Add sound

3. Add video

4. Create an animated navigation bar

5. Create character animations using inverse kinematics

6. Create 3D effects

5 CREATING SPECIAL EFFECTS

Introduction

Now that you are familiar with the basics of Flash, you can begin to apply some of the special features that can enhance a movie. Special effects can provide variety and add interest to a movie, as well as draw the viewer's attention to a location or event in the movie. One type of special effect is a spotlight that highlights an area(s) of the movie or reveals selected content on the Stage. You can use sound effects to enhance a movie by creating moods and dramatizing events. In addition, you can add sound to a button to provide feedback to the viewer when the button is clicked. Video can be incorporated into a Flash movie and effects such as fading in and out can be applied to the display of the video.

Another type of special effect is an animated navigation bar, for example, one that causes a drop-down menu when the user rolls over a button. This effect can be created using masks and invisible buttons.

Two new features of Adobe Flash CS4 are Inverse Kinematics and 3D Effects. Inverse Kinematics allows you to easily create character animations and even allows users to interact with the character when viewing the Flash movie. The 3D tools allow you to create 3D effects such as objects moving and rotating through 3D space.

Tools You'll Use

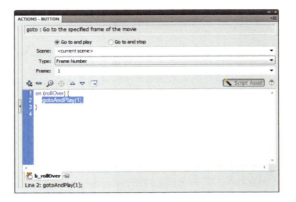

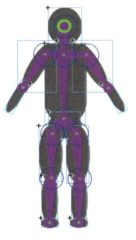

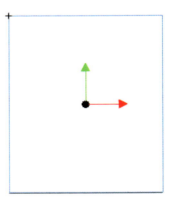

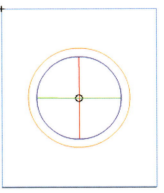

CREATE A
MASK EFFECT

Classic Car Club

 In this lesson, you will apply a mask effect.

Understanding Mask Layers

A **mask layer** allows you to cover up the objects on one or more layers and, at the same time, create a window through which you can view objects on those layer(s). You can determine the size and shape of the window and specify whether it moves around the Stage. Moving the window around the Stage can create effects such as a spotlight that highlights certain content on the Stage, drawing the viewer's attention to a specific location. Because the window can move around the Stage, you can use a mask layer to reveal only the area of the Stage and the objects you want the viewer to see.

You need at least two layers on the Timeline when you are working with a mask layer. One layer, called the mask layer, contains the window object through which you view the objects on the second layer below. The second layer, called the masked layer, contains the object(s) that are viewed through the window. Figure 1 shows how a mask layer works: The top part of the figure shows the mask layer with the window in the shape of a circle. The next part of the figure shows the layer to be masked. The last part of the figure shows the result of applying the mask. Figure 1 illustrates the simplest use of a mask layer. In most cases, you want to have other objects appear on the Stage and have the mask layer affect only a certain portion of the Stage.

The process for using a mask layer follows:

- Select an original layer that will become the masked layer—it contains the objects that you want to display through the mask layer window.
- Insert a new layer above the masked layer that will become the mask layer. A mask layer always masks the layer(s) immediately below it.
- Draw a filled shape, such as a circle, or create an instance of a symbol that will become the window on the mask layer. Flash will ignore bitmaps, gradients, transparency colors, and line styles on a mask layer. On a mask layer, filled areas become transparent and non-filled areas become opaque when viewed over a masked layer.

- Select the new layer and open the Layer Properties dialog box using the Timeline option from the Modify menu, then select Mask. Flash converts the layer to the mask layer.
- Select the original layer and open the Layer Properties dialog box using the Layer command on the Modify menu,

and then choosing Masked. Flash converts the layer to the masked layer.
- Lock both the mask and masked layers.
- To mask additional layers: Drag an existing layer beneath the mask layer, or create a new layer beneath the mask layer and use the Layer Properties dialog box to convert it to a masked layer.

- To unlink a masked layer: Drag it above the mask layer, or select it and select Normal from the Layer Properties dialog box.

FIGURE 1
A mask layer with a window

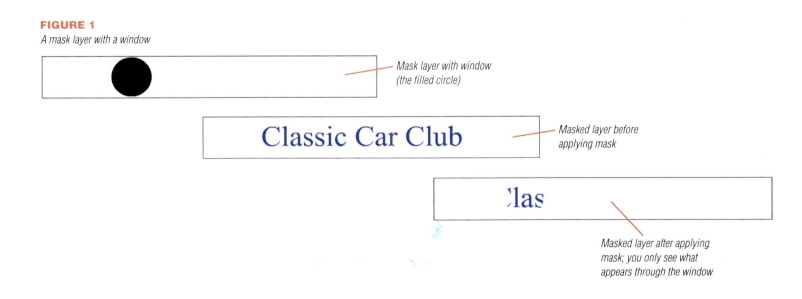

Mask layer with window
(the filled circle)

Classic Car Club

Masked layer before
applying mask

'las

Masked layer after applying
mask; you only see what
appears through the window

Create a mask layer

1. Open fl5_1.fla, then save it as **classicCC**.

2. Insert a **new layer**, name it **mask**, then click **frame 1** on the mask layer.

3. Select the **Oval tool** on the Tools panel, set the **Stroke Color** to **No Stroke** on the top row of the color palette.

4. Set the **Fill Color** to the **black color swatch** in the left column of the color palette.

5. Draw the **circle** shown in Figure 2, click the **Selection tool** on the Tools panel, then drag a **marquee** around the circle to select it.

6. Click **Insert** on the menu bar, click **Motion Tween**, then click **OK** to convert the drawing into a symbol so that it can be tweened.

7. Click **frame 40** on the mask layer, then drag the **circle** to the position shown in Figure 3.

8. Click **mask** on the Timeline to select the mask layer, click **Modify** on the menu bar, point to **Timeline**, then click **Layer Properties**.

9. Verify that the Show check box is selected in the Name section, click the **Lock check box** to select it, click the **Mask option button** in the Type section, then click **OK**.

   The mask layer has a shaded mask icon next to it on the Timeline.

10. Play the movie from frame 1 and notice how the circle object covers the text on the heading layer as it moves across the Stage.

    Note: The circle object will not become transparent until a masked layer is created beneath it.

You created a mask layer containing a circle object that moves across the Stage.

FIGURE 2
Object to be used as the window on a mask layer

FIGURE 3
Repositioning the circle

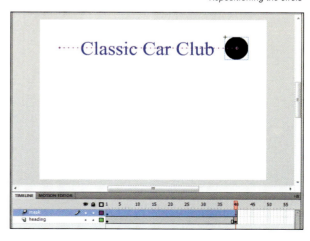

1. Click **heading** on the Timeline to select the heading layer, click **Modify** on the menu bar, point to **Timeline**, then click **Layer Properties** to open the Layer Properties dialog box.

2. Verify that the Show check box is selected in the Name section, click the **Lock check box** to select it, click the **Masked option button** in the Type section, compare your dialog box to Figure 4, then click **OK**.

   The text on the Stage seems to disappear. The heading layer title appears indented and has a shaded masked icon next to it on the Timeline.

3. Play the movie and notice how the circle object acts as a window to display the text on the heading layer.

4. Click **Control** on the menu bar, then click **Test Movie**.

5. View the movie, then close the Flash Player window.

6. Save your work, then close the movie.

You used the Layer Properties dialog box to create a masked layer.

FIGURE 4
The completed Layer Properties dialog box

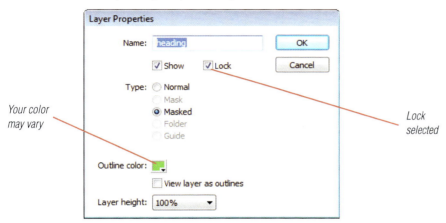

Your color may vary

Lock selected

ADD SOUND

What You'll Do

 In this lesson, you will add sound to an animation.

Incorporating Animation and Sound

Sound can be extremely useful in a Flash movie. Sounds are often the only effective way to convey an idea, elicit an emotion, dramatize a point, and provide feedback to a user's action, such as clicking a button. How would you describe in words or show in an animation the sound a whale makes? Think about how chilling it is to hear the footsteps on the stairway of a haunted house. Consider how useful it is to hear the pronunciation of "buenos dias" as you are studying Spanish. All types of sounds can be incorporated into a Flash movie: for example, CD-quality music that might be used as background for a movie; narrations that help explain what the user is seeing; various sound effects, such as a car horn beeping; and recordings of special events, such as a presidential speech or a rock concert.

The process for adding a sound to a movie follows:
- Import a sound file into a Flash movie; Flash places the sound file into the movie's library.
- Create a new layer.
- Select the desired frame on the new layer where you want the sound to play and drag the sound symbol to the Stage.

You can place more than one sound file on a layer, and you can place sounds on layers with other objects. However, it is recommended that you place each sound on a separate layer so that it is easier to identify and edit. In Figure 5, the sound layer shows a wave pattern that extends from frame 1 to frame 24. The wave pattern gives some indication of the volume of the sound at any particular frame. The higher spikes in the pattern indicate a louder sound. The wave pattern also gives some indication of the pitch. The denser the wave pattern,

the lower the pitch. You can alter the sound by adding or removing frames. However, removing frames may create undesired effects. It is best to make changes to a sound file using a sound-editing program.

You can use options in the Properties panel, as shown in Figure 6, to synchronize a sound to an event (such as clicking a button) and to specify special effects (such as fade in and fade out). You can import the following sound file formats into Flash:

- ASND (Windows or Macintosh)
- WAV (Windows only)
- AIFF (Macintosh only)
- MP3 (Windows or Macintosh)

If you have QuickTime 4 or later installed on your computer, you can import these additional sound file formats:

- AIFF (Windows or Macintosh)
- Sound Designer II (Macintosh only)
- Sound Only QuickTime Movies (Windows or Macintosh)
- Sun AU (Windows or Macintosh)
- System 7 Sounds (Macintosh only)
- WAV (Windows or Macintosh)

FIGURE 5

A wave pattern displayed on a sound layer

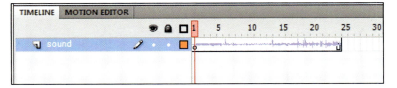

FIGURE 6

Sound Effect options in the Properties panel

Add sound to a movie

1. Open fl5_2.fla, then save it as **rallySnd**.

2. Play the movie and notice that there is no sound.

3. Click the **stopmovie layer**, insert a **new layer**, then name it **carSnd**.

4. Insert a **keyframe** in frame 72 on the carSnd layer.

5. Click **File** on the menu bar, point to **Import**, then click **Import to Library**.

6. Use the Import to Library dialog box to navigate to the drive and folder where your Data Files are stored, click the **CarSnd.wav file**, then click **Open** (Win) or **Import to Library** (Mac).

7. Display the Library Panel if it is not displayed.

8. Click **frame 72** on the CarSnd layer.

9. Drag the **CarSnd sound symbol** 🔊 to the Stage, as shown in Figure 7.

   After releasing the mouse button, notice the wave pattern that has been placed on the carSnd layer starting in frame 72.

   TIP The wave pattern may not appear on the layer until the movie is played one time.

10. Click **Control** on the menu bar, then click **Test Movie**.

11. Click the **Click to continue button** to test the sound.

12. Close the Flash Player window.

You imported a sound and added it to a movie.

FIGURE 7
Dragging the CarSnd symbol to the Stage

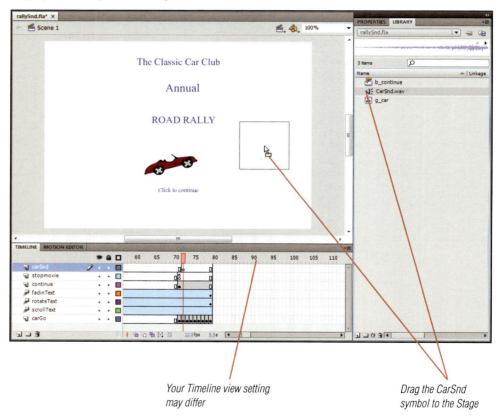

Your Timeline view setting may differ

Drag the CarSnd symbol to the Stage

FIGURE 8

The Timeline for the button with the sound layer

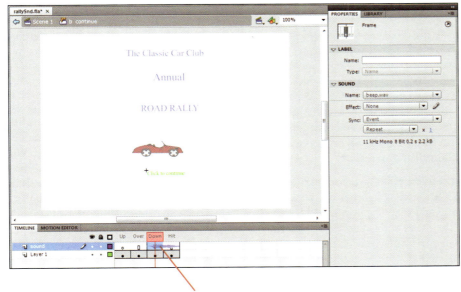

Sound wave pattern appears
in the selected frame

Add sound to a button

1. Click **frame 71** on the carSnd layer.

2. Click the **Selection tool** ⬉ on the Tools panel, drag a **marquee** around "Click to continue" to select the button, then double-click the **selection** to display the button's Timeline.

3. Insert a **new layer** above Layer 1, then name it **sound**.

4. Click the **Down frame** on the sound layer, click **Insert** on the menu bar, point to **Timeline**, then click **Blank Keyframe**.

5. Click **File** on the menu bar, point to **Import**, then click **Import to Library**.

6. Use the Import to Library dialog box to navigate to the drive and folder where your Data Files are stored, click the **beep.wav file**, then click **Open** (Win) or **Import to Library** (Mac).

7. Display the Properties panel, click the **Name list arrow** in the SOUND area, then click **beep.wav**.

8. Click the **Sync list arrow** in the Properties panel, click **Event**, then compare your screen to Figure 8.

9. Click **Scene 1** on the upper left of the edit window title bar to display the main Timeline.

10. Test the movie.

11. Click the **Click to continue button** and listen to the sounds, then close the Flash Player window.

12. Save your work, then close the movie.

You added a sound layer to a button, imported a sound, then attached the sound to the button.

VIDEO

What You'll Do

 In this lesson, you will import a video, add actions to video control buttons, and then synchronize sound to a video clip.

Incorporating Video

Adobe Flash allows you to import FLV (Flash video) files that then can be used in a Flash document. Flash provides several ways to add video to a movie, depending on the application and, especially, file size. Video content can be embedded directly into a Flash document, progressively downloaded, or streamed.

Embedded video becomes part of the SWF file similar to other objects, such as sound and graphics. A placeholder appears on the Stage and is used to display the video during playback. If the video is imported as a movie clip symbol, then the placeholder can be edited, including rotating, resizing, and even animating it. Because embedded video becomes part of the SWF file, the technique of embedding video is best used for small video clips in order to keep the file size small. The process for embedding video is to import a video file using the Import Video Wizard. Then, you place the video on the Stage and add controls as desired. Figure 9

shows a video placeholder for an embedded video. The video file (fireworks.mov) is in the Library panel and the video layer in the Timeline contains the video object.

Progressive downloading allows you to use ActionScript to load an external FLV file into a SWF file; the video then plays when the SWF file is played. With progressive downloading, the FLV file resides outside the SWF file. Therefore, the SWF file size can be kept smaller than when the video is embedded in the Flash document. The video begins playing soon after the first part of the file has been downloaded.

Streaming video provides a constant connection between the user and the video delivery. Streaming has several advantages over the other methods of delivering video, including starting the video quicker and allowing for live video delivery. However, streaming video requires the Flash Media Server, an Adobe software product designed specifically for streaming video content.

Using the Adobe Media Encoder

The Adobe Media Encoder is an application used by Flash to convert various video file formats, such as .mov, .avi, and .mpeg, to the FLV (Flash Video) format so the videos can be used with Flash. The Encoder allows you to, among other things, choose the size of the placeholder the video will play in, to edit the video, and to insert cue points that can be used to synchronize the video with animations and sound. Figure 10 shows the Encoder ready to convert the fireworks.mov video (Source Name) to fireworks.flv (Output File). The Start Queue button is used to start the process. When the conversion is complete, a green check mark is displayed in the Status column. The Adobe Media Encoder can be accessed through the Import Video Wizard.

Using the Import Video Wizard

The Import Video Wizard is used to import FLV files into Flash documents. The Wizard, in a step-by-step process, leads you through a series of windows that allows you to select the file to be imported and the deployment method (embed, progressive, streaming). In addition, you can specify whether or not to have the video converted to a movie clip symbol which allows you to animate the placeholder. The Wizard appears when you choose the Import Video command from the Import option on the File menu.

FIGURE 9

An embedded video

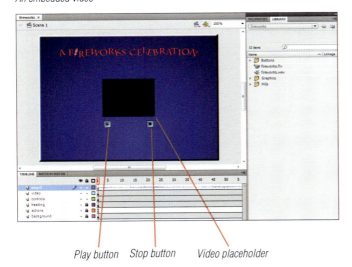

Play button   Stop button   Video placeholder

FIGURE 10

The Adobe Media Encoder

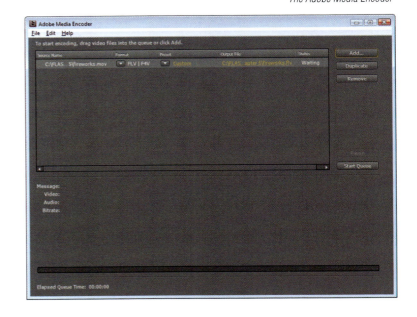

Import a video

1. Open fl5_3.fla, then save it as **fireworks**.

   Note: If the Missing Font Warning message appears, click Use Default.

   The movie has four layers and 85 frames. The actions layer has a stop action in frame 1. The heading layer contains the text object. The controls layer contains start and stop buttons that will be used to control the video. The background layer contains a blue gradient background object. The Library panel contains the two button symbols and a sound file as well as graphics and movie clip files.

2. Insert a **new layer** above the controls layer, name it **video**, then click **frame 1** on the video layer.

3. Click **File** on the menu bar, point to **Import**, then click **Import Video**.

   The Import Video Wizard begins by asking for the path to the video file and the desired method for importing the file, as shown in Figure 11.

4. Click the **Embed FLV in SWF and play in timeline option button**.

5. Click **Browse**, navigate to the drive and folder where your Data Files are stored, click **fireworks.mov**, then click **Open**.

   A message appears indicating that the video format is not valid for embedding video. You must convert the file to the FLV format.

   (continued)

FIGURE 11
The Import Video Wizard

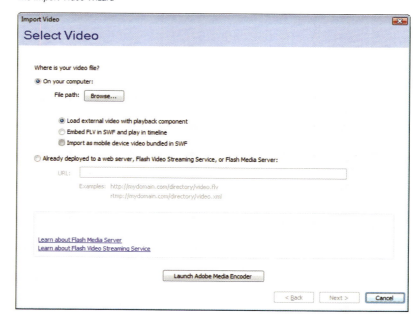

Creating Special Effects

FIGURE 12

The embed video options

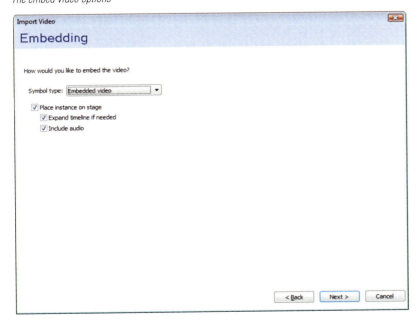

6. Click **OK**, then click the **Launch Adobe Media Encoder button**.

   Note: If a message about browsing to the file after it is converted opens, click OK.

   After several moments the encoder opens.

   Note: Click the Adobe Media Encoder button on the taskbar if the encoder does not open automatically in its own window.

7. Click **Start Queue**, when the process is done as indicated by a green check mark, close the encoder window.

8. Click **OK** to close the message window if one opens, then click the **Browse button**.

9. Click **fireworks.flv**, then click **Open**.

   Note: If you do not see fireworks.flv, navigate to the drive and folder where your solution file is stored.

   The Select Video screen now displays the path to the fireworks.flv file.

10. Click **Next** (Win) or **Continue** (Mac) in the Wizard.

    The Embedding window opens, which allows you to specify how you would like to embed the video.

11. Verify your settings match those in Figure 12.

12. Click **Next** (Win) or **Continue** (Mac).

13. Read the Finish Video Import screen, then click **Finish**.

    The video is encoded and placed on the Stage and in the Library panel.

You imported a video and then *specified the embed and encoding type.*

Attach actions to video control buttons

1. Test the movie, then click the **control buttons**.

   Nothing happens because there is a stop action in frame 1 and no actions have been assigned to the buttons.

2. Close the Flash Player window.

3. Open the Actions panel.

4. Click the **play button** on the Stage, then verify the playback – play button symbol appears at the lower left of the Script pane.

5. Turn on Script Assist if it is off.

6. Click the **Add a new item to the script button** ⊞ , point to **Global Functions**, point to **Timeline Control**, then click **play** as shown in Figure 13.

7. Click the **Stop button** on the Stage, then verify the playback - stop button symbol appears at the lower left of the Script pane.

8. Click the **Add a new item to the script button** ⊞ , point to **Global Functions**, point to **Timeline Control**, then click **stop**.

9. Close the Actions panel.

10. Test the movie, click the **play button**, then click the **stop button**.

    The video plays, however there is no sound.

11. Close the Flash Player window.

You assigned play and stop actions to video control buttons.

FIGURE 13
Using Script Assist to assign a play action to a button

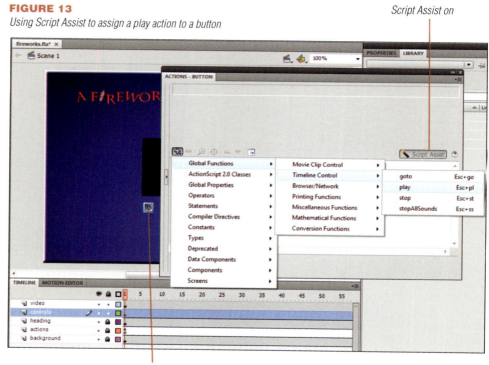

Script Assist on

Play button selected

FIGURE 14
The completed Properties panel

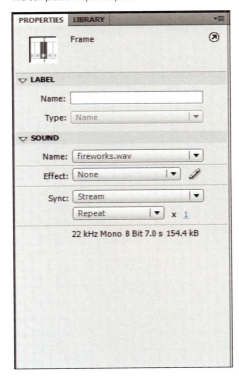

Synchronize sound to a video clip

1. Insert a **new layer** above the video layer, then name it **sound**.

2. Click **frame 1** on the sound layer.

3. Display the Properties panel, then display the SOUND area options.

4. Click the **Name list arrow** in the SOUND area, then click **fireworks.wav**.

5. Click the **Sync sound list arrow** in the SOUND area, click **Stream**, then compare your screen to Figure 14.

6. Test the movie, click the **play button**, then click the **stop button**.

7. Close the Flash Player window, save your work, then close the file.

You inserted a layer, then you synchronized a sound to the video clip.

CREATE AN ANIMATED
NAVIGATION BAR

What You'll Do

 In this lesson, you will work through the process to create one drop-down menu. A navigation bar has been provided as well as the necessary buttons.

Understanding Animated Navigation Bars

A common navigation scheme for a website is a navigation bar with drop-down menus, such as the one shown in Figure 15. Using a navigation bar has several advantages. First, it allows the developer to provide several menu options to the user without cluttering the screen, thereby providing more screen space for the website content. Second, it allows the user to go quickly to a location on the site without having to navigate several screens to find the desired content. Third, it provides consistency in function and appearance, making it easy for users to learn and work with the navigation scheme.

There are various ways to create drop-down menus using the animation capabilities of Flash and ActionScript. One common technique allows you to give the illusion of a drop-down menu by using masks that reveal the menu. When the user points to (rolls over) an option in the navigation bar, a list or "menu" of buttons is displayed ("drops down"). Then the user can click a button to go to another location in the website or trigger some other action. The dropping down of the list is actually an illusion created by using a mask to "uncover" the menu options.

The process is as follows:
- Create a navigation bar. This could be as basic as a background graphic in the shape of a rectangle with navigation bar buttons.
- Position the drop-down buttons. Add a layer beneath the navigation bar layer. Next, select an empty frame adjacent to the frame containing the navigation bar. Place the buttons on the Stage below their respective menu items on the navigation bar. If the navigation bar has an Events button with two choices, Road Rally and Auction, that you want to appear as buttons on a drop-down menu, position these two buttons below the Events button on the drop-down buttons layer.
- Add the animated mask. Add a mask layer above the drop-down buttons layer and create an animation of an object that starts above the drop-down buttons

and moves down to reveal them. Then change the layer to a mask layer and the drop-down buttons layer to a masked layer.

- Assign actions to the drop-down buttons. Select each drop-down button and assign an action, such as "on (release) gotoAndPlay."
- Assign a roll over action to the navigation bar button. The desired effect is to have the drop-down buttons appear when the user points to a navigation bar button. Therefore, you need to assign an "on rollOver" action to the navigation bar button that causes the playhead to go to the frame that plays the animation on the mask layer. This can be done using the Script Assist feature.
- Create an invisible button. When the user points to a navigation bar button,

the drop-down menu appears showing the drop-down buttons. There needs to be a way to have the menu disappear when the user points away from the navigation bar button. This can be done by creating a button on a layer below the masked layer. This button is slightly larger than the drop-down buttons and their navigation bar button, as shown in Figure 16. A rollOver action is assigned to this button so that when the user rolls off the drop-down or navigation bar buttons, he or she rolls onto this button and the action is carried out. This button should be made transparent so the user does not see it.

Using Frame Labels

Until now, you have worked with frame numbers in ActionScript code when creat-

ing a goto action. Frame labels can also be used in the code. You can assign a label to a frame as an identifier. For example, you could assign the label home to frame 10 and then create a goto home action that will cause the playhead to jump to frame 10. One advantage of using frame labels is that if you insert frames in the Timeline, the label adjusts for the added frames. So, you do not have to change the ActionScript that uses the frame label. Another advantage is that the descriptive labels help you identify parts of the movie as you work with the Timeline. You assign a frame label by selecting the desired frame and typing a label in the Frame text box in the Properties panel.

FIGURE 15
A website with a navigation bar with drop-down menus

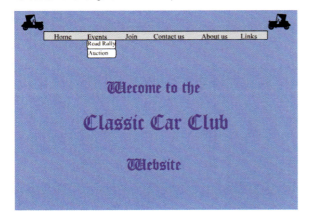

FIGURE 16
A button that will be assigned a rollOver action

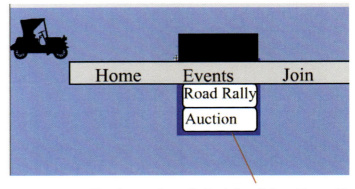

When the user rolls over the blue button with the pointer, a script is executed that causes the drop-down menu to disappear

Position the drop-down buttons

1. Open fl5_4.fla, then save it as **navBar**.

2. Click the **homeBkgrnd layer**, insert a **new layer**, then name it **roadRally**.

3. Click **frame 2** on the roadRally layer, then insert a **keyframe**.

4. Display the Library panel, open the Buttons folder, then drag the **b_roadRally button** to the position just below the Events button on the Navigation bar, as shown in Figure 17.

5. Insert a **new layer** above the homeBkgrnd layer, then name it **auction**.

6. Click **frame 2** on the auction layer, then insert a **keyframe**.

7. Drag the **b_auction button** from the Library panel and position it below the b_roadRally button.

8. Click the **Zoom tool** 🔍 on the Tools panel, then click the **Events button** on the Stage to enlarge the view.

9. Click the **Selection tool** ➤ on the Tools panel, then click each button and use the arrow keys to position them, as shown in Figure 18.

    The top line of the Road Rally button must overlap the bottom border of the navigation bar, and the bottom border of the Road Rally button must overlap the top border of the Auction button.

You placed the drop-down buttons on the Stage and repositioned them.

FIGURE 17
Positioning the b_roadRally button

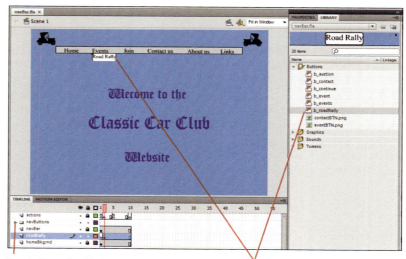

The expand icon indicates that this is a folder layer. In this case, all of navigation bar buttons are within this folder. Clicking the arrow reveals the contents of the folder.

Drag from library to here

FIGURE 18
Positioning the buttons

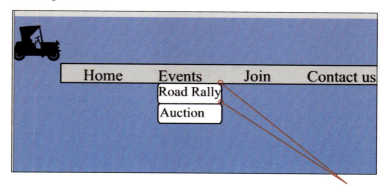

Make sure the button borders overlap

FIGURE 19
The drawn rectangle that covers the buttons

FIGURE 20
Dragging the rectangle above the buttons

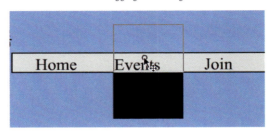

FIGURE 21
The rectangle positioned over the buttons

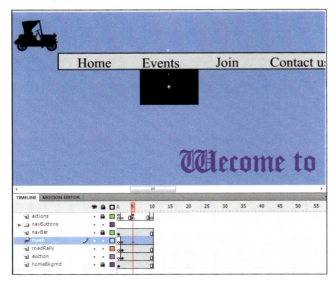

Add a mask layer

1. Click the **roadRally layer**, insert a **new layer** above the roadRally layer, then name it **mask**.

2. Click **frame 2** on the mask layer, then insert a **keyframe**.

3. Select the **Rectangle tool** ▭ on the Tools panel, set the **Stroke Color** to **none** ◻, then set the **Fill Color** to **black**.

4. Draw a **rectangle** that covers the buttons, as shown in Figure 19.

5. Click the **Selection tool** ▸ on the Tools panel, then drag the **rectangle** to above the buttons, as shown in Figure 20.

6. Verify the rectangle is selected, click **Insert** on the menu bar, click **Motion Tween**, then click **OK**.

7. Click **frame 5** on the mask layer, then insert a **keyframe**.

8. Use the **Selection tool** ▸ to move the **rectangle**, as shown in Figure 21.

9. Click **mask** on the Timeline, click **Modify** on the menu bar, point to **Timeline**, click **Layer Properties**, click the **Mask option button**, then click **OK**.

10. Click **roadRally** on the Timeline.

11. Click **Modify** on the menu bar, point to **Timeline**, click **Layer Properties**, click the **Masked option button**, then click **OK**.

12. Click **auction** on the Timeline, then repeat step 11.

13. Drag the **playhead** along the Timeline, notice how the mask hides and reveals the buttons.

You added a mask that animates to hide and reveal the menu buttons.

Assign an action to a drop-down button

1. Click **frame 2** on the roadRally layer, then click the **Road Rally button** to select it.

2. Open the **Actions panel** and verify the Script Assist button is selected and b_roadRally is displayed, as shown in Figure 22.

   b_roadRally in the lower-left corner of the Script pane indicates that the b_roadRally button symbol is selected on the Stage and that the ActionScript you create will apply to this object.

3. Click the **Add a new item to the script icon** ⊕, point to **Global Functions**, point to **Timeline Control**, then click **goto**.

4. Click the **Scene list arrow**, point to **Scene 2** as shown in Figure 23, then click.

   Scenes are a way to organize large movies. In this case Scene 2 contains the Road Rally screen for the website.

5. Verify the Type is set to Frame Number and the Frame is set to 1.

6. Collapse the Actions panel.

You used the Script Assist window to assign a goto action to a menu button.

FIGURE 22
The Actions panel with the b_roadRally button selected

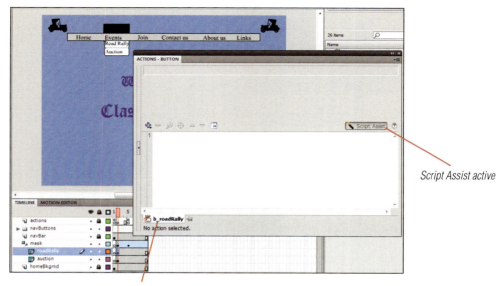

Script Assist active

b_roadRally button indicating the action to be created will be assigned to the button

FIGURE 23
Selecting the scene to go to

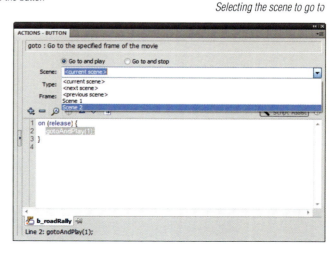

Creating Special Effects

FIGURE 24

Specifying a frame label

FIGURE 25

The completed Actions panel

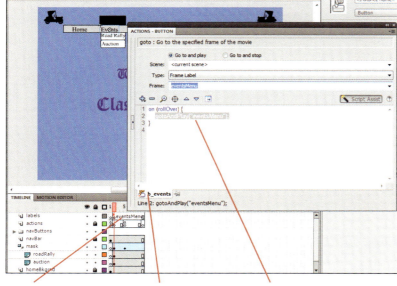

Frame label

b_event button symbol indicating the action will be assigned to
the button

gotoAndPlay("eventsMenu");

1. Insert a **new layer** at the top of the Timeline, name it **labels**, then insert a **keyframe** in frame 2 on the labels layer.

2. Display the Properties panel, click inside the **Name text box** in the LABEL area, then type **eventsMenu**, as shown in Figure 24.

3. Click the **Events button** on the Stage to select it.

4. Expand the Actions panel, then verify b_events is displayed in the lower-left corner of the Script pane.

5. Click the **Add a new item to the script icon**, point to **Global Functions**, point to **Movie Clip Control**, then click **on**.

6. Click the **Release check box** to deselect it, then click the **Roll Over check box** to select it.

7. Click the **Add a new item to the script icon**, point to **Global Functions**, point to **Timeline Control**, then click **goto**.

8. Click the **Type list arrow**, then click **Frame Label**.

9. Click the **Frame list arrow**, then click **eventsMenu**.

   Your screen should resemble Figure 25.

10. Click **Control** on the menu bar, then click **Test Movie**.

11. Point to **Events**, then click **Road Rally**.

12. Close the Flash Player window, collapse the Actions panel, then save your work.

You added a frame label and assigned a rollOver action using the frame label.

Add an invisible button

1. Click **Control** on the menu bar, click **Test Movie**, move the pointer over Events on the navigation bar, then move the pointer away from Events.

   Notice that when you point to Events, the drop-down menu appears. However, when you move the pointer away from the menu, it does not disappear.

2. Close the Flash Player window.

3. Insert a **new layer** above the homeBkgrnd layer, then name it **rollOver**.

4. Insert a **keyframe** in frame 2 on the rollOver layer.

5. Select the **Rectangle tool** on the Tools panel, verify that the Stroke Color is set to **none**, then set the **Fill Color** to **blue**.

6. Draw a **rectangle**, as shown in Figure 26.

7. Click the **Selection tool** on the Tools panel, then click the **blue rectangle** to select it.

8. Click **Modify** on the menu bar, then click **Convert to Symbol**.

9. Type **b_rollOver** for the name, click the **Type list arrow**, click **Button**, then click **OK**.

10. Expand the Actions panel.

(continued)

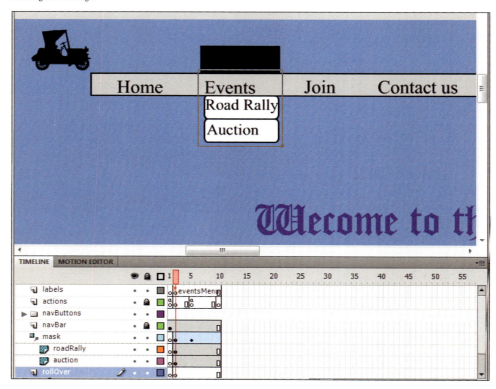

FIGURE 26
Drawing the rectangle

FIGURE 27
The Actions panel displaying Actionscript assigned to the b_rollOver button symbol

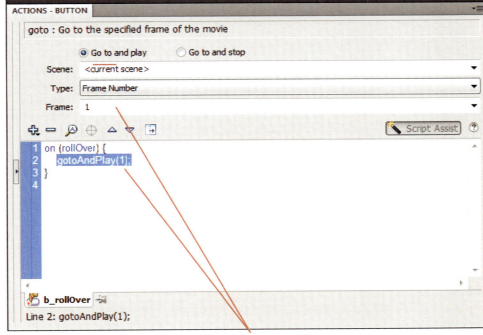

Frame 1 selected

11. Verify the rollOver button is selected and b_rollOver is displayed in the lower-left corner of the Script pane.

12. Click the **Add a new item to the script icon**, point to **Global Functions**, point to **Movie Clip Control**, then click **on**.

13. Click the **Release check box** to deselect it, then click the **Roll Over check box** to select it.

14. Click the **Add a new item to the script icon**, point to **Global Functions**, point to **Timeline Control**, then click **goto**.

15. Verify Frame 1 is specified, as shown in Figure 27.

16. Close the Actions panel.

17. Click the **Style list arrow** in the COLOR EFFECT area of the Properties panel, click **Alpha**, then set the percentage to **0**.

18. Click **Control** on the menu bar, then click **Test Movie**.

19. Point to **Events** to display the drop-down menu, then move the pointer away from Events.

   The drop-down menu disappears.

20. Close the Flash Player window, then save and close the movie.

21. Exit Flash.

You added a button and assigned a rollOver action to it, then made the button transparent.

CREATE CHARACTER ANIMATIONS
USING INVERSE KINEMATICS

What You'll Do

 In this lesson, you will use the bone tool to create a character animation and create a movie clip that can be manipulated by the viewer.

Understanding Inverse Kinematics

One way to create character animations is to use the frame-by-frame process in which you place individually drawn objects into a series of successive frames. You did this with the stick figure graphics in an earlier chapter. Those graphics were simple to draw. However, if you have more complex drawings, such as fill shapes that are more realistic, and if you want to create animations that show an unlimited number of poses, the time required to develop all of the necessary drawings would be considerable.

Flash provides a process that allows you to create a single image and add a structure to the image that can be used to animate the various parts of the image. The process is called **Inverse Kinematics (IK)** and involves creating an articulated structure of bones that allow you to link the parts of an image. Once the bone structure is created, you can animate the image by changing the position of any of

its parts. The bone structure causes the related parts to animate in a natural way. For example, if you draw an image of a person, create the bone structure, and then move the person's right foot, then all parts of the leg (lower leg, knee, upper leg) respond. This makes it easy to animate various movements.

Figure 28 shows a drawing of a character before and after the bone structure is added. Figure 29 shows how moving the right foot moves the entire leg. The image is made up of several small drawings, each one converted to a graphic symbol. These include a head, torso, upper and lower arms, upper and lower legs, hips, and feet.

Creating the Bone Structure

The bone structure can be applied to a single drawn shape, such as an oval created with the Flash drawing tools. More often it is applied to an image, such as a character, made up of several drawings. When this is the case, each drawing is converted to a graphic symbol or a movie clip symbol and then assembled to form the desired image. If you import a graphic, it needs to be broken apart using the Modify menu and the individual parts of the imported graphic converted to graphic symbols or movie clip symbols. If the imported graphic has only one part (such as a bitmap), it needs to be broken apart and treated as a single drawn shape.

Once the image is ready, you use the Bone tool to create the bone structure, called the armature, by clicking and dragging the Bone tool pointer to link one part of the image to another. You continue adding bones to the structure until all parts of the image are linked. For a human form you would link the head to the torso and the torso to the upper left arm and the upper left arm to the lower left arm, and so on. The bones in an armature are connected to each other in a parent-child hierarchy, so that adjusting the child adjusts the parent.

Animating the IK Object

As you are creating the bone structure, a layer named Armature_1 is added to the Timeline, and the image with the bone structure is placed in frame 1 on the layer. This new layer is called a **pose layer**. Each pose layer can contain only one armature and its associated image. Animating the image is done on this layer. When animating using inverse kinematics, you simply specify the start and end positions of the image. Flash interpolates the position of the parts of the image for the in-between frames. So, you can insert a keyframe in any frame after frame 1 on the Armature_1 layer and then change the position of one or more of the bones. This is referred to as creating a pose. When one bone moves, the other connected bones move in relation to it. Additional poses can be set along the Timeline by inserting keyframes and adjusting the bone structure. Animations of IK objects, other than those within movie clips, only allow you to change the shape, position, and ease in the animation.

FIGURE 28

Drawings showing before and after the bone structure is added

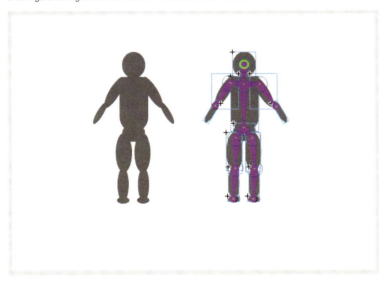

FIGURE 29

Moving the foot moves the other parts of the leg

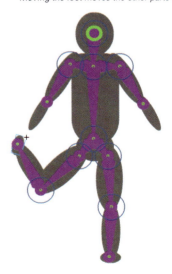

Creating a Movie Clip with an IK Object

Movie clips provide a great deal of flexibility when animating IK objects. You can change properties such as the color effect and you can nest one movie clip within another. So, you could have a movie clip of a character walking and nest another movie clip within it to have its mouth move. In addition, you can apply a motion tween to a movie clip. So, you could have a movie clip of a character walking and have it play within a motion tween which causes the character (movie clip) to jump over an obstacle.

Runtime Feature

Flash provides a runtime feature for manipulation of an IK object. That is, you can allow the user to click on the object and adjust the image. This is useful if you are creating a game or just wanting to provide some interaction on a website. The process is to click a frame on the Armature layer, then use the Properties panel to set the Type to Runtime. The runtime feature only works with IK structures connected to drawn shapes or movie clip symbols, not graphic or button symbols. In addition, only one pose can used. At the time this book was published, some browsers, such as Firefox, supported the runtime feature, but other browsers did not.

IK Objects

As you are working with IK objects, keep in mind the following:

- The Undo feature can be used to undo a series of actions such as undoing a mistake made when creating the bone structure.
- The bone structure may disappear as you are working on it. This could be caused by going outside the image as you are connecting the parts of the image. If the bone structure disappears, use the Undo feature to Undo your last action.
- To delete an individual bone and all of its children, click the bone and press [Delete]. You can select multiple bones to delete by holding down [Shift] and clicking each bone.
- To delete all bones, select the image and choose the Break Apart command from the Modify menu.
- To create IK animations, ActionScript 3.0 and Flash Player 10 need to be specified in the Publish Settings dialog box, which is displayed by choosing Publish Settings from the File menu.

Creating Special Effects

FIGURE 30

Connecting the head and torso

FIGURE 31

Connecting the torso and the upper arm

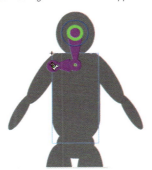

FIGURE 32

Connecting the upper and lower arms

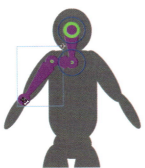

Note: If the bone structure disappears as you are working on it, use the Undo feature to undo your last action.

FIGURE 33

The completed bone structure

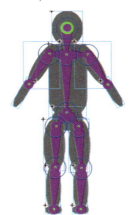

Create the bone structure

1. Open fl5_5.fla, then save it as **kicker**.

   This document has a graphic symbol made up of 13 individual drawings to form a character shape.

2. Use the **Selection tool** to drag a marquee around the image to select it.

   Notice the separate objects.

3. Click a blank area of the Stage to deselect the image.

4. Click the **Zoom tool** , then click the image to zoom in on it.

5. Scroll the Stage to view the head, then click the **Bone tool** on the Tools panel.

6. Point to the middle of the head, when the pointer changes to a bone with a cross , drag the **pointer** down to the torso as shown in Figure 30, then release the mouse button.

7. Point to the bottom of the bone, when the pointer changes to a bone with a cross , drag the **pointer** to the left as shown in Figure 31.

8. Point to the left end of the bone, when the pointer changes to a bone with a cross , drag the **pointer** down as shown in Figure 32.

   Notice that a bone connects two overlapping objects, such as the bone used to connect the upper arm and lower arm.

9. Using Figure 33 as a guide, complete the drawing of the other bones.

   Hint: Use the Undo command as needed if your connections do not match Figure 33.

10. Save your work.

You created a bone structure by connecting objects on the Stage with the Bone tool.

Animate the character

1. Change the view to **Fit in Window**.

2. Click **frame 10** on the Armature_1 layer, then insert a **keyframe**.

3. Click the **Selection tool**, then click a blank area of the Stage to deselect the object if it is selected.

4. Point to the **right foot**, when the pointer changes to a bone with a delta symbol, drag the pointer to position the foot as shown in Figure 34.

5. Point to the **right arm**, then use the pointer to position it as shown in Figure 35.

6. Use the pointer to position the left arm and left foot as shown in Figure 36.

   Hint: To position the left foot, move the left knee first, then move the left foot.

7. Click **frame 20** on the Armature_1 layer, then insert a **keyframe**.

8. Adjust the arms and legs as shown in Figure 37.

   Hint: Move the right leg to the position shown to create a kicking motion.

9. Click the **Free Transform tool** on the Tools panel, then drag a **marquee** around the image to select it.

10. Point to the **upper-right handle**, when the pointer changes to an arc, drag the pointer to the left as shown in Figure 38.

11. Test the movie, close the Flash Player window, then save the movie.

You animated the character by adjusting the armatures of the various bones.

FIGURE 34
Positioning the right foot

FIGURE 35
Positioning the right arm

FIGURE 36
Positioning the left arm and left foot

right leg

FIGURE 37
Positioning the left arm and left leg

right leg

FIGURE 38
Rotating the object

FIGURE 39
Increasing the length of the tween span

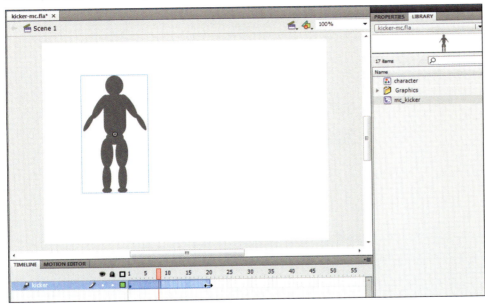

Create a movie clip of the IK

1. Click **File** on the menu bar, click **Save as**, type **kicker-mc**, then click **OK** [Win] or **Save as** [Mac].

2. Click **frame 1** on the Armature_1 layer.

3. Use the **Selection tool** ![selection tool icon] to drag a marquee around the entire image to select it.

4. Click **Modify** on the menu bar, then click **Convert to Symbol**.

5. Type **mc_kicker** for the name, select **Movie Clip** for the Type, then click **OK**.

6. Click **Armature_1** on the Timeline, then click the **Delete icon** ![delete icon].

7. Click **frame 1** on the kicker layer, display the Library panel, then drag the **mc_kicker** symbol to the Stage.

8. Insert a **Motion Tween**.

9. Drag the **tween span** on the Timeline to **frame 20**, as shown in Figure 39.

10. Click **frame 10** on the kicker layer.

11. Verify the object is selected, then press the **up arrow** [↑] on the keyboard 10 times.

12. Click **frame 20**, then press the **down arrow** [↓] on the keyboard 10 times.

13. Test the movie, close the Flash Player window, then save your work.

You created a movie clip and applied a motion tween to it.

Apply an ease value

1. Double-click the **mc_kicker symbol** in the Library panel to display the edit window, then scroll as needed to see the entire object.

2. Display the Properties panel.

3. Click **frame 10** on the Armature_2 layer.

4. Set the Ease Strength to **−100**.

5. Click the **Type list arrow** in the EASE area, then click **Simple (Fastest)**, as shown in Figure 40.

    Frame 10 is the start of the motion tween where the right leg begins to kick downward. Setting the ease value to −100 will cause the leg motion to start out slow and accelerate as the leg follows through to the end of the kicking motion. This is a more natural way to represent the kick than to have the leg speed constant throughout the downward motion and follow through.

6. Click **Scene 1** on the edit window title bar to return to the main Timeline.

7. Test the movie, close the Flash Player window, save your work, then close the file.

You added an ease value to the movie clip.

FIGURE 40
Setting the ease value

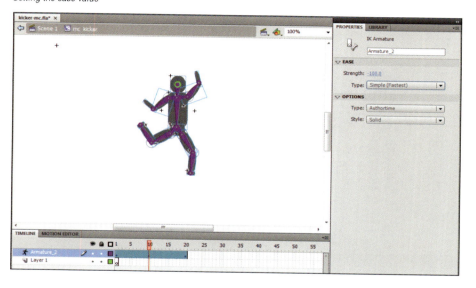

Creating Special Effects

FIGURE 41
The completed armature structure

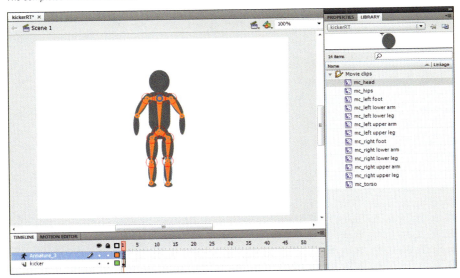

Set the play to runtime

1. Open fl5_6.fla, then save it as **kickerRT**.

   This is the same character used in the kicker movie, however it has been created using movie clips instead of graphic symbols. Also, only one pose is used.

2. Use the **Bone tool** to create the armature structure as shown in Figure 41.

3. Click **frame 1** on the Armature_3 layer, click the **Type list arrow** in the OPTIONS area of the Properties panel, then click **Runtime**.

4. Click **File**, point to **Publish Preview**, then click **Default -(HTML)** to display the movie in a browser, then drag the parts of the character, such as an arm or a leg.

   Hint: Press [F12] (Win) to display the movie in a browser.

5. Close your browser.

6. Save your work, then close the document.

You created an animated character, set the play to runtime and manipulated the character in a browser.

CREATE 3D
EFFECTS

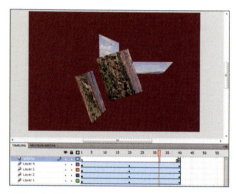

In this lesson, you will create a movie with 3D effects.

Flash allows you to create 3D effects by manipulating objects in 3D space on the Stage. Until now you have been working in two dimensions, width and height. The default settings for the Stage are 550 pixels wide and 400 pixels high. These are represented by an x axis (across) and a y axis (down). Any position on the Stage can be specified by x and y coordinates. The upper-left corner of the Stage has an x value of 0 and a y value of 0, and the lower-right corner has an x value of 550 and a y value of 400, as shown in Figure 42. In 3D space there is also a z axis that represents depth. Flash provides two tools, 3D Translation and 3D Rotation that can be used to move and rotate objects using all three axes. In addition, Flash provides two other properties that can be adjusted to control the view of an object. The Perspective Angle property controls the angle of the object and can be used to create a zooming in and out effect. The Vanishing Point property more precisely controls the direction of an object as it moves away from the viewer.

The Perspective Angle and the Vanishing Point settings are found in the Properties panel.

The 3D Tools

The 3D tools are available on the Tools panel. By default the 3D Rotation tool is displayed on the Tools panel. To access the 3D Translation tool, click and hold the 3D Rotation tool to open the menu. Toggle between these two 3D tools as needed.

The process for creating 3D effects is to create a movie clip (only movie clips can have 3D effects applied to them), place the movie clip on the Stage and then click it with either of the 3D tools. When you click an object with the 3D Translation tool, the three axes, X, Y, and Z appear on top of the object, as shown in Figure 43. Each has its own color: red (X), green (Y), and blue (Z). The X and Y axes have arrows and the Z axis is represented by a dot. You point to an arrow or the black dot and drag it to reposition the object.

When you click the object with the 3D Rotation tool, the three axes, X, Y, and Z appear on top of the object, as shown in Figure 44. Dragging the X axis (red) will flip the object horizontally. Dragging the Y axis (green) will flip the object vertically. Dragging the Z axis (blue) will spin the object. A forth option, the orange circle, rotates the object around the X and Y axes at the same time.

Using a Motion Tween with a 3D Effect

Creating 3D effects requires a change in the position of an object. A motion tween is used to specify where on the Timeline the effect will take place. This allows you to create more than one effect by selecting various frames in the tween span and making adjustments as desired. If you are animating more than one object, each object should be on its own layer.

FIGURE 42
The x and y coordinates on the Stage

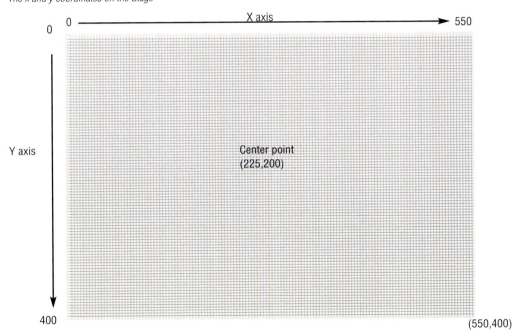

FIGURE 43
The 3D Translation tool

FIGURE 44
The 3D Rotation tool

Create a 3D animation

1. Open fl5_7.fla, then save it as **puzzle**.

   Note: The document opens with the ruler feature turned on and showing the vertical and horizontal lines that intersect at the center of the Stage.

2. Click **frame 1** on Layer 1, insert a **motion tween**, then drag the tween span to **frame 40**.

3. Click **frame 20** on Layer 1, then select the **3D Translation tool** ⚒ from the Tools panel.

4. Click the image in the upper-right corner of the Stage, point to the **green arrow**, then use the ☝ **pointer** to drag the image down to the horizontal ruler line.

5. Click the **red arrow**, then use the ☝ **pointer** to drag the image to the left, as shown in Figure 45.

6. Select the **3D Rotation tool** 🔴, point to the **green line Y axis** on the right side of the object, then drag the ☝ **pointer** down and to the left to flip the image horizontally.

7. Click **frame 40** on Layer 1, then use the **3D Translation tool** ⚒ to move the image to the position shown in Figure 46.

8. Use the **3D Rotation tool** 🔴 to drag the solid green line down and to the right, which flips the image again.

9. Click **frame 1** on Layer 2, insert a **motion tween**, then drag the tween span to **frame 40**.

10. Click **frame 20** on Layer 2, select the **3D Translation tool** ⚒, then drag the image to the position shown in Figure 47.

(continued)

FIGURE 45
Using the 3D Translation tool to position an object

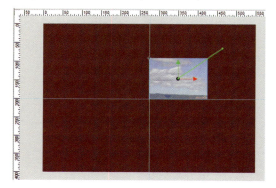

FIGURE 46
Using the 3D Translation tool to position the object again

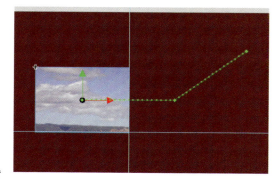

FIGURE 47
Using the 3D Translation tool to position a second object

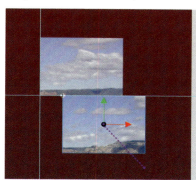

FIGURE 48
Using the 3D Translation tool to position the second object again

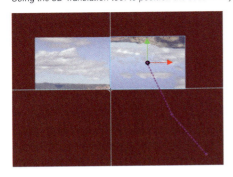

FIGURE 49
Using the 3D Translation tool to position a third object

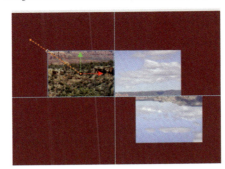

FIGURE 50
Using the 3D Translation tool to position the third object again

FIGURE 51
The completed 3D effects movie

11. Select the **3D Rotation tool** 🔵, then point to the **bottom red line X axis** and drag the line to the left and up to flip the image vertically.

12. Click **frame 40** on Layer 2, then use the **3D Translation tool** 🔧 to position the image as shown in Figure 48.

13. Use the **3D Rotation tool** 🔵 to flip the image vertically again.

14. Click **frame 1** on Layer 3, insert a **motion tween**, then increase the tween span to **frame 40**.

15. Click **frame 20** on Layer 3, select the **3D Translation tool** 🔧, then use the arrows to drag the image to the position shown in Figure 49.

16. Select the **3D Rotation tool** 🔵, then point to the **blue line Z axis** and drag the line to rotate the image clockwise 180 degrees.

17. Click **frame 40** on Layer 3, use the **3D Translation tool** 🔧 to position the image as shown in Figure 50, then use the **3D Rotation tool** 🔵 to rotate the image again.

18. Repeat steps 14–17 for Layer 4, making adjustments as needed such as
    * moving the image into the upper-right corner of the lower-left quadrant
    * using the orange circle and the 3D Rotation tool 🔵 two different times in two different frames, to rotate the X and Y axis simultaneously.

19. Use the 3D tools to make adjustments as needed so your screen resembles Figure 51.

20. Play the movie, close the Flash Player window, then save your work.

You created a movie with 3D effects.

Create a mask effect.

1. Start Flash, open fl5_8.fla, then save it as **skills demo5**.
2. Verify the frame rate is set to 12 and the Flash Publish Settings (accessed from the File menu) are set to Flash Player 10 and ActionScript 3.0.
3. Insert a new layer above the table layer, then name it **heading**.
4. Select frame 1 on the heading layer, then use the Text tool to create the Aces Wild heading with the following characteristics: size 48, color #006633, and Byington (or similar) font.
5. Use the Align command in the Modify menu to center the heading on the Stage.
6. Use the Selection tool to select the heading and then convert it to a graphic symbol with the name **g_heading**.
7. Insert a keyframe in frame 40 on the heading layer.
8. Insert a new layer above the heading layer, then name it **ending-heading**.
9. Insert a keyframe in frame 40 on the ending-heading layer.
10. Drag the g_heading symbol from the Library panel and position it on top of the heading on the Stage. Use the keyboard arrow keys as needed to position the g_heading symbol.
11. Lock the ending-heading layer.
12. Insert a new layer above the heading layer, then name it **circle**.
13. Select frame 1 on the circle layer, then use the Oval tool to create a black-filled circle that is

slightly larger in height than the heading text.
14. Place the circle to the left of the heading.
15. Convert the circle to a graphic symbol with the name **g_mask**.
16. Create a motion tween that moves the circle across and to the right side of the heading.
17. Extend the tween span in the Timeline to frame 40 (if necessary).
18. Change the circle layer to a mask layer and lock the layer.
19. Change the heading layer to a masked layer and lock the layer.
20. Insert keyframes in frame 40 on the table and the head and body layers.
21. Insert a new layer above the table layer, name it **stopmovie**, move the stopmovie layer below the table layer, then insert a keyframe in frame 40. (*Note:* You want to add a stop action to this frame. Because ActionScript 3.0 is needed when working with Inverse Kinematics and with the 3D feature, you cannot use the Script Assist feature of Flash. Rather, you must type the code directly into the Actions panel.)
22. Open the Actions panel, verify Script Assist is turned off and stopmovie: 40 is displayed in the lower left of the panel, then type **stop( );** for the code.
23. Test the movie, then save your work.

Create a character animation.

1. Select frame 1 on the Timeline, then use the Zoom tool to enlarge the view of the character.

2. Use the Bone tool to join the body with the upper and lower left arm, and the upper and lower right arm. (*Note:* The bone structure stops at the elbow on each arm.)
3. Select frame 6 on the Armature_1 layer.
4. Use the Selection tool to move the ends of the arms so that the lower left and lower right arms are horizontal and touch at the chest. This will cause the elbows to point out away from the body.
5. Select frame 12 on the Armature_1 layer.
6. Use the Selection tool to move the end of the right arm so that it is straight and pointing to the upper-left corner of the Stage.
7. Extend the Armature_1 layer to frame 40 (if necessary).
8. Select frame 40 on the Armature_1 layer.
9. Use the Selection tool to reposition the arms to their original positions, that is, so the arms are touching the table.
10. Change the view to Fit in Window.
11. Test the movie, then save your work.

Create a frame-by-frame animation.

1. Select frame 4 on the card layer, then insert a keyframe.
2. Use the arrow keys on the keyboard as needed to reposition the card so that it is at the end of the right arm.
3. Select frame 5 on the card layer, then insert a keyframe.
4. Use the arrow keys on the keyboard to reposition the card so that it is at the end of the right arm.

5. Repeat steps 3 and 4 in frame 6 through frame 12 on the card layer.

6. Select frame 13 on the card layer, then insert a blank keyframe.

7. Test the movie, close the Flash Player window, then save your work.

Create a 3D effect.

1. Insert a new layer above the card layer, then name it **ace3D**.

2. Select frame 12 on the ace3D layer, then insert a keyframe.

3. Drag the mc_aceD movie clip from the Library panel to the Stage, display the Properties panel, verify the Lock width and height values together icon is not a broken link, then resize the width to 10.6.

4. Reposition the ace to on top of the card held by the character.

5. Verify frame 12 on the ace3D layer is selected, then create a motion tween.

6. Verify the tween span on the Timeline extends from frame 12 through frame 40.

7. Select frame 40 on the ace3D layer.

8. Use the 3D Translation tool to reposition the card to the upper-left corner of the Stage in a diagonal line that extends from the character's right shoulder. (*Hint:* Use both the red and green arrows to move the card to create a diagonal line.)

9. Use the Free Transform tool and the Scale option at the bottom of the Tools panel to resize the card to a width of between 80 and 90.

10. Select frame 26 on the ace3D layer.

11. Use the 3D Rotation tool to add a 3D effect.

12. Select frame 40 on the ace3D layer.

13. Use the 3D Rotation tool to add a 3D effect that causes the card to display right side up, as seen in Figure 52.

14. Test the movie, close the Flash Player window, then save your work.

FIGURE 52
Completed Skills Review

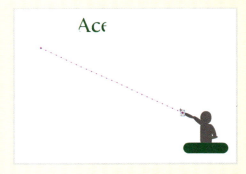

Add sound to a movie.

1. Insert a new layer at the top of the Timeline, then name it **sound**.

2. Insert a keyframe in frame 5 on the sound layer.

3. Drag introSound.wav from the Library panel to the Stage.

4. Insert a keyframe in frame 40 on the sound layer.

5. Test the movie, compare your movie to the images in Figure 52, close the Flash Player window, save your work, then close the file.

Work with video.

1. Open fl5_9.fla, then save it as **skillsdemo5-video**.

2. Add a new layer above the headings layer, then name it **video**.

3. Import tour-video.mov from the drive and folder where you store your Data Files to the Library, using the Import Video command, as an embedded video. (*Note:* You will need to use the Adobe Media Encoder to convert the file to the flv format, then you will need to browse to the drive and folder where you save your Solution Files to open the converted file.)

4. Verify that the video is in the Library panel and on the center of the Stage, note the number of frames needed to display the entire video. (*Hint*: Be sure to position the video placeholder, if necessary, to prevent overlapping the text subheading.)

5. Add a new layer, name it **controls**, then select frame 1 on the layer.

6. Use the Text tool to create a text box with the word **Play** beneath and to the left side of the video. Set the text characteristics to the following: family **Arial**, style **Narrow** (Win) or **Regular** (Mac), size **20** pt, and color **White**.

7. Convert the text to a button symbol with the name **b_play**.

8. Edit three stages of the button symbol, for example, make the color of the letters change when the mouse pointer is over the word Play.

9. Use the Actions panel and Script Assist to assign a play action to the button that plays the movie when the mouse is released.

10. Use the Text tool to create a text box with the word **Pause** beneath and to the right side of the video. Use the same text characteristics used for the Play button.

11. Convert the text to a button symbol with the name **b_pause**.

12. Edit the button symbol so that the color of the letters changes when the mouse pointer is over the word Pause.

13. Use the Actions panel to assign a stop action to the button when it is released.

14. Add a new layer, then name it **stopMovie**.

15. Add a stop action to frame 1 on the stopMovie layer.

16. Add a keyframe at the end of the movie on the headings layer.

17. Test the movie, compare your screen to Figure 53, close the Flash Player window, then save your work.

18. Exit Flash.

FIGURE 53
Completed Skills Review - video

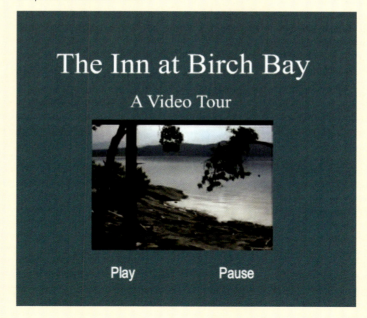

The Ultimate Tours travel company has asked you to design several sample animations for its website. Figure 54 shows a sample Cruises screen with a mask effect, as the spotlight rotates across the screen and highlights different ships. Complete the following for the Cruises screen of the Ultimate Tours website:

Add objects to the ultimatetours5 document.

1. Open fl5_10.fla, then save it as **assets**.
2. Open ultimatetours4.fla (the file you created in Chapter 4 Project Builder 1), and save it as **ultimatetours5**.
3. Insert a new layer at the top of the Timeline and select frame 1 on the layer.
4. Display the Library panel, then click the list arrow below the Library tab to display the list of open documents.
5. Select assets and drag each of the symbols in the Library panel to the Stage, delete the layer, click the assets tab, then close the assets file. (*Note*: This will add the objects from the assets file to the ultimatetours5 Library panel.)
6. Display the Library panel for ultimatetours5.

Add layers and objects to the Stage.

1. Insert a new layer at the top of the Timeline, then name it **background**.
2. Insert a keyframe in a frame that is higher than the last frame in the current movie (such as frame 100) on the background layer, then draw a dark gray rectangle (#333333) that covers the Stage.
3. Insert a keyframe that is at least 30 frames higher on the background layer (such as frame 130), then lock the layer. (*Note:* All of the subsequent layers will use the same frames (such as 100 to 130), so be sure to add keyframes to these frames as needed.)
4. Insert a new layer, name it **heading**, and create the Mystery Ships heading.
5. Insert a new layer, name it **lighthouse**, then place the g_lighthouse symbol on the Stage.

Add a motion tween and mask effect.

1. Insert a new layer, name it **searchlight**, and place the g_searchlight symbol to the left of the lighthouse.
2. Use the Free Transform tool to create a motion tween that causes the searchlight to rotate from the left to the right of the lighthouse.

(*Hint:* The searchlight will rotate (pivot) around the transformation point (small circle) of the graphic. You need to move the transformation point so it is at the narrow end of the graphic. To do this, select the graphic with the Free Transform tool to display the transformation point, then drag the point to the desired location (narrow end) on the graphic.)

3. Create a new layer for each of the three ships, name each layer appropriately (**ship1**, **ship2**, and **ship3**), and place them on the Stage so that the searchlight highlights them as it moves from left to right across the Stage.
4. Insert a new layer above the ship layers, name it **searchlight mask**, and using the g_searchlight symbol, add a motion tween that duplicates the one created in step 2.
5. Create a mask effect that has a searchlight as the mask and reveals the ships when the searchlight is over them. (*Note:* The two searchlight motion tweens are needed on different layers because one will become a mask and will not be visible in the movie.)

Add a sound and interactivity.

1. Insert a new layer, name it **sound**, insert a keyframe in frame 100 (or the appropriate frame) on the layer, then drag the sound file to the Stage.

2. Insert a new layer, name it **home button**, insert a keyframe in the last frame of the movie, then add the b_home button to the bottom center of the Stage.

3. Add an action to the home button to have the playhead go to frame 1 of the movie when the button is clicked.

4. Insert a new layer, name it **stopaction**, and add a stop action at the end of the movie.

5. Drag (scrub) the playhead on the Timeline to locate the Galapagos text (cruise heading layer for example), unlock the cruise heading layer (or layer that has the Galapogos text).

6. Change the Galapagos text to **Mystery Ships**, then create a button that changes color for the different phases and that jumps to frame 100 (or the appropriate frame) when the user clicks the Mystery Ships text.

7. Test the movie, then compare your image to the example shown in Figure 54.

8. Close the Flash Player window, then save your work.

FIGURE 54

Sample completed Project Builder 1

You have been asked to develop a website illustrating the signs of the zodiac. The introductory screen should have a heading with a mask effect and 12 zodiac signs, each of which could become a button. Clicking a sign button displays an information screen with a different graphic to represent the sign and information about the sign, as well as special effects such as sound, mask effect, and character animation (inverse kinematics). Each information screen would be linked to the introductory screen. (*Note:* Using the inverse kinematics feature requires ActionScript 3.0, therefore, you will start with a movie that has the ActionScript for the buttons and stop actions already developed.)

1. Open fl5_11.fla, save it as **zodiac5**, then change the frame rate to **12 fps**.
2. Test the movie and then study the Timeline to understand how the movie works.
3. Refer to Figure 55 as you complete the introductory screen with the following:
    - A new layer above the signs layer named **heading** with the heading, **Signs of the** that appears from frame 1 through frame 31
    - A new layer named **masked** that contains the word **Zodiac** and that appears from frame 1 through frame 31
    - A mask layer that passes across the heading Zodiac

(*Notes:* Use a fill color that can be seen on the black background. After creating the motion tween, drag the end of the tween span on the Timeline to frame 31. Be sure to set the Layer Properties for the mask and masked layers.)
    - A new layer that displays the word **Zodiac** in frame 31 only
(*Note:* Remove frames 32–80 from the layer by using the Remove Frames option from the Timeline command of the Edit menu.)
    - A new layer with a sound that plays from frame 1 through frame 31 as the mask is revealing the contents of the masked layer
4. Refer to Figure 55 as you complete the scorpio screen with the following:
(*Notes:* The scorpio screen starts in frame 51. Remove frames in other layers containing content that you do not want displayed after frame 31, such as the Zodiac heading.)
    - A new layer with the three-line heading
    - An inverse kinematics animation that moves the tail (*Note:* Be sure to connect the head to the tail.)
5. Test the movie, then save it.
6. Save the movie as **zodiac5-mc**.
7. Select frame 51 on the Armature1 layer and convert the IK animation to a movie clip.
8. Delete the Armature1 layer, then select frame 51 on the scorpio layer and drag the movie clip to the Stage.
9. Create a motion tween to animate the movie clip so the scorpion moves across the screen.

10. Test the movie, compare your screens to Figure 55, close the Flash Player window, then save the movie.

FIGURE 55
Sample completed Project Builder 2

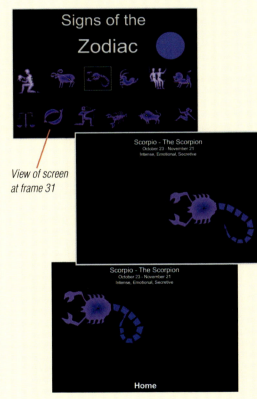

View of screen at frame 31

DESIGN PROJECT

Figure 56 shows the home page of a website. Study the figure and complete the following questions. For each question, indicate how you determined your answer.

1. Connect to the Internet, then go to *www.nikeid.com*.

   TIP: Use Figure 56 to answer the questions. Go to the site and explore several links to get a feeling for how the site is constructed.

2. Open a document in a word processor or open a new Flash document, save the file as **dpc5**, then answer the following questions. (*Hint*: Use the Text tool in Flash.)

   - Who's site is this and what seems to be the purpose of this site?
   - Who would be the target audience?
   - How might a character animation using inverse kinematics be used?
   - How might video be used?
   - How might a mask effect be used?
   - How might sound be used? How might 3D be used?
   - What suggestions would you make to improve the design and why?

FIGURE 56
Design Project

This is a continuation of the Portfolio Project in Chapter 4, which is the development of a personal portfolio. The home page has several categories, including the following:

- Personal data
- Contact information
- Previous employment
- Education
- Samples of your work

In this project, you will create several buttons for the Sample Animations screen and link them to their respective animations.

1. Open portfolio4.fla (the file you created in Portfolio Project, Chapter 4) and save it as **portfolio5**. (*Hint*: When you open the file, you may receive a missing font message, meaning a font used in this document is not available on your computer. You can choose a substitute font or use a default font.)

2. Display the Sample Animations screen. You will be adding buttons to this screen that play various animations. In each case, have the animation return to the Sample Animations screen at the end of the animation.

3. Add a button for a character animation so it appears on the Sample Animations screen, add a new layer and create a character animation (inverse kinematics) on that layer, then link the character animation button to the character animation.

4. Add a button for a mask effect so it appears on the Sample Animations screen, add new layers to create a mask effect (such as to the words My Portfolio) on that layer, add a sound that plays as the mask is revealing the contents of the masked layer, then link the mask effect button to the mask effect animation.

5. Add a button for an animated navigation bar so it appears on the Sample Animations screen, add a new layer and create an animated navigation bar on that layer, then link the navigation bar button to the animated navigation bar.

6. Test the movie, then compare your Sample Animation screen to the example shown in Figure 57.

7. Close the Flash Player window, then save your work.

FIGURE 57
Sample completed Portfolio Project

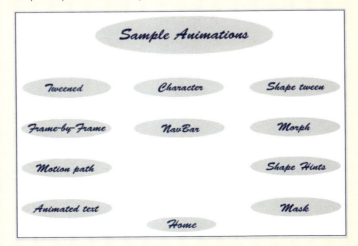

chapter

6

PREPARING AND
PUBLISHING MOVIES

1. Publish movies

2. Reduce file size to optimize a movie

3. Create a preloader

4. Use HTML Publish Settings

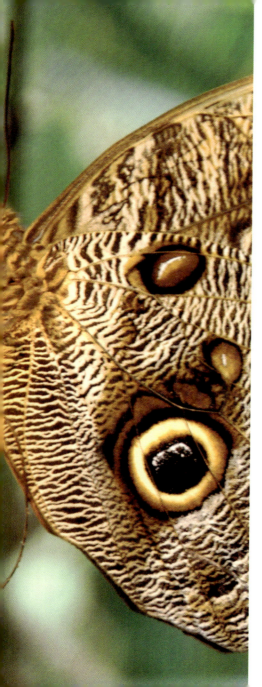

6 PREPARING AND
PUBLISHING MOVIES

Introduction

During the planning process for an Adobe Flash movie, you are concerned with, among other things, how the target audience will view the movie. The most common use of Flash is to develop movies that provide web content and applications. Flash provides several features that help you generate the files that are necessary for delivering movies over the Internet.

When you deliver content over the Internet, you want to provide compelling movies. However, it is important that you keep the file size down so that the movies play smoothly regardless of the user's connection speed. Flash allows you to test movies to determine where problems might arise during download and to make changes to optimize the movies.

Adobe provides a program, Device Central, that allows you to preview and test mobile content on an assortment of mobile devices. This is especially useful when designing Flash movies because of the reduced viewing size for mobile devices, such as cell phones, and the limited download speeds available for mobile devices. Using Device Central, you can specify the model of a cell phone and simulate the display of Flash movies for that phone. Then you can make adjustments in your movie to optimize the design and lighting, and even choose from an array of languages. Adobe provides a version of its Flash Player, Flash Lite, that is specifically developed to optimize the playing of Flash movies using mobile devices.

Tools You'll Use

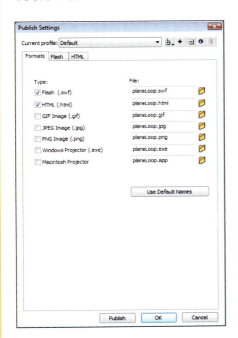

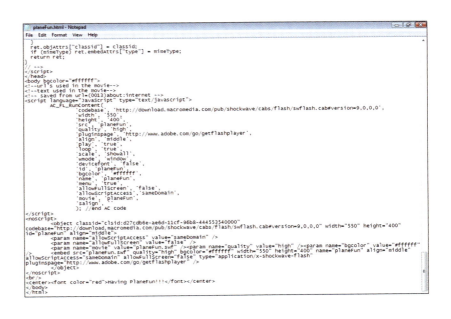

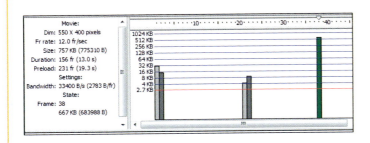

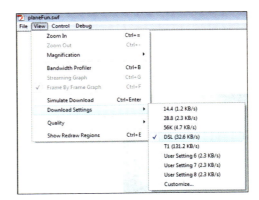

PUBLISH
MOVIES

What You'll Do

In this lesson, you will use the Flash Publish Settings feature to publish a movie, create a GIF animation, and create a JPEG image from a movie.

Using Publish Settings

The Flash Publish feature generates the files necessary to deliver the movies on the web. When you publish a movie using the default settings, a Flash (.swf) file is created that can be viewed using the Flash Player. In addition, an HTML file is created with the necessary code to instruct the browser to play the Flash file using the Flash Player. If you are not distributing the movie over the Internet, or if you know the Flash Player will not be available, you can use the Publish feature to create alternate images and stand-alone projector files.

Figure 1 shows the Publish Settings dialog box with a list of the available formats for publishing a Flash movie. By default, the Flash and HTML formats are selected and their related tabs are available. You can choose a combination of formats, and you can specify a different name (but not file extension) for each format. The GIF, JPEG, and PNG formats create still images that can be delivered on the web. The projector formats in the Publish Settings dialog box are executable files (which you created in Chapter 1). When you select a format, a tab appears. When you click a tab, the tab opens with settings specifically for the selected format. Figure 2 shows the Flash tab of the Publish Settings dialog box. You can choose settings for several options, including:

- A profile of selected settings that is saved for later use
- The version of the Flash Player

QUICKTIP

Not all features of Flash CS4 work when using Flash Player versions earlier than version 10.

- The version of ActionScript
- The quality for JPEG images and audio
- Other options, such as compressing the movie

FIGURE 1

The Publish Settings dialog box

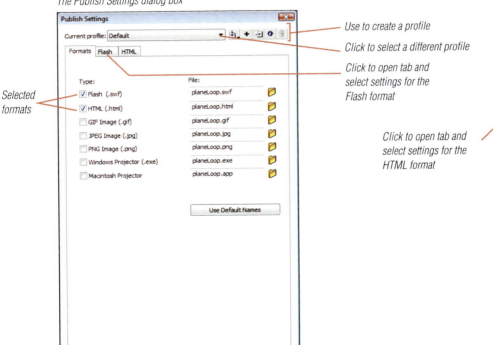

Selected formats

Use to create a profile

Click to select a different profile

Click to open tab and select settings for the Flash format

FIGURE 2

The Flash tab

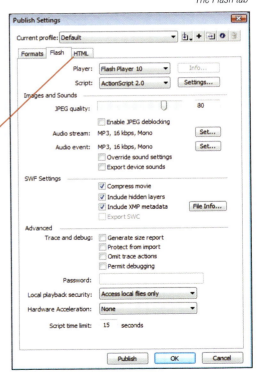

Click to open tab and select settings for the HTML format

Figure 3 shows the GIF tab in the Publish Settings dialog box. This tab appears after selecting GIF Image on the Formats tab. GIF files, which are compressed bitmaps, provide an easy way to create images and simple animations for delivery on the web. GIF animations are frame-by-frame animations created from Flash movie frames. Using this tab, you can change several settings, including the following:

- Specifying the dimensions in pixels (or you can match the movie dimensions)
- Specifying playback as a static image or an animated GIF
- Specifying whether an animation plays (loops) continuously or repeats a certain number of times
- Selecting from a range of appearance settings, such as optimizing colors and removing gradients

Using Publish Preview

You can use the Publish Preview command on the File menu to publish a movie and display the movie in either your default browser or the Flash Player. In addition, you can use this command to view HTML, GIF, JPEG, PNG, and Projector files.

FIGURE 3
The GIF tab

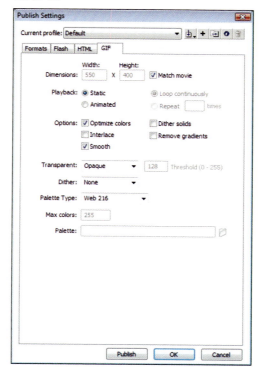

FIGURE 4

The three planeLoop files

The Flash document file

Your browser icon may vary

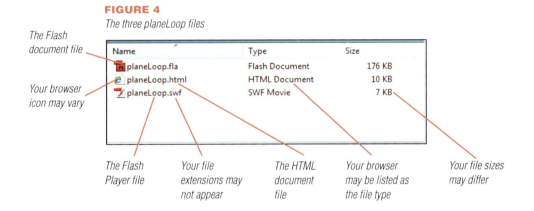

Name	Type	Size
planeLoop.fla	Flash Document	176 KB
planeLoop.html	HTML Document	10 KB
planeLoop.swf	SWF Movie	7 KB

The Flash Player file

Your file extensions may not appear

The HTML document file

Your browser may be listed as the file type

Your file sizes may differ

Publish using the default settings

1. Open fl6_1.fla from the drive and folder where your Data Files are stored, save it as **planeLoop**, then play the movie.

2. Click **File** on the menu bar, click **Publish Settings**, then verify the Formats tab is selected.

3. Verify that the Flash and HTML check boxes are the only ones selected, then click the **Flash tab**.

4. Verify that the version is set to Flash Player 10, and that the Compress movie check box under SWF Settings is selected.

5. Accept the remaining default settings, click **Publish**, then click **OK**.

6. Use your file management program to navigate to the drive and folder where you save your Data Files, then notice the three files with filenames that start with "planeLoop", as shown in Figure 4.

7. Display the Flash program, click **File** on the menu bar, point to **Publish Preview**, then click **Default - (HTML)**.

   The movie plays in a browser or in an HTML editor.

8. Close the browser or the HTML editor, then display the Flash program.

You published a movie using the default publish settings and viewed it in a browser.

Create a GIF animation from a movie

1. Click **File** on the menu bar, click **Publish Settings**, then click the **Formats tab**.

2. Click the **GIF Image (.gif) check box**, then click the **GIF tab**.

3. Click the **Match movie check box** to turn off this setting, double-click the **Width text box**, type **275,** double-click the **Height text box**, then type **200**.

4. Click the **Animated option button**, then review the remaining default settings as you compare your GIF tab with Figure 5.

5. Click **Publish**, then click **OK**.

6. Open your browser, then use the browser to open planeLoop.gif from the folder where you save your Data Files.

   TIP   Many browsers have an Open command on the File menu. Use this command to navigate and open files for display within the browser. If you do not see the gif file, change the file type to All Files.

7. Notice the GIF animation plays in the browser with the modified settings.

   Because the GIF file is not an SWF file, it does not require the Flash Player to play—it can be displayed directly in a web browser.

8. Close the browser, then display the Flash program.

You changed the publish settings for a GIF image, then created a GIF animation and viewed it in your web browser.

FIGURE 5

The completed GIF format dialog box

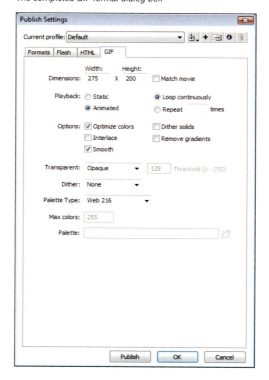

FIGURE 6

The JPEG image displayed in the browser

Your browser
may vary

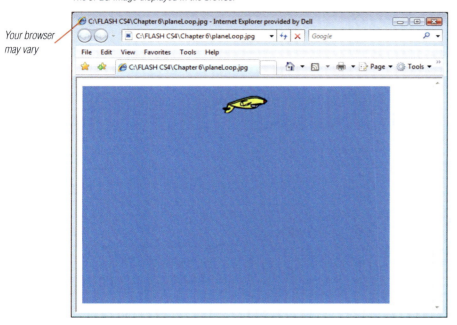

Create a JPEG image from a frame of a movie

1. Display the Flash program, then click **frame 10** on the plane layer.

2. Click **File** on the menu bar, then click **Publish Settings**.

3. Click the **Formats tab**, click the **GIF Image check box** to deselect it, then click the **JPEG Image check box** to select it.

   Deselecting the GIF format will prevent the GIF file from being created again.

4. Click the **JPEG tab**, accept the default settings, click **Publish**, then click **OK**.

5. Open your browser, then use the browser to open the planeLoop.jpg file from the folder where you save your Data Files.

   TIP   If you do not see the jpg file, change the file type to All Files.

6. Notice that the static JPEG image appears in the browser, as shown in Figure 6.

7. Close your browser, then display the Flash program.

8. Save your work, then close the movie.

You reviewed the default publish settings for a JPEG image, then created a JPEG image and viewed it in your web browser.

REDUCE FILE SIZE TO
OPTIMIZE A MOVIE

What You'll Do

In this lesson, you will test a movie and reduce its file size.

Testing a Movie

The goal in publishing a movie is to provide the most effective playback for the intended audience. This requires that you pay special attention to the download time and play-back speed. Users are turned off by long waits to view content, jerky animations, and audio that skips. These events can occur as the file size increases in relation to the user's Internet connection speed.

Flash provides various ways to test a movie to determine where changes/optimizations can improve its delivery. The following are guidelines for optimizing movies:

- Use symbols and instances for every element that appears in a movie more than once.
- Use tween animations rather than frame-by-frame animations when possible.
- Use movie clips rather than graphic symbols for animation sequences.
- Confine the area of change to a keyframe so that the action takes place in as small an area as possible.
- Use bitmap graphics as static elements rather than in animations.
- Group elements, such as related images.
- Limit the number of fonts and font styles.
- Use gradients and alpha trans-parencies sparingly.

When you publish a movie, Flash opti-mizes it using default features, including compressing the entire movie, which is later decompressed by the Flash Player.

Using the Bandwidth Profiler

When a movie is delivered over the Internet, the contents of each frame are sent to the user's computer. Depending on the amount of data in the frame and the user's connection speed, the movie may pause while the frame's contents down-load. The first step in optimizing a movie is to test the movie and determine which frames may create a pause during playback. The test should be done using a simulated Internet connection speed that is representative of the speed of your target audience. You can set a simulated speed using the **Bandwidth Profiler**, shown in Figure 7. The Bandwidth Profiler allows you to view a graphical representation of the size of each frame. Each bar represents a frame of the movie, and the height of the bar corresponds to the frame's size. If a bar extends above the red baseline, the movie may need to pause to allow the frame's contents to be downloaded. Figure 7 shows the following:

- Movie information: dimensions, frame rate, file size, duration, and preload
- Settings: simulated bandwidth (specified in the Debug menu option)
- State: selected frame number and size of contents in the frame

The Bandwidth Profiler shown in Figure 7 indicates that downloading frame 38 may result in a pause because of the large size of the contents in this frame in relationship to the connection speed and the frame rate. If the specified connection speed is correct for your target audience and the frame rate is needed to ensure acceptable animation quality, then the only change that can be made is in the contents of the frame.

Using the Simulate Download Feature

When testing a movie, you can simulate downloading Flash movies using different connection speeds. The most common connections are Dial-up, broadband (both DSL and cable), and T1. Dial-up is a phone connection that provides a relatively slow download speed. Broadband is a type of data transmission in which a wide band of frequencies is available to transmit more information at the same time. DSL provides a broadband Internet connection speed that is available through phone lines. DSL and cable are widely used by homes and businesses. T1 provides an extremely fast connection speed and is widely used in businesses, especially for intranet (a computer network within a company) applications. You can test the movie that you are developing at the different speeds to evaluate the download experience for potential users.

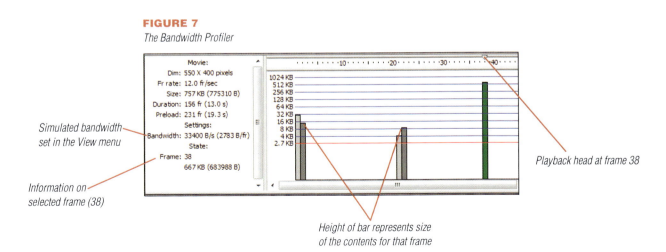

FIGURE 7
The Bandwidth Profiler

Simulated bandwidth set in the View menu

Information on selected frame (38)

Playback head at frame 38

Height of bar represents size of the contents for that frame

Play a movie stored on your computer in a browser

1. Open fl6_2.fla, then save it as **planeFun**.

2. Change the view to **Fit in Window**.

3. Click **File** on the menu bar, then click **Publish Settings**.

4. Verify the Flash and HTML check boxes on the Format tabs are selected, click **Publish**, then click **OK**.

5. Use your file management program to navigate to the drive and folder where you save your Data Files, then locate the planeFun.html file.

6. Double-click the **planeFun.html** file to open it in your browser.

7. Click the **Start button** and notice how the animation runs smoothly until the middle of the morphing animation, where there is a noticeable pause, as shown in Figure 8.

   The pause is caused by the browser waiting for the remaining contents of the movie to be downloaded. The pause may not be very long because the movie file is located on your computer (or a local network computer) and is not being downloaded from a remote web server. A user viewing this movie over a dial-up connection from a website would probably have a very long pause.

8. Close your browser, then return to the Flash program.

You played a movie in a browser and viewed the pause that occurs in the middle of the movie.

FIGURE 8
A pause in the movie

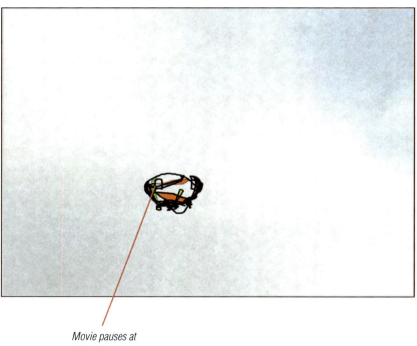

Movie pauses at this point

FIGURE 9
Selecting the connection speed for a simulated download

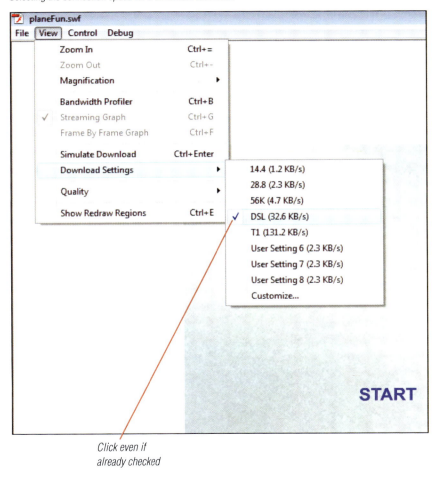

Click even if
already checked

Test the download time for a movie

1. Click **Control** on the menu bar, click **Test Movie**, then maximize the Flash Player window (if necessary).

2. Click **View** on the menu bar, point to **Download Settings**, then click **DSL (32.6 KB/s)**, as shown in Figure 9.

3. Click **View** on the menu bar, then click **Simulate Download**.

4. Click **Start**, then notice the pause in the movie when the plane morphs into the hot air balloon.

   You may have to wait several moments for the movie to continue.

5. Click **View** on the menu bar, point to **Download Settings**, then click **T1 (131.2 KB/s)**.

6. Click **View** on the menu bar, verify the Simulate Download feature is off (no check mark next to it), then click **Simulate Download** to turn on the feature.

   When you change a download setting, you need to be sure the Simulate Download feature is off, and then turn it on again to start the simulation with the new setting.

7. Click **Start**, then notice the pause in the movie is shorter with the simulated T1 line speed.

   TIP   If you don't notice a difference, turn the Simulate Download feature off and then on again.

You used the Flash Player window to simulate the download time for a movie using different connection speeds.

Use the Bandwidth Profiler

1. Verify that the Flash Player window is still open.

2. Click **View** on the menu bar, point to **Download Settings**, then click **DSL (32.6 KB/s)** to select it.

3. Click **View** on the menu bar, then click **Bandwidth Profiler**.

4. Click **View** on the menu bar, then verify Frame By Frame Graph is selected.

5. Click **View** on the menu bar, then click **Simulate Download**.

   Notice the green bar as it scrolls at the top of the Bandwidth Profiler to indicate the frames being downloaded. The bar pauses at frame 38, as shown in Figure 10.

6. Click **frame 37** on the Timeline, then notice that the only object in the frame is the morphing balloon, and its size is less than 1 KB.

7. Click **frame 38** on the Timeline, then notice the large color photograph.

   The frame setting in the State section indicates that the file size is over 600 KB. This image's large file size takes several moments to download and causes the pause in the movie.

8. Close the Flash Player window.

You used the Bandwidth Profiler to determine which frame causes a pause in the movie.

FIGURE 10

The Bandwidth Profiler indicating the pause at frame 38

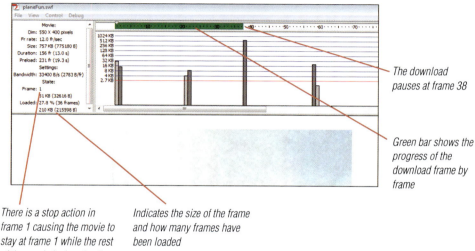

The download pauses at frame 38

Green bar shows the progress of the download frame by frame

There is a stop action in frame 1 causing the movie to stay at frame 1 while the rest of the movie is downloading

Indicates the size of the frame and how many frames have been loaded

Preparing and Publishing Movies

FIGURE 11
Positioning the cloud image

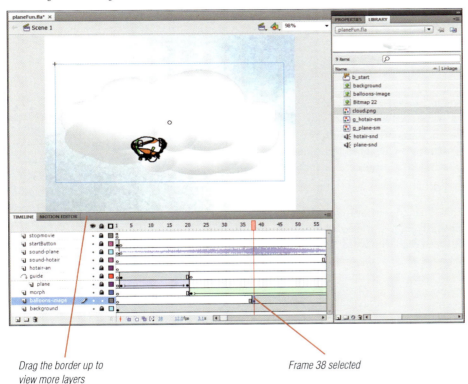

Drag the border up to view more layers

Frame 38 selected

1. Point to the **top border** of the Timeline, then, when the pointer changes to a double-arrow ↕ , drag the **top border** up to view the balloons-image layer.

2. Click **frame 38** on the balloons-image layer to view the image on the Stage.

   TIP If the layer name appears cut off, position the mouse over the right border of the layer area, then drag the border to the right until the name is fully visible.

3. Click the **balloon photographic image** on the Stage, click **Edit** on the menu bar, then click **Cut**.

   The balloon photograph is no longer visible on the Stage.

4. Display the Library panel.

5. Verify frame 38 is selected, then drag the **cloud graphic symbol** from the Library panel to the center of the Stage, as shown in Figure 11.

6. Click **Control** on the menu bar, click **Test Movie**, then maximize the Flash Player window if it is not already maximized.

7. Click **View** on the Flash Player window menu bar, click **Simulate Download**, wait for the download to finish, then click **Start**.

   Notice the movie no longer pauses.

8. Click **frame 38** on the Timeline in the Flash Player window and notice that the file size is now just above the 8 KB line.

9. Close the Flash Player window.

10. Save your work, then close the movie.

You replaced an image that had a large file size with one having a small file size to help optimize a movie.

CREATE A
PRELOADER

What You'll Do

In this lesson, you will create a preloader for the planeFun movie. Ten frames have been added to the beginning of the movie and labels have been added to the start and ending frames of the movie.

Preloading a Movie

One way to improve the playback performance of large or complex movies is to preload the movie frames. Preloading frames prevents the browser from playing a specified frame or series of frames until all of the frames have been downloaded. Commonly, a **preloader** frame includes a simple animation that starts in frame 1 and loops until the rest of the movie has been downloaded. The animation could consist of the words "Please wait" flashing on the screen, the word "Loading" with a series of scrolling dots, or the hand of a clock sweeping around in a circle. The purpose of the animation is to indicate to the viewer that the movie is being loaded. The animation is placed on its own layer. A second layer contains the ActionScript code that checks to see if the movie has been loaded and, if not, causes a loop which continues until the last frame of the movie has been loaded.

For example, assume a movie has 155 frames. An additional 10 frames could be added to the beginning of the movie for the preloader, and the preloader animation would run from frames 1 to 10. A label, such as **startofMovie**, would be added to frame 11 (the first frame of the actual movie). Another label, such as **endofMovie**, would be added to frame 165, the last frame of the entire movie. Then the following ActionScript code would be placed in frame 1 of the movie on the preloaderScript layer:

```
ifFrameLoaded ("endofMovie") {
    gotoAndPlay ("startofMovie");
}
```

This is a conditional statement that checks to see if the frame labeled endofMovie is loaded. If the statement is true, then the next line of the script is executed and the playhead goes to the frame labeled startofMovie. This script is placed in frame 1 on the preloaderScript layer. So each time the playhead is on frame 1, there is a check to see if the entire movie has been downloaded. If the condition is false, the playhead moves on to frames 2, 3, 4, and so on. Then the following ActionScript code would be placed in frame 10.

gotoAndPlay (1);

This creates a loop. When the movie first starts, the playhead is on frame 1 and there is a check to see if the movie has been loaded. If not, the playhead continues to frame 10 (playing the preloader animation) where this script (gotoAndPlay (1);) causes it to loop back to frame 1 for another check. The looping process continues until all movie frames have been loaded.

Figure 12 shows the Timeline that displays the two preloader layers after the preloader has been created.

FIGURE 12
The completed preloader with the animation and ActionScript

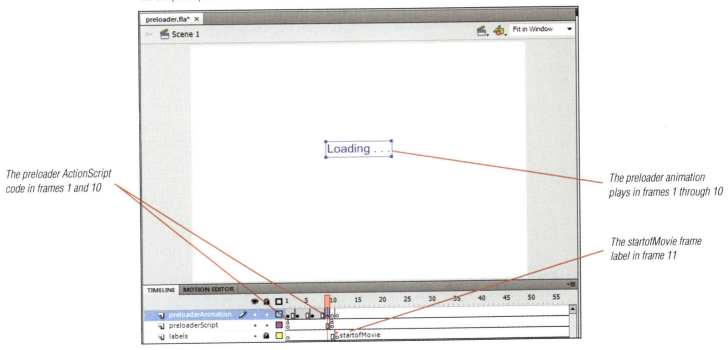

The preloader ActionScript code in frames 1 and 10

The preloader animation plays in frames 1 through 10

The startofMovie frame label in frame 11

Add layers for a preloader

1. Open fl6_3.fla, then save it as **preloader**. This movie is similar to the planeFun.fla movie except that the first 10 frames contain no content, and the movie again contains the larger graphic file of the hot air balloons.

2. Change the view to **Fit in Window**.

3. Click the **labels layer** at the top of the Timeline, then click the **New Layer icon** to insert a new layer.

4. Name the new layer **preloaderScript**.

5. Insert a **new layer**, above the preloaderScript layer, then name it **preloaderAnimation**.

6. Click **frame 10** on the preloaderAnimation layer, then insert a **keyframe**.

7. Insert a **keyframe** in frame 10 on the preloaderScript layer.

   Your screen should resemble Figure 13.

You added two layers that will be used to create a preloader. One layer will contain the ActionScript and the other layer will contain the animation for the preloader.

FIGURE 13

The preloader layers added to the Timeline

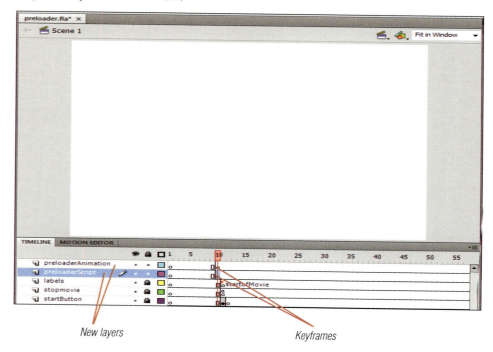

New layers

Keyframes

FIGURE 14

The Actions panel displaying preloaderScript:1 indicating the layer and frame

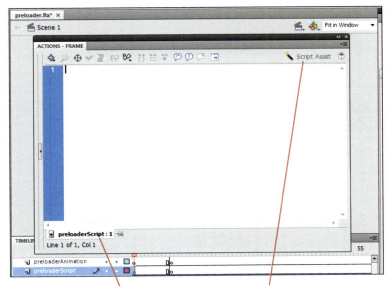

The ActionScript that is to be developed will be applied to frame 1 on the preloaderScript layer

Script Assist feature is off

FIGURE 15

The ActionScript code to check if the last frame in the movie has been downloaded

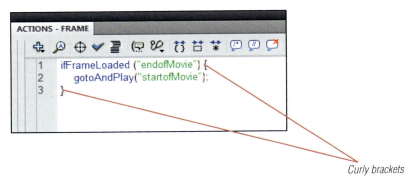

Curly brackets

Add actions to the preloader

1. Open the Actions panel, then turn off the Script Assist feature if it is on.

2. Click **frame 1** on the preloaderScript layer.

3. Verify the preloaderScript:1 is displayed in the lower-left corner of the Actions panel Script pane, as shown in Figure 14.

4. Click inside the **Actions panel Script pane**, then type the following code, matching use of capital letters, spacing, and punctuation exactly.

   ifFrameLoaded ("endofMovie") {
       gotoAndPlay ("startofMovie");
   }

   Your screen should match Figure 15.

5. Click **frame 10** on the preloaderScript layer, then verify preloaderScript:10 is displayed in the lower-left corner of the Actions panel Script pane.

6. Click inside the **Actions panel Script pane**, then type the following code.

   gotoAndPlay (1);

7. Close the Actions panel.

You added actions to frames on the preloaderScript layer that create a loop. The loop includes a check to see if the entire movie has been loaded and, if so, jumps to a starting place in the movie.

Create the preloader animation

1. Click **frame 1** on the preloaderAnimation layer.
2. Click the **Text tool** T on the Tools menu, click in middle of the Stage, then type **Loading**.
3. Double-click to select **Loading**, then use the Properties panel to set the font to **Arial**, the size to **20**, and the color to **blue**.
4. Insert a **keyframe** in frame 3 on the preloaderAnimation layer.
5. Using the **Text tool** T , point to the right of the g in Loading, then click to set an insertion line.
6. Press the **spacebar**, then type a **period [.]**.
7. Insert a **keyframe** in frame 6 on the preloaderAnimation layer.
8. Point to the right of the period, then click to set an insertion line.
9. Press the **spacebar**, then type a **period [.]**.
10. Repeat Steps 7 through 9 using frame 9. Your screen should resemble Figure 16.
11. Click **frame 10** on the preloaderAnimation layer, click **Insert** on the menu bar, point to **Timeline**, then click **Blank Keyframe**.

    Inserting a blank keyframe prevents the contents of the previous frame from being inserted into the frame.
12. Drag the **playhead** back and forth across frames 1 through 10 and view the animation.

    This animation causes the word Loading to appear, followed by three dots. You can create any animation for the preloader and use as many frames as desired.

You created an animation that will play as the playhead loops waiting for the movie to load.

FIGURE 16
The text used in the preloader animation

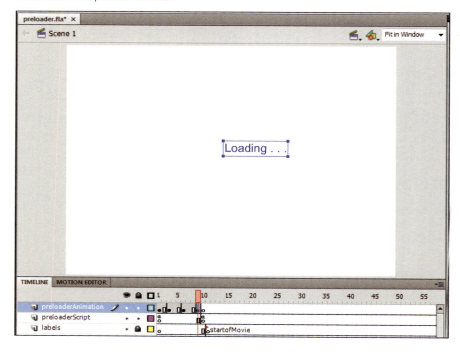

FIGURE 17

The Bandwidth Profiler showing the delay in downloading frame 48

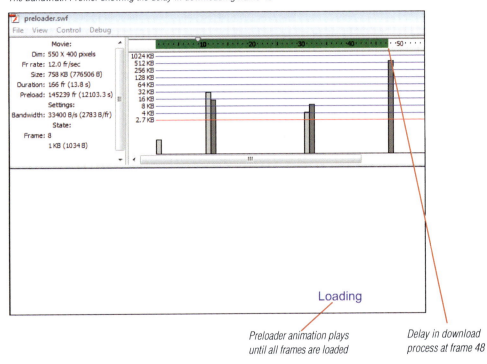

Preloader animation plays
until all frames are loaded

Delay in download
process at frame 48

1. Click **Control** on the menu bar, then click **Test Movie**.

2. Maximize the Flash Player window if it is not already maximized.

3. Click **View** on the menu bar, then click **Bandwidth Profiler** to display it if it is not already displayed.

4. Click **View** on the menu bar, point to **Download Settings**, then verify that DSL (32.6 KB/s) is selected.

5. Click **View** on the menu bar, then click **Simulate Download**.

    Notice the playhead loops, causing the preloader animation Loading... to play over and over in the Flash Player window as the frames are loaded. There is a delay in downloading frame 48, as shown in Figure 17, as the large jpg file is loaded. Once all frames are loaded, the screen with the Start button appears in the Flash Player window.

6. Repeat Step 5 twice (to turn off and then turn on the Simulated Download feature) to run the simulation again, then drag the **scroll bar** on the Bandwidth Profiler to the right to view the last frames of the movie.

7. Close the Flash Player window.

8. Save and close the movie.

You tested the preloader by simulating a download and you viewed the information on the Bandwidth Profiler during the simulation.

USE HTML
PUBLISH SETTINGS

What You'll Do

Having PlaneFun!!!

 In this lesson, you will use the HTML Publish Settings to align the Flash movie window in a browser window and change the code of an HTML document.

Understanding HTML Publishing Options

During the publishing process, Flash automatically creates an HTML document that allows a Flash movie to be displayed on the web. When you test a Flash movie, you see it in the Flash Player window. When you see a Flash movie on the web, you see it in a Flash movie window in your browser. The Flash Player window has controls for manipulating the movie. The Flash movie window has no controls, instead, all information on how the Flash movie should play and how the Flash movie window should look are in the HTML code for the web page.

The HTML code specifies, among other things, the movie's background color, its size, and its placement in the browser window. In addition, the attributes for the OBJECT (Internet Explorer for Win) and EMBED (all other browsers for Win and Mac) tags are specified in the HTML document. These tags are used to direct the browser to load the Flash Player. The HTML options from the Publish Settings dialog box can be used to change these settings.

A description of the HTML options follows:

Template—Flash provides several templates that create different HTML coding. For example, selecting Flash HTTPS creates HTML coding suitable for a secure HTTP connection.

Dimensions—This option sets the values for the Width and Height attributes in the OBJECT and EMBED tags and is used to set the size of the Flash movie window in the browser. You can choose to match the size of the movie, enter the size in pixels, or set the movie dimensions as a percentage of the browser window.

Playback—These options control the movie's playback and features, including:
- Paused at start—pauses the movie until the user takes some action.
- Loop—repeats the movie.
- Display menu—displays a shortcut menu (with options such as zoom in and out, step forward and back, rewind, and play) when the user right-clicks (Win) or [control] clicks (Mac) the movie in the browser.

- Device font (Win)—allows you to substitute system fonts for fonts not installed on the user's computer.

Quality—This option allows you to specify the quality of the appearance of objects within the frames. Selecting low quality increases playback speed, but reduces image quality, while selecting high quality results in the opposite effect.

Window Mode—This option allows you to specify settings for transparency, positioning, and layering.

HTML alignment—This option allows you to position the movie in the browser window. Center alignment is the default setting.

Scale—If you have changed the movie's original width and height, you can use this option to place the movie within specified boundaries.

Flash alignment—This option allows you to align the movie within the Flash movie window.

Determining Movie Placement in a Browser Window

When you publish a movie for delivery on the Internet, you need to be concerned with where in a browser window the movie will appear. The placement is controlled by settings in the HTML document. You can specify the settings when you publish the movie. A Flash movie is displayed within a Flash movie window. You can have the Flash movie window match the size of the movie or use the HTML tab in the Publish Settings dialog box to specify a different size. Figure 18 shows the relationships among the movie dimensions, the Flash movie window, the browser window, and the HTML settings. In this example, the dimensions for the Flash movie window are set to Percent (Width:

50%, Height: 25%). This means that the Flash movie window will span only half of the width of the browser and that the height of the Flash movie window will be one quarter of the height of the Flash movie. The original height of the Flash movie is 400 px, so 25 percent of that height is 100 px. The HTML alignment, that is where the Flash movie window appears in the browser, is set to right. The Flash alignment, that is where the Flash movie appears in the Flash movie window, is also set to right.

When you reduce the percent of one Flash movie window dimension below 100, the other Flash movie dimension is reduced to keep the same aspect ratio. In this example, the Flash movie window height of 25 percent causes the Flash movie height to be resized to 100. Then, the Flash movie width is resized to 100 to maintain the same 1:1 aspect ratio (as the original dimensions, which were 400 x 400).

FIGURE 18

Relationships among the Flash movie dimensions, Flash movie window and browser window, and the HTML settings

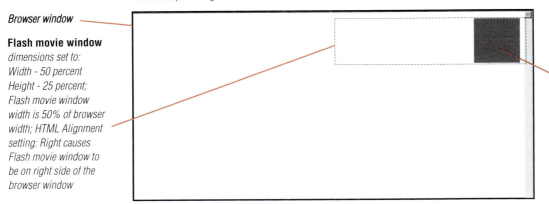

Browser window

Flash movie window
dimensions set to:
Width - 50 percent
Height - 25 percent;
Flash movie window
width is 50% of browser
width; HTML Alignment
setting: Right causes
Flash movie window to
be on right side of the
browser window

Flash Movie
dimensions set to:
Width - 400 px
Height - 400 px
Actual display size is
100 x 100 caused
by Flash movie window
dimensions;
Flash Alignment Horizontal
setting: Right causes Flash
movie to be on right side of
the Flash movie window

Change HTML publish settings

1. Open planeFun.fla, click **File** on the menu bar, then click **Publish Settings**.

2. Click the **HTML tab**.

3. Click the **Dimensions list arrow**, then click **Percent**.

4. Double-click the **Height text box**, type **50**, then compare your settings on the HTML tab to Figure 19.

    Specifying 100 percent for the width and 50 percent for the height causes the Flash movie window to be as wide as the browser window and approximately one-half the height of the browser window.

5. Verify the Flash alignment Horizontal option is set to Center.

6. Click **Publish**, then click **OK**.

7. Click **File** on the menu bar, point to **Publish Preview**, then click **Default-(HTML)**.

8. Click the **Start button**, then view the movie.

    TIP The Flash movie window, which is transparent to the visitor, is the full width of the browser because the width setting of the movie window was specified as 100% in the HTML settings. The Flash movie is centered within the Flash movie window in the browser because the horizontal alignment for the Flash movie was specified as centered. The vertical setting has no effect on the placement of the Flash movie because the movie height is the same height as the Flash movie window height.

9. Close the browser.

You resized the Flash movie window by changing the HTML publish settings, which in turn resized the Flash movie.

FIGURE 19
Changing the HTML publish settings

This affects the size of the Flash movie window in the browser

This affects the placement of the Flash movie window in the browser. Default is center alignment

This affects the placement of the Flash movie in the Flash movie window

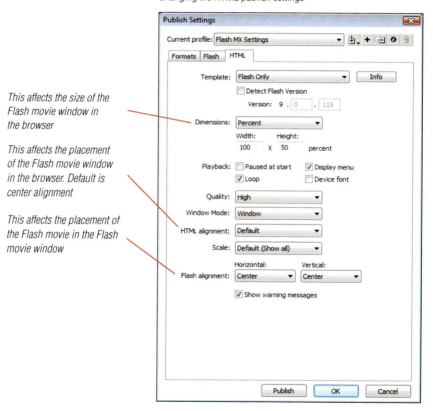

FIGURE 20
Changing the HTML code

```
 planeFun-caption.html - Notepad
File  Edit  Format  View  Help
            'quality', 'high',
            'pluginspage', 'http://www.adobe.com/go/getflashplayer',
            'align', 'middle',
            'play', 'true',
            'loop', 'true',
            'scale', 'showall',
            'wmode', 'window',
            'devicefont', 'false',
            'id', 'planeFun',
            'bgcolor', '#ffffff',
            'name', 'planeFun',
            'menu', 'true',
            'allowFullScreen', 'false',
            'allowScriptAccess','sameDomain',
            'movie', 'planeFun',
            'salign', '',
            ); //end AC code
</script>
<noscript>
        <object classid="clsid:d27cdb6e-ae6d-11cf-96b8-444553540000"
codebase="http://download.macromedia.com/pub/shockwave/cabs/flash/swflash.cab#version=9,0,0,0"
width="100%" height="50%" id="planeFun" align="middle">
        <param name="allowScriptAccess" value="sameDomain" />
        <param name="allowFullScreen" value="false" />
        <param name="movie" value="planeFun.swf" /><param name="quality" value="high" /><param
name="bgcolor" value="#ffffff" />        <embed src="planeFun.swf" quality="high" bgcolor="#ffffff"
width="100%" height="50%" name="planeFun" align="middle" allowScriptAccess="sameDomain"
allowFullScreen="false" type="application/x-shockwave-flash"
pluginspage="http://www.adobe.com/go/getflashplayer" />
        </object>
</noscript>
<br/>
<h3><center><font color="red">Having PlaneFun!!!</font></center></h3>
</body>
</html>
```

Your code may vary

Edit an HTML document

1. Open a text editor such as Notepad (Win) or TextEdit (Mac).

2. Click **File** on the text editor menu bar, click **Open**, change the Files of type to **All Files** (if necessary), navigate to planeFun.html, verify the Ignore rich text commands check box is checked (Mac), click **planeFun.html**, click **open** in the text editor window, then maximize the editor window as needed.

3. Scroll to the bottom of the window, click to the left of </body>, then press **[Enter]** to insert a blank line above </body>.

4. Click the blank line, type **
, then press **[Enter] (Win) or **[return]** (Mac).

5. Type **<h3> <font color="red">Having PlaneFun!!!</font> </h3>**, then compare the text you typed with the boxed text in Figure 20.

6. Save the file with the file name **planeFun-caption.html**, then close the text editor.

7. Use your file management program to navigate to the folder where you save your Data Files, then double-click **plane Fun-caption.html** to open the movie in your browser.

   The text you added appears centered on the screen in red.

8. Close your browser.

9. Close the movie.

10. Exit Flash.

You edited an HTML document to display format-ted text below the Flash movie.

Publish using default settings.

1. Start Flash, open fl6_4.fla, then save it as **skillsdemo6**. (*Notes*: When you open the file, you may receive a warning message that the font is missing. You can replace this font with the default, or with any other appropriate font on your computer. If a message appears indicating that you need QuickTime, you will need to install the program to continue.)
2. Open the Publish Settings dialog box.
3. Verify that the Formats tab is selected and the Flash and HTML options are the only Format types checked.
4. Click Publish, then click OK to close the dialog box.
5. Use your file management program to navigate to the drive and folder where your Data Files are stored to view the skillsdemo6.html and skillsdemo6.swf files.
6. Return to the Flash program.
7. Use the Publish Preview feature to display the movie in a browser or HTML editor.
8. Close your browser or HTML editor.
9. Save your work.

Create a JPEG image.

1. Select frame 60 on the Timeline.
2. Open the Publish Settings dialog box.
3. Click the Formats tab (if necessary), click the JPEG Image check box, then click the JPEG tab.
4. Click Publish, then click OK to close the dialog box.
5. Use your file management program to navigate to the folder with the JPEG file.

6. Open your browser, and then open the JPEG file.
7. Close the browser, return to the Flash program, then save your work.

Test a movie.

1. Click Control on the menu bar, then click Test Movie to view the movie in the Flash Player window.
2. Turn off the loop feature. (*Hint*: Click Control, then deselect the Loop check box.)
3. Set the Download Setting to DSL (32.6 KB/s) if it is not already set to that setting.
4. Display the Bandwidth Profiler if it is not already displayed, click View on the menu bar, then click Frame By Frame Graph if it is not already selected.
5. Use controls on the Control menu to rewind the movie. (Notice the bar on the Timeline for frame 1 is just under 256 KB, which is way above the red base line. The large photo is in frame 1, which could cause the movie to have a slow start.)
6. Close the Flash Player window.

Optimize a movie.

1. Select frame 1 on the sedona-photo layer, verify the image is selected on the Stage, then delete the image.
2. Replace the image with the sedona-sm from the Library panel.
3. Position the sedona-sm image approximately two-thirds of the way down the Stage and centered across the Stage.
4. Save the movie.

5. Test the movie within the Flash Player window by simulating a DSL download (Notice the bar on the Timeline for frame 1 is under 32 KB. This allows the movie to start more quickly.)
6. Close the Flash Player window.

Change HTML publish settings.

1. Display the Publish Settings dialog box, and then click the HTML tab.
2. Change the Dimensions to Percent, then change the width to **100%** and the height to **40%**.
3. Click Publish, then click OK to close the dialog box.
4. Use the Publish Preview feature to view the movie in a browser.
5. Close the browser.
6. Save your work.

Edit an HTML document.

1. Open a text editor.
2. Open the skillsdemo6.html file, then save it as **skillsdemo6-caption.html**.
3. Scroll to the end of the window, insert a blank line above the </body> tag.
4. Type **
**, then press [Enter] to insert a new line.
5. Type **<h3> <font color="green">Beautiful Northern Arizona</font> </h3>**.
6. Save your work.
7. Display skillsdemo6-caption.html in your browser.
8. Close the browser.
9. Close the text editor.

Add a background.

1. Verify skillsdemo6.fla is the active file, then insert a new layer and move it below the sedona-photo layer.
2. Name the new layer **background**.
3. Select frame 1 on the background layer.
4. Display the Library panel (if necessary).
5. Drag the g_background graphic symbol to the center of the Stage.
6. Click the last frame on the Timeline associated with content so your screen looks like Figure 21.
7. Save your work, then use the Publish Preview feature to view the movie in a browser.

Add a preloader.

1. Click frame 1 on the Timeline.
2. Click Edit on the menu bar, point to Timeline, then click Select All Frames.
3. Point to any frame on the Timeline and drag the frames to the right so they start in frame 11.
4. Insert a new layer and name it **labels**.
5. Click frame 11 on the labels layer to select it, insert a keyframe, then display the Properties panel and type **startofMovie** in the Name text box in the LABEL area.
6. Insert a keyframe in frame 70 on the labels layer and type **endofMovie** in the Name text box in the LABEL area.
7. Add a new layer and name it **preloader Script**.

8. Insert an ifFrameLoaded action in frame 1 to check if all the frame have been loaded and, if so, go to and play the startofMovie frame. Also, insert a gotoAndPlay(1) action in frame 10 on the preloader Script layer to cause a loop in the preloader frames.
9. Add a new layer and name it **preloader Animation**, then have the words "**Please wait**" appear in the first four frames and not appear in the last six frames of the ten frames used for the preloader. This will cause the words Please wait to flash until all the frames are loaded.
10. Test the movie, and use the Simulate Download feature to view the preloader.
11. Save your work, then exit Flash.

FIGURE 21

Completed Skills Review

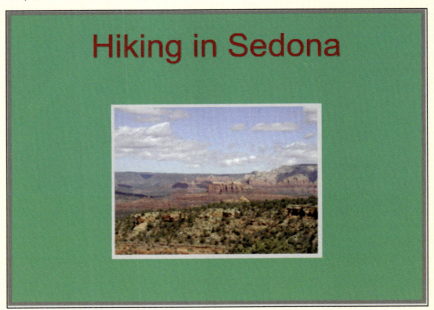

The Ultimate Tours travel company has asked you to create a website, a GIF animation, and a JPEG image using movies you created in previous chapters.

1. Open ultimatetours5.fla (the file you created in Chapter 5 Project Builder 1) and save it as **ultimatetours6**.
2. Use the Publish Settings dialog box to publish the movie using the default setting for the Flash and HTML formats.
3. Use the Publish Preview feature to display the movie in the browser.
4. Display the GIF format tab in the Publish Settings dialog box, and make a change in the dimensions.
5. Create a GIF animation.
6. Display the GIF animation in your browser.
7. Create a JPEG image of the Mystery Ships screen, as shown in Figure 22.
8. Display the JPEG image in your browser.
9. Make a change in the HTML publish settings, then display the movie in your browser.
10. Edit the HTML document using a text editor to add caption.
11. Save the edited HTML file as **ultimatetours6-caption.html**, then display the movie in your browser.
12. Save the ultimatetours6.fla file.

FIGURE 22
Sample completed Project Builder 1

In this project you will choose a Flash movie you developed from this book or one you developed on your own. You will make changes to the publish settings, create a GIF animation, a JPEG image, and edit the HTML document. Figure 23 shows a JPEG image with a caption for a sample movie.

FIGURE 23

Sample completed Project Builder 2

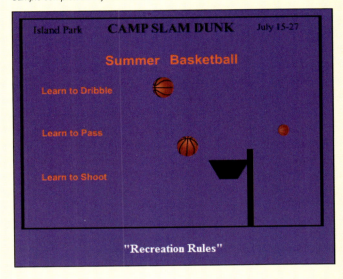

1. Open a movie you developed from this book or one you developed on your own, then save it as **publish6**.
2. Use the Publish Settings dialog box to publish the movie using the default setting for the Flash and HTML formats.
3. Use the Publish Preview feature to display the movie in the browser.
4. Display the GIF format tab in the Publish Settings dialog box, and make a change in the dimensions.
5. Create a GIF animation.
6. Display the GIF animation in your browser.
7. Create a JPEG image of the last frame of the movie.
8. Display the JPEG image in your browser.
9. Make a change in the HTML publish settings, then display the movie in your browser.
10. Edit the HTML document using a text editor to add a caption.
11. Save the edited HTML file as **publish6-caption.html**, then display the movie in your browser.
12. Save the publish6.fla file.

Preparing and Publishing Movies

Figure 24 shows the home page of a website. Study the figure and complete the following questions. For each question, indicate how you determined your answer.

1. Connect to the Internet, go to *www.yha.com.au/itinerary/index.cfm?*

2. Open a document in a word processor or open a new Flash movie, save the file as **dpc6**, then answer the following questions. (*Hint*: Use the Text tool in Flash.)

   ■ What seems to be the purpose of this site?

   ■ Who would be the target audience?

   ■ How might the Bandwidth Profiler be used when developing this site?

   ■ Assuming there is a pause in the playing of a Flash movie on the site, what suggestions would you make to eliminate the pause?

   ■ What would be the value of creating a GIF animation from one of the animations on the site?

■ What would be the value of creating a JPEG image from one of the animations on the site?

■ What suggestions would you make to improve the design, and why?

FIGURE 24
Design Project

This is a continuation of the Portfolio Project in Chapter 5, which is the development of a personal portfolio. In this project, you will create a website and a JPEG image with the movies you have created.

1. Open portfolio5.fla (the file you created in Portfolio Project, Chapter 5) and save it as **portfolio6**. (*Hint* : When you open the file, you may receive a warning message that the font is missing. You can replace this font with the default, or with any other appropriate font on your computer.)

2. Use the Publish Settings dialog box to publish the movie using the default settings for the Flash and HTML formats.

3. Use the Publish Preview feature to display the movie in the browser.

4. Create a JPEG image of the first frame of the movie.

5. Display the JPEG image in your browser, and compare it to the example shown in Figure 25.

6. Use the Bandwidth Profiler to display a frame-by-frame graph of the movie and to determine which frame may cause a pause in the movie at a 28.8 (2.3 KB/s) connection speed. (*Note:* Specifying 28.8 (2.3 KB/s) as the connection speed enables you to identify any pauses and practice using the Bandwidth Profiler.)

7. Make a change in the movie to help optimize it.

8. Make a change in the HTML publish settings, then display the movie in your browser.

9. Edit the HTML document using a text editor to add a caption.

10. Save the edited HTML file as **portfolio6-caption.html**, then display the movie in your browser.

11. Save portfolio6.fla.

FIGURE 25
Sample completed Portfolio Project

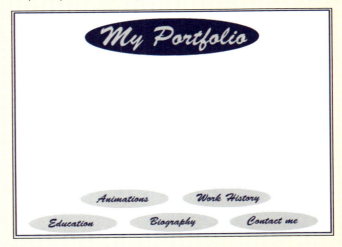

IMPORTING AND
MODIFYING GRAPHICS

1. Understand and import graphics

2. Break apart bitmaps and use bitmap fills

3. Trace bitmap graphics

4. Use the Deco tool with imported graphics

7 IMPORTING AND
MODIFYING GRAPHICS

Introduction

Graphics are vital to websites and applications. A single drawing, chart, or photograph can illustrate what might take many pages of narrative text to communicate. In the end, the image may do a better job of creating a lasting impression or establishing a mood. Within your movies, you may often find yourself wanting to use a logo or image that originated in another application. In previous chapters, you learned to create graphics using the drawing tools on the Tools panel. As you have seen in previous chapters, you are not limited to just what you can draw within your movie. You can also import and even animate vector and bitmap graphics that have been created or modified in other applications.

Importing vector graphics from an application such as Adobe Fireworks or Adobe Illustrator is easy—the vector graphics are treated almost the same as if you created them in Adobe Flash.

Importing bitmap graphics is easy, too, but working with them can be more difficult. Using bitmap graphics can increase the file size of your movies dramatically, resulting in slower download times. When considering images for your movies, it is most efficient to use vector graphics or to create graphics directly within Flash.

In this chapter, you will practice importing graphics that have been created outside the Flash environment. For those who are "artistically-challenged," importing graphics from other applications can often help to make up for less-than-perfect drawing skills. You can import a wide variety of vector and bitmap graphics, including drawings and photographs. Once the graphics are in your library, you can place them on the Stage, where you can trace them, break them apart, use them to fill an object, optimize them, and animate them.

Tools You'll Use

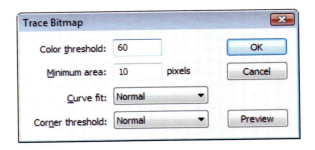

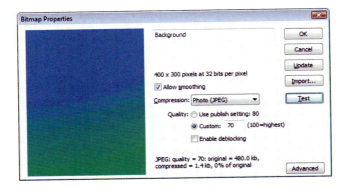

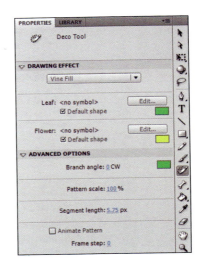

UNDERSTAND AND IMPORT GRAPHICS

What You'll Do

 In this lesson, you will import graphics from several different drawing and image-editing programs.

Understanding the Formats

Because Flash is a vector-based application, all graphics and motion within the application are calculated according to mathematical formulas. This vector-based format results in a smaller file size, as well as a robust ability to resize movies without a notable loss in quality.

When you import bitmapped graphics, some of the vector-based benefits change dramatically. A bitmap graphic, also called a **raster graphic**, is based on pixels, not on a mathematical formula. Importing multiple bitmap graphics increases the file size of your movie and decreases flexibility in terms of resizing the movie.

Flash gives you the ability to import both vector and bitmap graphics from applications such as Adobe Fireworks, Illustrator, and Photoshop. In many cases, you can retain features, such as layers, transparency, and animation, when you import graphics.

Importing Different Graphic Formats: An Overview

There are several ways of bringing external graphics into your movie, including import or cut and paste. Generally, the best way to bring a graphic into your movie is to **import** it by selecting the Import option on the File menu. Then you can choose the Import to Stage command to have the graphic placed on the Stage or choose the Import to Library command to have the graphic placed only in the library. Next, you navigate to the graphic of your choice. Figure 1 displays the Import to Library dialog box with the All Files option selected.

If the original graphic has layers, Flash can create new layers associated with that graphic in your document, depending on the file type and the settings you specify when you import the graphic. Flash automatically places the additional layers on the Timeline or inside a movie clip symbol, when applicable.

If you are importing large numbers of graphics, you can import a group of graphics (of the same file type and from a single folder), all of which will automatically use the same settings, enabling you to choose your import preferences just once.

For some file formats, you can also copy and paste across applications. This is a quicker process than importing. However, it provides less flexibility. For example, when you copy and paste across applications, the graphic becomes a flattened bitmap. So, the contents of layers are not available to be manipulated and the advantages of vector graphics, such as smaller file sizes and resizing without distortion, are lost.

Using Fireworks PNG Files

You can import Fireworks PNG files as flattened bitmap graphics or as editable objects. If you choose to import a PNG file as a flattened graphic, Flash will automatically convert the graphic to a bitmap image.

When you insert a PNG file as an editable object, it retains its vector format as well as its layers, transparency features, and filters

FIGURE 1

Import to Library dialog box

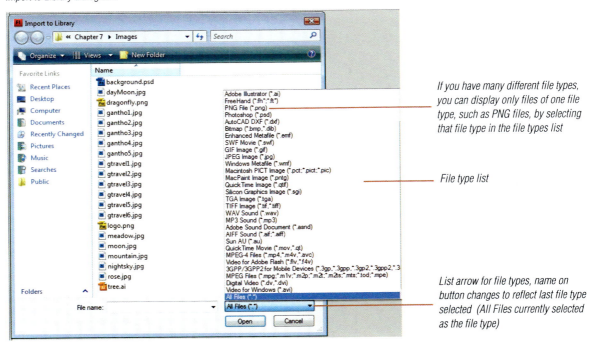

If you have many different file types, you can display only files of one file type, such as PNG files, by selecting that file type in the file types list

File type list

List arrow for file types, name on button changes to reflect last file type selected (All Files currently selected as the file type)

(such as bevels). If you click the Keep all paths editable option, Flash imports the PNG file as a movie clip symbol. All the features of the PNG file will be intact inside the movie clip symbol that is stored in the library. Paths are the segments, such as lines, of a graphic that can be individually edited. To edit features of an imported file, open the movie clip in the edit window and make the changes.

Fireworks uses Pages to contain selected layers, which in turn contain the paths. Pages also contain the settings such as size, color, and image resolution that are applied to different parts of a graphic. For example, in a picture of a child on a bike, one page might contain the settings for the bike and the other page might contain the settings

for the child. If a PNG file has more than one page, you can specify which pages to import. Figure 2 shows the Import Fireworks Document dialog box, which you use to set the import settings for a PNG file.

Importing Adobe Illustrator Files

Adobe Illustrator is an excellent program for creating artwork that is to be imported into Flash. Illustrator AI files are vector-based. So, when imported as a movie clip, they preserve most of their attributes including filters (such as drop shadows) and blends (such as transparency settings). In addition, Flash allows you to convert Illustrator graphic layers to Flash layers. This allows quite a bit of flexibility when editing and animating an Illustrator file in Flash.

Importing Adobe Photoshop Files

Flash also allows you to import Photoshop PSD files into a Flash document. One advantage of using Photoshop to create graphics and enhance photographs is that the drawing and selection tools, as well as the photo-retouching features, allow you to produce more creative and complex images. The Photoshop tools allow you to create high-quality artwork before you import the graphic into Flash. A key feature of importing PSD files is that you can choose to have the Photoshop layers imported as Flash layers. This allows you to edit individual parts of an image, such as animating text, or to use the entire graphic, such as creating a button using a

FIGURE 2
Import Fireworks Document dialog box

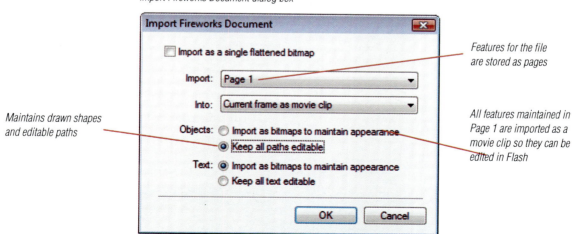

Maintains drawn shapes and editable paths

Features for the file are stored as pages

All features maintained in Page 1 are imported as a movie clip so they can be edited in Flash

photograph, once the graphic is in your Flash document.

The process for importing Photoshop files into Flash follows. First, open a Flash document and select the Import option from the File menu. Then, choose to import to the Stage or to the library, and then navigate to and select the PSD file you want to import. An Import dialog box opens, as shown in Figure 3. Here you decide whether or not you want to be able to edit the contents (text, image, background, etc.) of each PSD layer. If you choose not to make a layer editable, the contents are flattened as a bitmap image. If you choose to make a layer editable, a movie clip symbol that contains the graphic information is created using the layer contents. When importing to the Stage, other options allow you to specify that the contents of the imported file retain the same relative position they had in Photoshop and that the Flash Stage resize so it is the same size as the Photoshop document.

Importing Bitmaps

Flash allows you to use and modify imported bitmaps in a variety of ways. You can control the size, compression, and **anti-aliasing** of an imported bitmap. Anti-aliasing is the process of smoothing the edges of a graphic so they appear less jagged. This is done by blending colors. For example, if there is a black graphic on a white background, the pixels on the edges of the graphic would be turned to shades of gray. You can also use a bitmap as a fill or convert a bitmap to a vector by tracing it or breaking it apart.

Once you import a bitmap, it becomes an element in the library. To edit the graphic from the Library panel, double-click the object to open the Bitmap Properties dialog box. Using the dialog box, you can compress the graphic and allow for smoothing (anti-aliasing) on the graphic.

If an instance of a bitmap symbol is on the Stage, you can use the Properties panel to numerically change the dimensions of the graphic on the Stage as well as swap it for another graphic and edit the bitmap in an outside application.

FIGURE 3

Photoshop Import "background.psd" to Stage dialog box

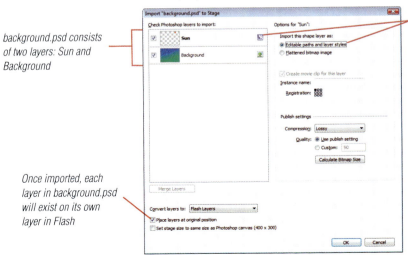

background.psd consists of two layers: Sun and Background

Once imported, each layer in background.psd will exist on its own layer in Flash

Sun layer is selected; it is converted to a movie clip so its features will be editable

Import a layered Fireworks PNG file as a movie clip symbol

1. Start Flash, create a new **Flash (ActionScript 2.0) document**, save it as **gsamples**, then verify the Stage size is 550 × 400 pixels.

2. Display the Library panel.

3. Click **File** on the menu bar, point to **Import**, click **Import to Stage**, then navigate to the drive and folder where your Data Files are stored.

4. Click the **list arrow** for the file types, click **PNG File (*.png)**, click **dragonfly.png**, then click **Open** (Win) or **Import** (Mac).

   | TIP If you have difficulty finding the file types list arrow, refer to Figure 1.

5. In the Import Fireworks Document dialog box, verify the Import as a single flattened bitmap check box is deselected and the Into: option is set to Current frame as movie clip.

6. Click the **Keep all paths editable option button** in the Objects area to select it, then click **OK**.

7. Set the view to **Fit in Window**, click the **Pasteboard**.

8. Click the **expand arrow** ▶ next to the Fireworks Objects folder in the Library panel, then continue to expand folders until there are no more to expand, as shown in Figure 4.

9. Click the **collapse arrow** ▼ next to the Fireworks Objects folder in the Library panel.

10. Name Layer 1 as **dragonfly**.

You imported a Fireworks PNG file as a movie clip to the Stage, which automatically generated a folder containing the movie clip and supporting files in the Library panel.

FIGURE 4
Imported Fireworks PNG graphic file

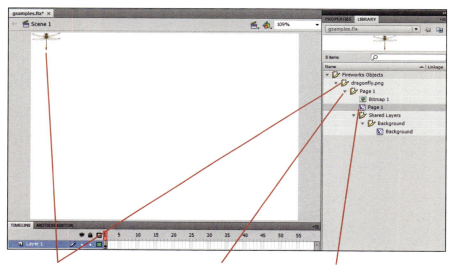

Importing the PNG file to the Stage automatically generated the dragonfly.png folder in the Library panel

The Page folder containing the features (size, color, etc.) of the graphic.

The movie clip containing any editable paths

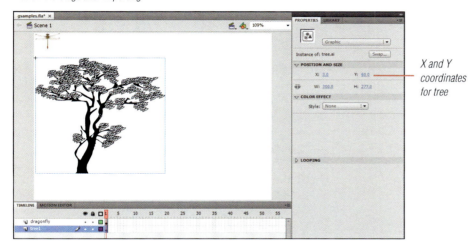

FIGURE 5

Tree on the Stage after importing

X and Y coordinates for tree

1. Click **File** on the menu bar, point to **Import**, then click **Import to Library**.

2. Click the **list arrow** for the file types, click **Adobe Illustrator (*.ai)**, click **tree.ai**, then click **Open** (Win) or **Import to Library** (Mac). The Import "tree.ai" to Library dialog box appears.

3. Verify the Convert layers to option is set to Flash Layers, then verify both Import unused symbols and Import as a single bitmap image check boxes are deselected.

4. Click **OK**.

   A new graphic symbol, tree.ai, appears in the Library panel.

5. Insert a **new layer**, name it **tree1**, then drag the **tree1 layer** beneath the dragonfly layer.

6. Verify that frame 1 of the tree1 layer is selected, then drag the **tree.ai graphic symbol** from the Library panel to the left side of the Stage beneath the dragonfly.

7. Display the Properties panel, then verify the Lock width and height values together symbol ⊕ is broken.

8. Change the width to 300 and the height to 277.

9. Set the X: coordinate to **3.0** and the Y: coordinate to **60.0**.

10. Compare your screen to Figure 5.

You imported an Illustrator file to the library, dragged the graphic symbol to the Stage, and then resized and repositioned it.

Import an Adobe Photoshop file saved in PSD format

1. Click **File** on the menu bar, point to **Import**, then click **Import to Stage**.

2. Click the **list arrow** for the file types, click **Photoshop (*.psd)**, click **background.psd**, then click **Open** (Win) or **Import** (Mac).

   The Import to Stage dialog box opens. A check mark next to a layer means the layer will be imported.

3. Click the **Background layer** (not its check box), then verify Flattened bitmap image is selected.

4. Click the **Sun layer** (not its check box), then click **Editable paths and layer styles**.

5. Verify the Convert layers to option is set to Flash Layers, then verify the Set stage size to … option is deselected, as shown in Figure 6.

6. Click **OK**, notice the two layers that are added to the Timeline, then press **[Esc]** to deselect the newly inserted graphics.

7. Click the **Sun layer**, then click the **Delete icon** 🗑.

8. Drag the **Background layer** to below the tree1 layer.

9. Click the **background graphic** to select it, then use the Properties panel to change the width to **550** and the height to **400**.

10. Verify the X: coordinate is set to 0.0 and the Y: coordinate is set to 0.0.

    Your screen should resemble Figure 7.

11. Click the **Lock/Unlock layer icon** to lock the Background layer.

You imported a PSD file to the library, resized it, set its position on the Stage, and then locked its layer.

FIGURE 6

Completed Photoshop Import "background.psd" to Stage dialog box

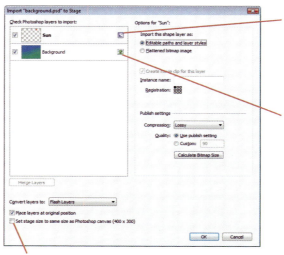

Sun layer is converted to a movie clip, which contains all the settings associated with the Sun layer

Background layer converted to a graphic symbol; its settings are not editable

Set stage size option not selected

FIGURE 7

The imported graphics placed on the Stage

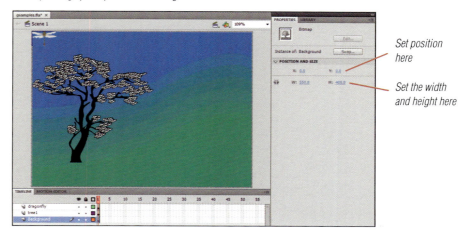

Set position here

Set the width and height here

FIGURE 8
Bitmap Properties dialog box

Original size of graphic; changing the size of the object on the Stage does not affect the original bitmap symbol

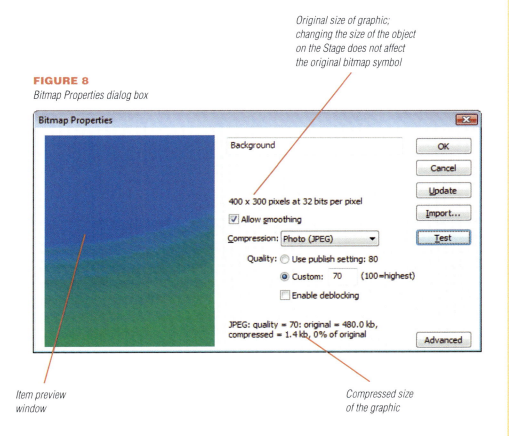

Item preview window

Compressed size of the graphic

1. Display the Library panel, then double-click the **background.psd Assets folder** to display the objects and their symbols.

2. Right-click (Win) or [control] click (Mac) the **Background bitmap symbol** in the Library panel, then click **Properties** to open the Bitmap Properties dialog box.

3. Click the **Allow smoothing check box** to select it.

4. Verify that Photo (JPEG) is selected for Compression, then click the **Custom option button** in the Quality area.

5. Type **100** in the Custom text box, then click **Test**.

   Notice the compressed size of the graphic is approximately 25 kb.

6. Change the Custom setting to **70**, then click **Test**.

   Your screen should resemble Figure 8. The Compressed size of the graphic has been reduced to less than 2 kb, with no significant reduction in the appearance of the image.

7. Click **OK**.

8. Save your work.

You compared the file sizes of different compressions and then compressed a bitmap file.

BREAK APART BITMAPS
AND USE BITMAP FILLS

What You'll Do

▶ *In this lesson, you will break apart bitmap graphics and manipulate bitmap fill graphics to create new effects.*

Breaking Apart Bitmaps

Bitmap graphics, unlike vector graphics, are made up of groups of pixels. You can break apart a bitmap graphic and edit individual pixels. Breaking apart a bitmap graphic allows increased flexibility in how you can use it within a movie. If you are planning to use unmanipulated photographs or graphics, there is no need to break apart a bitmap graphic. Once you do break apart a bitmap graphic, you can select different areas of the graphic to manipulate them separately from the graphic as a whole, including deleting the area or changing its color.

Using the Lasso Tool and the Magic Wand Tool

The Lasso tool lets you select an irregularly shaped part of a graphic, which you can then move, scale, rotate, or reshape. The Magic Wand tool is available in the Options area of the Tools panel when the Lasso tool is selected. You can use the Magic Wand tool to select areas of similar color in a bitmap graphic you have broken apart. In the properties for the Magic Wand tool, you can specify a color similarity threshold for the Magic Wand (a higher number means more matching colors will be selected).

QUICKTIP

Introducing bitmaps will always increase the file size of your movie, resulting in increased download times for the users.

Using Bitmap Fills

Until now, you have been applying solid colors and gradient fills to objects. Flash allows you to apply a bitmap fill to any drawn shape or text that has been broken apart. A **bitmap fill** is created by breaking apart a bitmap graphic and using it to fill another graphic. To do this, you break apart a bitmap graphic, use the Eyedropper tool to select the graphic and then use the Paint Bucket tool to apply the bitmap fill to a different graphic.

Figure 9 shows different bitmap fill effects. You can apply a bitmap fill to any drawn shape. If necessary, Flash will tile (repeat) the bitmap to fill the shape. You can use the Gradient Transform tool to change the size, shape, rotation, and skew of your fill, which allows you to position the original graphic exactly as you want it in the new shape.

In addition to filling shapes with a bitmap, you can also apply your bitmaps as a fill by using the Brush tool. This process involves breaking apart the bitmap graphic, selecting it with the Eyedropper tool, and then choosing a Brush tool and brush size. When you begin painting, you will see your bitmap graphic as a fill.

Selecting a Bitmap Fill with the Color Panel

If the bitmap graphic you want to use for a fill is not on the Stage, you can use the Color panel to select it. The process is to open the Color panel, choose Bitmap as the Type of fill, and then select the bitmap of your choice from the library area. If you select a bitmap fill through the Color panel, you do not have to break apart the bitmap. Figure 10 shows the Color panel with a bitmap fill selected.

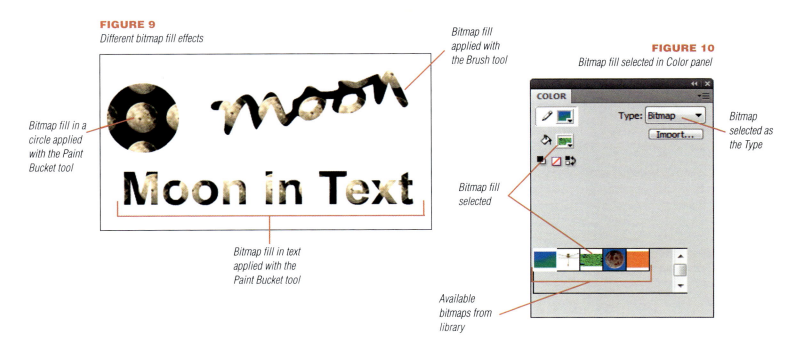

FIGURE 9
Different bitmap fill effects

Bitmap fill applied with the Brush tool

Bitmap fill in a circle applied with the Paint Bucket tool

Bitmap fill in text applied with the Paint Bucket tool

FIGURE 10
Bitmap fill selected in Color panel

Bitmap selected as the Type

Bitmap fill selected

Available bitmaps from library

Break apart a bitmap

1. Verify that the gsamples.fla document is open, click **File** on the menu bar, point to **Import**, then click **Import to Library**.

2. Click the **list arrow** for the file types, click **JPEG Image (*.jpg)**, click **moon**, then click **Open** (Win) or **Import to Library** (Mac).

3. Insert a **new layer**, move it to just above the background layer, then name it **moon**.

4. Click **frame 1** on the moon layer, then drag the **moon graphic symbol** to the Stage, as shown in Figure 11.

5. Verify the moon is selected, click **Modify** on the menu bar, then click **Break Apart**.

6. Click the **Selection tool** , then click the **Pasteboard** to deselect the moon graphic.

7. Click the **Lasso tool** on the Tools panel, then click the **Magic Wand Settings tool** in the Options area of the Tools panel.

8. Click the **Smoothing list arrow** in the Magic Wand Settings dialog box, click **Pixels**, change the Threshold to **20**, then click **OK**.

9. Click the **Magic Wand tool** in the Options area of the Tools panel, point to the **blue background** of the moon graphic as shown in Figure 12, then click to select the blue background.

10. Click **Edit** on the menu bar, then click **Cut**.

11. Click the **Selection tool** , drag the **moon graphic** to the upper-right corner of the Stage, click the **Pasteboard**, then compare your Stage to Figure 13.

You broke apart and edited a bitmap graphic.

FIGURE 11
Moon on Stage after importing

FIGURE 12
Using the Magic Wand to select the background color

FIGURE 13
Positioning the moon graphic

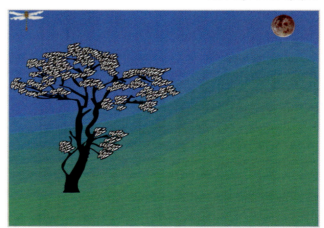

FIGURE 14
Selecting a bitmap fill

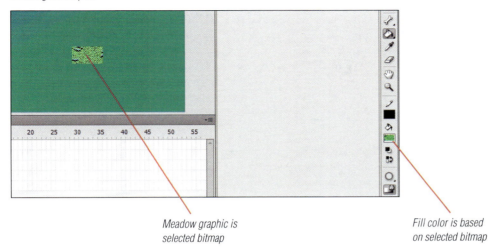

Meadow graphic is
selected bitmap

Fill color is based
on selected bitmap

FIGURE 15
Filling a shape with a bitmap

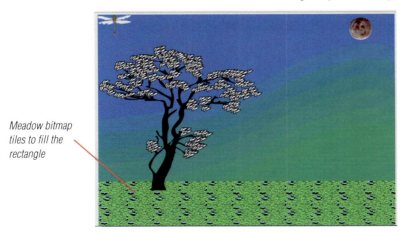

Meadow bitmap
tiles to fill the
rectangle

Lesson 2   Break Apart Bitmaps and Use Bitmap Fills

Use and edit a bitmap fill

1. Click **File** on the menu bar, point to **Import**, click **Import to Library**, then open **meadow.jpg**.

2. Insert a **new layer**, move it to just below the tree1 layer on the Timeline, then name it **meadow**.

3. Click **frame 1** of the meadow layer, then drag the **meadow graphic symbol** from the Library panel to an empty area of the Stage.

4. Click **Modify** on the menu bar, then click **Break Apart**.

5. Click the **Eyedropper tool** on the Tools panel, click the **meadow graphic** on the Stage, then compare your screen to Figure 14.

   TIP   The Eyedropper tool lets you select a fill from an existing object so you can apply it to another object. Notice the color swatch for the Fill color tool in the Tools panel displays the meadow pattern.

6. Click the **Selection tool** on the Tools panel, then verify the meadow graphic on the Stage is selected.

7. Click **Edit** on the menu bar, then click **Cut** to remove the graphic from the Stage.

8. Select the **Rectangle tool** on the Tools panel, then set the Stroke color to **No color** .

9. Using Figure 15 as a guide, draw a **rectangle** covering a small part of the tree trunk across the bottom of the Stage.

   The rectangle fills with a tiling bitmap of the meadow.

10. Save your work.

You used the Eyedropper tool to select a fill from an object, then applied the fill to another object.

TRACE BITMAP
GRAPHICS

What You'll Do

▶ *In this lesson, you will trace a bitmap graphic to create vectors and special effects.*

Understanding Tracing

Tracing is an outstanding feature if you are illustration-challenged or if you need to convert a bitmap graphic into a vector graphic for animation purposes. When you apply the trace function, you turn a pure bitmap into vector paths and fills with varying degrees of detail. If you keep all the detail in a graphic, you end up with very detailed, intricate vector paths, which tend to increase file size. If you remove some of the detail, you can turn a photograph into a more abstract-looking drawing, which usually requires less file size.

Once traced, you can remove the original graphic from the library and work with only the traced paths and shapes, thereby reducing the movie's file size. The traced shapes act just like shapes you have drawn, with fills, lines, and strokes that you can manipulate and change. Tracing allows a graphic to act as a graphic drawn directly in Flash, which is why you are able to select vector fills based on color and change the color. You can also select vector paths (lines) and

manipulate the paths to alter the shape of a graphic.

> **QUICK**TIP
> Tracing bitmaps can often take a long time, especially if it is a detailed trace or a large graphic.

One of the challenges with using the trace feature comes when you try to animate a traced graphic. Tracing creates paths and shapes, but every piece of the original graphic remains on one layer. To animate or tween between pieces of the shape, you often have to isolate parts of the object onto their own layers. Figure 16 shows the before and after effects of tracing a graphic. In this example, you can see how tracing makes the original photograph appear more abstract. Figure 17 shows the traced graphic cut up for animation.

Using the Trace Settings

It is possible to trace a graphic using very detailed or less detailed settings. Your traced graphic will look more like the original graphic if you retain more detail.

If you want the traced graphic to look more abstract, use less detail. Remember, the greater the detail, the greater the file size. In Figure 18, three different trace effects are created by adjusting the trace values.

There are four options that affect how detailed the trace will appear: Color threshold, Minimum area, Curve fit, and Corner threshold. Color threshold compares two side-by-side pixels; if the difference is less than the color threshold, the two are considered the same color. Color threshold options include integers between 1 and 500. Minimum area sets the number of surrounding pixels to consider, with options between 1 and 1000. Curve fit determines how smoothly outlines are drawn. Corner threshold works with sharp edges to retain them or smooth them out. Figure 19 shows the Trace Bitmap dialog box.

QUICKTIP

You can no longer trace a bitmap graphic once you break it apart.

FIGURE 17
Dividing a traced graphic by color

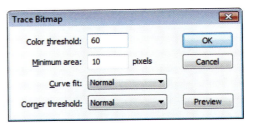

Sections of the moon selected by color and moved

FIGURE 16
Before and after tracing a bitmap

FIGURE 18
Three different effects with different trace settings

FIGURE 19
Trace Bitmap dialog box

Trace a bitmap graphic

1. Click the **Selection tool** ![selection tool icon] on the Tools panel, click the **moon graphic** on the Stage to select it, then press **[Delete]**.

2. Click **frame 1** on the moon layer to select the frame, then drag the **moon.jpg graphic** from the Library panel to the upper-right corner of the Stage.

3. Verify that the moon is selected, click **Modify** on the menu bar, point to **Bitmap**, then click **Trace Bitmap**.

4. Click the **Color threshold text box**, type **60**, click the **Minimum area text box**, type **10**, then verify the settings for Curve fit and Corner threshold are set to Normal.

5. Click **OK**, click the **Pasteboard** to deselect the moon, then compare your graphic to Figure 20.

6. Click the **Zoom tool** ![zoom tool icon] on the Tools panel, then click the **moon** to enlarge it, as shown in Figure 21.

You traced a bitmap graphic and zoomed in on it.

FIGURE 20
The traced bitmap graphic

Bitmap graphic traced

FIGURE 21
Zooming in on the moon

Importing and Modifying Graphics

FIGURE 22
Specifying a fill color

New fill color

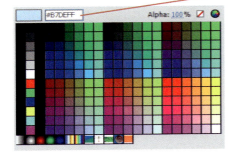

FIGURE 23
Changing the fill color

FIGURE 24
The completed screen

Your moon may
appear different

Lesson 3   Trace Bitmap Graphics

Edit a traced bitmap graphic

1. Click the **Selection tool** ➤ on the Tools panel.

2. Click the **Paint Bucket tool** ◇ on the Tools panel.

   Your Paint Bucket tool may display a lock. This is a modifier that can be used to create the appearance of masks revealing the underlying bitmap. You can toggle the lock off and on using the Lock Fill option at the bottom of the Tools panel. You can complete these steps with the Paint Bucket tool locked or unlocked.

3. Set the Fill color to **#B7DEFF**, as shown in Figure 22, then press **[Enter]**.

4. Click various parts of the moon graphic with the Paint Bucket tool ◇ to change the color to resemble Figure 23.

   Note: Click Edit on the menu bar, then click Undo to use the undo command, as needed.

5. Click the **Selection tool** ➤ on the Tools panel.

6. Click **View** on the menu bar, point to **Magnification**, then click **Fit in Window**.

   Your screen should resemble Figure 24.

7. Save your work, then close the document.

You edited a traced bitmap graphic by changing the color of parts of the bitmap.

USE THE DECO TOOL WITH
IMPORTED GRAPHICS

What You'll Do

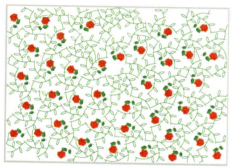

 In this lesson, you will use the Deco tool to create and animate decorative patterns.

Understanding the Deco Tool

The Deco tool is used to create decorative patterns that incorporate imported graphics and those drawn in Flash. These patterns can be animated and added to a movie to create special effects. There are three effects you can generate with the Deco tool: Vine Fill, Grid Fill, and Symmetry Brush. These effect options are available in the Properties panel when the Deco tool is selected from the Tools panel.

Using the Vine Fill Effect

Figure 25 shows a pattern created using the Vine Fill effect. There are two parts of the Vine Fill effect that you can specify which graphic to use: the leaf and the flower. In Figure 25, the default leaf and flower are used. To change one or the other, click the corresponding Edit button and select the graphic you want to use. You can also use the advanced options to change the branch color, branch length, pattern scale, and segment length.

Using the Grid Fill Effect

Figure 26 shows a pattern created using the Grid Fill effect. You can change which graphic is used to create the Grid Fill effect. In Figure 26, a black square graphic has been used to create the Grid Fill effect. In addition to changing the graphic used, you can change the horizontal and vertical spacing and the pattern scale.

Using the Symmetry Brush Effect

Figure 27 shows a pattern created using the Symmetry Brush effect. This option allows you to arrange symbols around a central point. The green handles shown in the figures are used to add more symbols, add more

Importing and Modifying Graphics

symmetries (such as additional circles), and change the position of the symmetries.

Animating the Patterns

Any pattern created using the Deco tool can be selected, converted to a graphic or movie clip symbol, and animated by inserting a motion tween or using another animation process in Flash. Because the Vine Fill effect grows the pattern, patterns created using the Vine Fill effect can be animated by simply selecting the Animate Pattern option in the Properties panel. This will add keyframes to the Timeline corresponding to the segments created as the pattern grows.

Hint: After selecting the Deco tool on the Tools panel, if the Properties panel does not display the Deco tool properties, click the Selection tool, then click the Deco tool.

FIGURE 25
Pattern created using the Vine Fill effect

FIGURE 26
Pattern created using the Grid Fill effect

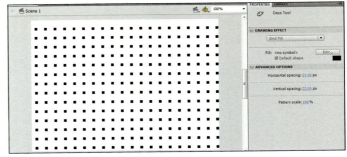

FIGURE 27
Pattern created using the Symmetry Brush effect

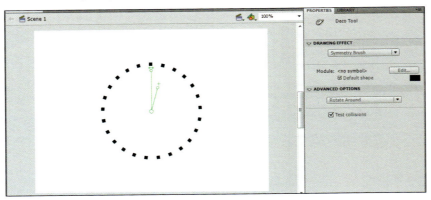

Lesson 4   Use the Deco Tool with Imported Graphics

Creating a screen design with the Deco tool

1. Open fl7_1.fla, then save it as **deco1.fla**.

    This document has an imported graphic (rose.jpg) that has been converted to a graphic symbol.

2. Click the **Deco tool** on the Tools panel, then display the Properties panel.

3. Verify your settings are the same as those shown in Figure 28.

4. Click the **Stage** to create the design.

5. Click **Edit** on the menu bar, then click **Undo Deco Tool**.

6. Click the **Deco tool**, then click the **Edit button** in the Properties panel Flower area.

7. Click **rose** in the Swap Symbol dialog box as shown in Figure 29, then click **OK**.

8. Point to the middle of the Stage, then click the mouse button.

9. Test the movie and notice that there is no animation, then close the Flash Player window.

10. Click **Edit** on the menu bar, click **Undo Deco Tool**, then click the **Deco tool**.

11. Click the **Animate pattern check box** in the ADVANCED OPTIONS area of the Properties panel to select it, point to the middle of the Stage, then click the mouse button.

    Notice the keyframes on the Timeline.

12. Test the movie, notice the animation, then close the Flash Player window.

13. Save your work, then close the document.

You created a design with the Deco tool, swapped graphics, then animated the design.

FIGURE 28
Settings for the Vine Fill effect

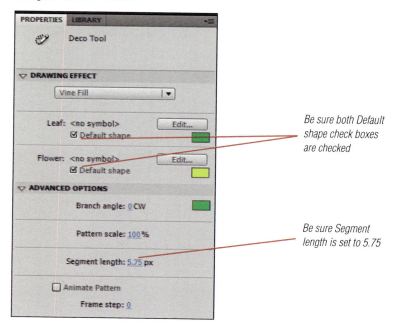

Be sure both Default shape check boxes are checked

Be sure Segment length is set to 5.75

FIGURE 29
The Swap Symbol dialog box

FIGURE 30
Pointing to above the vertical handle

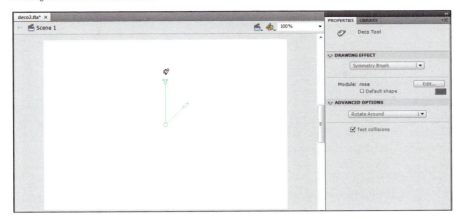

FIGURE 31
Dragging the pointer to the left to display more roses

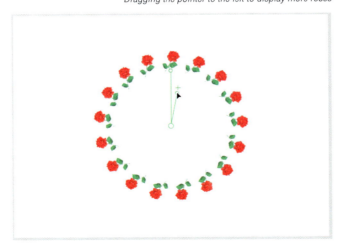

Using the Symmetry brush

1. Open fl7_1.fla, then save it as **deco2.fla**.

2. Verify the Deco tool is selected, click the **list arrow** in the DRAWING EFFECT area, then click **Symmetry Brush**.

3. Click the **Edit button** for Module in the DRAWING EFFECT area, verify rose is selected in the Swap Symbol dialog box, then click **OK**.

4. Point to above the **vertical handle** as shown in Figure 30, then click to display the circle of roses.

5. Point to between the open circle and the + on the diagonal handle, when the pointer changes to a delta symbol ▶, slowly drag the pointer to the left to display more roses as shown in Figure 31, then release the mouse button.

6. Click the **Selection tool** ▶ on the Tools panel, then draw a marquee around the roses to select them.

7. Click **Modify** on the menu bar, click **Convert to Symbol**, name the symbol **g_circle-of-roses**, select **Graphic** as the type, then click **OK**.

8. Create a motion tween and increase the tween span on the Timeline to **40**.

9. Use the Properties panel to set the rotation to **30** and the direction to **CW**.

10. Test the movie, close the Flash Player window, save your work, close the document, then exit Flash.

You used the Symmetry brush to create a circle of graphic symbols, change the number of symbols, and animate the circle.

Import graphics.

1. Create a new Flash document with a size of **550 × 400** pixels and a white background color, the view set to Fit in Window, the frame rate to **12** fps, then save it as **skillsdemo7**.
2. Make sure the Library panel is open.
3. Import the logo.png file from the drive and folder where your Data Files are stored to the library with the following settings:
   Import: Page 1
   Into: Current frame as movie clip
   Objects: Keep all paths editable
   Text: Keep all text editable
4. Import dayMoon.jpg to the library.
5. Import mountain.jpg to the library.
6. Import nightsky.jpg to the library.
7. Save your work.

Break apart bitmaps and use bitmap fills.

1. Rename Layer 1 **nightsky**.
2. Select frame 1 on the nightsky layer, drag the nightsky graphic to the Stage and break it apart.
3. Click the nightsky graphic with the Eyedropper tool, then delete the nightsky graphic from the Stage.
4. Use the Rectangle tool to create a rectangle (with nightsky for the fill and no stroke color) that spans the width of the Stage and covers the top half of the Stage.
5. Insert a new layer, name it **logo**, select frame 1 on the logo layer, and drag the logo graphic symbol to the upper-left corner of the Stage.
6. Create a new layer named **mountain**, select frame 1 on the mountain layer, and drag the mountain symbol to the bottom-center of the Stage.
7. Use the Properties panel to change the width of the mountain so that it is as wide as the Stage, 550 pixels, then move the mountain graphic so it is flush with the bottom and sides of the Stage.
8. Lock the nightsky and logo layers.
9. Save your work.

Trace bitmap graphics.

1. Trace the mountain graphic, using settings of **100** for Color threshold, **10** for Minimum area, and Normal for Curve fit and Corner threshold.
2. Deselect the graphic.
3. Verify the Fill color on the Tools panel displays the nightsky and the Stroke color is set to none.
4. Use the Paint Bucket tool to change the blue sky, in the background of the mountain, to stars.
5. Lock the mountain layer.
6. Save your work.

Create an animated pattern.

1. Insert a new layer at the top of the Timeline and name it **moons**.
2. Add a keyframe to frame 30 of each layer except the moons layer.
3. Select frame 1 of the moons layer.
4. Drag the dayMoon graphic to the Stage and break it apart.
5. Click the Lasso tool on the Tools panel, click the Magic Wand Settings button in the Options area of the Tools panel, set the Threshold to **10** and the Smoothing to Pixels.
6. Use the Magic Wand to select the blue background, then delete the background.
7. Use the Selection tool to select the dayMoon and convert it to a graphic symbol with the name g_dayMoon.
8. Delete the graphic from the Stage.

9. Select the Deco tool, set the Drawing Effect to Symmetry Brush, then change the graphic for the Module to the g_dayMoon graphic symbol.
10. Click just above the vertical handle to display the moons.
11. Use the Selection tool to click one of the moons to select all of them, then convert them to a graphic symbol with the name g_circle-of-moons.

12. With the graphic selected, insert a motion tween and extend the tween span in the Timeline to frame 30.
13. Use the Properties panel to set the rotation to **3** times.
14. Drag the moons layer to below the mountain layer.
15. Test the movie, then close the Flash Player window.
16. Compare your movie to Figure 32, then save your work.
17. Exit Flash.

FIGURE 32
Completed Skills Review

Ultimate Tours is rolling out a new "summer in December" promotion in the coming months and wants a Flash website to showcase a series of tours to Florida, Bermuda, and the Caribbean. The website should use bright, "tropical" colors and have a family appeal. Though you will eventually animate this site, Ultimate Tours would first like to see still pictures of what you are planning to do.

1. Open a new Flash document, then save it as **ultimatetours7**.
2. Set the movie properties, including the size and background color if desired.
3. Create the following text elements on separate layers:
   - A primary headline **Ultimate Tours Presents…** with an appropriate font and treatment.
   - A subheading **Our new "Summer in December" Tour Packages!** in a smaller font size.
4. Import the following JPG files from the drive and folder where your Data Files are stored to the Library panel (alternately, you can create your own graphics, obtain graphics from your computer or the Internet, or create graphics from scanned media):

   gtravel1.jpg gtravel4.jpg
   gtravel2.jpg gtravel5.jpg
   gtravel3.jpg gtravel6.jpg

5. Move three of the graphics to the Stage, each on its own layer, to create an appealing vacation collage, arranging and resizing the graphics as appropriate. (*Hint*: Some of the sample files have a white background. If you want to include one of these graphics and your Stage has a different background color, try breaking the graphic apart, then using the Magic Wand tool to erase the background of the graphic.)
6. Trace one of the graphics on the Stage to create an artistic effect and reduce file size, then delete the traced graphic from the Library panel.

FIGURE 33
Sample completed Project Builder 1

7. Create three round or square objects that will eventually become buttons—use a graphic from the Library panel as a bitmap fill for each object. Resize or skew the bitmap fill as appropriate.
8. Apply a bitmap fill to some or all the letters in the title. (*Hint*: To add a bitmap fill to text, you must first convert the characters to shapes by breaking apart the text two times.)
9. Lock all the layers.
10. Save your work, then compare your image to the example shown in Figure 33.

You have been asked to create several sample designs for the home page of a new student art, poetry, and fiction anthology website called AnthoArt. This website will showcase artwork that includes painting, woodcuts, and photography, as well as writing (including poetry and fiction).

1. Open a new movie and save it as **anthoart7**.
2. Set the movie properties, including the size and background color if desired.
3. Import the following JPG files from the drive and folder where your Data Files are stored to the Library panel (alternately, you can create your own graphics, obtain graphics from your computer or the Internet, or create graphics from scanned media):
   gantho1.jpg
   gantho2.jpg
   gantho3.jpg
   gantho4.jpg
   gantho5.jpg
4. Using a combination of tracing and breaking apart graphics, create a collage on the Stage from at least four graphics.
5. Create the title **AnthoArt**, using a bitmap fill for some or all of the letters.
6. Create an Enter button, using one of the graphics as a bitmap fill.
7. Save your work, then compare your movie image to the example shown in Figure 34.

FIGURE 34
Sample completed Project Builder 2

DESIGN PROJECT

Figure 35 shows the home page of the NASA website. Study the figure and complete the following. For each question, indicate how you determined your answer.

1. Connect to the Internet, type the URL *www.nasa.gov/missions/highlights/index.html,* then click Current Missions in the left navigation pane.

2. Open a document in a word processor or open a new Flash document, save the file as **dpc7**, then answer the following questions. (*Hint*: Use the Text tool in Flash.)

   ■ Are photographs used well in this website? Why or why not?

   ■ Could the goals and intent of the website be accomplished without the use of photographs?

   ■ Do the graphics contribute to the design of the site? If so, how?

   ■ Which file format do you think was used for the graphics?

   ■ Can you guess what file format the logo was before it was brought into Flash? Or, do you think it was recreated in the application?

   ■ Do you think the graphics in this site should be changed in any way? How?

   ■ Who do you think is the target audience for this website?

FIGURE 35
Design Project

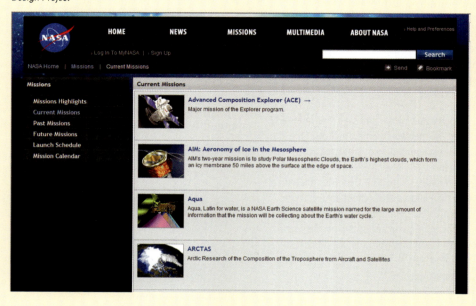

To showcase your broad range of skills, you want to add some web-related work to your portfolio. This will allow you to improve upon and continue to use websites and artwork you created previously. You will need to take screen captures of the websites you have built and convert the graphics into JPEGs using a graphics editor. Try to create at least four samples of your work.

1. Open a new Flash document, then save it as **portfolio7**.
2. Add a heading and colors as desired.
3. Import from the drive and folder where your Data Files are stored to the Library panel at least four samples of your work; the samples might be in a variety of file formats.
4. Place the samples on the Stage.
5. Resize the graphics so you can fit all four of them on the Stage at one time.
6. Add a sentence below or next to each graphic describing the graphic.
7. Save your work, then compare your movie to the example shown in Figure 36.

FIGURE 36
Sample completed Portfolio Project Page

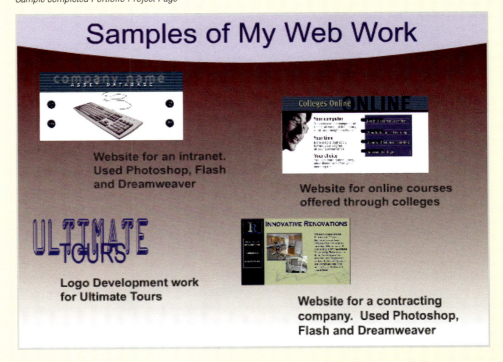

chapter

BUILDING COMPLEX
ANIMATIONS

1. Plan for complex movies and animations

2. Create an animated graphic symbol

3. Create a movie clip symbol

4. Animate buttons using movie clip symbols

ADOBE FLASH CS4

8 BUILDING COMPLEX
ANIMATIONS

Introduction

As your movies become more complex and you begin utilizing more advanced features of Flash, planning your work is critical. Part of the planning process is determining how to develop a clean Timeline, that is, with objects that are easy to recognize and manipulate, and how to optimize file size by reusing symbols as much as possible.

Creating animated graphic symbols and movie clip symbols can help meet both goals. A well-built movie consists of many small pieces of animation put together and often, of movies nested within movies. While the concept of movies

within movies might sound confusing, it is actually very logical from a file management, media management, and animation perspective. Building movies with 40 layers and lengthy tween spans can be unwieldy. The alternative is to split the many animations on the Stage into smaller, reusable pieces, and then insert these smaller pieces as needed. Creating Flash movies using reusable pieces such as movie clip symbols, allows you to have fewer motion tweens and layers in the movie. Creating animated graphic symbols and movie clip symbols also allows you greater flexibility in adding ActionScript to elements, as well as in placing elements on and off the Stage.

Tools You'll Use

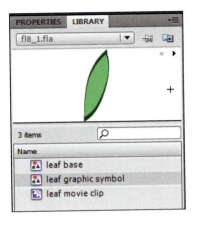

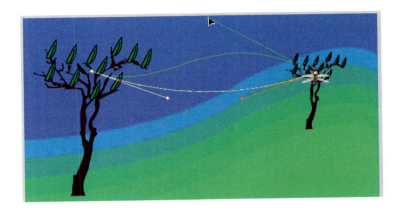

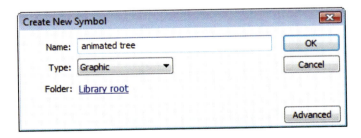

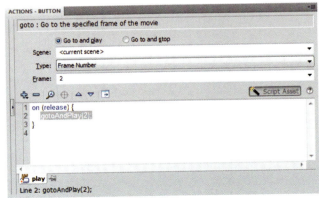

PLAN FOR COMPLEX MOVIES
AND ANIMATIONS

What You'll Do

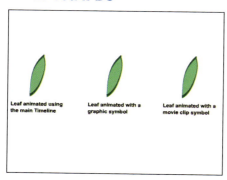

Leaf animated using
the main Timeline

Leaf animated with a
graphic symbol

Leaf animated with a
movie clip symbol

In this lesson, you will work with and compare animated graphic and movie clip symbols.

Making Effective Use of Symbols and the Library Panel

It is important to sketch out in advance what you are trying to accomplish in a movie. In addition to making development work easier, planning ahead will also allow you to organize your Library panel with more accuracy. Consider the following questions as you plan your project:

- Are there any repeated elements on the Stage? If yes, you should make them into graphic symbols. Graphic symbols should include any still element that is used on the Stage more than once. Graphic symbols might also be elements that you want to be able to tween. Keep in mind one graphic symbol can contain other graphic symbols.

- Are there any repeating or complex animations, or elements on-screen that animate while the rest of the movie is still? If so, make these animated graphic symbols or movie clip symbols.

- What kind of interactivity will your Flash movie have? You can assign ActionScript to button symbols and to movie clip symbols, but not to graphic symbols. You should use button symbols for elements used for navigation or elements that you want to be clickable. Button symbols can contain both graphic and movie clip symbols inside them.

Remember, your Library panel should house all of the building blocks for your movies. To build a logical Library panel, you should have a solid plan in place for the different elements you expect to use.

Understanding Animated Graphic Symbols

Just as you can create a graphic symbol from multiple objects on the Stage, you can convert an entire multiple-frame, multiple-layer animation into a single **animated graphic symbol** that you can store in the Library panel. Creating a single animated graphic symbol removes all of the associated keyframes, layers, and tweening of the animation from your Timeline, which results in a much cleaner Timeline. Animated graphic symbols can also reduce file size if you expect to use the animation in more than one place in a movie.

Compare the two Timelines in Figure 1. On the left is a tree animated through the main Timeline; each individual leaf on the tree has its own layer. On the right is a Timeline for a movie with the same animation, but with the leaves grouped into an animated graphic symbol and appearing on a single layer.

An animated graphic symbol is tied to the Timeline of the movie in which you place the symbol. This means there must be enough frames on the Timeline for the animation to run, and that if the movie stops, so does the animation.

Understanding Movie Clip Symbols

A **movie clip symbol**, which is essentially a movie within a movie, is a more robust way to store complex animations in the Library panel. The biggest difference between a movie clip symbol and an animated graphic symbol is that the movie clip symbol retains its own independent Timeline when you insert an instance of the symbol into a movie. Even if the main

FIGURE 1
Comparing Timelines

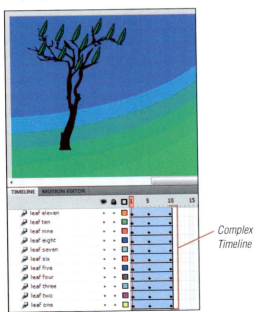

Complex Timeline

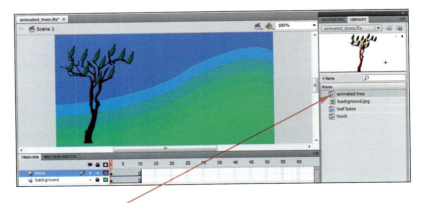

Animated graphic symbol contains the animation for all the leaves

Lesson 1   Plan for Complex Movies and Animations

FLASH 8-5

Timeline stops, the movie clip keeps going, endlessly repeating like a film loop.

Consider Figure 2, which looks like a drawing of a still living room. However, if it were animated, the fire could be crackling and the candles flickering. To create the animation for these elements (the fire and the candle flame), each one of these animated elements might reside in its own movie clip symbol (one containing the fire animation and a different one containing the candle

flame). That way, when placed on the Stage in a movie, each of the movie clip symbols would move according to its own independent Timeline, as well as only taking up one layer and, potentially, only one keyframe on the Timeline. Not only does this help to organize the different pieces of a movie, it also allows you to isolate animated elements and have animations repeat. For example, the animation of the candle flame could be done by using a few frames in which the

flame is moved back and forth one time. The animation could be converted to a movie clip with its own Timeline. This allows the movie clip to be repeated (independent of the main Timeline) giving the flame a fluttering effect.

In this lesson, you will view the same animation (animated leaf) created in three different ways: using the main Timeline, a graphic symbol, and a movie clip.

FIGURE 2
Using movie clip symbols

You could create one movie clip symbol of a flickering flame, and use it to animate all three candles

You could create one movie clip symbol of the fire, which would continuously crackle and move as fires do

FIGURE 3

Adding an animated graphic symbol to the Stage

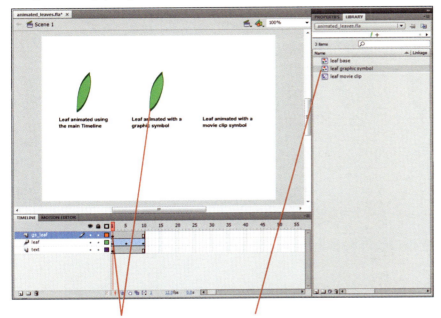

Animated graphic symbol
instance on the Timeline and
on the Stage

Leaf graphic symbol
in the Library panel

1. Open fl8_1.fla, then save it as **animated_leaves**.
2. Display the Library panel.
3. Press [**Enter**] (Win) or [**return**] (Mac) to play the animation.

   The motion tween in the leaf layer on the Timeline causes the leaf to move.
4. Right-click (Win) or [control] click (Mac) the **leaf graphic symbol** in the Library panel, then click **Edit**.
5. Press [**Enter**] (Win) or [**return**] (Mac) to play the animation.

   This is the same animation as the one on the main Timeline. It was developed by creating a new graphic symbol (named leaf graphic symbol) of the leaf, copying the motion tween on the main Timeline, and pasting it into the Timeline of this leaf graphic symbol.
6. Click **Scene 1** at the top left of the work-space to return to the main Timeline.
7. Insert a **new layer** above the leaf layer, then name it **gs_leaf**.
8. Click **frame 1** on the gs_leaf layer, then drag the **leaf graphic symbol** from the Library panel to the Stage above the text, as shown in Figure 3.

   The animated graphic symbol version of the leaf still takes up 10 frames on the Timeline, but the symbol's motion tween (blue shading and keyframe on the Timeline) does not display because it is saved as part of the symbol.
9. Press [**Enter**] (Win) or [**return**] (Mac) to view the animations.

You opened a graphic symbol animation in the edit window and you moved an instance of an ani-mated graphic symbol to the Stage.

Work with a movie clip symbol

1. Insert a **new layer** above the gs_leaf layer, name it **mc_leaf**, then drag the **leaf movie clip symbol** from the Library panel to the Stage above the text, as shown in Figure 4.

2. Click **frame 1** on the mc_leaf layer, then press **[Enter]** (Win) or **[return]** (Mac) to view the animations.

   The movie clip symbol version of the leaf does not move because movie clips on the Stage play only when you export, publish, or test the movie. You will learn in a later lesson how to create this movie clip symbol.

3. Click **Control** on the menu bar, then click **Test Movie** to test the movie.

   All three leaves animate in place continually.

4. Close the Flash Player window.

You placed an instance of a movie clip symbol on the Stage, then tested the movie.

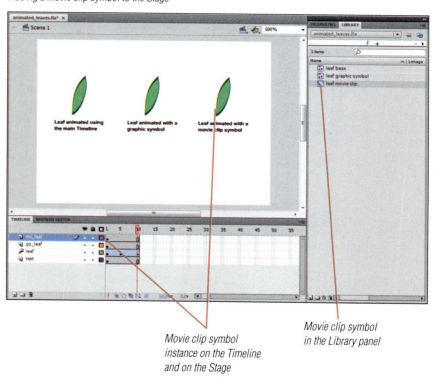

FIGURE 4

Adding a movie clip symbol to the Stage

Movie clip symbol
instance on the Timeline
and on the Stage

Movie clip symbol
in the Library panel

FIGURE 5

Inserting a **stop** action using the Actions panel

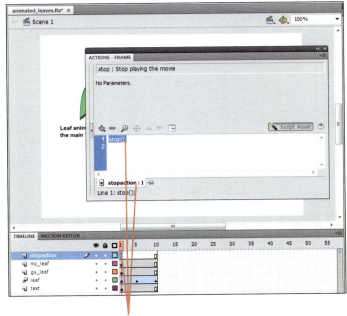

Stop action assigned
to frame 1 on the
action layer

1. Insert a **new layer** above the mc_leaf layer, then name it **stopaction**.

2. Open the Actions panel, then click **frame 1** on the stopaction layer.

3. Verify the Script Assist button is turned on.

4. Verify that stopaction:1 is displayed in the lower left of the Actions panel Script pane.

   This indicates that the ActionScript code will be assigned to frame 1 on the stopaction layer.

5. Click the **Add a new item to the script button** 🔧 in the Script Assist window, point to **Global Functions**, point to **Timeline Control**, then click **stop**.

   Your screen should resemble Figure 5.

6. Click **Control** on the menu bar, then click **Test Movie**.

   Only the movie clip symbol moves because it has an independent Timeline; the stop action stopped the main Timeline, upon which the other two instances of the leaf are dependent.

7. Close the Flash Player window.

8. Close the Actions panel.

9. Save your work, then close the movie.

You assigned a stop action to the Timeline and tested the movie.

CREATE AN ANIMATED
GRAPHIC SYMBOL

What You'll Do

In this lesson, you will convert an animation on the Timeline into an animated graphic symbol.

Using Graphic Symbols for Animations

Most of the time, you will want to use movie clip symbols instead of animated graphic symbols to store animations. However, there are some situations where creating an animated graphic symbol is useful, such as a sequential animation you want to play only one time, rather than repeat continuously like a movie clip. Or, you might want an animation to synchronize with other elements on the Stage, and because animated graphic symbols use the main Timeline, it can be easier to achieve this effect. Also, you can preview animated graphic symbols you place on the Stage right from the Flash editing environment by dragging the playhead back and forth across the Timeline (also called **scrubbing**). This makes animated graphic symbols easy to test within a Flash movie.

You create an animated graphic symbol in the same way you create a static graphic symbol, by choosing the Graphic option in the Create New Symbol dialog box. In the Library panel, an animated graphic symbol looks the same as a static graphic symbol. However, when you select the animated graphic symbol or a movie clip symbol, it is displayed with Stop and Play buttons in the Item Preview window in the Library panel. You can click these buttons, shown in Figure 6, for testing purposes.

Copying Motion Tweens, Frames, and Layers from the Timeline

Despite good preliminary planning, you may end up drawing and animating objects in a movie, and decide later that the animation would be better placed inside an animated graphic or movie clip symbol.

Fortunately, it is easy to copy motion tweens, frames, and layers from the main Timeline and paste them into a new symbol.

To copy multiple layers and frames from within a movie to a symbol, first select the layers and keyframes that you want to copy. To select multiple frames in one or more layers, click the first frame you want to select, and then drag to the last frame. Also, you can click the first frame, press and hold [Shift], and then click the last frame to select the frames and those in-between frames.

To select noncontiguous layers, click the name of the first layer you want to select, press and hold [Ctrl] (Win) or [command] click (Mac), and then click each layer name. To select contiguous layers, click the first layer name, and then press and hold [Shift] and click the last layer name to select the layers and all in-between layers. Figure 7 shows a selection across multiple frames and layers. Once you select the frames, click Edit on the menu bar, point to Timeline, and then click Cut or Copy Frames. Create or open the symbol, place the insertion point in a keyframe, click Edit on the menu bar, point to Timeline, and then click Paste Frames. Flash pastes each individual layer from the original movie into the Timeline for the symbol, and even maintains the layer names.

Note that you cannot copy sound or inter-activity in an animation from the main Timeline to an animated graphic symbol. If you want to include sound or interactivity in an animation, you should create a movie clip symbol instead of a graphic symbol.

FIGURE 6

Stop and Play buttons in the Library panel Item Preview window

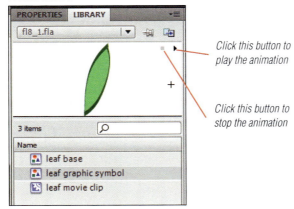

Click this button to play the animation

Click this button to stop the animation

FIGURE 7

Multiple frames and layers selected

Delete objects from the Timeline

1. Open fl8_2.fla, then save it as **animated_trees**.
2. Verify the Library panel is open, drag the **border** at the top of the Timeline up to display the trunk and all eleven leaf layers, then set the view to **Fit in Window**.
3. Play the movie.

   The leaves animate on 11 separate layers.
4. Click the **trunk layer** to select it, press **[Shift]**, click **leaf eleven layer**, then release **[Shift]**.

   The trunk layer, all numbered leaf layers, and all frames in each layer on the Timeline are selected, as shown in Figure 8.

   TIP You can press and hold [Ctrl] (Win) or [command] (Mac), then click one or more layer names to select all frames in each layer you click.
5. Click **Edit** on the menu bar, point to **Timeline**, then click **Cut Frames**.

   The tree is no longer visible on the Stage. Notice that you cut the frames but not the layers from the main Timeline.

You selected and then cut the frames on the layers on the Timeline that made up the tree.

Move frames to create an animated graphic symbol

1. Click **Insert** on the menu bar, then click **New Symbol**.
2. Type **animated tree** in the Name text box, verify Graphic is selected as the type, as shown in Figure 9, then click **OK**.

   You are now in the edit window for the animated tree graphic symbol.

(continued)

FIGURE 8
Selecting frames on the main Timeline

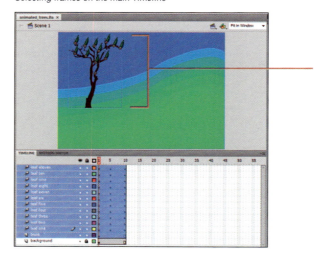

Selecting the frames on the Timeline also selects the elements on the Stage

FIGURE 9
The Create New Symbol dialog box

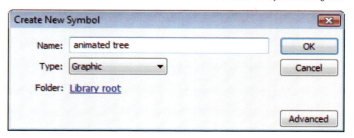

FIGURE 10
Moving an instance of the tree symbol to the Stage

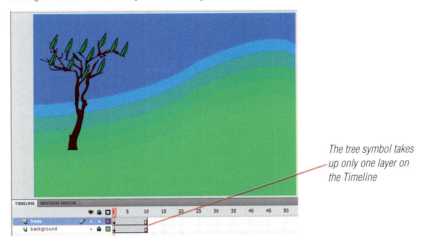

The tree symbol takes
up only one layer on
the Timeline

FIGURE 11
Resizing the second instance of the tree symbol

*Hover over one of the
corners of the tree until
the cursor appears as
a two-headed arrow,
then drag to resize; use
the Selection tool to
reposition the image
after it is resized*

Lesson 2   Create an Animated Graphic Symbol

3. Click **frame 1** on Layer 1, click **Edit** on the menu bar, point to **Timeline**, then click **Paste Frames**. The tree trunk and leaves appear on the Stage.

4. Play the movie, then click **Scene 1** at the top left of the workspace to return to the main Timeline.

5. Select all the layers, except the background layer, then click the **Delete icon** 🗑 to delete them.

6. Click **ESSENTIALS** on the menu bar, then click **Reset 'Essentials'**.

You pasted frames from the main Timeline into a graphic symbol to create an animated graphic symbol. You then deleted the layers from the main Timeline.

Move an animated graphic symbol to the Stage

1. Insert a **new layer** above the background layer, then name it **trees**.

2. Click **frame 1** on the trees layer, then drag the **animated tree graphic symbol** from the Library panel to the left side of the Stage, as shown in Figure 10.

3. Play the movie.

4. Click **frame 1** on the trees layer, then drag another instance of the **animated tree graphic symbol** from the Library panel to the right side of the Stage.

5. Click the **Free Transform tool** 📐 on the Tools panel, click the **Scale option button** ◺ in the Options area of the Tools panel, click a **corner sizing handle** on the tree, then drag to resize the tree to the size shown in Figure 11.

6. Play the movie and watch the leaves animate on the Stage.

7. Save your work, then close the movie.

You created two instances of an animated graphic symbol on the Stage.

FLASH 8-13

CREATE A MOVIE CLIP SYMBOL

What You'll Do

In this lesson, you will create a movie clip symbol and nest movie clip symbols within one another.

Using Movie Clip Symbols for Animations

Movie clip symbols are usually the most efficient choice for creating and storing complex animations. The main advantage of movie clip symbols is that they maintain their own independent Timeline, which is especially useful for animating continuous or looping actions. Movie clip symbols require only one frame in the main movie, regardless of the complexity of the animation, which can make it easier to work with the Timeline.

Movie clip symbols offer many other sophisticated features not available with animated graphic symbols. For instance, you can add sound and associate ActionScript statements to movie clip symbols, or you can create an animation for a movie clip in the main Timeline (such as a motion tween) while another movie clip continues to play its own animation on its independent Timeline. For example, you could have an animation of a plane flying across the screen developed as a motion tween on the main Timeline. At the same time, you could have an animation of a spinning windmill developed as another movie clip that plays continuously. In addition, you can use movie clip symbols to animate a button.

To start building a movie clip symbol, create a new symbol and then choose Movie Clip in the Create New Symbol dialog box. You can create the movie clip animation from scratch, or cut and copy frames and layers from the main Timeline, as you did with the animated graphic symbol in the previous lesson. You can also copy a motion tween from another animated object and paste it to a movie clip symbol.

QUICKTIP
While you're working with the main Timeline, you see only a static image of the first frame of a movie clip symbol on the Stage. To view the full animation, you must export, publish, or test the movie.

Nesting Movie Clips
As you learned in Chapter 4, a movie clip symbol is often made up of many other movie clips, a process called **nesting**.

You can nest as many movie clip symbols inside another movie clip as you like. You can also place a symbol, graphic, or button inside a movie clip symbol. Figure 12 shows a diagram of nesting.

Nesting movie clips creates a **parent-child relationship** that will become increasingly important as you enhance the interactivity of your movies and begin to deploy more sophisticated ActionScript statements. When you insert a movie clip inside another movie clip, the inserted clip is considered the child and the original clip the parent. These relationships are hierarchical, as indicated in Figure 12. Keep in mind that if you place an instance of a parent clip into a movie and then change it, you will also affect the nested child clip. Any time you change the instance of a parent clip, the associated child clips update automatically. For example, if you have a car that is the parent clip and it has wheels that are child clips and you resize the car, the wheels resize proportionally.

The Movie Explorer panel, shown in Figure 13, allows you to inspect the nesting structure of your entire movie. This is a useful reference to print, so as you work on a movie, you can easily view the movie's structure and see which elements are nested inside each other. You can also apply a filter to view just the elements you want. To access the Movie Explorer, click Window on the menu bar, then click Movie Explorer.

The Options menu lets you perform a variety of actions on the elements listed in the Movie Explorer. For example, you can go to the element on the Stage and Timeline, find the element in the Library panel, or open all panels relevant to the element so you can edit the object using the panels.

FIGURE 12
Diagram of a nested movie clip animation

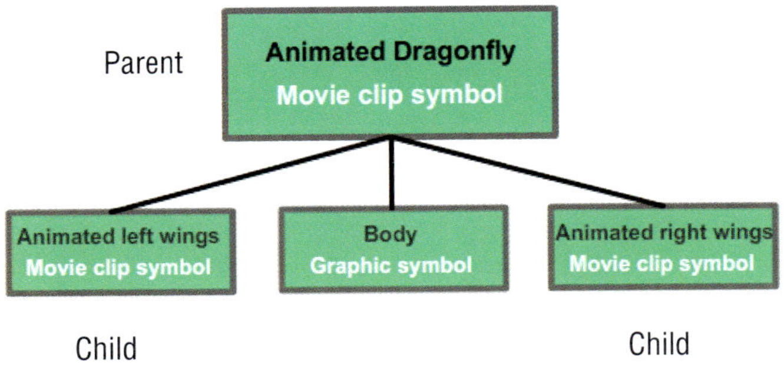

FIGURE 13
Movie Explorer panel

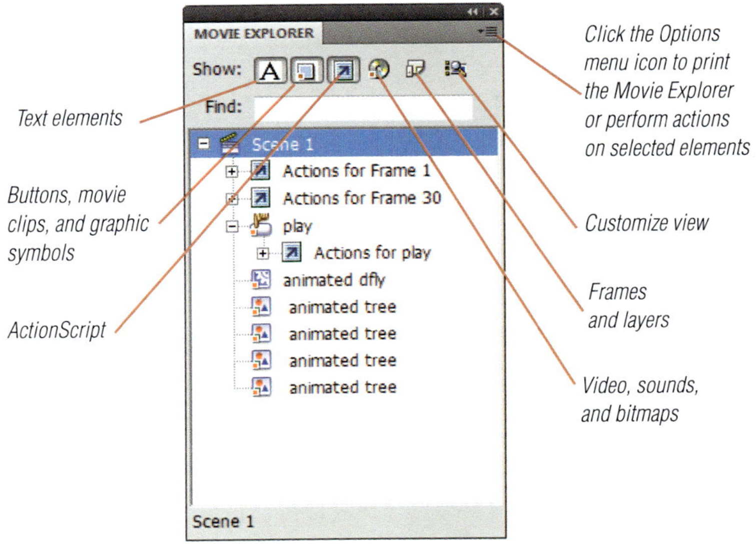

Create a movie clip symbol

1. Open fl8_3.fla, save it as **dragonfly**, then change the frame rate to 10 fps.

2. Display the Library panel, then notice the symbols.

   The Library panel contains the dfly body, left wings, and right wings graphic symbols, as well as the animated left wings movie clip symbol. These symbols will form the basis of your movie clip.

3. Click the **animated left wings movie clip symbol** in the Library panel, then click the **Play button** ▶ in the Item Preview window.

   The wings appear to flutter. Next, you will create another movie clip symbol to animate a set of right wings for the dragonfly.

4. Click **Insert** on the menu bar, then click **New Symbol**.

5. Type **animated right wings** in the Name text box, select **Movie Clip** for the type, then click **OK** to display the edit window.

6. Click **frame 1** on Layer 1 on the Timeline, then drag the **right wings graphic symbol** from the Library panel to the center of the Stage so that the circle is over the centering cross-hair, as shown in Figure 14.

7. Display the Properties panel, click **frame 1** on the Timeline, then click the **wings**.

8. Change the x and y coordinates to **0**.

(continued)

FIGURE 14
Positioning the wings in the edit window

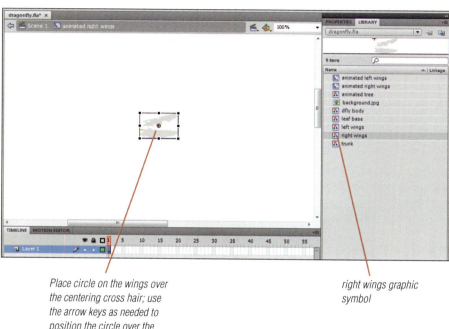

Place circle on the wings over the centering cross hair; use the arrow keys as needed to position the circle over the centering cross hair

right wings graphic symbol

FIGURE 15

Setting values for frame 5 of the motion tween

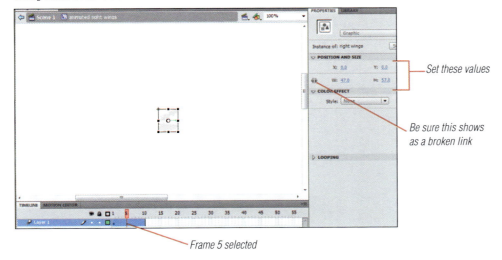

Set these values

Be sure this shows
as a broken link

Frame 5 selected

FIGURE 16

Assembled animated dragonfly

9. Click **Insert** on the menu bar, then click
   Motion Tween.

10. Click **frame 5** on the Timeline, click the **wings**,
    then use the Properties panel to set the fol-
    lowing values: X: **0**, Y: **0**, W: **47**, H: **57**, as
    shown in Figure 15.

11. Click **frame 10** on the Timeline, click the
    wings, then use the Properties panel to set the
    following values: X: **0**, Y: **0**, W: **84**, H: **57**.

12. Play the animation.

13. Click **Scene 1** at the top left of the workspace
    to return to the main Timeline.

*You created a movie clip symbol containing a
motion tween animation.*

Nest movie clip symbols

1. Click **Insert** on the menu bar, then click
   New Symbol.

2. Type **animated dfly** in the Name text box,
   verify Movie Clip is selected for the type,
   then click **OK**.

3. Drag the **dfly body graphic symbol** from the
   Library panel to the center of the Stage.

4. Drag the **animated left wings movie clip
   symbol** from the Library panel to the Stage,
   then attach it to the upper-left side of the
   dragonfly's body.

5. Drag the **animated right wings movie clip
   symbol** to the upper-right side of the body.

   Compare your image to Figure 16.

6. Click **Scene 1** at the top left of the workspace to return to the main Timeline.

*You nested two movie clips inside a new movie
clip symbol.*

Move the movie clip symbol to the Stage, rotate, and resize it

1. Insert a **new layer** above the trees layer, then name it **dragonfly**.

2. Click **frame 1** on the dragonfly layer, then drag the **animated dfly movie clip symbol** from the Library panel so it is on top of the left tree on the Stage, as shown in Figure 17.

3. Play the movie.

   Because the dragonfly is an animated movie clip, the animation does not play on the Stage.

4. Test the movie to view the animation, then close the Flash Player window.

5. Verify the dragonfly graphic on the Stage is selected.

6. Click **Modify** on the menu bar, point to **Transform**, then click **Scale and Rotate**.

7. Type **180** for the Rotate value, then click **OK**.

8. Display the Properties panel, click **frame 1** on the dragonfly layer, then click the **dragonfly**.

9. Change the width to **43** and the height to **32** in the Properties panel, then use the Selection tool ![selection tool] to place the dragonfly so it is centered on the branches.

You added an instance of a movie clip symbol to the Stage, rotated it 180 degrees, and resized it.

Animate an instance of a movie clip and resize an object

1. Click **frame 1** on the dragonfly layer, click **Insert** on the menu bar, then click **Motion Tween**.

FIGURE 17
Animated dragonfly instance placed on the Stage

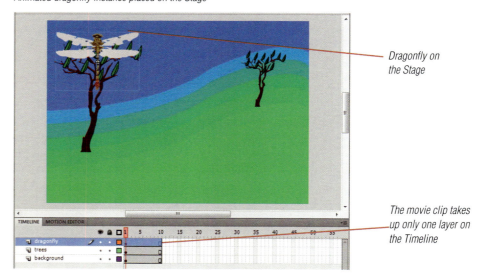

Dragonfly on the Stage

The movie clip takes up only one layer on the Timeline

FIGURE 18
Reshaping the path with the Selection tool

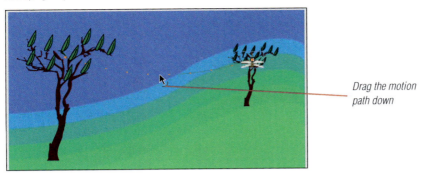

Drag the motion
path down

FIGURE 19
Dragging the Bezier handle up to complete the curve

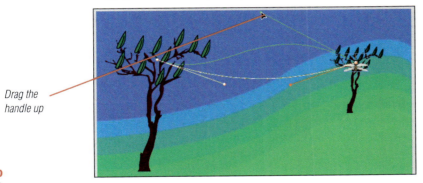

Drag the
handle up

FIGURE 20
Completed path

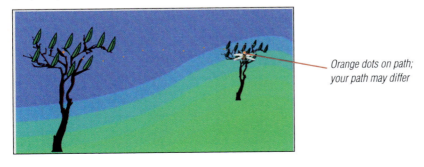

Orange dots on path;
your path may differ

Lesson 3   Create a Movie Clip Symbol

2. Click **frame 10** on the dragonfly layer, then drag the **dragonfly** to the leaves on the small tree.

3. Click the **Selection tool** ⬚, point to the middle of the motion path, when the pointer changes to ⬚, drag the **path** down, as shown in Figure 18.

4. Click the **Subselection tool** ⬚, point to the left end of the motion path, when the pointer changes to an arrow with an unfilled square ⬚ click to display the Bezier handles.

5. Point to the right-side handle, when the pointer changes to a delta symbol ▶, drag the **handle** up to the position shown in Figure 19.

6. Click the **solid path** with the Subselection pointer with a filled square ⬚, then move the path down slightly.

   Notice the orange dots from the original path are now on the reshaped path, as shown in Figure 20.

7. Click **frame 1** on the dragonfly layer, then click **Orient to path** in the Properties panel.

8. Click the **Free Transform tool** ⬚, then rotate a corner handle to align the front of the dragonfly to the path.

9. Click **frame 10** on the dragonfly layer, click the **dragonfly**, then resize the dragonfly to width **22** and height **16**.

10. Drag the **tween span** on the dragonfly layer to **frame 30**, then insert keyframes in frame 30 on the other layers.

11. Test the movie, close the Flash Player window, then save your work.

You animated and resized an instance of a movie clip.

ANIMATE BUTTONS USING
MOVIE CLIP SYMBOLS

What You'll Do

In this lesson, you will create an animated button and put together a short interactive movie using ActionScript.

Understanding Animated Buttons

As you learned in a previous chapter, a button symbol does not have the standard Timeline, but instead has four states associated with it. You can animate a button by nesting a movie clip symbol inside any one of the three visible states of the button: Up, Over, or Down—although Up and Over are the most common placements.

Depending on the state in which you nest the symbol, you will have different results. If you nest the animation inside the Up state, the movie/button will continue to animate as long as the button is visible on the Stage in the main Timeline. If you nest the movie inside the Over state, the animation will be visible only when the user's mouse is over the button. If the animation is nested inside the Down state, the users will see only a brief flicker of animation when they click the mouse. The first two are the most common and both have obvious interface benefits as well—if your

users see something animated, they are more inclined to interact with it and discover it is actually a button.

Building an Animated Button Symbol

To build an animated button symbol, you need at least two symbols in the Library panel. First, you need to create a movie clip symbol with the animation. In building this animation, make sure you design it to repeat cleanly, especially if you plan to use it in the Up state of a button. Once you have built the movie clip symbol, you need to create a button symbol in which to nest the animation. Remember, because movie clips have independent Timelines, the clip will run continually while the button symbol is on the Stage, even if the main movie pauses or stops. Figure 21 shows the Information bar for the edit window of a movie clip symbol nested inside a button.

As with a movie clip, you must publish the movie or test it within Flash to see the animation of a button. The Enable Simple Buttons option will not play the movie clip—you will see only a static view of the first frame of the clip.

Creating an Interactive Movie

Adding interactivity to a movie simply means you are asking your user to be involved in the movie in some way other than watching it. It can be as simple as adding a button for a user to click or giving the user a choice to make. Interactivity can also be complex, for example, the game shown in Figure 22 in which a user must assemble a puzzle. Because adding interactivity means you are forcing users to become involved in your movie, you are more likely to hold your users' interest.

You can also create complex interactions by using ActionScript in combination with movie clip symbols. With ActionScript, you can set up movie clips to play, pause, or perform other actions based on user input such as clicking the mouse or pressing a key on the keyboard, similar to the interactions you can create with a button. You can also use ActionScript to instruct movie clips to perform actions without waiting for user input and to jump to specific frames on the Timeline of a movie clip symbol.

FIGURE 21

Movie clip symbol nested inside a button

FIGURE 22

Interactive game created with symbols, buttons, and ActionScript

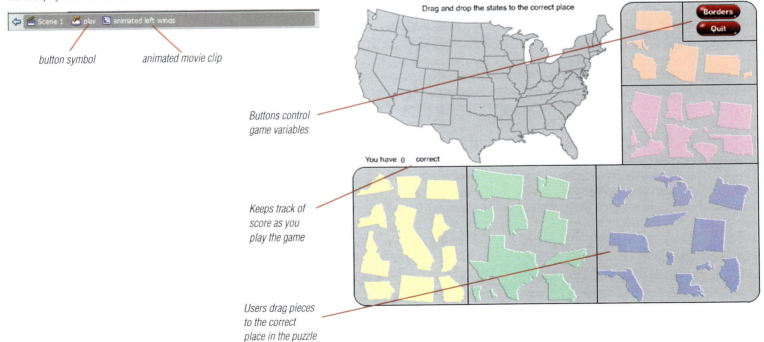

button symbol *animated movie clip*

Buttons control game variables

Keeps track of score as you play the game

Users drag pieces to the correct place in the puzzle

Drag and drop the states to the correct place

You have 0 correct

Create an animated button by nesting an animation in the button's Up state

1. Verify that the dragonfly document is open, click **Insert** on the menu bar, then click **New Symbol**.

2. Type **play** in the Name text box, change the Type to **Button**, then click **OK**.

3. Click the **Up frame** on Layer 1, click the **Text tool** T on the Tools panel, then click the **Text tool pointer** ⊤ in the center of the Stage.

4. Use the Properties panel to change the Character family to **Verdana**, the style to **bold**, the size to **24**, and the color to **black**.

   Note: If you see Dynamic Text or Input Text at the top of the Properties panel, click the list arrow next to the phrase you see and then select Static Text.

5. Type **PLAY**.

6. Click the **Selection tool** ▶ on the Tools panel, drag the **animated left wings movie clip symbol** from the Library panel to the left of the word "PLAY," then drag the **animated right wings movie clip symbol** from the Library panel to the right side of the word, as shown in Figure 23.

(continued)

FIGURE 23
Adding the animated wings to the text

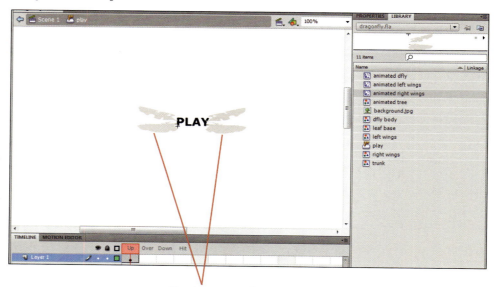

The wings are nested movie clip symbols

FIGURE 24
Setting the Hit area

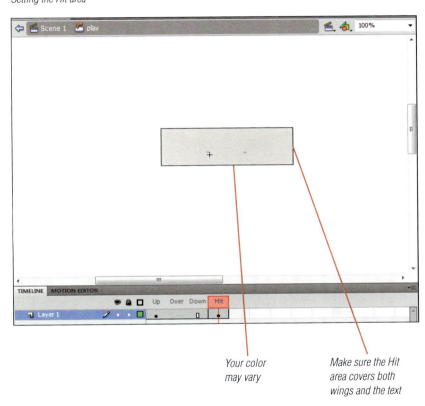

Your color
may vary

Make sure the Hit
area covers both
wings and the text

7. Click the **Selection tool** on the Tools panel, click the word **PLAY** on the Stage, click the **Text (fill) color box** on the Properties panel, position the Eyedropper pointer (Mac pointer may differ) over a wing, then click.

   TIP When you move the Eyedropper pointer to the Stage, do not pass over any other clickable element in the Properties panel. If, as you move the Eyedropper pointer, the pointer changes to a shape other than the Eyedropper, go back and click the Text (fill) color box and try again.

   The text and the wings are now the same color.

8. Insert a **keyframe** in the Hit frame of the button Timeline, select the **Rectangle tool** on the Tools panel, then draw a box around both sets of wings and the text, as shown in Figure 24.

   TIP Remember that the Hit state is invisible on the Stage, but defines the clickable area of a button.

9. Click the **Selection tool** on the Tools panel.

10. Click **Scene 1** at the top left of the work-space to return to the main Timeline.

You created a button symbol and placed an animation inside the Up state of the button symbol.

Place the animated button on the Stage

1. Insert a **new layer** above the dragonfly layer, name it **button**, then click **frame 1** on the button layer.

2. Drag the **play button symbol** from the Library panel underneath the right tree on the Stage, as shown in Figure 25.

3. Insert a **new layer** above the button layer, then name it **actions**.

4. Open the Actions panel, then click **frame 1** on the actions layer.

5. Verify that the Script Assist button is selected and that actions:1 is displayed at the lower left of the Actions panel Script pane.

6. Click **Add a new item to the script button** 🔁 in the Script Assist window, point to **Global Functions**, point to **Timeline Control**, click **stop**, then collapse the Actions panel.

7. Click **Control** on the menu bar, then click **Test Movie**.

   The wings flutter on the animated button. Notice that while the dragonfly's wings also move, the dragonfly does not fly on the motion path, nor do the leaves on the trees animate. This is because both the dragonfly's motion and the leaves are dependent on the main Timeline, which is stopped on frame 1.

8. Close the Flash Player window.

You placed an animated button on the Stage and added a stop action.

FIGURE 25
Placing the button on the Stage

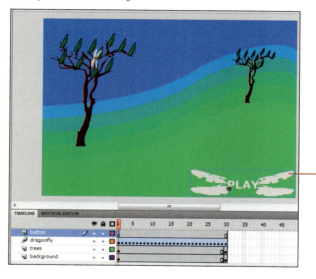

The animated button is made up of text and two movie clip symbols

FIGURE 26

Adding the button action in the Actions panel

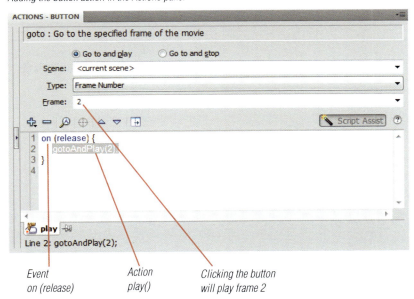

Event
on (release)

Action
play()

Clicking the button
will play frame 2

Add a button action

1. Click the **Selection tool** ![cursor] , then click the **Play button** on the Stage to select it.

2. Display the Actions panel, then verify that the play button symbol is displayed in the lower left of the Actions panel Script pane.

3. Click **Add a new item to the script button** ![plus] in the Script Assist window, point to **Global Functions**, point to **Movie Clip Control**, then click **on**.

4. Click **Add a new item to the script button** ![plus] , point to **Global Functions**, point to **Timeline Control**, then click **goto**.

5. Change the Frame number to **2**, as shown in Figure 26.

6. Click **frame 30** on the actions layer, click **Insert** on the menu bar, point to **Timeline**, then click **Blank Keyframe**.

7. Click **Add a new item to the script button** ![plus] in the Script Assist window, point to **Global Functions**, point to **Timeline Control**, click **stop**, then close the Actions panel.

8. Click **Control** on the menu bar, then click **Test Movie**.

   Notice the dragonfly in the tree and the Play button are animated. This is because they are movie clips and use their Timelines, which are independent of the main Timeline.

9. Click the **Play button**.

   Notice that the movie plays to the end—the leaves on the trees animate and the dragonfly flies on the motion path, which are actions associated with the main Timeline.

10. Close the Flash Player window, save your work, close the movie, then exit Flash.

You added actions to the movie, creating interactivity.

Plan for complex movies and animations, and create an animated graphic symbol.

1. Start Flash, open fl8_4.fla from the drive and folder where your Data Files are stored, then save it as **skillsdemo8**. (*Hint*: When you open the file, you may receive a missing font message, meaning a font used in this document is not available on your computer. You can choose a substitute font or use a default font.)

2. Verify the frame rate is set to **12** fps. In this Flash document, you will create a movie that will display a clock (a movie clip) with a minute hand (a movie clip) and an hour hand (a movie clip) that are rapidly spinning. The clock will be a button so that when the user clicks the clock it displays wings (two movie clips) and flies around the screen. All of the necessary graphic objects are available in the Library panel. The movie currently has a background graphic (water and clouds) and a text title (Time Flies).

Create movie clip symbols.

1. Create a new movie clip symbol named **mc_minuteHand**.

2. Verify you are in the edit window for the mc_minuteHand movie clip, then drag the g_minute hand graphic symbol to the Stage.

3. Click the Free Transform tool and verify the object is selected.

4. Change the view to 200%, then drag the transformation point (circle) of the object to the bottom of the object. This will set the pivot point for the object as it spins around.

5. Click frame 1, then create a motion tween.

6. Drag the end of the tween span in the Timeline back to frame 5.

7. Verify frame 5 is selected, then use the Properties panel to set the rotate value to 1 and the direction to clockwise.

8. Play the movie clip, then return to the main Timeline.

9. Create a new movie clip symbol named **mc_hourHand**.

10. Verify you are in the edit window for the mc_hourHand movie clip, then drag the g_hour hand graphic symbol to the Stage.

11. Change the view to 200%, then drag the transformation point (circle) to the bottom of the object, which is actually to the left.

12. Click frame 5, then insert a keyframe.

13. Click Modify on the menu bar, click Transform, click Scale and Rotate, set the rotate value to 30 degrees, then click OK.

14. Click frame 10, insert a keyframe, then set the rotate value to 30 degrees.

15. Repeat step 14 for frames 15, 20, 25, 30, 35, 40, 45, 50, 55, and 60. (*Hint*: Do not just copy and paste frames because the action of rotating the hand will not be copied and pasted to the new frames.)

16. Play the movie clip, then return to the main Timeline.

17. Create a new movie clip symbol named **mc_clock**.

18. Verify you are in the edit window for the mc_clock movie clip, rename Layer 1 **clockFace**, then drag the g_clock face graphic symbol to the Stage.

19. Add a new layer, name it **hourHand**, drag the mc_hourHand movie clip to the middle of the clock.

20. Add a new layer, name it **minuteHand**, drag the mc_minuteHand movie clip to the middle of the clock so that the bottoms of the objects overlap.

21. Add a new layer below the clockFace layer, name it **wings**, then drag the mc_left wings to the upper-left side of the clock.

22. Drag the mc_right wings to the upper-right side of the clock.

23. Use the Free Transform tool and the arrow keys to rotate the wings as needed to place the wings to your satisfaction.

24. Insert keyframes in frame 60 on all the layers, then return to the main Timeline.

25. Add a layer, name it **clock**, insert a keyframe in frame 2 on the layer.

26. Drag the mc_clock movie clip symbol to the lower middle of the Stage.

Animate the movie clip symbol.

1. Verify frame 2 on the clock layer is selected, then create a motion tween.

2. Select frame 60 on the clock layer, then drag the clock to the upper-left corner of the Stage.

3. Use the Selection tool to reshape the motion path to an arc.

4. Use the Subselection tool to display the Bezier handles and reshape the motion path to an S curve.

5. Use the Properties panel to resize the clock to approximately one-fourth of its original size, then compare your screen to Figure 27.

Animate buttons with movie clip symbols.

1. Display the mc_clock symbol in the edit window.

2. Select the clock and hands layers (not the wings layer). (*Hint*: If the wings are selected, recheck to be sure you placed the wings on the wings layer and not one of the other layers.)

3. Click Edit on the menu bar, point to Timeline, click Copy Frames, then return to the main Timeline.

4. Create a new movie clip symbol with the name **mc_clockButton**.

5. Verify you are in the edit window for the mc_clockButton symbol, click frame 1, click Edit on the menu bar, point to Timeline, click Paste Frames, then return to the main Timeline.

6. Create a new button symbol with the name **b_clockButton**, then insert the mc_clockButton symbol into the Up state of the button.

7. Insert a keyframe in the Hit state of the button, return to the main Timeline, insert a new layer above the clock layer, then name it **button**.

8. Click the Edit Multiple Frames icon at the bottom of the Timeline to display the contents of the first few frames.

9. Select frame 1 on the button layer, drag the button symbol to the Stage and place it directly on top of the clock. (*Hint*: Use the arrow keys to align the two clocks.)

10. Turn off the Edit Multiple Frames feature.

11. Remove frames 2-60 on the button layer.

12. Insert a new layer above the button layer, name it **stopaction**, then insert a stop action in frame 1. (*Hint*: Be sure Script Assist is selected.)

13. Add a goto action to the button on the Stage, and specify **2** as the frame to go to. (*Hint*: Be sure the button symbol is displayed in the lower left of the Actions panel Script pane.)

14. Test your movie, compare your screen to Figure 28, then click the button to see the animation.

15. Save your work.

16. Exit Flash.

FIGURE 27
Motion path for clock movie clip symbol

FIGURE 28
Completed Skills Review

Ultimate Tours has decided it wants to add animation to the opening page of its "Summer in December" website, which is promoting a series of tours to Florida, Bermuda, and the Caribbean. The management would like the animation to draw attention to the company name and to the navigation button (which in this case is the sun graphic), so visitors will click to find out more information about specific tours. Though the site is still at an early stage, they would like to see some prototypes of potential animations. The company would like a new look that differs from the prototype developed in Chapter 7 (ultimatetours7.fla).

1. Start a new Flash document and save it as **ultimatetours8**.
2. On paper, plan how you might add animations to this page that will fulfill the criteria Ultimate Tours has established.
3. Build the animation you have planned for emphasizing the company name. For example, you might convert the text of the company name ("Ultimate Tours") to a graphic symbol, then create a movie clip symbol in which the text dissolves and reappears, changes color, rotates, or moves across the screen.
4. Build the animation you have planned that will encourage visitors to click the continue button. For example, you might create an animation of a yellow ball representing the sun rolling out from the heading. Then, you could create a direction line telling visitors to click the sun to continue. (*Note*: For this project, the button does not have to be active.)
5. Save your work, then compare your image to the example shown in Figure 29.

FIGURE 29
Sample completed Project Builder 1

You have been asked to create a short interactive movie on ocean life for the local elementary school, which is planning a visit to an oceanographic institute. This project should be colorful, interactive, and full of images that appeal to 7–12-year-old students.

The opening page of the site should show some images of sea creatures which, when clicked, lead to more information. You must include at least three clickable objects on this opening page.

1. Obtain some images of fish, coral, and other ocean creatures from resources on your computer or the Internet, or from scanned media.
2. Create a new Flash document, then save it as **ocean_life8**.
3. Set the document properties, including the size and background color, if desired.
4. Create animated movie clips for at least three ocean creatures. Use different types of animation for these movie clips. For example, you might use motion tweening to move, resize, or rotate objects, or fade them in or out.
5. Create buttons for the ocean creature images using your animated movies in the Up state and also designating a Hit state. (*Hint*: Be creative about the appearance of the buttons—use different shapes and sizes, or try cropping and making the images themselves clickable.)
6. Place the three buttons on the Stage.
7. Add some explanatory text.
8. Save your work and compare your image to the example shown in Figure 30.

FIGURE 30
Sample completed Project Builder 2

The starfish movie clip contains the graphic image of the starfish and a motion tween that causes the starfish to rotate and get larger as it rotates

Click an image to learn about these ocean creatures...

Figure 31 shows a birthday card created in Flash. Study the figure and complete the following. For each question, indicate how you determined your answer.

1. Connect to the Internet, then go to www.rubberchickencards.com/content.php/action/play_card/id/197/.
2. Open a document in a word processor or create a new Flash document, save the file as **dpc8**, then answer the following questions. (*Hint*: Use the Text tool in Flash.)
   - Without seeing the source file in this movie, make a list of objects you believe to be in the Library panel and why you think they should be stored there.
   - Do you think all the images in this work were drawn in Flash? Explain.
   - What in this movie could be animated?
   - Would you use animated graphic symbols or movie clip symbols to create the animations? Explain.
   - Are there any animated graphic symbols or movie clip symbols you could create once and use in multiple places?
   - What other buttons would you add and why?
   - Suppose you want to create an animation in which one jester strums his lute, some text appears and then dissolves, the other jester bangs his tambourine, more text appears and dissolves, then both jesters play simultaneously while the words "Happy Birthday" float across the screen. Plan a strategy for creating this animation that will streamline the Timeline, reuse symbols to conserve file size, and allow you to easily set up the timing of the sequence so the text appears at the appropriate time.

FIGURE 31
Design Project

PORTFOLIO PROJECT

To add some pizzazz to your existing portfolio, you want to change the navigation on your home page. Your goal is to have visitors mouse over the navigation buttons and see an animation that you hope will better entice employers and potential clients with your skills. The animation should be fairly subtle and elegant, and showcase your animation skills.

1. Start a new Flash document and save it as **portfolio8**.
2. Create a movie clip symbol named **animated button**.
3. Inside the movie clip symbol create an animation that would be appropriate for the mouse-over of your primary navigation buttons in the portfolio.
4. Open each of your button symbols and place the animation in the Over state.
5. Save your work, then compare your movie to the example shown in Figure 32.

FIGURE 32
Sample completed Portfolio Project

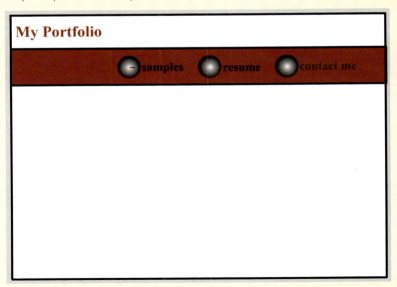

chapter **9**

USING ACTIONSCRIPT

1. Work with the Actions panel

2. Work with targets and movie clip symbols

3. Create interactive movie clip symbols

4. Define variables

A D O B E F L A S H C S 4

chapter **9** USING
ACTIONSCRIPT

Introduction

In the previous chapters, you began working with ActionScript, the built-in scripting language for Flash. In this chapter, you will explore more of the ways in which ActionScript can take your movies to the next level of interactivity and sophistication. For example, you can apply ActionScript code to an object that changes the appearance of that object based on the actions a user takes. Or, you can use ActionScript code to create a form that captures user data and displays it elsewhere in your site.

You can use ActionScript code to add actions to a frame, to any object such as a button, or to a movie clip symbol. Since ActionScript is a type of programming language, using exact syntax—spelling action names correctly and including the necessary parameters—is essential. The Actions panel, in which you add ActionScript to frames and objects, helps ensure that your ActionScript follows the required syntax and runs efficiently. You are already familiar with the Script Assist feature, which was used in earlier chapters. In this chapter, you will generate ActionScript code with and without the Script Assist feature.

Tools You'll Use

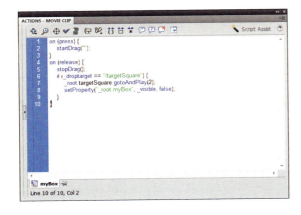

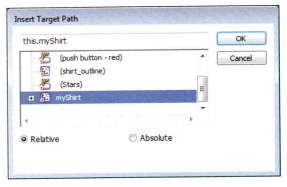

WORK WITH THE
ACTIONS PANEL

What You'll Do

In this lesson, you will use ActionScript and frame labels to create navigation to specific frames on the Timeline.

Using the Actions Panel

The Actions panel is used to build the ActionScript code that enhances a movie by adding complex interaction, playback control, and data manipulation.

The Actions panel has three panes, as shown in Figure 1:

- **Actions toolbox pane**—provides the categories of actions that can be selected to build ActionScript code. For example, the Global Functions category contains Timeline controls, such as stop and goto.
- **Script navigator pane**—provides a list of elements (objects, movie clips, frames) that contain scripts used in the movie. It can be used to quickly locate an object, such as a button, and display its code in the Script pane.
- **Script pane**—displays the code and a toolbar for editing the code. Also, it displays the Script Assist dialog box at the top of the Script pane when Script Assist is active.

Two useful buttons on the Script pane toolbar are the Check syntax button and the Auto format button. Clicking the Check syntax button checks for any errors in the syntax of the coding and, if found, displays a list. Clicking the Auto format button formats the code in accordance with ActionScript formatting conventions. This may add spaces, lines, and indents to make the code more readable.

Script Assist

There are two ways to work with the Actions panel, either with the Script Assist feature turned on or turned off.

Script Assist is good for basic actions, such as goto, when working with ActionScripts 1.0 and 2.0. You merely use the Script Assist menus and dialog boxes to select the desired actions and the code is written for you. Script Assist is useful if you have limited knowledge of ActionScript. However, when using Script Assist, you are limited in the actions you can work with and you cannot edit code directly in the

Script pane. With Script Assist turned off, you build the ActionScript code by selecting actions listed in folder categories in the Actions toolbox pane. As with Script Assist, the code is generated as you make your selections. However, unlike Script Assist, you can type directly into the Script pane to create and edit code. This allows greater flexibility, more control, and, for those with some programming experience, the ability to write code that creates more sophisticated interactions and animations.

As you have already seen in earlier chapters, you can create code by switching between the two modes. That is, start with Script Assist on to generate some code, and then turn Script Assist off to complete the code by typing in the Script pane.

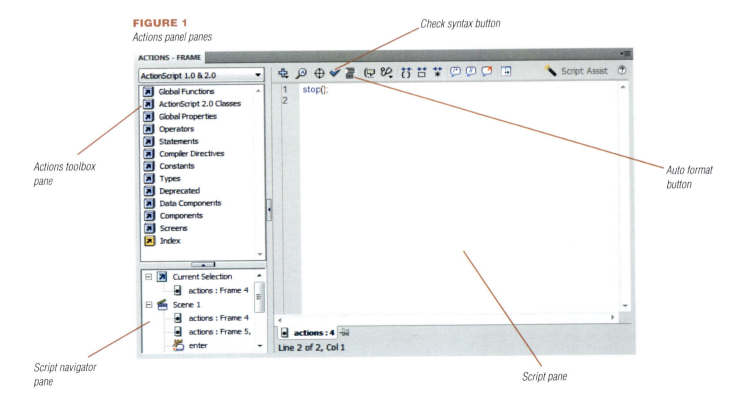

FIGURE 1
Actions panel panes

Check syntax button

Actions toolbox pane

Auto format button

Script navigator pane

Script pane

Configuring the Actions Panel

There are two windows, left and right, in the Actions panel. The left window displays the Actions toolbox pane and the Script navigator pane. The right window displays the Script pane where the ActionScript code is displayed and edited. You will need to display the right window at all times. You can collapse and expand the left window by clicking the Expand/Collapse arrow between the windows. Figure 2 shows the Actions panel with the Actions toolbox pane and Script navigator pane collapsed. You can resize the left window by dragging the border between the two windows. Before writing any code, be sure to check the element (button, frame, movie clip, object) that is displayed in the lower left of the Script pane to verify it is the element to which you want to apply the code.

Writing ActionScript Code

There are certain syntax rules you must follow when writing ActionScript. You must use exact case for action names; for example, when typing the gotoAndPlay action, be sure to capitalize the "A" and "P."

A semicolon (;) terminates an ActionScript statement. Functions or parameters for an action are enclosed in parentheses. Text strings appear between quotation marks. To group actions, you enclose them in curly brackets—{}— as shown in Figure 3 on the next page.

After you finish entering actions, you should click the Check syntax button above the Script pane to check the code and display errors in an output window.

If you need help, you can display code hints. Code hints give the syntax or possible parameters for an action in a pop-up window as you are entering the action. To see a code hint, type the action statement, and then type an opening parenthesis. To dismiss the code hint, type a closing parenthesis or press [Esc]. To disable the code hints, click Edit on the menu bar, click Preferences, and then click to deselect the Code Hints check box in the ActionScript category.

Referencing the Timeline in Actions

One of the most common uses of Action-Script is to create navigation buttons that jump between frames based on a user action, such as a click of the mouse. Referencing a specific frame allows you to break your movies out of the sequential movement of the Timeline. You can use either a frame number or frame label to reference the Timeline in actions. A **frame label** is simply a text name for a keyframe.

Frame labels have an advantage over frame numbers, in that adding or deleting frames won't disrupt any navigation or frame references you have already included in

FIGURE 2

The Actions panel with the Actions toolbox pane and Script navigator pane collapsed

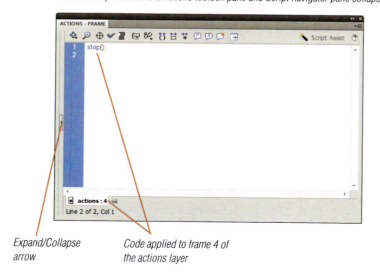

Expand/Collapse arrow

Code applied to frame 4 of the actions layer

actions because the label remains attached to the frame even if the frame moves.

ActionScript 2.0 and 3.0

The latest version of Flash ActionScript is 3.0. This powerful, sophisticated scripting program provides a great deal of flexibility when creating applications and can result in quicker playback for the viewer. However, ActionScript 3.0 (AS3) requires knowledge of object-oriented programming. Therefore, it is primarily used by Flash developers who create applications by writing scripting code. ActionScript 2.0 (AS2) has most of the functionality of AS3. And, the Script Assist feature of AS2 allows those with minimal programming expertise to create complex applications.

When you start a new Flash document, you are given the choice of specifying that ActionScript 2.0 or 3.0 be used. If you are working with a document that is started as an AS3 document, you can change to AS2 in two ways. First, using the Actions panel, you can select ActionScript 1.0 & 2.0 from a list in the Actions toolbox pane. Second, you can select the Publish Settings command on the File menu to open the Publish Settings dialog box, and then select the Flash tab. Then you can select the desired ActionScript version from a list, as shown in Figure 4.

FIGURE 4

Selecting the ActionScript version

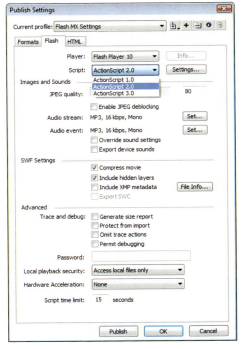

Parameters enclosed in parentheses

FIGURE 3

Example of ActionScript code

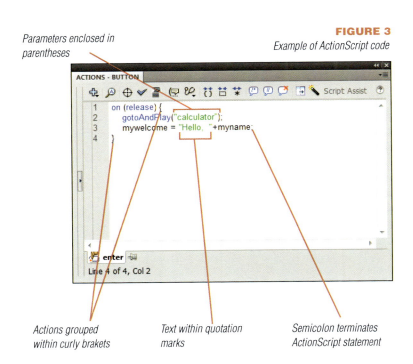

Actions grouped within curly brakets

Text within quotation marks

Semicolon terminates ActionScript statement

Lesson 1   Work with the Actions Panel

Create a frame label

1. Open fl9_1.fla from the drive and folder where your Data Files are stored, then save it as **sale**.

2. Drag the **playhead** through the Timeline to see the parts of the movie.

   There are four different screens: in frames 1, 5, 10, and 15. There are also four stop actions in the corresponding frames on the actions layer, which stop the movie after each screen is displayed.

3. Insert a new **layer** above the buttons layer, then name it **labels**.

4. Insert a **keyframe** in frame 10 on the labels layer.

5. Open the Properties panel, click **frame 10** on the labels layer, click the **Name text box** in the LABEL area on the Properties panel, type **try_out** for the frame label, press **[Enter]** (Win) or **[return]** (Mac), then compare your Properties panel to Figure 5.

6. Insert a **keyframe** in frame 15 on the labels layer, click the **Name text box** in the Properties panel, name the frame **one_on_one**, then press **[Enter]** (Win) or **[return]** (Mac).

   A flag symbol in frame 15 on the labels layer indicates a frame label has been inserted.

   You added a new layer and used the Properties panel to create frame labels.

FIGURE 5
Creating a frame label

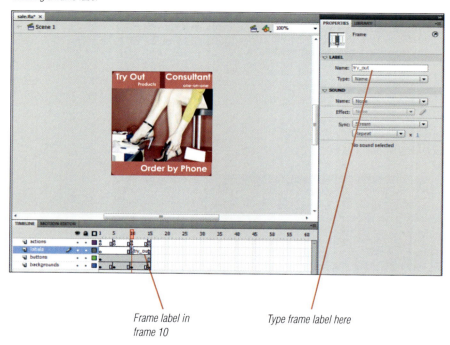

Frame label in frame 10

Type frame label here

FIGURE 6

Adding a `goto` action that references a frame label

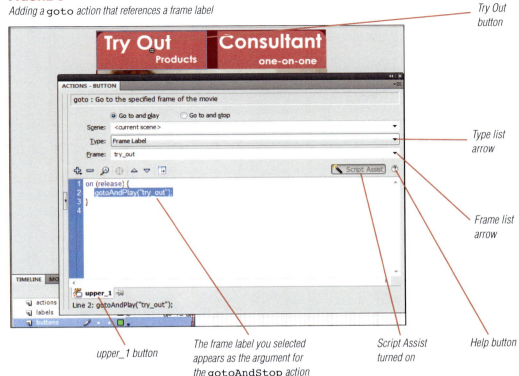

Try Out button

Type list arrow

Frame list arrow

Help button

Script Assist turned on

upper_1 button

The frame label you selected appears as the argument for the `gotoAndStop` action

Use frame labels with actions

1. Set the view to **Fit in Window**, then click the **Try Out button** on the Stage to select it.

2. Open the Actions panel, then verify that Script Assist is turned on.

3. Verify the button symbol and upper_1 is displayed at the bottom left of the Script pane.

   The button is named upper_1.

4. Click the **Add a new item to the script button** ⚎ , point to **Global Functions**, point to **Movie Clip Control**, then click **on**.

5. Click the **Add a new item to the script button** ⚎ , point to **Global Functions**, point to **Timeline Control**, then click **goto**.

6. Click the **Type list arrow**, then click **Frame Label**.

7. Click the **Frame list arrow**, click **try_out**, then compare your screen to Figure 6.

8. Click **Control** on the menu bar, click **Test Movie** to test the movie, then click the **Try Out button**.

   The movie jumps to the shoes product frame.

9. Close the Flash Player window.

You created navigation by referencing an action to a frame label.

Getting help on ActionScript

If you're not sure what an action does or if you need some guidance on which parameters to use, the Help panel can provide more information. To display the Help panel, highlight an action in the Actions panel, then click the Help button. An explanation of the action, along with details about its usage and parameters, appears in a separate panel. You can navigate this panel to show information about other actions in the same way you navigate the Actions panel.

Lesson 1   Work with the Actions Panel

1. Click the **Script Assist button** to turn it off.

2. Click the **View Options button** ▼≡ on the Actions panel.

3. Verify that Line Numbers has a check mark next to it, then click the **Stage** to close the Options menu.

   Note: The ActionScript code disappears from the Script pane because the object is no longer selected.

4. Click the **Consultant button** on the Stage, then verify the upper_2 button symbol is displayed in the lower left of the Script pane.

5. Click next to 1 in the Script pane, then type **// navigation for button**.

   This comment will be ignored when the ActionScript runs. Comments that explain the intent of your ActionScript can help when troubleshooting, and they are especially important if you are working collaboratively on a movie.

6. Press **[Enter]** (Win) or **[return]** (Mac) to insert a new line, then type **on(**.

   The code hint list appears, displaying the options for the action.

   | TIP   You can also click the Show code hint button to display the code hint list.

7. Double-click **release** to select it, type **)** to end the function, press **[Spacebar]**, then type **{** as shown in Figure 7.

8. Press **[Enter]** (Win) or **[return]** (Mac) to move to line 3, then type **gotoAndStop(**.

(continued)

FIGURE 7
Adding an `on(release)` action

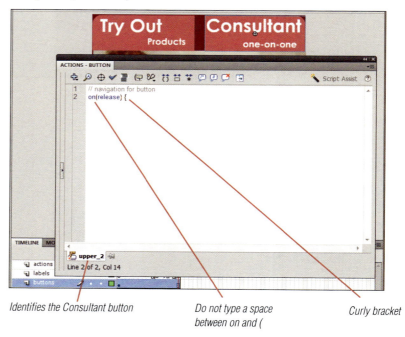

Identifies the Consultant button

Do not type a space between on and (

Curly bracket

Adding a comment to the code

You can add a comment to your ActionScript by placing a slash and an asterisk (/*) at the beginning and an asterisk and a slash (*/) at the end of one or more lines of text. Any code between the set of symbols will be ignored when the ActionScript runs. If your comment is only a single line, you can alternatively place two slashes (//) at the beginning of the line, and that line will be ignored when the ActionScript runs. Comments are helpful reminders as to your intentions as you write the code.

FIGURE 8

Adding a `gotoAndStop` *action*

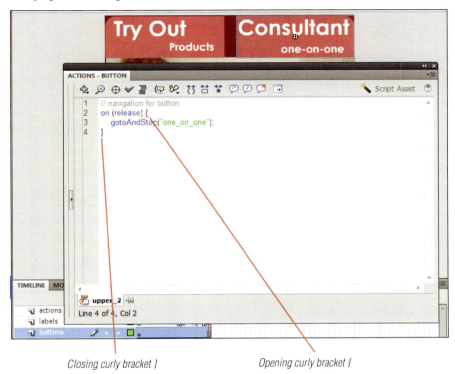

Closing curly bracket }　　　　　　*Opening curly bracket {*

Typing code in the Actions panel

ActionScript code needs to be precisely entered into the Actions panel—this includes spacing between parts of the code. In some cases, added spaces may cause an error when the code is executed. In most cases, using the Auto format feature will automatically format the code with the correct spacing. It is recommended to always use the Auto format feature.

A code hint appears, displaying the syntax for the action.

> TIP Be sure to use exact case when typing actions.

9. Immediately after the opening parenthesis, type **"one_on_one");**.

   The quotation marks indicate that one_on_one is a frame label. This code instructs the program to stop at the frame labeled one_on_one when the Consultant button is clicked. The semicolon indicates the end of a line of code.

10. Press **[Enter]** (Win) or **[return]** (Mac) to move to Line 4, then type **}**.

11. Click the **Auto format button** ≣ at the top of the Script pane, then click the **Check syntax button** ✔.

    If an error message appears, check your screen with Figure 8 and make changes as necessary.

12. Click **OK** to continue.

13. Test the movie, then click the **Consultant button**.

    The movie jumps to the consultation frame.

    Note: If the Consultant button does not work, check your code carefully. It needs to be precise. Make sure that the curly brackets are used as specified.

14. Close the Flash Player window, close the Actions panel, save your work, then close the file.

You created navigation by writing code using a frame label in the Actions panel, and you checked the format and syntax of the script.

WORK WITH TARGETS AND
MOVIE CLIP SYMBOLS

What You'll Do

In this lesson, you will use ActionScript to control movie clip Timelines.

Working with Movie Clips

Most large Flash documents include many movie clip symbols. Using movie clips helps you better manage your document by breaking complex tasks into smaller components, and also lets you reuse content and reduce file size. Another advantage to movie clips is you can use actions with them, allowing you greater control over the objects on the Stage.

You can set up the actions you associate with movie clips to run when a user performs an action, to run automatically when the movie plays, or to run when a condition is met, such as if the movie clip has been dropped on top of another movie clip. Some common uses of ActionScript with movie clip symbols include creating actions that run a specific frame within the movie clip symbol's Timeline, and making a movie clip draggable, so users can move it in games, shopping carts, or simulations.

QUICKTIP

The ActionScript that you associate with movie clips will run only when you test, export, or publish your movie.

Referencing Movie Clip Symbols as ActionScript Targets

To control movie clip symbols and their Timelines with ActionScript, you must target the movie clips, or refer to them by path and name. Since actions are associated with specific instances of objects, you cannot just use the movie clip symbol name that appears in the Library panel. Instead, you must use the Properties panel to create an instance name for the movie clip to which you want to refer. You can target movie clip symbols at any level, even movie clips nested inside other movie clips.

The "with" action lets you target a movie clip on which to perform other actions. You can specify the movie clip symbol either by typing a path and name directly using dot syntax, which is explained in the following paragraph, or by clicking the Insert a target path button. The Insert Target Path dialog box, shown in Figure 9, displays movie clip symbol names hierarchically. You can click the plus sign next to a name to see nested movie clips.

In addition, Flash allows you to use **dot syntax** to create targets. A dot (.) identifies the hierarchical nature of the path to a movie clip symbol, similar to the way slashes are used to create a path name to a file in some operating systems. For example, "myShirt.myPattern", as shown in the ActionScript statement in Figure 10, refers to a movie clip symbol named myPattern nested within the symbol myShirt. You can also use dot syntax in an ActionScript statement to set actions and variables for a movie clip. For example, "square._x = 150" sets the X-axis position of a movie clip symbol named square to 150.

There are also three special terms: _root, _parent, and this, which you can use when creating target paths with dot syntax. _root refers to the main Timeline. You can use _root to create an absolute path, or a path that works downward from the top level of a movie. _parent refers to the movie clip in which the current clip is nested. You can use _parent to create a relative path or a path that works backward through the hierarchy. (_parent essentially means "go up one level from where I currently am.") Relative paths are helpful when writing ActionScript you intend to reuse for multiple objects. The term this in a dot syntax statement refers to the current Timeline.

FIGURE 9
Insert Target Path dialog box

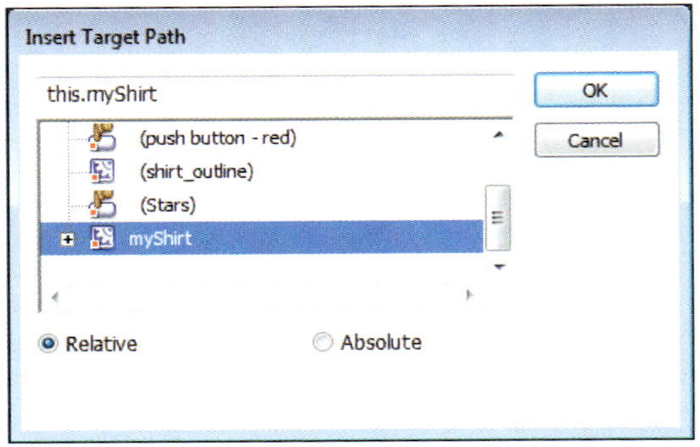

FIGURE 10
ActionScript statement using dot syntax

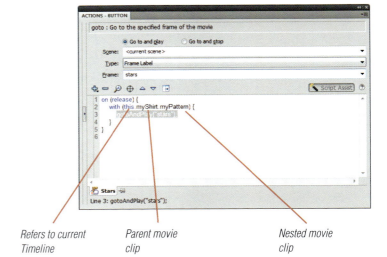

Refers to current Timeline

Parent movie clip

Nested movie clip

Assign an instance name to a movie clip symbol

1. Open fl9_2.fla, then save it as **shirt**.

2. Click the **Selection tool** ▶ on the Tools panel (if necessary), then double-click the **yellow shirt** on the Stage to open the shirt_color movie clip symbol.

   The yellow shirt on the Stage is an instance of the shirt_color movie clip. This movie clip symbol has a layer (shirt) that changes the color of the shirt, a layer (actions) that includes actions to stop the clip after each frame, and a layer (pattern) that includes a nested movie clip to change the pattern of the shirt. When you click the shirt on the Stage, you are selecting the movie clip instance. When you double-click the shirt, you are displaying the movie clip in an edit window.

3. Drag the **playhead** along the movie clip Timeline to see how the shirt changes color, then click **Scene 1** at the top left of the workspace to return to the main Timeline.

4. Click the **shirt** on the Stage to select it.

5. Display the Properties panel, then verify shirt_color is displayed after the phrase Instance of.

   This indicates that the shirt is an instance of the shirt_color movie clip, which is available in the Library panel.

6. Click the **Instance Name text box**, type **myShirt** for the instance name, then press **[Enter]** (Win) or **[return]** (Mac).

   The shirt on the Stage is an instance of the movie clip shirt_color. Specifying an instance name (as shown in Figure 11) is required when you want to target the movie clip in your ActionScript.

   You viewed a movie clip in the edit window and then assigned an instance name to the movie clip.

FIGURE 11
Naming a movie clip symbol instance

myShirt is the name for the instance of the shirt_color movie clip

Type the instance name in this text box

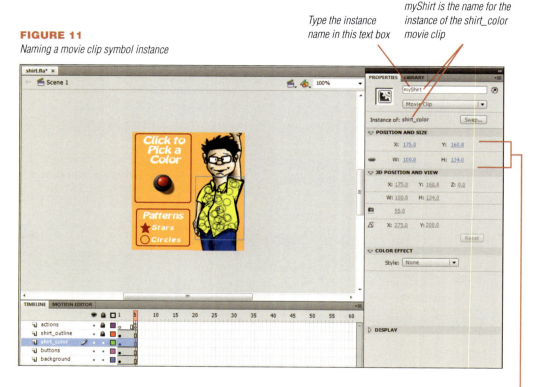

The X and Y coordinates on your screen may differ

FIGURE 12

Movie clip symbol instance name in Insert Target Path dialog box

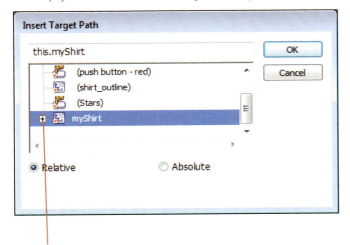

Symbol may differ on your screen

FIGURE 13

ActionScript to change the color of the shirt on button release

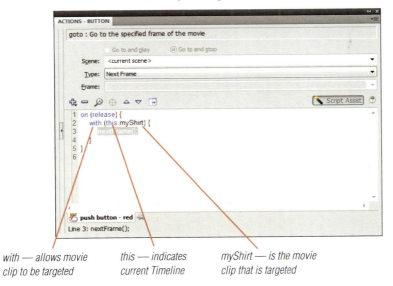

with — allows movie clip to be targeted

this — indicates current Timeline

myShirt — is the movie clip that is targeted

Use Script Assist to control the Timeline of a movie clip symbol

1. Click the **red button** on the Stage (under the words "Click to Pick a Color"), display the Actions panel, then verify the push button - red button symbol is displayed in the lower left of the Script pane.

2. Click **Script Assist** to turn it on.

3. Click the **Add a new item to the script button** ⚡, point to **Global Functions**, point to **Movie Clip Control**, then click **on**.

4. Click the **Add a new item to the script button** ⚡, point to **Statements**, point to **Variables**, then click **with**.

   Now you need to specify the movie clip to be targeted with the action.

5. Click inside the **Object text box**, click the **Insert a target path button** ⊕ to open the Insert Target Path dialog box, scroll the list, click the **myShirt movie clip instance symbol**, as shown in Figure 12, then click **OK**.

6. Click the **Add a new item to the script button** ⚡, point to **Global Functions**, point to **Timeline Control**, then click **goto**.

7. Click the **Type list arrow**, click **Next Frame**, then compare your image to Figure 13.

8. Test the movie, then click the **red button** repeatedly.

   Each time you click the button, the shirt color changes.

9. Close the Flash Player window, then collapse the Actions panel.

You used Script Assist to write ActionScript code to control the Timeline of a movie clip symbol.

Use Script Assist to control the Timeline of a nested movie clip symbol

1. Verify that the Selection tool ![selection tool icon] is selected, double-click the **shirt** on the Stage, double-click the **shirt** (now in the edit window) to open the pattern_shirt nested movie clip symbol, then compare your image to Figure 14.

   The pattern_shirt movie clip symbol (nested inside the shirt_color movie clip symbol) changes the pattern of the shirt. It includes two frame labels, "circles" and "stars."

2. Drag the **playhead** along the movie clip symbol Timeline to see how the shirt pattern changes.

3. Click the **shirt_color movie clip link** at the top of the workspace to return to the shirt_color edit window.

4. Click the **shirt** on the Stage to select an instance of the pattern_shirt movie clip symbol, display the Properties panel, click the **Instance Name text box**, type **myPattern** for the instance name, then press **[Enter]** (Win) or **[return]** (Mac).

   TIP   The Properties panel changes the settings for the currently selected object, the pattern_shirt movie clip. To select a nested movie clip, the parent movie clip must be open.

5. Click **Scene 1** at the top left of the workspace to return to the main Timeline.

6. Click the **Stars button** on the Stage (under the word "Patterns") to select the Stars button.

7. Display the Actions panel, then verify that the Stars button symbol is displayed in the lower left of the Script pane.

   (continued)

FIGURE 14
Timeline of a nested movie clip symbol

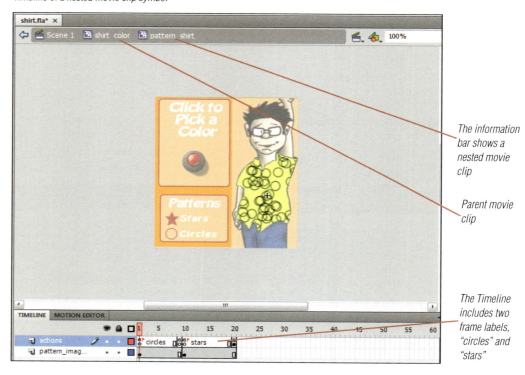

The information bar shows a nested movie clip

Parent movie clip

The Timeline includes two frame labels, "circles" and "stars"

FIGURE 15

Nested movie clip symbol in the Insert Target Path dialog box

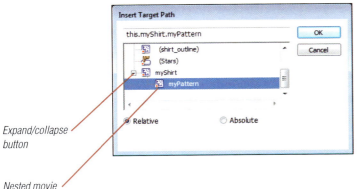

Expand/collapse button

Nested movie clip symbol

FIGURE 16

Referencing a frame label in the nested movie clip symbol `gotoAndPlay` *action*

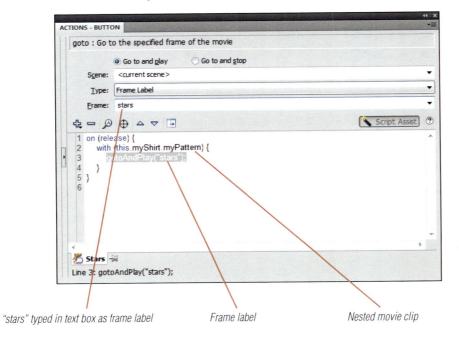

"stars" typed in text box as frame label   Frame label   Nested movie clip

8. Click the **Add a new item to the script button** ⊞ , point to **Global Functions**, point to **Movie Clip Control**, then click **on**.

9. Click the **Add a new item to the script button** ⊞ , point to **Statements**, point to **Variables**, then click **with**.

10. Click inside the **Object text box**, click the **Insert a target path button** ⊕ , click ⊞ (Win) or **triangle** (Mac) to expand the myShirt path, click the **myPattern movie clip symbol**, as shown in Figure 15, then click **OK**.

A path (this.myShirt.myPattern) is inserted into the nested movie clip symbol in dot syntax format.

11. Click the **Add a new item to the script button** ⊞ , point to **Global Functions**, point to **Timeline Control**, then click **goto**.

12. Click the **Type list arrow**, click **Frame Label**, click in the **Frame text box**, delete the frame number, type **stars** in the Frame text box, then compare your Actions panel to Figure 16.

13. Test the movie, then click the **Stars button**.

The shirt pattern changes to stars.

14. Close the Flash Player window, then save your work.

You used Script Assist to create ActionScript code to control the Timeline of a nested movie clip symbol.

Copy ActionScript between objects

1. Turn off Script Assist.

   Turning off Script Assist allows you to edit the code.

2. Right-click (Win) or [control] click (Mac) in the **Script pane**, then click **Select All** to select the ActionScript, as shown in Figure 17.

3. Right-click (Win) or [control] click (Mac) the selection, then click **Copy**.

4. Click the **Circles button** on the Stage to select it, then verify circles and the button symbol are displayed in the lower left of the Script pane.

5. Click in the **Script pane**, right-click (Win) or [control] click (Mac), then click **Paste**.

(continued)

FIGURE 17
Selecting the ActionScript to copy

Using ActionScript

FIGURE 18

Replacing the frame label in the gotoAndPlay action

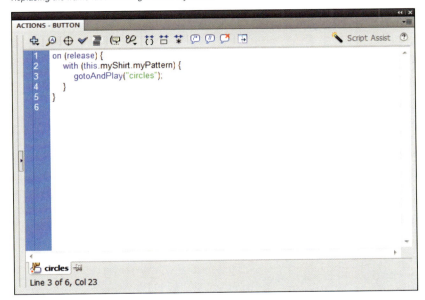

6. Double-click the word **stars** in the Script pane to select it, press **[Delete]**, then type **circles**, as shown in Figure 18.

7. Test the movie, click the **Stars button**, then click the **Circles button**.

   The shirt pattern changes to stars when you click the Stars button. The shirt pattern changes to circles when you click the Circles button.

8. Close the Flash Player window, close the Actions panel, save your work, then close the document.

You copied and edited ActionScript code.

CREATE INTERACTIVE
MOVIE CLIP SYMBOLS

What You'll Do

 In this lesson, you will use ActionScript to make a movie clip draggable and change the properties of a movie clip based on user actions.

Understanding Interactive Movie Clips

Using ActionScript with movie clip symbols offers many opportunities for creating a richer user experience. With the startDrag and stopDrag actions, you can make a movie clip draggable while a movie is playing; that is, you can allow a user to click the movie clip and then move it to another location on the screen. You have probably seen draggable movie clips in games created with Flash, as shown in Figure 19, or in user interface features such as scroll bars and sliders in web applications created with Flash.

Another action, _droptarget, extends the draggable movie clip feature by allowing Flash to determine if a movie clip has collided with (been placed on top of) another movie clip or a specified area on the Stage. When the _droptarget code is used, Flash can then take another set of actions based on where the user has dragged the clip.

ActionScript statements can also change the properties of movie clip symbols as a movie is playing. You can control such properties as position, rotation, color, size, and whether the movie clip is visible or hidden. Actions that change movie clip properties are often used in combination with actions that test for user input or interactions. For example, you can create ActionScript that makes a movie clip disappear when it is dragged onto another movie clip.

Creating Conditional Actions

If-then statements are familiar to anyone who has had minimal programming exposure. ActionScript includes an if action that can test whether certain conditions have been met and, if so, can perform other actions. (You used an If statement when creating a preloader in a previous chapter.) Such conditional statements offer many possibilities for building more interactive movies. You should enclose all the actions you want Flash to carry out in brackets following the if action. If the conditions are not met, the actions in the brackets are ignored, and Flash jumps to the next action.

When creating conditions in ActionScript, you must use two equal signs (==). A single equal sign (=) sets a variable to a specific value. For example, $x=9$ in ActionScript sets a variable named x to the value 9, but $x==9$ is a conditional state-ment that checks if the variable x has a value of 9, and if so, performs another action. Figure 20 shows an example of a conditional statement.

QUICK TIP

ActionScript includes many other actions for creating conditional statements and loops, such as **else**, which lets you specify actions to run when an if statement is false, and **do while**, which lets you specify a set of actions to run continuously until a certain condition is met. See the Help feature for more information.

FIGURE 19

Draggable movie clips in a Flash game

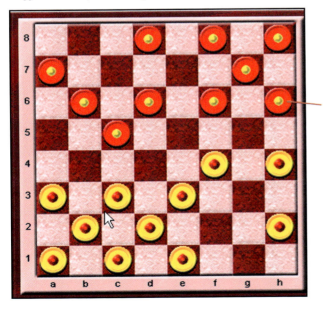

Each checker is a movie clip symbol, which you can drag to a square

FIGURE 20

Example of a conditional ActionScript statement

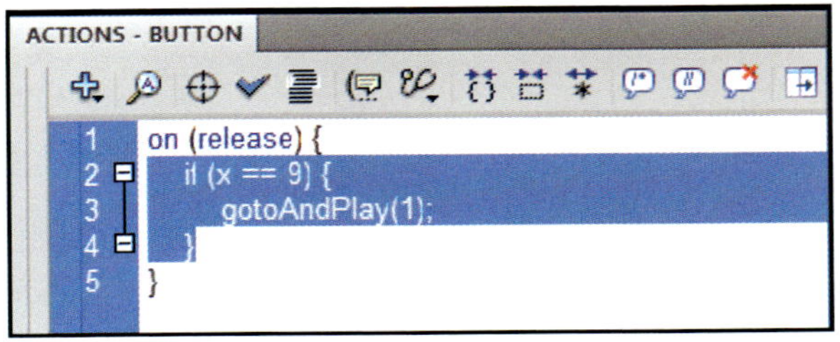

```
ACTIONS - BUTTON
1  on (release) {
2    if (x == 9) {
3      gotoAndPlay(1);
4    }
5  }
```

Use ActionScript to make a movie clip symbol draggable

1. Open fl9_3.fla, then save it as **shapes**.

2. Drag the **playhead** through the Timeline.

   This movie contains two frame labels, "start" and "play", which are associated with two separate screens. The actions layer contains stop actions that correspond to each screen. All the shapes on the "play" screen are movie clip symbols.

3. Click **frame 7** on the Timeline to display the play screen, click the **black square** in the Start Bin, then display the Actions panel.

4. Verify the square and the movie clip symbol are displayed in the lower left of the Script pane, and that Script Assist is active.

5. Click the **Add a new item to the script button** , point to **Global Functions**, point to **Movie Clip Control**, then click **on**.

6. Click the **Release check box** to deselect it, then click the **Press check box** to select it.

7. Click the **Add a new item to the script button** , point to **Global Functions**, point to **Movie Clip Control**, then click **startDrag**.

8. Click the **closing curly bracket** in Line 3 to select it, as shown in Figure 21.

9. Click the **Add a new item to the script button** , point to **Global Functions**, point to **Movie Clip Control**, then click **on**.

   The on (release) action is inserted after the closing curly bracket, indicating the start of a new action.

   (continued)

FIGURE 21
Selecting the curly bracket

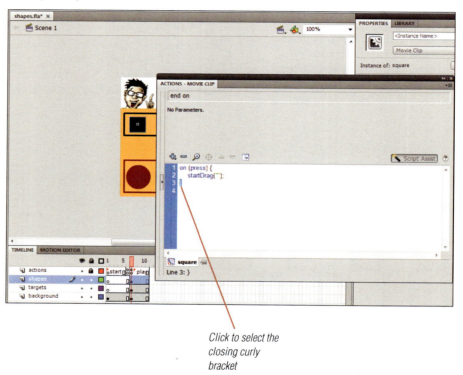

Click to select the closing curly bracket

FIGURE 22
ActionScript to make the movie clip draggable

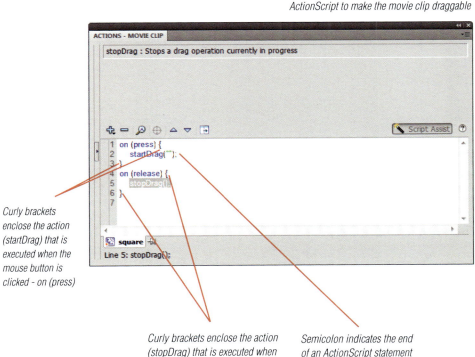

Curly brackets enclose the action (startDrag) that is executed when the mouse button is clicked - on (press)

Curly brackets enclose the action (stopDrag) that is executed when the mouse button is released - on (release)

Semicolon indicates the end of an ActionScript statement

10. Click the **Add a new item to the script button**
⊕ , point to **Global Functions**, point to **Movie Clip Control**, click **stopDrag**, then compare your image to Figure 22.

11. Test the movie, click the **Start button**, then drag and drop the **square** around the screen.

12. Close the Flash Player window, then close the Actions panel.

> TIP   To make the other two movie clip symbols draggable, you could select each symbol and then copy and paste between Script panes. The same ActionScript will work for all three symbols.

You made a movie clip symbol draggable.

Create a conditional action

1. Double-click the **yellow square** in the Drop Bin on the Stage to open the square movie clip, then drag the **playhead** along the movie clip Timeline.

   This movie clip symbol has two states: one with the square filled in, and one with just an outline. In the following steps, you'll create a conditional statement that moves the movie clip to frame 2 when a user drops the square from the Start Bin onto the square in the Drop Bin.

2. Click **Scene 1** to display the main Timeline.

3. Click the **yellow square** to select it, display the Properties panel, then click the **Instance Name text box** in the LABEL area.

4. Type **targetSquare** for the instance name, then press **[Enter]** (Win) or **[return]** (Mac).

   You must name the square so it can be referenced in the ActionScript code.

5. Click the **black square** to select it, then display the Actions panel.

(continued)

6. Click the **Script Assist button** to turn this feature off.

   You need to turn off Script Assist in order to enter text into the Script pane.

7. Click the end of the **StopDrag line** in the Script pane (after the semicolon) in Line 5, press **[Enter]** (Win) or **[return]** (Mac) to create a new line, then type the following ActionScript with no spaces, as shown in Figure 23: **if(_droptarget=="/targetSquare")**.

   This line creates a condition. If the square from the Start Bin is placed on top of the square in the Drop Bin, then perform the next set of actions in curly brackets.

8. Press **[Enter]** (Win) or **[return]** (Mac) to create a new line, then type the following ActionScript:

   {_root.targetSquare.gotoAndPlay(2);}.

   This line of ActionScript plays frame 2 of the targetSquare movie clip.

   > TIP   Use curly brackets at the beginning and end of the code.

9. Click the **Auto format button**, be sure your code matches the code in Figure 24, test the movie, click the **Start button**, then drag and drop the **black square** from the Start Bin onto the yellow square.

   Flash plays the second frame of the targetSquare movie clip, which changes the square in the Drop Bin to just an outline.

10. Close the Flash Player window, then close the Actions panel.

You created a conditional ActionScript statement that plays a specified frame in a movie clip symbol when two movie clips collide.

FIGURE 23
ActionScript to create a conditional statement

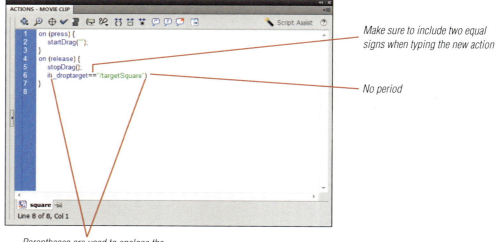

Make sure to include two equal signs when typing the new action

No period

Parentheses are used to enclose the conditional part of the conditional statement

FIGURE 24
Actions to execute if the conditional statement is true

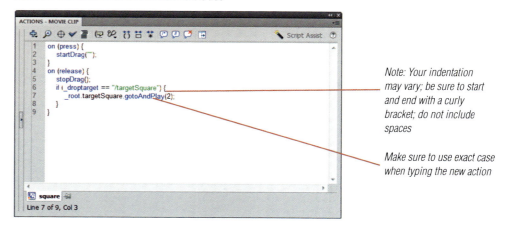

Note: Your indentation may vary; be sure to start and end with a curly bracket; do not include spaces

Make sure to use exact case when typing the new action

Using ActionScript

FIGURE 25
ActionScript to hide the square

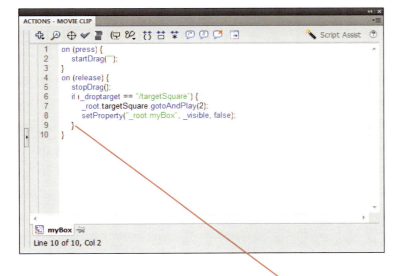

ACTIONS - MOVIE CLIP

```
1   on (press) {
2       startDrag("");
3   }
4   on (release) {
5       stopDrag();
6       if (_droptarget == "/targetSquare") {
7           _root.targetSquare.gotoAndPlay(2);
8           setProperty("_root.myBox", _visible, false);
9       }
10  }
```

Script Assist

myBox
Line 10 of 10, Col 2

*Make sure to type the new action
inside the line-closing curly bracket*

Understanding the / (slash) in the _droptarget action

_droptarget was first introduced in Flash Version 4.0, before dot syntax was available, and when only slash syntax was supported. The slash in "/targetSquare" is the equivalent of _root in dot syntax: it tells Flash where the movie clip is relative to the main Timeline. Other actions may also require paths that use slash syntax; be sure to check the Help panel when using a new action. Flash includes an eval action with which you can convert dot syntax paths to slash syntax in an ActionScript statement.

Use ActionScript to change the properties of a movie clip symbol

1. Click the **black square** in the Start Bin, open the Properties panel, then name the instance of the movie clip symbol **myBox**.

   You must name the square so you can reference it in ActionScript.

2. Display the Actions panel, verify that the black square is still selected and that **myBox** is displayed in the lower left of the Script pane.

3. Click the **Script pane** after the semicolon at the end of the gotoAndPlay code on Line 7, then press **[Enter]** (Win) or **[return]** (Mac) to create a new line.

   Line 8 is now blank and the line-closing curly bracket moves down one line.

4. On the blank line 8, which is before the line-closing curly bracket, type the following ActionScript:

   setProperty("_root.myBox", _visible, false);

5. Click the **Auto format button** ≣ in the Script pane, then compare your ActionScript to Figure 25.

6. Test the movie, click the **Start button**, then drag and drop the **square** from the Start Bin onto the square in the Drop Bin.

   The black square becomes invisible.

7. Close the Flash Player window, save your work, then close shapes.fla.

You created an ActionScript statement that hides a movie clip symbol when a condition is met.

DEFINE VARIABLES

What You'll Do

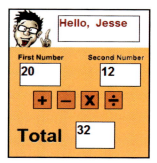

 In this lesson, you will use ActionScript to create interactive text and number variables.

Understanding Variables

A **variable** is a container that holds information. Variables are dynamic; that is, the information they contain changes depending on an action a user takes or another aspect of how the movie plays. A Flash game that keeps track of scores is an example of using variables, as is a form in which a user enters credit card information while making an online purchase.

You create variables in ActionScript with the setvar action or by using an equal sign (=). You do not have to specify a data type for the variable when you create it, but it is good practice to give the variable an initial value so you can keep track of how it changes as you use it in expressions. To create a **string variable**, which is a sequence of characters including letters, numbers, and punctuation, place quotation marks around the string. For example, the ActionScript statement `myExam = "Pop Quiz"` creates a variable named myExam and assigns the string Pop Quiz to it. To create a **number variable**, just write the number. For example, `myScore = 93` creates a number variable named myScore and assigns the number 93 to it. No quotation marks are needed around a number variable.

Flash includes the following data types for variables: String, Number, Boolean, Object, Movieclip, Null, and Undefined. See the Flash Help system for a full explanation of each type.

QUICKTIP

To ensure your ActionScript will run correctly, do not include spaces in variable names.

Using Text Fields to Collect User Information

One of the most powerful uses of variables is to collect and work with information from users. To do this, you create input and dynamic text fields.

An **input text field** takes information entered by a user and stores it as a variable. To create an input box, first create a text box using the Text tool on the Tools panel, then open the Properties panel.

You then change the text type to Input and assign a variable name, as shown in Figure 26. You can also set other properties, such as whether the input box appears with a border, or the maximum number of characters allotted for user input.

A **dynamic text field** displays information derived from variables. A dynamic text field can be used together with an input text field. For example, you could have a user enter his/her name into an input text field in one part of a movie and have the name displayed in a dynamic field in another part of the movie. You use the Text tool and Properties panel to create a dynamic text field. If you want exactly what a user has typed to appear in the dynamic text field (for example, a name to appear on a series of pages), assign the dynamic text field the same name as the input text field. If you want to manipulate variables using ActionScript before displaying them in the dynamic text field (for example, adding a greeting with a person's name), assign the field a unique name. (*Note*: When the Input and Dynamic text fields are used to assign numbers to variables, the Flash Publish Settings must be set to ActionScript 2.0 and Flash Player version 6.)

Understanding Expressions

Expressions are formulas for manipulating or evaluating the information in variables. This can range from string expressions that concatenate (join together) user and system-derived text (as in a paragraph that inserts a user's name right in the text) to numeric expressions that perform mathematical calculations like addition, subtraction, or incrementing a value. Flash also lets you enter logical expressions that perform true/false comparisons on numbers and strings, with which you can create conditional statements and branching.

Note that some expressions have different results depending on whether they are performed on string or number variables. For example, the comparison operators $>$, $>=$, $<$, and $<=$ determine alphabetical order when used with string variables, and the mathematical operator $+$ concatenates strings.

Figure 27 shows an expression in which the value in one variable (secondNumber) is subtracted from the value of another variable (firstNumber) and the result is assigned to a third variable (myTotal).

FIGURE 26
Using the Properties panel to create an input text field

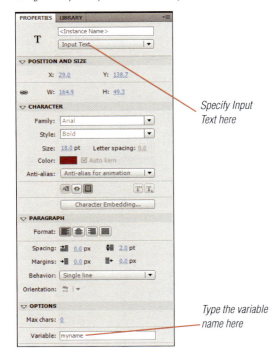

Specify Input Text here

Type the variable name here

FIGURE 27
Example of an expression used for a calculation

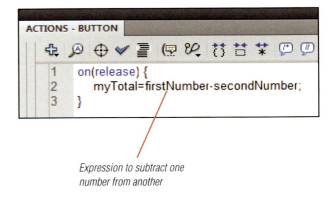

Expression to subtract one number from another

Create an input text box

1. Open fl9_4.fla, then save it as **math**.

2. Drag the **playhead** through the Timeline.

   This movie has two screens, an introduction that allows you to type in a name, and a screen to enter numbers and perform calculations.

3. Click **frame 1** on the background layer, then click the **Text tool** T on the Tools panel.

4. Display the Properties panel, then make the following changes: Family: **Arial**; Style: **Bold**; Size: **18**; Color: **#990000**.

5. Click the **Text type list arrow** in the Properties panel, click **Input Text**, click the **Show border around text button** 🖽 to turn it on, then verify the Behavior is set to Single line.

6. Draw a **text box** as shown in Figure 28.

   TIP   Use the pointer to move the box. Use the handles to resize the box.

7. Verify the input text box is selected on the Stage, display the OPTIONS area on the Properties panel, click the **Variable text box**, type **myname**, press **[Enter]** (Win) or **[return]** (Mac), then compare your screen to Figure 29.

8. Test the movie.

   A white input text box appears.

9. Close the Flash Player window.

You created an input text box in which users can type their name. You also specified the formatting for the input text.

FIGURE 28
Drawing the text box for the input text field

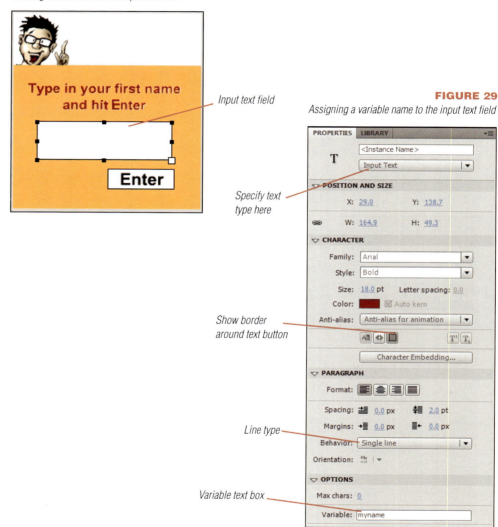

Input text field

FIGURE 29
Assigning a variable name to the input text field

Specify text type here

Show border around text button

Line type

Variable text box

Using ActionScript

FIGURE 30

Drawing the text box for the dynamic text field

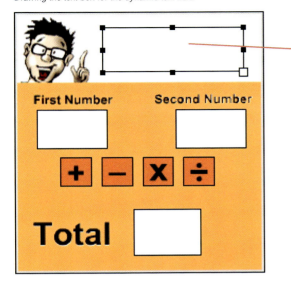

Text box that will
become a dynamic
text field

First Number   **Second Number**

+ — X ÷

Total

FIGURE 31

Creating the dynamic text field

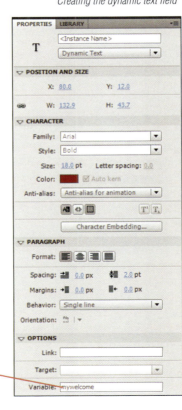

Type variable
name here

Create a dynamic text box

1. Click the **Selection tool** on the Tools panel, then click **frame 5** on the background layer.

2. Click the **Pasteboard** to deselect the objects.

3. Click the **Text tool** T on the Tools panel, click the **white area** next to the character, then draw a **text box** in the white area of the Stage to the right of the cartoon character, as shown in Figure 30.

4. Click the **Selection tool** on the Tools panel, then verify the text box is selected.

5. Display the Properties panel.

6. Click the **Text type list arrow**, click **Dynamic Text**, display the OPTIONS area of the Properties panel if it is not already displayed, click the **Variable text box**, type **mywelcome**, as shown in Figure 31, then press **[Enter]** (Win) or **[return]** (Mac).

You created a dynamic text box to hold the name the user enters.

Use ActionScript to collect and modify string variables

1. Click **frame 1** on the buttons layer, then click the **Enter button** on the Stage.

2. Display the Actions panel, then verify that the enter button symbol and name are displayed in the lower left of the Script pane.

3. Turn off Script Assist (if necessary).

4. In the Script pane, click at the **end of Line 2** after the semicolon, press **[Enter]** (Win) or **[return]** (Mac) to create a new blank line after Line 2 but before the closing curly bracket, then type the following line of ActionScript: **mywelcome = "Hello, "+myname;**.

   When the user clicks the Enter button, this ActionScript takes the name the user has entered in the myname input field, prefaces it with the word "Hello", then places the text string in the mywelcome dynamic text box.

5. Click the **Check syntax button** ✔ in the Script pane, then click **OK**.

   If there are errors in the code, check your code and be sure it matches the code in Figure 32.

6. Click the **Auto format button** ☰ in the Script pane.

7. Test the movie, click the **name input field**, type **Jesse**, then click **Enter**.

   The name "Jesse" appears in the dynamic text field, prefaced by "Hello".

8. Close the Flash Player window, then close the Actions panel.

You used ActionScript to modify a text variable and place it in a dynamic text box.

FIGURE 32
ActionScript to populate the mywelcome dynamic text box

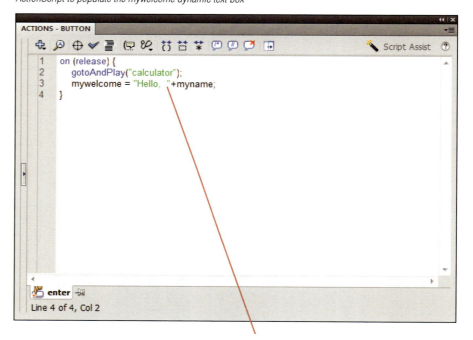

Make sure to include a space between the comma and closing quotation mark

FIGURE 33

ActionScript for subtraction operation

```
ACTIONS - BUTTON

1  on(release) {
2      myTotal=firstNumber-secondNumber;
3  }


     minus_button

Line 3 of 3, Col 2
```

FIGURE 34

The working formula

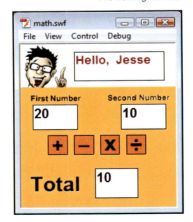

Use ActionScript to collect and perform a mathematical operation on a numeric variable

1. Click **frame 5** on the Timeline to display the second screen.

   This screen already contains two input text boxes (First Number and Second Number) and a dynamic text box (Total).

2. Verify the Selection tool ▸ on the Tools panel is selected, click the **subtraction button**, then display the Actions panel.

3. Verify that the minus_button symbol and name are displayed in the lower left of the Script pane, then type the three lines of ActionScript in the Script pane, as shown in Figure 33.

   When the user clicks the subtraction button, this ActionScript subtracts the number the user has typed in the secondNumber input field from the number in the firstNumber input field, then places the result in the myTotal dynamic text field.

4. Check the syntax and auto format the code.

5. Test the movie, type **Jesse**, click the **Enter button**, type **20** in the First Number box, type **10** in the Second Number box, click the **subtraction button**, then compare your screen to Figure 34.

6. Close the Flash Player window.

You used ActionScript to create a mathematical operation that works with variables.

Copying ActionScript code

1. Right-click (Win) or [control] click (Mac) the **ActionScript code** in the Script pane, then click **Select All**.

2. Right-click (Win) or [control] click (Mac) the **ActionScript code** in the Script pane, then click **Copy**.

3. Click the **multiplication button** on the Stage, verify the multiplication button symbol and name are displayed at the lower left of the Script pane, right-click (Win) or [control] click (Mac) in the Script pane, then click **Paste**.

4. Double-click the **minus sign** between firstNumber and secondNumber, type * (an asterisk), then compare your Script pane to Figure 35.

5. Click the **division button** on the Stage, verify the division button symbol and name are displayed at the lower left of the Script pane, click in the **Script pane**, right-click (Win) or [control] click (Mac), then click **Paste**.

6. Double-click the **minus sign**, then type / (forward slash).

   The forward slash is the division operator.

7. Test the movie, type **Jesse**, click the **Enter button**, then experiment with entering numbers in the input boxes and clicking the subtraction, multiplication, and division buttons.

8. Close the Flash Player window.

You copied ActionScript code from one object to another and made a change in the code.

FIGURE 35
ActionScript for multiplication operation

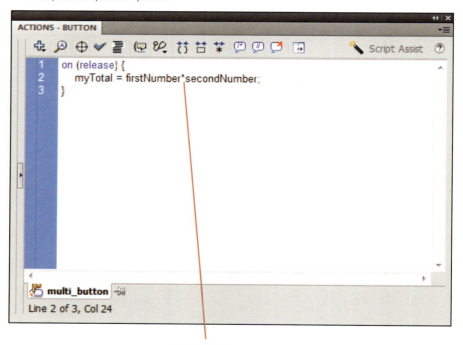

* (asterisk) is the multiplication operator

FIGURE 36

FIGURE 36

ActionScript utilizing the Number function

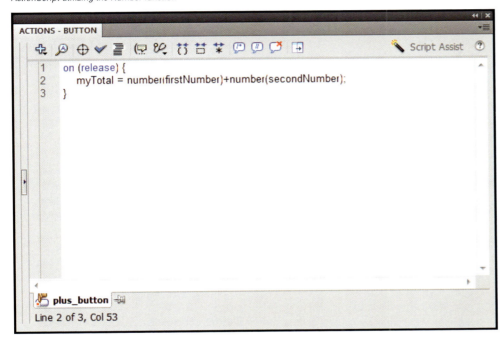

Use the Number function to create an addition operation for numeric variables

1. Click the **addition button** on the Stage, then display the Actions panel.

2. Verify the plus_button button symbol and name are displayed in the lower left of the Script pane.

3. Click in the **Script pane**, right-click (Win) or [control] click (Mac), then click **Paste**.

4. Edit the second line of the ActionScript to the following and as shown in Figure 36: **myTotal=number(firstNumber)+number (secondNumber);**.

   The number function indicates the variable in parentheses is a number, which ensures an addition operation, rather than a concatenation. For example, without the number function, if the user inputs 20 and 10, the + would cause the Total box to display 2010 instead of 30.

5. Test the movie, type **Jesse**, click the **Enter button**, then experiment with typing numbers in the input boxes and clicking the plus sign.

6. Close the Flash Player window, save your work, then close the file.

7. Exit Flash.

You used the Number function to create an addition operation in ActionScript.

Work with actions.

(*Hint*: Use the Check syntax and Auto format features when typing ActionScript code.)

1. Start Flash, open fl9_5.fla, then save it as **skillsdemo9**.
2. Use the playhead to look at all the frames in the movie. (*Hint*: This movie includes three different screens, starting in frames 1, 5, and 10. There are stop actions in frames 4, 9, and 15.)
3. Use the Properties panel to label frame 5 on the title_screens layer **seasonChange**.
4. Click frame 1 on the Timeline, unlock the buttons layer, select the Start button, then use the Actions panel to create a link to the seasonChange frame when a user clicks the button. (*Hint*: Use the Script Assist feature and the goto action to create the link.)
5. Test the movie, then save your work.

Work with targets and movie clip symbols.

1. Unlock all layers, then click frame 5 on the Timeline.
2. Double-click the tree on the Stage, then move the playhead through the Timeline of the movie clip symbol. The movie clip symbol animates the changing seasons.
3. Return to the main Timeline, click the tree, then use the Properties panel to name this instance of the seasons_animated movie clip **change**.

4. Select the green button to the right of the word "Seasons", then use the Actions panel to add actions that will play the movie clip when a user clicks the button. (*Hint*: This requires a Play command which cannot be inserted using Script Assist. Type the following directly into the Script pane:

    on(release) { with (change) { play(); } }

    Then use the Auto format and Check syntax features to check your entry.)
5. Test the movie, click the Start button to move to the second screen, then click the green button repeatedly. (*Hint*: Each time you click the button, the season changes.)
6. Close the Flash Player window, then save your work.

Create interactive movie clip symbols.

1. Click frame 10 on the Timeline.
2. Select the scarf movie clip symbol on the left side of the Stage, then use the Properties panel to name this instance of the scarf movie clip **scarf**.
3. Select the winter movie clip symbol in the upper-right corner of the screen, then use the Properties panel to name this instance of the winter_graphic movie clip **winter_mc**.
4. Click the red scarf on the left side of the Stage to select the scarf movie clip, then use the Actions panel to add startDrag and stopDrag actions that allow users to drag the scarf.

(*Hint*: Use Script Assist to include an on (press) action with the startDrag action, and after completing the startDrag command, click the closing bracket (}), then continue to specify an *on(release)* action for the stopDrag.)

5. Use the Actions panel to add an if action to the scarf movie clip symbol that uses _droptarget to test whether the scarf has been placed on top of the movie clip instance named winter_mc. (*Hint*: Turn off Script Assist and insert a blank line below the stopDrag line, then type the code.)
6. Use the Actions panel to add a setProperty action to the scarf movie clip symbol that turns the scarf invisible if it is dropped onto the winter_mc movie clip. (*Hint*: Remember to enclose the action within the closing curly bracket of the on (release) action.)
7. Test the movie, click the More button and drag the scarf to the winter scene, close the Flash Player window, then save your work.

Define variables.

1. Click frame 1 on the title_screens layer.
2. Below the "All About Seasons" title, insert the text **What is your favorite season?** using these settings: family: Arial, size: 14, style: Bold, color: black, Show border around text is deselected (off), then resize the box as needed so the question fits on one line.

3. Directly beneath the text, create an input text field with the variable name **mySeason**. Click the Show border around text button to select (turn on) this feature. (*Hint*: Be sure to type the variable name in the "Variable" field in the OPTIONS area on the Properties panel, not the Instance Name field.)

4. Click frame 5 on the title_screens layer.

5. Below the "All About Seasons" title, create a dynamic text field with the variable name **mySeasonText**. (*Hints*: Verify the Show border around text button is deselected. Select the Multiline option as the Behavior in the PARAGRAPH area on the Properties panel and change the font size as needed to ensure that all the dynamic text is displayed.)

6. Click frame 1 on the Timeline, select the Start button, then use the Actions panel to create ActionScript which, upon a click of the button, the words **My favorite season is** followed by the season the user typed in the mySeason input field are displayed in the mySeasonText dynamic text field. (*Hint*: Be sure to insert the new action before the closing curly bracket of the on (release) action, and to include a space at the end of the "My favorite season is" text.)

7. Test the movie, compare your screens to Figure 37, then save your work. (*Hint*: If you do not see all of the text when you test the movie, make the text box larger and then run the test again.)

8. Exit Flash.

FIGURE 37
Completed Skills Review

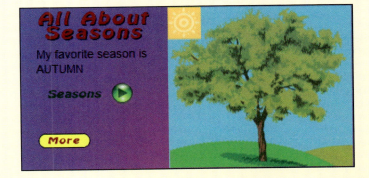

Ultimate Tours wants to add pages to their website that will provide information for the Package Tour of the month. The information will include the destination, features for various types of accommodations, and costs per week. Ultimate Tours would like the pages to be interactive and allow the visitor to enter a name (which is displayed later), enter the number of adults (used to calculate the cost) going on the trip and select the type of accommodations (used to calculate the cost). It would also like the pages to have some visual interest beyond just a series of text and numbers so that it is engaging to the visitor.

1. Open ultimatetours8.fla (the file you created in Chapter 8 Project Builder 1) and save it as **ultimatetours9**.

2. Change the Flash Publish Settings to Player 6.
3. Create a second page that will be displayed when the visitor clicks the sun navigation button on the home page. The second page is a movie clip. (*Hint*: To create a movie clip page, create a new movie clip symbol and use the edit window to design the page. Then return to the main Timeline, insert a keyframe where the new page will appear, drag the movie clip from the Library panel and align it on the Stage.)
4. Refer to Figure 38 as you include the following on the second page. Be sure to include all elements and to check spelling and punctuation.
   - A background that is the same as the home page but that has been dimmed (e.g. set the brightness to 55)
   - A heading with the destination, Cozumel

- A static text box with the text: **Enter your name:**; followed by an input text field that allows the visitor to enter a name
- A static text box with the text: **Enter number of adults:**; followed by an input text field that allows the visitor to enter a number (the number of adults going on the trip)
- Two buttons used to display the features of each type of accommodation (Deluxe and Standard). When the Deluxe button is clicked a list of features appears and a variable is assigned a value that is checked when the calculation for the package cost is calculated. When the Standard button is clicked a different list of features appears and the same variable is assigned a different value that is checked when the package cost is calculated
- A continue button that displays a third page.

FIGURE 38

Sample completed Project Builder 1

Using ActionScript

5. Include the following on the third page:
   - Same background and heading as on the second page
   - A dynamic text field that displays a message (such as Welcome) followed by the name from the input text field on page 2
   - A static text block that displays the words **Total cost: $**
   - A dynamic text field that follows the words Total cost: $ and displays a number that is calculated from the number of adults times the rate for the type of accommodation selected (2000 for Deluxe and 1500 for Standard)
   - The selected accommodation type and list of features
   - A home button that when clicked displays the home page
6. The hierarchy for the movie clips follows:

- The entire second page is a movie clip
  - The rectangle that contains the accommodation features
    - The Deluxe room features
    - The Standard room features
7. Buttons and their functions include:
   - A Deluxe button
     - Displays the features of the Deluxe accommodation
     - Assigns a value to a variable that is checked with the if statement in the Package Price button
   - A Standard button
     - Displays the features of the Standard accommodation
     - Assigns a value to a variable that is checked with the if statement in the Package Price button
   - A "Click to see your Package Price" button
     - Displays the Welcome text and name entered into the input field

- Uses if statements to determine accommodation amount (2000 or 1500) to use in the calculation for the package cost
- Calculates the package cost by multiplying the accommodation amount times the number of adults from the input text field
- Causes the display of the package cost in the dynamic text field
- Jumps to a frame that displays the appropriate objects
- Home button
  - Displays the home page
8. Save your work, then compare your image to the example shown in Figure 38.

You work in the multimedia department of a university. A professor asks you to build an interactive study guide in Flash that includes a series of test questions. The professor would like to see a prototype of a multiple choice style test question with two choices, similar to the following:

What is the periodic symbol of oxygen?

1. Ox
2. O

The professor would like you to build in feedback telling students whether the answer they supply is correct or incorrect. (In this case, the correct answer is choice 2, "O".)

1. Create a new Flash ActionScript 2.0 document, then save it as **test_question9**.
2. Set the Flash Publish Settings to Flash Player 6.
3. Set the movie properties, including the size and background color, if desired.
4. Use the Text tool on the Tools panel to create a multiple-choice-style question of your own, or use the example given in this Project Builder. The question should have two choices.
5. Create an input text field in which a student can type an answer.
6. Create a text label for the field that reads **Your answer:**
7. Create a Submit button near the input field.
8. Create two feedback screens. One screen should indicate an answer is correct, and the other that an answer is incorrect.
9. Attach ActionScript to the Submit button which, upon a click of the button, uses if actions to compare the number the student typed in the input text field with the correct answer, then sends the student to the appropriate "correct" or "incorrect" screen.
10. Create a Start Again button that uses ActionScript to return the student to the original question and also sets the input text field to blank. (*Hint:* You can set the input text field to blank by assigning "" to the variable. The quotation marks with nothing between them clears the input text field.)
11. Create a Next Question button for the Great Job! screen that displays a blank screen with a heading "Placeholder for next question". Set the input field to blank when this button is clicked.
12. Save your work, then compare your movie to the example shown in Figure 39.

FIGURE 39

ActionScript utilizing the Number function

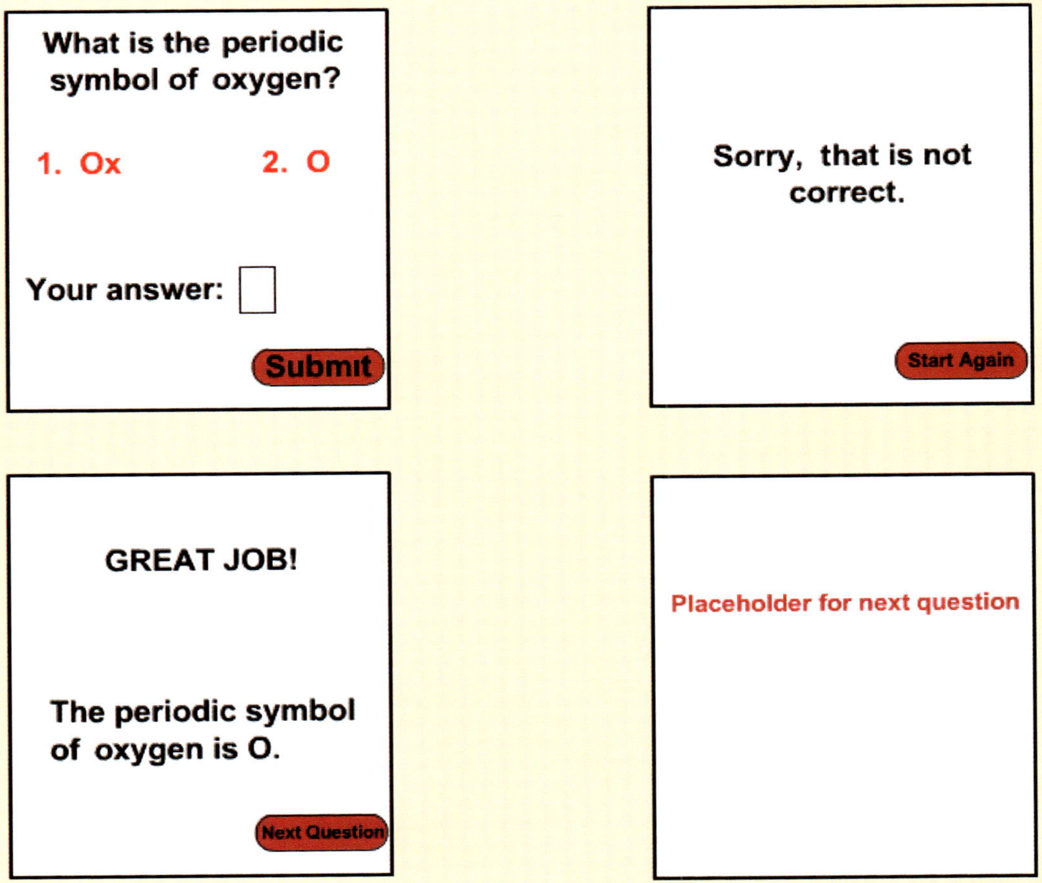

What is the periodic symbol of oxygen?

1. Ox   **2. O**

Your answer: ☐

Submit

Sorry, that is not correct.

Start Again

GREAT JOB!

The periodic symbol of oxygen is O.

Next Question

Placeholder for next question

Figure 40 shows a page from a website created using Flash. Study the figure and complete the following. For each question, indicate how you determined your answer.

1. Connect to the Internet, type the URL *www.nyphilkids.org/games/main.phtml?*, click instrument Frenzy, then read and follow the directions on the screen to play the game.

2. Open a document in a word processor or create a new Flash document, save the file as **dpc9**, then answer the following questions. (*Hint*: Use the Text tool in Flash.)

   - In this game, the visitor uses the arrow keys on the keyboard to move the maestro back and forth. The maestro has to catch the instrument as it drops. The visitor then moves the maestro to the correct bin for the captured instrument and presses the down arrow to drop it in the bin by category (woodwind, brass, percussion, strings). If the instrument is dropped into the correct bin, the visitor is awarded points. Missed catches are also tabulated. What are some of the actions that might be used to enable the user to drag and drop an instrument to the correct bin rather than using the arrow keys?
   - Which elements of the movie must be movie clip symbols? Would all the movie clips need instance names?
   - What actions might be used to allow the visitor to enter a name at the beginning of the game and have the name displayed at the end of the game?
   - When the question mark (?) button near the lower right of the screen is clicked, instructions for playing the game appear. How would you create this navigation?
   - Suppose you wanted the text "Good job!" to appear for one second each time a visitor successfully dragged an instrument into the correct bin. How might you go about creating this effect?

FIGURE 40
Design Project

In a previous chapter, you created a page for your portfolio website that contained thumbnail pictures of work samples. Another way to highlight your work might be to create a slide show, which would display a different sample each time the visitor clicks a button. Such a strategy could motivate the visitor to look at more samples, and would allow you to display a larger area of the sample without forcing the visitor to follow a link.

1. Open portfolio8.fla, then save it as **portfolio9.fla**.
2. Create a series of screen shots with at least four samples of your work, or use the screen shots you created for the Portfolio Project at the end of Chapter 7.
3. Create a new page with the title **Samples of My Web Work**.
4. Create a new movie clip symbol that includes a series of screens each with a sample of your work and some explanatory text. Each sample and associated text should appear in a separate frame.
5. Add stop actions to each frame in the movie clip symbol.
6. Return to the main Timeline and add the movie clip symbol in the center of the Samples of My Web Work page. Use the Properties panel to name the instance of the movie clip symbol **samples**.

7. Add a button with the text **Next slide** on the Samples of My Web Work page, then program the Over and Down states for the button in any way you'd like.
8. Attach ActionScript to the button which, upon a click, will advance the samples movie clip one frame.

FIGURE 41
Sample completed Portfolio Project

9. If desired, create navigation from your current samples page to the main portfolio page, then back to the samples page from the main portfolio page. Use ActionScript and frame labels to create the navigation.
10. Save your work, then compare your movie to the example shown in Figure 41.

chapter

10

ADDING
SOUND

1. Work with sound

2. Specify synchronization options

3. Modify sounds

4. Use ActionScript with sound

10 ADDING SOUND

Introduction

Like animation and interactivity, sound is an important tool you can use to express a message and make your site appealing to visitors. In an earlier chapter, you added sound to the Timeline and to a button. In this chapter, you will see that there is much more you can do with sound in Flash. For example, you can set a short sound clip to play continuously, creating a musical backdrop for your movie. Or, you can synchronize sound with an animation or movie clip, perhaps providing a voice-over that explains what's happening on the screen.

Sound can add significantly to the size of published movies, so you should plan ahead and try to use sound strategically. Apply sound only where it will have the most impact. Flash includes a number of compression options that can help you achieve a balance between sound quality and file size in your movies. Effective and judicious use of sound is a key ingredient in making a Flash site a truly multimedia experience.

Tools You'll Use

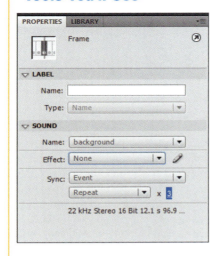

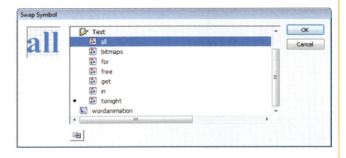

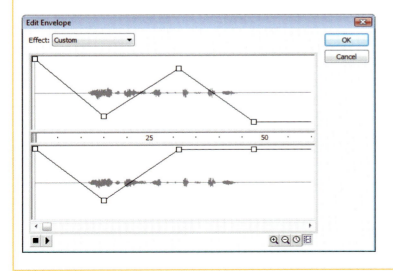

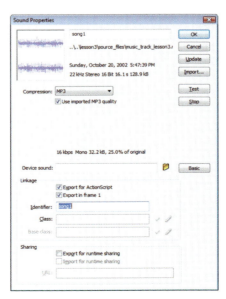

WORK WITH
SOUND

What You'll Do

 In this lesson, you will add background music to a movie and work with layering and repeating sounds.

Importing Sound Files

Before you can add sound to an object or the Timeline in Flash, you must import the file that contains the sound. Flash stores sounds in the Library panel. Table 1 shows the types of sound files you can import. In addition to imported sound files, Flash provides dozens of sound effects such as sirens wailing, dogs barking, and lightning cracking. These are found in the Common Libraries panel on the Windows menu.

Adding a Sound to the Timeline

When you want a sound to play in the background, rather than tie it to a specific object on the Stage like a button, you can add an instance of the sound to a frame in the Timeline. You can select a keyframe on a layer on the Timeline and then drag a sound from the Library panel to the Stage to add the sound to the selected keyframe, or you can select a keyframe on a layer on

TABLE 1: Sound Files that Flash Imports		
sound type	Windows	Mac
Adobe Soundbooth (.asnd)	Yes	Yes
Waveform Audio File (.wav)	Yes	Yes, requires QuickTime
Audio Interchange File (.aiff), (.aif)	Yes, requires QuickTime	Yes
MPEG-1 Audio level 3 (.mp3)	Yes	Yes
Sound only QuickTime movies (.mov), (.qt)	Yes, requires QuickTime	Yes, requires QuickTime
System 7 sounds (.snd)	No	Yes, requires QuickTime
Sound Designer II (.sd2)	No	Yes, requires QuickTime
SunAU (.au)	Yes, requires QuickTime	Yes, requires QuickTime

the Timeline and then add a sound to the selected keyframe through the Properties panel. Using the Properties panel is the recommended method because you can select the sound file you want to use, set the number of times you want the sound file to repeat, and set effects related to the sound file, such as fade in and fade out.

QUICKTIP

Although you can add sounds to layers that contain other objects and actions, keeping sounds on their own layers helps organize your movie and makes it easier to edit the sounds.

Sounds are represented on the Timeline by either a straight or waveform line, as shown in Figure 1. The approximate duration of the sound is indicated by the number of frames the line occupies. Although the line extends no further than the last frame, the duration of the sound may be longer than the duration of the movie, that is, if the last frame that contains sound is beyond the last frame that contains the movie.

FIGURE 1
A sound on the Timeline

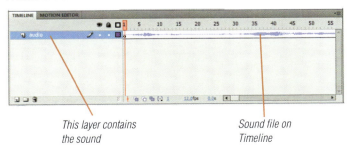

This layer contains the sound

Sound file on Timeline

You can play multiple sounds at once by placing the sounds on different layers. For example, you might have background music that plays continuously, but then play accent sounds at various points to act as a supplement or counterpoint to the background. You can stagger where each sound begins by creating a keyframe at a later point on the Timeline, and then adding the sound to this keyframe. You can also add multiple instances of the same sound to different layers.

QUICKTIP

If you do not have a stop action at the end of the movie and the movie starts over, any sounds in the movie will also restart; this can cause overlapping if the first set of sounds has not yet finished playing.

Understanding Event Sounds

By default, sounds you add in Flash are considered **event sounds**. Event sounds are like movie clip symbols in that they play independently of the Timeline. The sound starts in the keyframe to which you add it,

but it can continue playing even after the last frame in the main Timeline is played. In addition, event sounds may play at a faster or slower rate than indicated by the frames on the Timeline, depending on the speed of the computer on which the movie is played.

Event sounds have an advantage in that you can use them as many times as you like in a movie, with no increase in the file size of your published movie. However, when a movie is played over the web, event sounds do not begin until the entire sound file is downloaded; this may cause a disconnect between sound and images for some users.

There is another type of sound in Flash, called **streaming sound**. Streaming sounds are similar to animated graphic symbols because they are closely tied to the main Timeline; whatever its length, a streaming sound stops at the end of the movie. Streaming sounds can also start playing as your computer downloads them. You will work with streaming sounds in the next lesson.

Repeating Sounds

The Repeat feature lets you replay a sound a specified number of times. This is useful in certain situations, such as creating background music for a movie. If you want your audio to loop continuously, you can select the Loop option by clicking the Repeat list arrow in the SOUND area on the Properties panel, and then selecting Loop.

The default repeat setting is 1, indicating that the sound will play one time.

Add sound to a Timeline

1. Open fl10_1.fla from the drive and folder where your Data Files are stored, then save it as **nightclub**.

2. Display the Library panel, open the Audio folder to display the list of audio files, click **accent1**, then click the **Play button** ▶ in the Item Preview area at the top of the Library panel to preview the sound.

3. Preview the **accent2** and **background** sounds.

4. Insert a **new layer** above the actions layer, then name it **audiobackground**.

5. Click **frame 1** on the audiobackground layer, display the Properties panel, click the **Name list arrow** in the SOUND area, click **background**, then verify that Event appears in the Sync sound list box, as shown in Figure 2.

   Flash adds the sound file to the layer, as indicated by the blue horizontal line through the frames on the audiobackground layer.

   TIP   When you click the Name list arrow in the SOUND area, a list appears of all sound files that have been imported into the Library panel. The Library panel already contains several sounds.

6. Test the movie.

   The background music sound clip plays, ending after about 13 seconds, which is how long it takes to play the sound file one time.

7. Close the Flash Player window.

   You added a sound to the Timeline and verified it was an event sound.

FIGURE 2

Selecting a sound file in the Properties panel

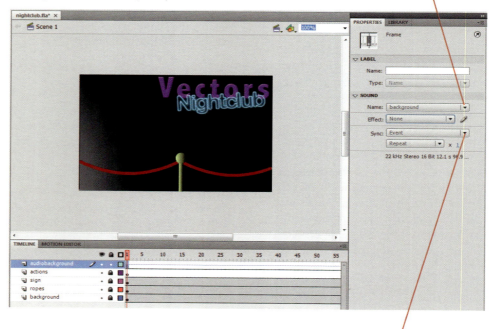

Click the list arrow to see a list of sounds in the Library panel

If necessary, click the list arrow and then select Event

FIGURE 3
A Timeline with layered sounds

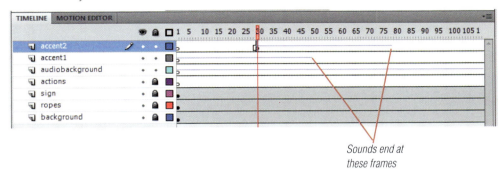

Sounds end at
these frames

1. Insert a **new layer** above the audiobackground layer, then name it **accent1**.

2. Click **frame 1** on the accent1 layer, click the **Name list arrow** in the SOUND area on the Properties panel, click **accent1**, then verify that Event appears in the Sync list box.

3. Insert a **new layer** above the accent1 layer, then name it **accent2**.

4. Insert a **keyframe** in frame 30 on the accent2 layer.

5. Click the **Frame view button** at the top-right side of the Timeline, then click **Tiny** to display more frames.

6. Click the **Name list arrow** in the SOUND area on the Properties panel, click **accent2**, verify that Event appears in the Sync list box, then compare your screen to Figure 3.

7. Test the movie.

    All three sound files play simultaneously for a short time. However, since the sound clips are of different durations, they do not all play to the end of the movie.

    | TIP   When you look at the Timeline, sound lines are blue and layer border lines are black.

8. Close the Flash Player window.

You layered sounds of different durations.

Create a repeating sound

1. Click **frame 1** on the audiobackground layer, verify that Repeat is displayed in the SOUND area on the Properties panel, change the Number of times to repeat to **3**, then compare your screen to Figure 4.

   The sound line on the audiobackground layer now stretches to the end of the movie, frame 200.

2. Click **frame 1** on the accent1 layer, then use the Properties panel to change the Number of times to repeat to **5**.

3. Click **frame 30** on the accent2 layer, then use the Properties panel to change the Number of times to repeat to **4**.

   Since the accent2 sound starts in a later keyframe than the accent1 sound, you do not have to repeat it as many times to have it play until the end of the movie.

4. Lock the three audio layers.

(continued)

FIGURE 4
Specifying the number of times a sound repeats

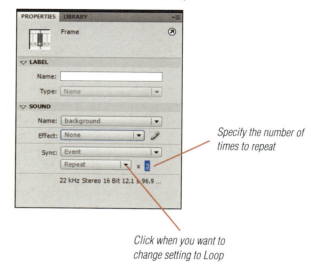

Specify the number of times to repeat

Click when you want to change setting to Loop

FIGURE 5

Sounds in Timeline extend to end of movie

5. Drag the **playhead** to frame 200 in the Timeline, as shown in Figure 5.

   All the sounds now extend to the same ending frame, frame 200, which is the end of the animation of the sign.

6. Test the movie and let it play until all the sounds stop.

   The sound files play simultaneously during the animation of the sign. You can tell the animation has ended when the words "Vectors Nightclub" stop flashing. The blue lines on the Timeline representing the sound waves end at frame 200, the last frame of the movie. However, because the sounds are event sounds, they continue to play even after the playhead reaches frame 200, each stopping only when it reaches the end of the number of repetitions you specified.

7. Click the **Frame view button** ▾☰ at the top left of the Timeline, then click **Normal** to display fewer frames.

8. Close the Flash Player window.

9. Save your work.

You set three sounds to repeat, which causes them to play simultaneously to the same ending frame, frame 200.

Lesson 1   Work with Sound

SPECIFY SYNCHRONIZATION
OPTIONS

What You'll Do

In this lesson, you will synchronize a streaming sound with an animation, and you will set a button to play a sound in the Over state and stop playing the sound in the Up state.

Understanding Synchronization Options

As you've seen, Event is the default synchronization sound option in the Properties panel. You can also choose from one of three other synchronization options: Start, Stop, and Stream, as shown in Figure 6.

Understanding Streaming Sounds

Unlike event sounds, streaming sounds are tied to the Timeline and the number of frames in the Timeline. When you add a sound and set it to be streaming, Flash breaks up the sound into individual sound clips and then associates each clip with a specific frame on the Timeline. The frame rate of your movie determines the number of clips that Flash creates. If the sound is longer than the number of frames on the Timeline, the sound still stops at the end of the movie.

On the web, streaming sounds will start to play as soon as a computer has downloaded a part of the sound file; this provides a usability advantage over event sounds. However, unlike event sounds, streaming sounds increase the file size of your movie each time the sounds are repeated, which means you should use them only when necessary. It is especially recommended that you do not set streaming sounds to loop, that is to play continuously.

One important use of streaming sounds is to synchronize animation and audio, since the sounds can be better coordinated with the Timeline during both development and playback. If the computer playing a movie is slow, Flash will skip frames of an animation to maintain synchronization with a streaming sound. To avoid a jumbled or jerky playback, you should try to keep your animation simple when using streaming sound.

QUICKTIP

Once you set a sound to be streaming, you can preview the sound by dragging the playhead through the Timeline.

Understanding the Start and Stop Synchronization Options

Start sounds act just like event sounds, but they will not play again if an instance of the sound is already playing. The Start option is often used with sounds associated with buttons or with movies that loop back to the beginning, in order to avoid overlapping sounds.

The Stop option lets you end an event sound at a specific keyframe. For example, you can start a sound in frame 1 and then stop it playing in frame 40, even if the sound is of a much longer duration. You create a keyframe in the frame where you want to apply a Stop option, then you specify the name of the sound you want to stop in the Properties panel. If you want to stop multiple sounds, you must insert separate

Stop options in keyframes on each sound layer. Flash indicates a Stop option with a small square in the keyframe, as shown in Figure 7.

QUICKTIP

You can stop a streaming sound at a specific frame by adding a keyframe on the sound's layer. You can stop an event sound by adding a stop action to a keyframe. Event sounds will continue to play through a keyframe unless it includes a Stop option.

FIGURE 6
The Sync sound options in the Properties panel

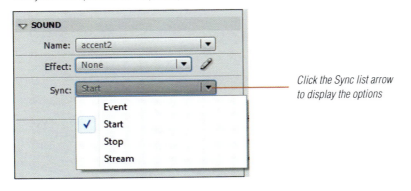

Click the Sync list arrow to display the options

FIGURE 7
A Stop option on the Timeline

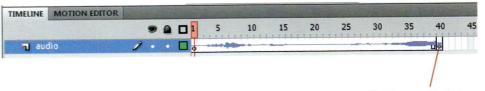

The blue square indicates a stop action

Set synchronization to the Stream option

1. Verify that the nightclub.fla movie is open, click **Insert** on the menu bar, then click **New Symbol**.

2. Type **wordanimation** in the Name text box, select **Movie Clip** for the Type, then click **OK**.

3. Rename Layer 1 on the edit window Timeline as **audio**.

4. Insert a **keyframe** in frame 50.

5. Display the Actions panel, then verify Script Assist is turned off and audio:50 appears in the lower left of the Script pane.

6. Click the **Add a new item to the script button**, point to **Global Functions**, point to **Timeline Control**, click **stop**, then compare your Script pane to Figure 8.

   Inserting a keyframe creates a movie clip of sufficient length (frames 1–50) for the sound to play, and adding a stop action to the keyframe stops the movie clip Timeline from repeating.

7. Close the Actions panel, click **frame 1** on the audio layer, click the **Name list arrow** in the SOUND area on the Properties panel, then click **bitmaps_free_vo**.

8. Click the **Sync list arrow**, click **Stream**, then compare your screen to Figure 9.

9. Press **[Enter]** (Win) or **[return]** (Mac), then listen to the audio.

   The sound file plays, "Tonight all bitmaps get in for free."

You created a movie clip, specified a stop action, added a sound, and set the synchronization of a sound to streaming.

FIGURE 8
Adding a **stop** *action*

FIGURE 9
The streaming sound in the Timeline and Properties panel

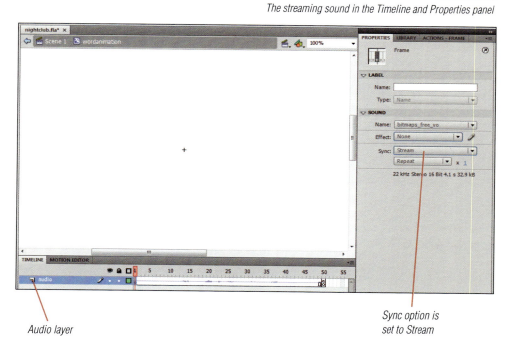

Audio layer

Sync option is
set to Stream

FIGURE 10

The Swap Symbol dialog box

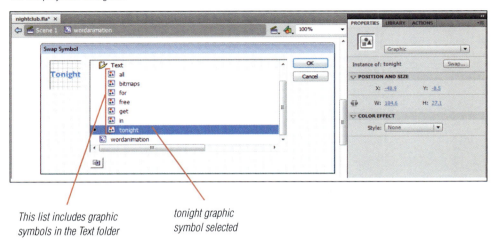

This list includes graphic symbols in the Text folder

tonight graphic symbol selected

1. Insert a **new layer** above the audio layer in the wordanimation movie clip, then name it **text**.

   You will add text that synchronizes with a voice-over.

2. Insert a **keyframe** in frame 13 on the text layer, display the Library panel, open the Text folder to view the text graphic symbols, then drag the **tonight graphic symbol** approximately to the middle of the Stage.

3. Display the Properties panel, change the X value to **−48.9**, change the Y value to **−8.5**, then press **[Enter]** (Win) or **[return]** (Mac).

   The word Tonight appears centered on the Stage.

4. Click the **Selection tool** ↖ on the Tools panel, insert a **keyframe** in frame 19 on the text layer, click the word **Tonight** on the Stage to select it, click the **Swap button** in the Properties panel to open the Swap Symbol dialog box as shown in Figure 10.

   TIP The Swap Symbol dialog box lets you replace an object on the Stage with a different object, keeping all other properties the same, including any actions you have assigned to the original object.

   (continued)

5. Click the **all graphic symbol** in the Swap Symbol dialog box, as shown in Figure 11, then click **OK**. Flash replaces the instance of the tonight graphic symbol with an instance of the all graphic symbol.

6. Insert a **keyframe** in frame 23 on the text layer, click the word **all** on the Stage to select it, click the **Swap button**, click the **bitmaps graphic symbol** in the Swap Symbol dialog box, then click **OK**.

7. Insert a **keyframe** in frame 31 on the text layer, click the word **Bitmaps** on the Stage to select it, click the **Swap button**, click the **get graphic symbol** in the Swap Symbol dialog box, then click **OK**.

8. Insert a **keyframe** in frame 32 on the text layer, click the word **Get** on the Stage to select it, click the **Swap button**, click the **in graphic symbol** in the Swap Symbol dialog box, then click **OK**.

9. Insert a **keyframe** in frame 35 on the text layer, click the word **in** on the Stage to select it, click the **Swap button**, click the **for graphic symbol** in the Swap Symbol dialog box, then click **OK**.

10. Insert a **keyframe** in frame 37 on the text layer, click the word **for** on the Stage to select it, click the **Swap button**, click the **free graphic symbol** in the Swap Symbol dialog box, click **OK**, then compare your Timeline to Figure 12.

11. Click **frame 1** on the Timeline, then press **[Enter]** (Win) or **[return]** (Mac), to view the words as they synchronize with sound.

12. Click **Scene 1** at the top left of the workspace to return to the main Timeline.

You created a text animation, then synchronized the appearance of each word in the animation with a voice-over saying the word.

FIGURE 11
Selecting a symbol to swap

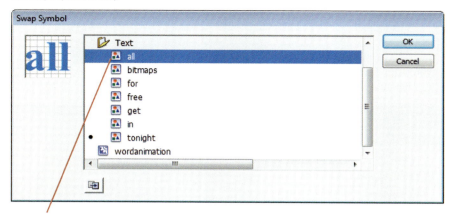

all graphic symbol selected

FIGURE 12
The wordanimation movie clip symbol Timeline

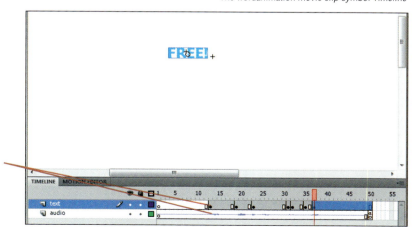

The keyframes containing graphic symbols on the text layer synchronize with the spoken words on the audio layer

Adding Sound

FIGURE 13

Movie clip symbol on the Stage

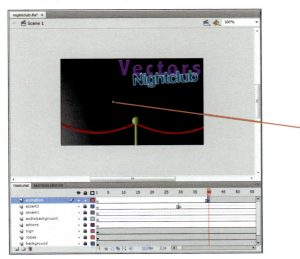

Drag the wordanimation
movie clip symbol to
this location

1. Insert a **new layer** above the accent2 layer, then name it **animation**.

2. Insert a **keyframe** in frame 40 on the animation layer.

3. Display the Library panel, then drag the **wordanimation movie clip symbol** from the Library panel to the left side of the Stage, as shown in Figure 13.

4. Click **Control** on the menu bar, then click **Test Movie** to test the movie.

   The words and streaming sounds appear synchronized.

5. Close the Flash Player window.

6. Save your work.

7. Close the movie.

You added an animation synchronized with sound to the Stage.

Set synchronization to the Start option

1. Open fl10_2.fla, then save it as **supertips**.

2. Display the Library panel, open the buttons folder, then double-click the **gel Right button** to display the edit window.

3. Drag the **playhead** through the Timeline.

   The gel Right button symbol currently has four layers, which create the visual effects of the button.

4. Insert a **new layer** above the button-arrow layer, name it **audio**, then insert a **keyframe** in the Over frame on the audio layer.

5. Display the Properties panel, click the **Name list arrow** in the SOUND area, then click **accent2**.

   Flash adds the sound file, as indicated by the straight line on the audio layer, which will start to play once you move the mouse pointer over the button, and will continue to play even after you move off the button.

6. Click the **Sync list arrow**, click **Start**, then compare your screen to Figure 14.

7. Click **Scene 1** at the top left of the work-space to return to the main Timeline.

8. Click **Control** on the menu bar, then click **Test Movie** to test the movie, position the mouse pointer over a button, then move the mouse pointer off the button.

   The music starts playing when you hover over a button, and continues even if you move the mouse pointer away from the button.

9. Close the Flash Player window.

You added sound to the Over state of a button.

FIGURE 14

Inserting a Start option in the Over state of a button

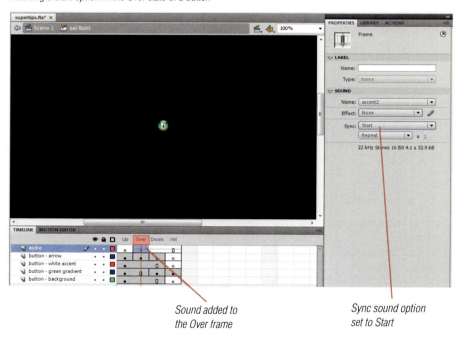

Sound added to
the Over frame

Sync sound option
set to Start

Adding Sound

FIGURE 15

Inserting a Stop option in the Up state of a button

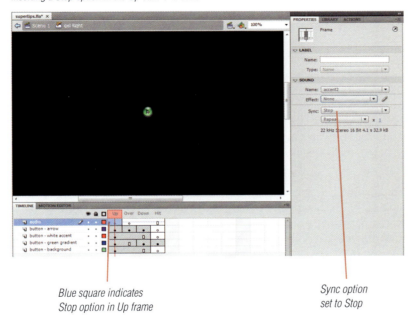

Blue square indicates
Stop option in Up frame

Sync option
set to Stop

1. Display the Library panel, then double-click the **gel Right button** in the Library panel to open it in the edit window.

2. Click the **Up frame** on the audio layer.

3. Display the Properties panel, click the **Name list arrow** in the SOUND area, then click **accent2**.

4. Click the **Sync list arrow**, click **Stop**, then compare your screen to Figure 15.

5. Click **Scene 1** at the top left of the work-space to return to the main Timeline.

6. Click **Control** on the menu bar, then click **Test Movie** to test the movie.

7. Position the mouse pointer over a button, then move the mouse pointer off the button.

   The music stops playing when you move the mouse pointer away from the button.

8. Close the Flash Player window.

9. Save your work, then close the file.

You directed a sound to stop when a button is in the Up state.

MODIFY
SOUNDS

What You'll Do

In this lesson, you will edit when one sound begins and create a custom sound effect for another sound.

Editing Sounds for Length

In most cases, you will want to edit and enhance sounds in a sound-editing program before you import them into Flash. However, Flash does include some basic editing features you can use on sounds you have already imported.

You can trim the length of a sound file using the Edit Envelope dialog box, shown in Figure 16. By moving the Time In and Time Out controls, you can set where the sound file will start and stop playing. Adjusting the controls lets you delete unwanted sounds and remove silent sections at the start and end of sounds, which reduces the file size of the published movie. You can preview the edits you make to a sound by clicking the Play button at the bottom-left corner of the Edit Envelope dialog box. Other buttons in this dialog box let you zoom the display of the sound in or out and set the units in the center of the dialog box to seconds or frames, which can help you determine the length of event sounds and make frame-by-frame adjustments to streaming sounds.

Changing Sound Effects

Flash includes the following effects you can apply to sounds:

- Left Channel plays the sound only in the left channel or speaker.
- Right Channel plays the sound only in the right channel or speaker.
- Fade Left to Right gradually shifts the sound from the left channel to the right channel over the duration of the sound.
- Fade Right to Left gradually shifts the sound from the right channel to the left channel over the duration of the sound.
- Fade In ramps up the volume of the sound as it begins to play.
- Fade Out diminishes the volume of the sound as it ends.

You can set these options either in the Properties panel of the frame to which you have added the sound, or in the Edit Envelope dialog box for the sound.

An additional option—Custom—lets you create your own volume variations over the duration of a sound. By clicking the channel sound line and then moving the envelope

Adding Sound

handle toward the top (to make the sound louder) or bottom (to make the sound lower), you can specify up to eight locations where you want the sound to fade in, fade out, or play at less than 100% volume. For stereo sounds, you can set different custom envelopes for the two channels. Figure 17 shows a custom volume envelope.

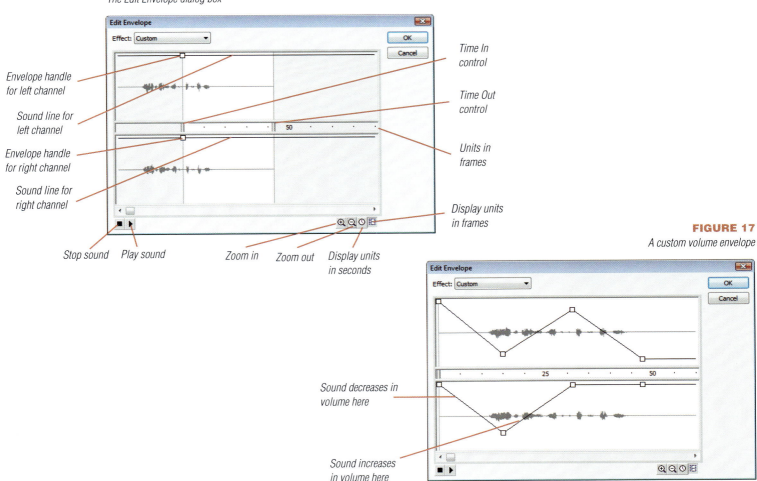

FIGURE 16

The Edit Envelope dialog box

Envelope handle for left channel

Sound line for left channel

Envelope handle for right channel

Sound line for right channel

Stop sound   Play sound

Zoom in   Zoom out   Display units in seconds

Time In control

Time Out control

Units in frames

Display units in frames

FIGURE 17

A custom volume envelope

Sound decreases in volume here

Sound increases in volume here

Edit a sound using the Time In control

1. Open nightclub.fla, then save it as **vectors.fla**.

2. Insert a **new layer** above the animation layer, then name it **voice_intro**.

3. Click **frame 1** on the voice_intro layer, click the **Name list arrow** in the SOUND area on the Properties panel, click **hello_vo**, click the **Sync list arrow**, then click **Stream**.

4. Test the movie, then close the Flash Player window.

5. Click the **Edit sound envelope button** 🖉 in the Properties panel, click the **Effect list arrow**, then click **Custom**.

    You will edit the sound file so it plays only the words "Vectors Nightclub."

6. Click the **Frames button** 🗒 in the Edit Envelope dialog box (if necessary).

7. Click the **Zoom Out button** 🔍 repeatedly until you can see the entire sound with the frames, as shown in Figure 18.

8. Click and drag the **Time In control** to frame 30, then compare your image to Figure 19.

9. Click the **Play sound button** ▶ in the Edit Envelope dialog box.

    Only the last two words of the sound, "Vectors Nightclub," should play. If necessary, adjust the Time In control.

10. Click **OK** to close the Edit Envelope window, then test the movie.

11. Close the Flash Player window.

You changed the point at which a sound begins playing.

FIGURE 18
Zooming the hello_vo sound in the Edit Envelope dialog box

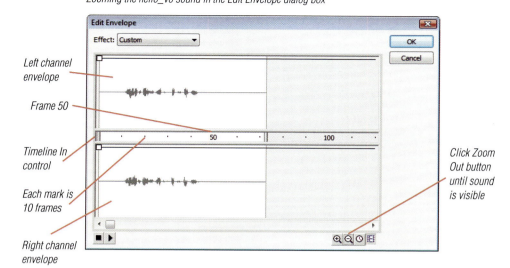

Left channel envelope

Frame 50

Timeline In control

Each mark is 10 frames

Right channel envelope

Click Zoom Out button until sound is visible

FIGURE 19
Trimming the length of a sound

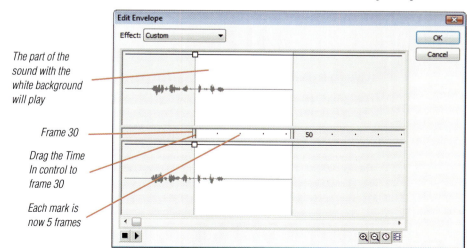

The part of the sound with the white background will play

Frame 30

Drag the Time In control to frame 30

Each mark is now 5 frames

FIGURE 20

Decreasing the volume of both channels

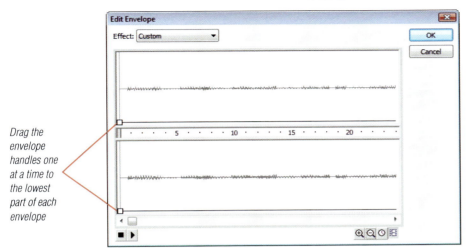

Drag the envelope handles one at a time to the lowest part of each envelope

FIGURE 21

Increasing the volume of the left channel

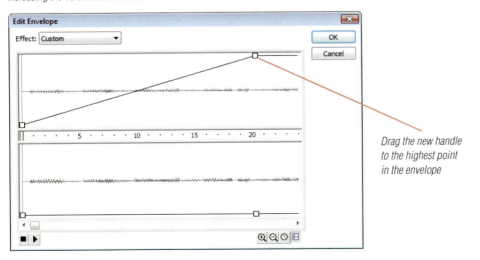

Drag the new handle to the highest point in the envelope

Edit envelopes to create custom volume effects

1. Click **frame 1** on the audiobackground layer.

2. Click the **Effect list arrow** in the Properties panel, then click **Custom**.

   Note: You can also select Custom using the list arrow in the Edit Envelope dialog box.

3. Click the **Zoom Out button** 🔍 (if necessary) until the frames display 5, 10, 15, and 20, drag the **envelope handle** for the left channel and the **envelope handle** for the right channel down to the lowest point to decrease the sound in both channels, then compare your dialog box to Figure 20.

4. Click the **left channel sound line** on frame 20.

   New envelope handles appear on frame 20 for both the left and right channel envelope sound lines.

5. Drag the **new handle** on the left channel up to the highest point, as shown in Figure 21.

6. Drag the **new handle** on the right channel up to its highest point.

7. Click the **Play sound button** ▶ in the Edit Envelope dialog box.

   The music fades in gradually in both channels.

8. Click the **Stop sound button** ■, click **OK** in the Edit Envelope dialog box, save your work, then close the movie.

You established a fade in effect for a sound file by dragging envelope handles to create a custom envelope.

USE ACTIONSCRIPT WITH
SOUND

What You'll Do

 In this lesson, you will use ActionScript to play and stop sounds.

Understanding ActionScript and Sound

ActionScript and sound are a powerful combination. You can use actions to set how and when sounds play in a movie, and to start or stop sounds in response to user interactions. You can also use actions to trigger an event such as navigating to a frame or scene based on when a sound ends.

To reference a sound from the Library panel in ActionScript, you must assign a **linkage identifier string** and create a **sound object**. You use the Sound Properties dialog box, shown in Figure 22. In the dialog box, you make sure a sound in the Library panel that is referenced in ActionScript will be exported for use by the ActionScript, and you also assign a linkage identifier string, which is the name you will use to identify the sound in ActionScript. The identifier string may be the same as the sound name.

A sound object is a way for ActionScript to recognize and control a sound. Creating a sound object is similar to creating an instance of a sound on the Stage, except it happens entirely in ActionScript. First, you create the object using the code for the new Sound action, and then you

Sound and movie clip symbols

Another way to control sound through ActionScript is to embed the sound in a movie clip symbol. You must still create a sound object in ActionScript, but you specify the movie clip symbol instance name as part of the new Sound action, rather than using attachSound. For example, the following line of ActionScript creates a sound object called "music" and attaches a movie clip symbol named "Verdi" to it. The movie clip symbol contains the sound.

```
music=newSound(verdi)
```

attach a sound to the object using the Sound.attachSound action, where Sound is the sound object and attachSound is followed by the linkage identifier (which links the sound file to the sound object). You reference the sound using the linkage identifier string, as shown in Figure 23.

Starting and Stopping Sounds with ActionScript

Once you have created a sound object and attached a sound to it, you can begin controlling the sound using ActionScript.

The Sound.start action starts a sound playing. When using this action, you substitute the name of a sound object for "Sound." For example, if you have a sound object named "BackgroundMusic," you would include the action BackgroundMusic.start to play the sound. Sound.start includes optional parameters that let you specify a sound offset (for example, if you want to start playing a sound that is 15 seconds long at the 10-second mark) and also the number of times to repeat the sound.

The stopAllSounds action stops all sounds currently playing, regardless of whether the sound is an event or streaming sound. It's a good idea to include a stopAllSounds action at the end of a movie, especially if the movie uses event sounds.

QUICKTIP

There is also a Sound.stop action you can use to stop the playing of a specific sound object.

QUICKTIP

If you do not want the sound to start over from the beginning, you can use the Sound.setVolume action to temporarily mute a sound without stopping it, then increase the volume again at a later point in the movie.

FIGURE 22
The Sound Properties dialog box

Click check box to export a sound that does not appear on the Timeline

Linkage identifier string in Identifier text box

FIGURE 23
Example of ActionScript to create a sound object

Sound object music created using new Sound action code

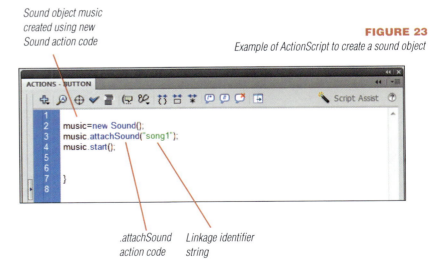

.attachSound action code

Linkage identifier string

Link a sound file with a movie

1. Open fl10_3.fla, then save it as **levels**.

2. Click **Control** on the menu bar, then click **Test Movie**.

3. Click the **start button**, then click the **mute button**.

   The animation plays and stops, but there is no sound.

4. Close the Flash Player window.

5. Display the Library panel, right-click (Win) or [control]-click (Mac) the **song1 audio file**, then click **Properties**.

   The Sound Properties dialog box opens.

6. Click the **Advanced button** (if necessary) to display the Linkage area, then click the **Export for ActionScript check box** to select it, as shown in Figure 24.

   When you click the check box, Flash adds the sound name to the Identifier field and automatically selects the Export in frame 1 check box.

   | TIP   The identifier is the name you will use to reference this sound clip in ActionScript.

7. Click **OK**.

You used the Sound Properties dialog box to create a linkage identifier string and to make sure a sound will be exported for ActionScript.

FIGURE 24

Using the Sound Properties dialog box to export a sound and create an identifier string

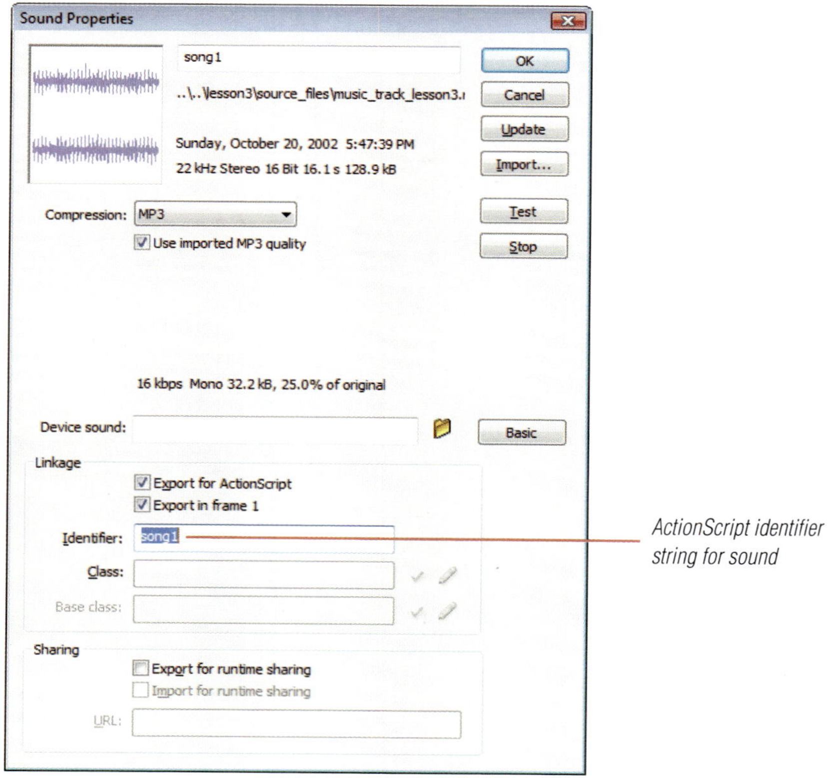

ActionScript identifier string for sound

FIGURE 25

ActionScript to create a new sound object

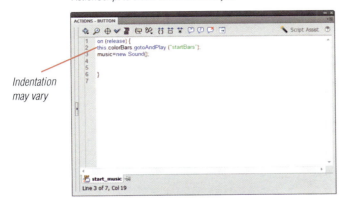

Indentation
may vary

1. Click the **Selection tool** ![arrow] on the Tools panel, click the **start button** to select it, then open the **Actions panel**.

   The current ActionScript code causes the playhead to go to the frame labeled startBars when the start button is clicked. The startBars frame is the start of the animation.

2. Verify that Script Assist is turned off, then verify that the start_music button symbol appears in the lower left of the Script pane.

3. Click the **View Options button** ![icon] in the Actions panel, then click **Line Numbers** if it does not already have a check mark next to it.

4. Click the end of Line 2 in the Script pane (after the semicolon), press **[Enter]** (Win) or **[return]** (Mac) to create a new Line 3, then type **music=new Sound();**.

   Your screen should look like Figure 25. Be sure you have a space between new and Sound. This ActionScript statement creates a new sound object named "music."

5. Press **[Enter]** (Win) or **[return]** (Mac) to create a new Line 4, then type **music.attachSound("song1");**.

   This ActionScript statement attaches song1 to the sound object based on the linkage identifier.

   Note: A list of actions appeared as you were typing the code. You can double-click an action to insert it into the code as a shortcut.

   (continued)

Lesson 4   Use ActionScript with Sound

6. Press **[Enter]** (Win) or **[return]** (Mac) to create a new Line 5, then type **music.start();**, as shown in Figure 26.

   This ActionScript statement plays the sound object.

7. Click **Control** on the menu bar, click **Test Movie** to test the movie, click the **start button**, then click the **mute button**.

   The sound file plays when you click start; when you click mute, the color bars stop playing, but the sound file does not.

8. Close the Flash Player window.

You wrote an ActionScript for a button that creates a sound object, attaches a sound to the object, and plays the sound.

Stop sounds using ActionScript

1. Collapse the Actions panel, click the **mute button** on the Stage to select it, then display the Actions panel.

2. Verify that the mute button symbol appears in the lower left of the Script pane.

3. Click **Line 4** in the Script pane of the Actions panel.

4. Click the **Add a new item to the script button** ⊕, point to **Global Functions**, point to **Timeline Control**, click **stopAllSounds**, then compare your screen to Figure 27.

5. Collapse the Actions panel, click the **start button** on the Stage to select it, then display the Actions panel and verify that the start_music button symbol appears in the lower left of the Script pane.

(continued)

FIGURE 26
ActionScript to play a sound object

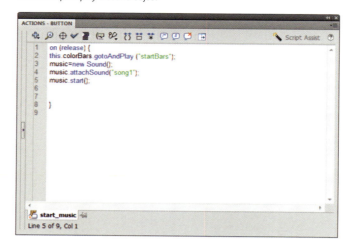

FIGURE 27
ActionScript to stop all sounds when mute button is clicked

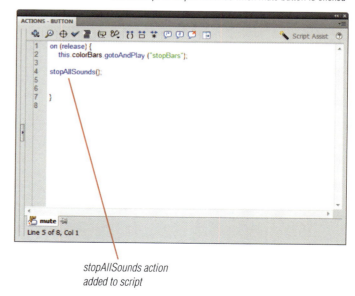

stopAllSounds action added to script

FIGURE 28

ActionScript to stop currently playing sounds before starting sound

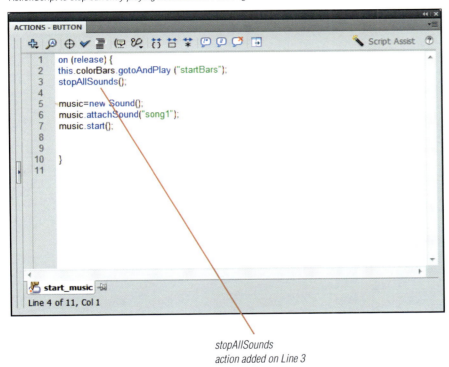

```
ACTIONS - BUTTON

     1    on (release) {
     2    this.colorBars.gotoAndPlay ("startBars");
     3    stopAllSounds();
     4
     5    music=new Sound();
     6    music.attachSound("song1");
     7    music.start();
     8
     9
    10    }
    11
```

start_music
Line 4 of 11, Col 1

stopAllSounds
action added on Line 3

6. Click the end of Line 2 in the Script pane of the Actions panel, then press **[Enter]** (Win) or **[return]** (Mac) to create a blank Line 3.

7. Click the **Add a new item to the script button** ⊹ , point to **Global Functions**, point to **Timeline Control**, click **stopAllSounds**, then compare your screen to Figure 28.

   Inserting stopAllSounds ensures that the sound starts at the beginning each time the visitor clicks the button and that multiple copies of the sound file do not play at the same time.

8. Close the Actions panel, click **Control** on the menu bar, then click **Test Movie**.

9. Click the **start button**, click the **mute button**, then click the **start button** again.

   The music plays when you click start, then stops when you click mute.

10. Close the Flash Player window, save your work, then close the movie.

You added actions to stop sounds from playing.

Work with sounds.

1. Start Flash, open fl10_4.fla, then save it as **skillsdemo10**.

2. Move the playhead through the Timeline of the movie. Notice there are two screens that are partially completed. The callouts in Figure 29 indicate the types of changes you will make to the movie.

3. Insert a new layer above the buttons layer, then name it **ambient1**.

4. Click frame 1 on the ambient1 layer, then select the background_loop1 sound from the Name list in the SOUND area on the Properties panel, which adds it to frame 1 on the ambient1 layer.

5. Set the synchronization for the sound on the ambient1 layer to Event, then set the number of times to repeat to **10**.

6. Insert a new layer above the ambient1 layer, then name it **ambient2**.

7. Click frame 1 on the ambient2 layer, then select the background_loop2 sound from the Name list in the SOUND area on the Properties panel, which adds it to frame 1 on the ambient2 layer.

8. Set the synchronization for the sound on the ambient2 layer to Event, then set the number of times to repeat to **10**.

9. Insert a new layer above the ambient2 layer, name it **song**, then add an instance of the song1 sound to frame 15 on the song layer. (*Hint*: Insert a keyframe in frame 15 before you add the sound.)

10. Set the synchronization for the sound on the song layer to Event, then set the number of times to loop to **10**.

11. Save your work.

FIGURE 29
Completed Skills Review

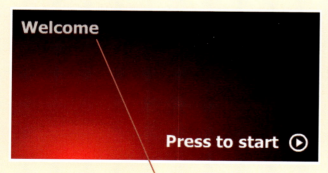

Voice-over and background music begin when screen is displayed; voice-over is synchronized with words

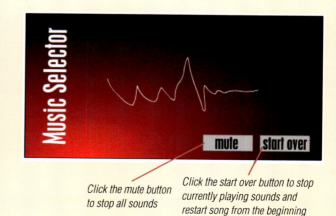

Click the mute button to stop all sounds

Click the start over button to stop currently playing sounds and restart song from the beginning

Adding Sound

Specify synchronization options.

1. Create a new movie clip symbol named **animated_text**.

2. Name Layer 1 of the animated_text movie clip symbol **audio**, click frame 1 on the audio layer, select the music_selector_audio sound from the Name list in the SOUND area on the Properties panel, which adds it to frame 1 on the new layer, then set the synchronization to Stream.

3. Insert a keyframe in frame 75 on the audio layer, then add a stop action to the keyframe. (*Hint*: Adding a keyframe lets you see the full streaming sound. Adding the stop action keeps the movie clip from repeating.)

4. Insert a new layer above the audio layer, name it **text**, insert a keyframe in frame 13 on the layer, then drag the Welcome graphic symbol from the Text folder in the Library panel to the Stage.

5. Display the Properties panel, change the value in the X text box to **–58.5** and the value in the Y text box to **–16.7**, then press [Enter] (Win) or [return] (Mac).

6. Insert a keyframe in frame 17 on the text layer, select the word "Welcome" on the Stage, click the Swap button on the Properties panel, click the "to" graphic symbol, then click OK.

7. Insert a keyframe in frame 20 on the text layer, select the word "to" on the Stage, click the Swap button on the Properties panel, click the "the" graphic symbol, then click OK.

8. Insert a keyframe in frame 23 on the text layer, select the word "the" on the Stage, click the Swap button on the Properties panel, click the "music" graphic symbol, then click OK.

9. Insert a keyframe in frame 27 on the text layer, select the word "Music" on the Stage, click the Swap button on the Properties panel, click the "selector" graphic symbol, then click OK.

10. Insert a blank keyframe in frame 45 on the text layer.

11. Play the movie clip symbol.

12. Return to the main Timeline.

13. Create a new layer above the song layer, name it **animation**, click frame 1 on the new layer, then add an instance of the animated_text movie clip symbol from the Library panel to anywhere on the Stage.

14. Display the Properties panel for the movie clip symbol instance, change the value in the X text box to **120** and the value in the Y text box to **40**, then press [Enter] (Win) or [return] (Mac).

15. Click frame 1 on the buttons layer, double-click the right arrow button on the Stage to open it, click the Down frame, then use the Properties panel to add an instance of the Plastic Click sound to the frame and set the synchronization to Start.

16. Click the Up frame, add an instance of the Plastic Click sound to the frame, then set the Sync sound to Stop.

17. Return to the main Timeline, test the movie, then save your work.

Modify sounds.

1. Open the animated_text movie clip in the edit window, then click frame 1 on the audio layer.

2. Display the Properties panel, then click the Edit sound envelope button on the Properties panel.

3. Show units in Frames, then zoom out the view in the Edit Envelope dialog box until you can see the waveform for the entire sound, as shown in Figure 30.

4. Play the sound.

5. Drag the Time Out control (located on the Timeline at the end of the waveform, about frame 70) left to approximately frame 31, then play the sound in the Edit Envelope dialog box to verify that the word "online" does not play.

6. Click OK, then return to the main Timeline.

7. Click frame 1 on the ambient1 layer, then click the Edit sound envelope button on the Properties panel.

8. Play the sound.

9. Reduce the volume by dragging the envelope handles in both channels so the sound line is just above the bottom of the envelope, as shown in Figure 31.

10. Play the sound. (*Hint*: If you do not hear the sound, drag the envelope handles up slightly. Adjust the sound lines as needed until you hear the sound playing softly.)

11. Click OK to accept changes and close the Edit Envelope dialog box.

12. Click frame 1 on the ambient2 layer, then click the Edit sound envelope button on the Properties panel.

13. Play the sound.

14. Drag the envelope handles in both channels to just above the bottom of the envelope, then play the sound.

15. Click OK to accept changes and close the Edit Envelope dialog box.

16. Save your work.

FIGURE 30
The Edit Envelope dialog box

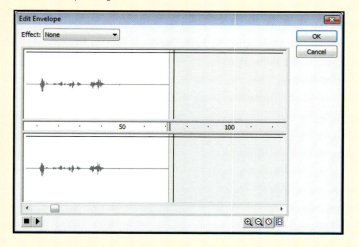

FIGURE 31
Volume adjusted by changing placement of sound line in each channel

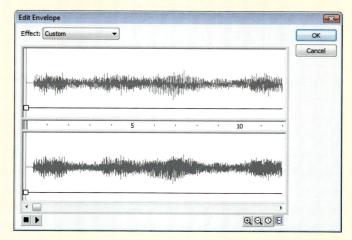

Use ActionScript with sounds.

1. Click the right arrow button on the Stage to select it, open the Actions panel, turn off Script Assist if it is on, then click the beginning of Line 2 in the Script pane.

2. Add a stopAllSounds action to the beginning of Line 2, before the gotoAndPlay action, then use the Check syntax and Auto format buttons to check your code.

3. Click frame 15 on the Timeline to display the second screen.

4. Select the song1 sound in the Sounds folder in the Library panel, then display the Sound Properties dialog box for the song1 sound symbol. (*Hint*: Click the Options list arrow in the Library panel, then click Properties.)

5. Select the Export for ActionScript check box in the Linkage area of the Sound Properties dialog box, then click OK.

6. Click the mute button on the Stage to select it, then in the Script pane add an

on (release) action to the button. As the statements for the on (release) action, add a stopAllSounds action, then a gotoAndPlay action that plays the frame named mute in the waveform movie clip symbol. *Note*: This requires the following *with* statement.
with (waveform) {
                    gotoAndPlay("mute");}

7. Use the Check syntax and Auto format buttons to check your code.

8. Click the start over button on the Stage to select it, then in the Script pane add an on (release) action to the button. As a statement for the on (release) action, add a gotoAndPlay action that plays the frame "start" in the movie clip symbol named waveform. *Note*: This requires the following *with* statement:
with (waveform) {
                    gotoAndPlay("start");}

9. Use the Check syntax and Auto format buttons to check your code.

10. In the Script pane for the start over button, add the following additional statements for the on (release) action: a stopAllSounds action after the gotoAndPlay action to stop all currently playing sounds, then add actions to start playing the sound with the linkage identifier song1. *Note*: You can use the following code to create a sound object, use attachSound to attach the song1 sound to the sound object, then use the start action to start the sound.
stopAllSounds();
           music = new Sound();
           music.attachSound("song1");
           music.start();

11. Use the Check syntax and Auto format buttons to check your code.

12. Test the movie, then save your work.

13. Close the file, then exit Flash.

Ultimate Tours would like you to create a banner promoting its "Japan on a Budget" tours. The graphics for the banner are complete; now you need to add music and a voice-over. Ultimate Tours would like a musical background to play continuously while the banner is displayed, and they have also provided a voice-over they would like to be synchronized with text on the screen, as shown in Figure 32. Finally, Ultimate Tours would like an accent sound to play when a visitor clicks the navigation button on the banner.

1. Open fl10_5.fla, then save the file as **ultimatetours10**.
2. Test the movie and notice the text banner that appears across the screen against a series of background images.
3. Insert a new layer above the text animation layer, name it **audio**, use the Properties panel to add the sound named ultimate_background to frame 1 on the layer, then set synchronization to Event.
4. Set repetition for the sound to **2** to ensure the music plays the entire time the banner is displayed.
5. Display the Library panel, open the movie clips folder, then open the words movie clip symbol in the edit window.
6. Insert a new layer above the text layer, name it **audio**, use the Properties panel to add the

ultimate_voiceover sound to the layer, then set synchronization to Stream.
7. Move the keyframes that control when each word of text appears on the Stage to synchronize with when the word is spoken in the voice-over. (*Hint*: Use the playhead to hear the streaming sound and use the wave pattern as a clue to when a sound is played. Drag the keyframes on the text layer to create the synchronization effect.)
8. Return to the main Timeline, unlock the button layer, then edit the arrow button to play

the Switch Small Plastic sound when a visitor clicks the button. (*Hint*: Be sure to specify an Event sound.)
9. Return to the main Timeline, test the movie, then close the Flash Player window.
10. Select frame 1 on the audio layer, then use the Edit Envelope dialog box to reduce the volume of the ultimate_background sound.
11. Test the movie.
12. Save your work.

FIGURE 32
Sample completed Project Builder 1

*Voice-over is synchronized
with appearance of words*

*Sound plays when
visitor clicks button*

You work for a software game company. Your newest game, "Match the Shapes," will be developed in Flash and marketed to preschoolers. You are working on a prototype of the game to show upper management. You have already completed the visual aspects of the prototype; now you must add sound.

1. Open fl10_6.fla, then save it as **game_prototype10**.

2. Test the movie to see how the matching game works, then close the Flash Player window.

3. Add a new layer named **ambient**, then using the Properties panel, add the ambient_audio sound as an event sound. Repeat the sound 10 times to ensure it plays the entire time the visitor is viewing the screen. Set the Effect in the Properties panel to Fade in.

4. Test the movie, click the Start button and notice how the sound continues, then close the Flash Player window.

5. Add a stopAllSounds action that stops the sound from playing when a visitor navigates to the second screen of the site. (*Hint*: You can add the action to the Start button just before the gotoAndPlay code or to the first frame of the second screen on the actions layer.)

6. Create a movie clip symbol that synchronizes the welcome_voiceover sound from the Library panel with the words "Welcome to

Match the Shapes." You will need to create the text objects for each word. Alternatively, create another sort of animation, such as a motion tween from off the Stage for the words, and synchronize this animation with the streaming sound. (*Hint*: Be sure to include a stop action in the last frame of the movie clip symbol, so the movie clip doesn't play continuously. Also, be sure to end the movie clip on the main Timeline before the second screen.)

7. Add an instance of the movie clip symbol to the first screen of the movie.

FIGURE 33
Sample completed Portfolio Project

Background music plays during voice-over/text synchronized animation

Button sound plays when the button is clicked

8. Add Switch Small Plastic sound from the Properties panel to the Down state of the Start button on the first screen of the site.

9. On the second screen of the movie, attach ActionScript to the square, triangle, and circle in the Start Bin that, when a visitor correctly places the shape on its corresponding shape in the Drop Bin, stops any currently playing sounds, then plays the sound named match, which can be found in the library. (*Hint*: Remember to first create a linkage identifier for the match sound, then create a sound object in the ActionScript for each instance where you want to play the sound.)

10. Test the movie.

11. Save your work and compare your screen to Figure 33.

Voice-over plays when visitor successfully drops a shape onto the correct position in the drop bin

Figure 34 shows a page from a website that might have been created using Flash. Study the figure and complete the following. For each question, indicate how you determined your answer.

1. Connect to the Internet, then go to *www.americaslibrary.gov/cgi-bin/page.cgi/jp/bball/early_2*.

2. Open a document in a word processor or open a new Flash document, save the file as **dpc10**, then answer the following questions. (*Hint*: Use the Text tool in Flash.)

   ■ Currently, this site does not have any sounds. How might sound be used to enhance this site?

   ■ If this site were created in Flash, how might you incorporate sounds?

   ■ What user controls might be appropriate when including sound in a Flash movie and why?

FIGURE 34
Sample Design Project

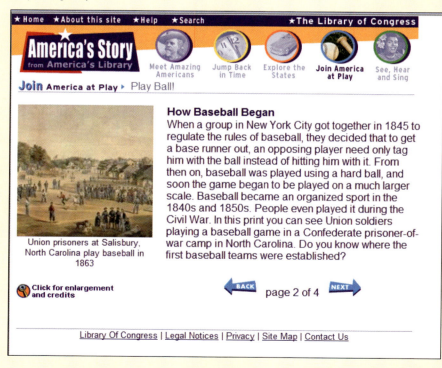

In the previous chapter, you created a slide show for your work samples, which displayed a different sample each time the visitor clicked a button. Now add sound to the slide show. If you have access to sound-recording software, you can record your own voice-overs that describe the samples being shown. You can import sound clips or use the sounds found in the Sounds area of the Common Libraries panel. Alternatively, use can use the sample files provided in this chapter as musical background sounds.

1. Open portfolio9.fla, then save it as **portfolio10**.
2. Use sound files from the Common Libraries panel, or import to the Library panel sound files you have acquired or created, such as voice-overs describing your work, or import the following sound files from the drive and folder where your Data Files are stored:
   accent1.mp3
   accent2.mp3
   background.mp3
   portfolio_voiceover.wav
3. Open the samples movie clip symbol, add a new layer named **audio**, and then add a different sound to each frame of the movie clip, except frame 1. You can use either voice-over clips that describe the sample, or the voice introduction and musical backgrounds provided in the sample files and listed in step 2.

4. If you used the sample files, set repetition for each musical background sound to **50**, to ensure the music plays continuously for the entire time the visitor views the page.
5. If you are using the musical backgrounds, experiment with adding effects to the sounds, such as fades or shifts between channels.

FIGURE 35
Sample completed Portfolio Project

6. Add a stopAllSounds action to keep the different sounds from overlapping as the visitor clicks the "Next slide" button. (*Hint*: You should add the action to the button, not the movie clip symbol.)
7. Test the movie.
8. Save your work, then compare your movie to Figure 35.

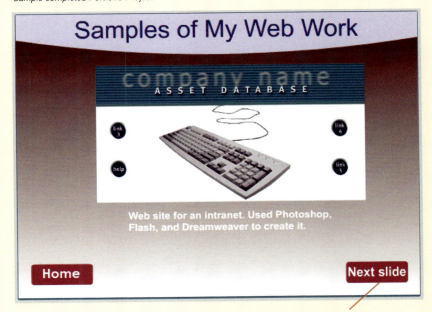

Voice-over or background music begins when page is displayed; new voice-over or music begins when visitor clicks button to view next slide

Adding Sound

ADOBE FLASH CS4

USING ADVANCED
ACTIONSCRIPT

1. Create complex interactivity

2. Use ActionScript to create external links

3. Load new movies

4. Work with conditional actions

  # USING ADVANCED ACTIONSCRIPT

Introduction

In this chapter, you will continue to build on your knowledge of ActionScript, with an emphasis on adding actions that encourage user interaction and enhance the user experience. For example, you can replace the mouse cursor with a custom cursor; track user interactions and offer feedback based on the data you gather; and send information you collect from users to another website or program for processing. Breaking your movies into multiple, smaller movies and then using ActionScript to load these movies when appropriate, can help you better organize a large website and provide users relief

from lengthy downloads. Conditional actions let you implement complex branching in your movies; looping actions help streamline your ActionScript and provide a way to repeat a set of actions based on a value provided by the user or on a task you want the user to perform.

With all the new actions and cool techniques you will see in this chapter, remember that you're still just scratching the surface of ActionScript. The more you research and experiment, the more surprised you will be by all you can accomplish with ActionScript, and the more your users will appreciate your efforts.

Tools You'll Use

```
on (release) {
    getURL("mailto:webmaster@server.com", "_self");
}
```

```
on (release) {
    loadMovieNum("frog.swf", 2);
}
```

ACTIONS - BUTTON

```
on (release) {
    if (pass == "letmein") {
        gotoAndStop(2);
    } else {
        n++;
        feedback = "Sorry. Tries left: " +(3-n);
        pass = "";
        if (n == 3) {
            gotoAndStop(3);}
    }
}
```

login
Line 7 of 12, Col 13

ACTIONS - BUTTON

```
on(release) {
    n = 0;
    while (n < amount) {
        duplicateMovieClip ("_root.face","face_"+n,n);
        setProperty ("face_"+n._x, random(250));
        setProperty ("face_"+n._y, random(200));
        n++;
    }
}
```

duplicate_bt
Line 9 of 10, Col 2

CREATE COMPLEX INTERACTIVITY

What You'll Do

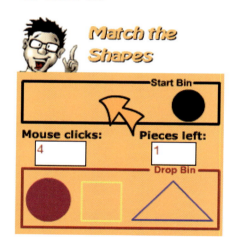

In this lesson, you will use ActionScript to create a custom cursor and count user interactions.

Creating a Custom Cursor

Creating a custom cursor is a fun way to make a Flash site distinctive. You might create a cursor with your face on it for a personal site, or you can tie the cursor into the theme of the site, such as using a picture of a yo-yo for an e-business site selling toys. You can also integrate a custom cursor with the purpose of the site: for example, in a game site, the custom cursor might be a cartoon figure the user has to lead through a maze with the mouse. The custom cursor can be a graphic, photograph, or even an animation. The only requirement is that it be a movie clip symbol.

The first step toward implementing a custom cursor is to hide the regular cursor.

You do this with the mouse.hide action. There is a corresponding mouse.show action you can use to redisplay the cursor at any point.

There are two ways to add your custom cursor to a movie. In both methods, the custom cursor is an instance of a movie clip symbol. The first method uses the startDrag action. As you add this action to an instance of the movie clip symbol, you should select the Lock mouse to center option. This option centers the hidden mouse pointer beneath the custom cursor so both the mouse pointer and the custom cursor move when the user drags the mouse. Figure 1 shows the ActionScript for this method.

Using mouse coordinate information

There are many ways to use the mouse coordinate information returned by the _xmouse and _ymouse actions to enhance interaction. For example, you might create ActionScript that changes the color of an object or screen area whenever the user passes the mouse over it or that creates a panoramic view of an automobile or other product as the user moves the mouse.

A second method for creating a custom cursor uses actions that determine the X and Y coordinates of the hidden mouse pointer, and then sets the coordinates of your custom cursor to the same position. As the user moves the mouse, the values constantly are updated, so the custom cursor tracks where the mouse would be on the screen if it wasn't hidden. The _xmouse and _ymouse actions return the coordinates of the mouse pointer; the _x and _y actions control the coordinates of an instance of a movie clip symbol. Figure 2 shows the ActionScript for a custom cursor implemented using this method.

Tracking User Interactions

One aspect of interactivity involves responding to user actions, such as jumping to a different point in a movie when a user clicks a button. Another aspect involves providing users with individual feedback based on the actions they take or information they supply. This can be as simple as creating a dynamic text box to display the user's name in a greeting, as you did in Chapter 9. You can also use ActionScript to gather and display more complex information, such as the number of times a user clicks the mouse or a user's progress in a game or quiz. Collecting such information presents many opportunities to offer users custom feedback. Tracking interactions can also provide you with insight on the way people work with your site.

The increment and decrement actions are useful when tracking user interactions. The **increment action**, ++ (two plus signs), adds 1 unit to a variable or expression; the **decrement action**, – – (two minus signs), subtracts 1 unit. For example, the ActionScript statement x++ is the equivalent of the expression $x=x+1$. Both add 1 to the variable. You might use the increment operator to keep track of and display the number of correct answers a user has given during an online test.

QUICKTIP

The increment and decrement operators are also useful when setting up the number of times to run a conditional loop. For example, you might want to allow a user to attempt to answer a question a specified number of times before providing the correct answer.

FIGURE 1

ActionScript to create a custom cursor using `startDrag`

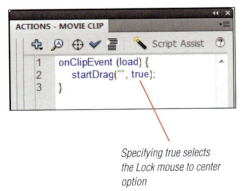

Specifying true selects the Lock mouse to center option

FIGURE 2

ActionScript to create a custom cursor by setting X and Y coordinates

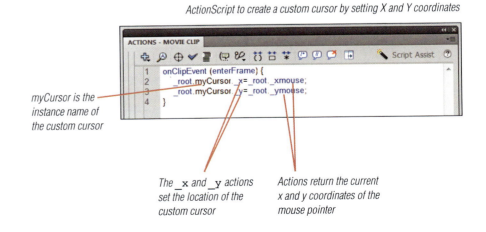

myCursor is the instance name of the custom cursor

The _x and _y actions set the location of the custom cursor

Actions return the current x and y coordinates of the mouse pointer

Hide the cursor

1. Open fl11_1.fla from the drive and folder where your Data Files are stored, then save it as **interactive**.

2. Drag the **playhead** to view the contents of the frames.

3. Click **frame 1** on the actions layer, then open the Actions panel.

4. Verify Script Assist is turned off and actions:1 appears in the lower left of the Script pane.

5. Click the **View Options button** ▾≡ in the Actions panel, then verify that Line Numbers is selected.

6. Type the following in the Script pane, as shown in Figure 3: **Mouse.hide()**.

   TIP Text can only be typed in the Script pane when Script Assist is off.

7. Test the movie.

   The mouse cursor is not visible.

8. Close the Flash Player window.

9. Collapse the Actions panel.

You used ActionScript to hide the mouse cursor.

FIGURE 3
ActionScript to hide the mouse

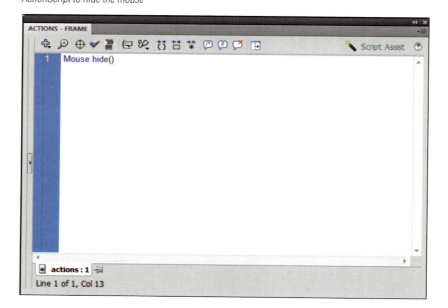

Using onClipEvent

onClipEvent determines when to run actions associated with an instance of a movie clip. Options include running the actions when the movie clip instance is first loaded onto the Timeline, upon a mouse event, upon a key press, or upon receiving data. You can associate different options with the same movie clip instance.

FIGURE 4

Instance of custom cursor movie clip symbol on the Stage

The custom cursor

FIGURE 5

Naming the movie clip instance

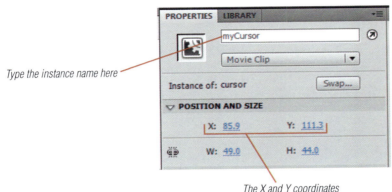

Type the instance name here

The X and Y coordinates on your screen may differ

FIGURE 6

ActionScript to create the custom cursor

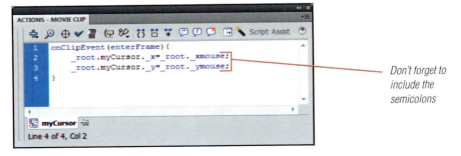

Don't forget to include the semicolons

Create a custom cursor using X and Y coordinates

1. Insert a **new layer** above the shapes layer, name it **cursor**, then click **frame 1**.

2. Display the Library panel, open the movie_clips folder, then drag the **cursor movie clip symbol** to the center of the Stage, as shown in Figure 4.

3. Click the **cursor movie clip symbol** to select it, display the Properties panel, click the **Instance Name text box**, type **myCursor**, press [Enter] (Win) or [return] (Mac), then compare your screen to Figure 5.

4. Display the Actions panel, verify myCursor appears in the lower left of the Script pane, click **line 1** of the Script pane, type **onClipEvent (enterFrame) {**, then press [Enter] (Win) or [return] (Mac).

5. Type **_root.myCursor._x=_root._xmouse;** then press [Enter] (Win) or [return] (Mac).

6. Type **_root.myCursor._y=_root._ymouse;** then press [Enter] (Win) or [return] (Mac).

7. Type **}**, then compare your Script pane to Figure 6.

8. Click **Control** on the menu bar, click **Test Movie** to test the movie, then use the custom cursor to click the button on the first screen and to drag and drop the shapes on the second screen.

   TIP The cursor reverts to the shape for your operating system when you position the mouse pointer on the title bar or menu bar of the Flash Player window.

9. Close the Flash Player window.

You used ActionScript to designate an instance of a movie clip symbol to act as the mouse cursor using X and Y coordinates.

Track user interactions with the increment operator

1. Collapse the Actions panel, click **frame 7** on the background layer, click the **Pasteboard** to deselect all objects, click the **Text tool** T on the Tools panel, then display the Properties panel.

   TIP Collapse and display the Actions panel as needed.

2. Set the text properties to: Family: **Arial**; Style: **Regular**; Size: **14**; Text fill color: **#990000**.

3. Click the **Text type list arrow**, click **Dynamic Text**, click the **Show border around text button** to select it, then, using Figure 7 as a guide, draw a **text box** below the words Mouse clicks.

   TIP If the text box overlaps other elements on the screen, click the Selection tool on the Tools panel after drawing the text box, then use the mouse or arrow keys to move the box.

4. Click the **text box** to select it, click the **Variable text box** in the OPTIONS area of the Properties panel, type **myClicks**, then press **[Enter]** (Win) or **[return]** (Mac).

5. Click **frame 7** on the actions layer, display the Actions panel, then verify actions:7 is displayed in the lower left of the Script pane.

6. Type **myClicks = 0;** on Line 1 in the Script pane, as shown in Figure 8.

   This ActionScript resets the value of the myClicks variable to 0 each time a user navigates to the page.

   (continued)

FIGURE 7
Drawing the dynamic text box

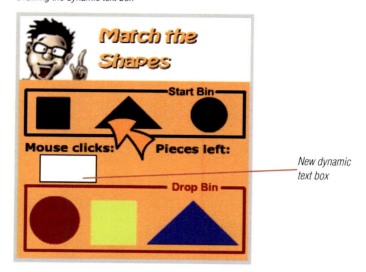

New dynamic text box

FIGURE 8
ActionScript to set the initial value of the variable to 0

Using Advanced ActionScript

FIGURE 9

ActionScript to count mouse clicks

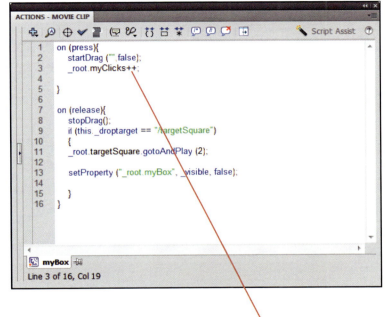

```
ACTIONS - MOVIE CLIP
                                                    Script Assist
 1   on (press){
 2       startDrag ("",false);
 3       _root.myClicks++;
 4
 5   }
 6
 7   on (release){
 8       stopDrag();
 9       if (this._droptarget == "/targetSquare")
10       {
11       _root.targetSquare.gotoAndPlay (2);
12
13       setProperty ("_root.myBox", _visible, false);
14
15       }
16   }

myBox
Line 3 of 16, Col 19
```

New line of ActionScript;
be sure to include two
plus signs (++) followed
by a semicolon (;)

7. Click the **Selection tool** on the Tools panel, click the **black square** in the Start Bin to select it, then verify that the myBox movie clip symbol is displayed in the lower left of the Script pane.

8. Click at the **end of Line 2** in the Script pane, then press **[Enter]** (Win) or **[return]** (Mac) to create a blank line.

9. Type **_root.myClicks++;** on Line 3 in the Script pane, as shown in Figure 9.

   This ActionScript increases the value of the myClicks variable by one each time the mouse is clicked. Including _root in the target path ensures that Flash looks for the variable at the main Timeline level.

10. Test the movie, click the **Start button**, then click the **black square** in the Start Bin repeatedly.

   The value in the Mouse clicks: dynamic text box, that is, the box that is keeping track of mouse clicks, is updated each time you click the square.

11. Close the Flash Player window, then repeat steps 7, 8, and 9 to add the ActionScript that increases the value of the myClicks variable by one each time the mouse is clicked for the black triangle (myTriangle) and black circle (myCircle) in the Start Bin.

12. Test the movie, click the **Start button**, click each shape, then close the Flash Player window.

You used the increment operator action to maintain a count of the number of times a user clicks the mouse on a set of objects.

Track user interactions with the decrement operator

1. Collapse the Actions panel, then click **frame 7** on the background layer.

2. Click the **Text tool** T on the Tools panel, click the **Pasteboard** to deselect all objects, then draw a **text box** below the words Pieces left, as shown in Figure 10.

   The new text box will be a dynamic text box with the same settings you specified for the Mouse clicks dynamic text box.

3. Verify that the text box is selected, click the **Variable text box** in the Properties panel, type **myPieces**, then press **[Enter]** (Win) or **[return]** (Mac).

4. Click **frame 7** on the actions layer, display the Actions panel, verify actions:7 appears in the lower left of the Script pane, click at the **end of Line 1** in the Script pane, then press **[Enter]** (Win) or **[return]** (Mac) to create a blank line.

5. Type **myPieces = 3;** on Line 2 in the Script pane, as shown in Figure 11.

   This ActionScript resets the value of the myPieces variable to 3 each time a user navigates to the page.

6. Click the **Selection tool** ▸ on the Tools panel, double-click the **yellow square** in the Drop Bin to open the movie clip symbol in the edit window, then click **frame 2** on Layer 1 on the edit window Timeline.

   In this movie clip, frame 2 appears when a shape from the Start Bin is successfully dropped on a shape in the Drop Bin.

(continued)

FIGURE 10
Drawing a second dynamic text box

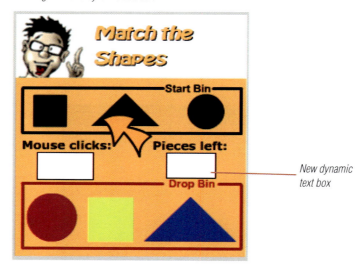

New dynamic text box

FIGURE 11
ActionScript in line 2 resets the value of the myPieces variable to 3

FIGURE 12

ActionScript to decrement a variable as pieces are successfully matched

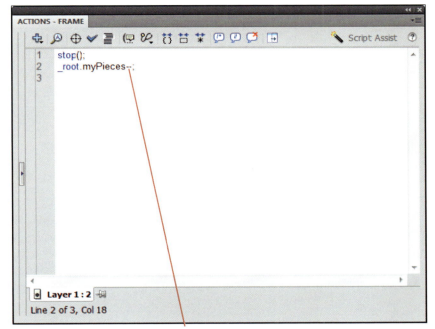

New line of ActionScript;
be sure to include two
minus signs (--) followed
by a semicolon (;)

7. Display the Actions panel, verify Layer 1:2 appears in the lower left of the Script pane, click at the **end of Line 1** in the Script pane, press **[Enter]** (Win) or **[return]** (Mac) to create a blank line, then type **_root.myPieces– –;** on Line 2 in the Script pane, as shown in Figure 12.

   This ActionScript decreases the value of the myPieces variable by one each time frame 2 is displayed, which will count down the number of pieces still left to match.

   TIP You can press the hyphen key on the keyboard to type – (a minus sign).

8. Click **Scene 1** at the top left of the workspace to return to the main Timeline.

9. Test the movie, click the **Start button**, then drag the **black square** to the yellow square.

   The value in the Pieces left: dynamic text box changes to 2 when you match the square, but is not updated if you drag the other shapes because you have not written the ActionScript to decrement for the other shapes yet.

10. Close the Flash Player window, then repeat steps 6 and 7 for the red circle (targetCircle) and blue triangle (targetTriangle) in the Drop Bin.

11. Test the movie, close the Flash Player window, save your work, then close the movie.

You used the decrement action to maintain a count of the user's score in the game.

USE ACTIONSCRIPT TO
CREATE EXTERNAL LINKS

What You'll Do

 In this lesson, you will create e-mail and web page links.

Creating a Link to a Website

Many websites contain links to other sites. You might create links to lead the user to a related site or just to another site you want to share. The getURL action, shown in Figure 13, lets you open another file or jump from a button or movie clip symbol to another website. The new site or file can appear in the same browser window as your site or in a new window. Table 1 displays the target options for a website and external file links.

QUICKTIP

You can also enter the HTML file name of a specific window or frame as a target. This might be appropriate if you have multiple links on a page and want a separate window to open for the first link the user follows, but not for subsequent links.

When you use getURL to lead to another website, you must supply the URL for the file. Make sure to include the entire URL, including the protocol prefix, for example, *http://www.adobe.com*, which is known as

TABLE 1: Target options for website links

Option	Opens site or link in:
_self	The current window
_blank	A new window
_parent	The parent of the current frame (a frame is a part of a web page)
_top	The top-level frame in the current window

an absolute path. If you are creating a link to a file, you can include an **absolute path**, which specifies the exact location of the file, or a **relative path**, which indicates location based on the current location of your movie file. For example, to jump to a file you include in the same server folder to which you will be publishing, you can include just the file name, without any path.

Creating a Mailto: Link

You can also use getURL to create a mail link from a button or movie clip symbol. When a user clicks an e-mail link, a new e-mail message window opens, with an address field you have specified already filled in. If you want to create an e-mail link from text, not a button or movie clip symbol, you can use the Properties panel.

To create an e-mail link, include mailto: and then the e-mail address in the URL field of the getURL action. To test an e-mail link, you must display your movie in a browser by clicking File on the main menu, and then clicking Publish Preview. The e-mail link is not active in the Flash Player window.

Posting Information to a Website

The best kind of communication is two-way, and along with displaying a website, getURL can send variables to another application or a Common Gateway Interface (CGI) script located on a web server. The application or script can perform actions by using, storing, or responding to the variables—creating instant feedback that can be displayed on a user's site. Forms with user surveys and shopping carts are examples of posting information. Figure 14 shows a form to send an e-mail message.

There are two options when sending variables: GET and POST. Both methods collect all the variables defined at the main Timeline level of a movie and send them to the URL you specify in the getURL action for processing. GET is best for small amounts of information because it can send a string of up to 1,024 characters. Information sent using GET is less secure because the variables are appended to the URL string, and so they appear in the Address field of the browser. POST can accommodate more variables, and is more secure because the variables are collected and sent in a file. POST is the recommended way to send data to a script.

FIGURE 13

Using `getURL` to link to a website

FIGURE 14

A form used to send an e-mail message

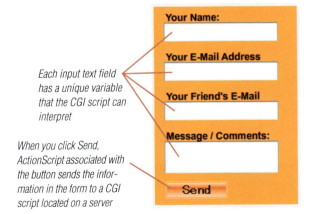

Each input text field has a unique variable that the CGI script can interpret

When you click Send, ActionScript associated with the button sends the information in the form to a CGI script located on a server

Create a website link

1. Open fl11_2.fla, then save it as **links**.

2. Click the **Selection tool** on the Tools panel, click the **Visit our Web site button** to select it, then open the Actions panel.

3. Verify the web link button appears in the lower-left corner of the Script pane, then turn on **Script Assist**.

   The following steps use Script Assist to create code for a website link.

   Note: Throughout this lesson Mac users will need to turn Script Assist off and then type code directly in the Script pane. Win users can use either method.

4. Click the **Add a new item to the script button**, point to **Global Functions**, point to **Movie Clip Control**, then click **on**.

5. Click the **Add a new item to the script button**, point to **Global Functions**, point to **Browser/Network**, then click **getURL**.

6. Click inside the **URL text box**, then type **http://www.adobe.com**.

7. Click the **list arrow** for the Window option, click **_self**, then compare your Script pane to Figure 15.

8. Collapse the Actions Panel, test the movie, then click the **Visit our Web site button**.

   The Adobe website opens in a browser window.

   Hint: If you are not connected to the Internet, you will not be able to view the site.

9. Close the browser window, then close the Flash Player window.

You created a button that links to a website.

FIGURE 15

ActionScript to create a website link

FIGURE 16

ActionScript to create an e-mail link

```
ACTIONS - BUTTON

getURL : Tell Web browser to navigate to specified URL

    URL:    mailto:webmaster@server.com          [ ] Expression
    Window: _self                             ▼    [ ] Expression
    Variables: Don't send                        ▼

    🔁 ➖ 🔍 ⊕ △ ▽ 🔲              [🪄 Script Assist]  ⑦

1  on (release) {
2      getURL("mailto:webmaster@server.com", "_self");
3  }
4

📄 email_button  📝
Line 2: getURL("mailto:webmaster@server.com", "_self");
```

Sending an e-mail through the web

To send an e-mail completely through the web, you can collect the recipient and message information for the e-mail in variable fields, and then send the variables to a CGI (Common Gateway Interface) script for processing. Common mail scripts include mailform.pl and tellafriend.cgi. See your webmaster or network administrator for information about scripts available on your server.

1. Click the **E-mail us at webmaster@server.com button** to select it.

    TIP It's good practice to include the e-mail address as part of a link, in case your user wants the address for future reference.

2. Expand the Actions panel, click the **Add a new item to the script button** 🔁 , point to **Global Functions**, point to **Movie Clip Control**, then click **on**.

3. Click the **Add a new item to the script button** 🔁 , point to **Global Functions**, point to **Browser/Network**, then click **getURL**.

4. Click inside the URL text box, then type **mailto:webmaster@server.com**.

5. Click the **list arrow** for the Window option, click **_self**, then compare your Script pane to Figure 16.

6. Click **File** on the menu bar, point to **Publish Preview**, then click **Default – (HTML)**.

    The movie opens in a browser window.

7. Click the **E-mail us at webmaster@server.com button**.

    A new e-mail message window opens in your default e-mail program, with the To: field already filled in.

    TIP If an e-mail message window does not appear, your current computer may not have access to an e-mail program. If a security warning appears, click Allow.

8. Close the mail message window, do not save changes if prompted to do so, then close the browser window.

9. Save your work, then close the movie.

You created a button with a link to an e-mail address.

Post information to a website

1. Open fl11_3.fla, then save it as **search**.

2. Click **frame 1** on the heading layer, then click the **Pasteboard** to deselect any selected objects.

3. Click the **Text tool** T on the Tools panel, display the Properties panel, then set the properties to: Family: **Arial**; Style: **Regular**; Size: **18**; Text (fill) color: **#000000**.

4. Click the **Text type list arrow**, click **Input Text**, click the **Show border around text button** ▣ to select it, then draw a **text box** below the Yahoo! graphic, as shown in Figure 17.

5. Click the **Variable text box** in the Properties panel, type **p**, then press **[Enter]** (Win) or **[return]** (Mac).

   p is a variable used in the CGI script to which you will be sending information. The script conducts a search using the information in the p variable.

6. Click the **Selection tool** ↖ on the Tools panel, click the **search button** to select it, then display the Actions panel.

7. Verify submit appears in the lower left of the Script pane and that Script Assist is on, click the **Add a new item to the script button** ⊕, point to **Global Functions**, point to **Movie Clip Control**, then click **on**.

(continued)

FIGURE 17
Drawing the text box to collect the variable information

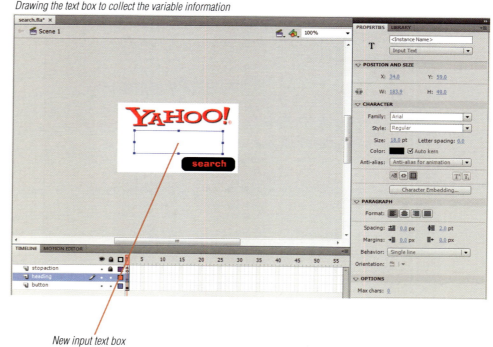

New input text box

FIGURE 18

ActionScript to send variable information to a CGI script

8. Click the **Add a new item to the script button** ⊞ , point to **Global Functions**, point to **Browser/Network**, then click **getURL**.

   Note: Mac users will need to turn off Script Assist and type in the code.

9. Click inside the URL text box, then type **http://search.yahoo.com/bin/search**.

10. Click the **Window list arrow**, then click **_self**.

11. Click the **Variables list arrow**, click **Send using GET** to enter the CGI script location and name, then compare your Script pane to Figure 18.

12. Test the movie, type **ActionScript** in the input text box, then click the **search button**.

   The Yahoo! Search website opens, with the Search field already filled in and search results displayed. You can see the format in which the GET option sent the variable by looking in the Address field of the browser. "search" is the name of the CGI script to which you sent the variable p. The URL includes the search term.

13. Close the browser window, close the Flash Player window, save your work, then close the movie.

You sent information to a CGI script.

LOAD NEW
MOVIES

What You'll Do

 In this lesson, you will load new movies into and unload movies from the Flash Player.

Understanding Multiple Movies

In previous chapters, you have seen how you can use scenes and movie clip symbols to break large movies into smaller, more manageable components. Another strategy is to split a single movie into a number of different movies, and then use ActionScript to load the movies as needed. For example, you might have a site with a number of discrete areas, not all of which are of interest to every user. By splitting each area into its own movie, you can save download time for the user because, instead of having to download a large movie for the entire site, the movie for each area will be downloaded only when the user visits it. Multiple movies can create smoother transitions between pages because the new movies load into the current HTML page. Using multiple movies can also help you keep organized during development of a movie, especially if different people are working on different parts of the movie. Figure 19 shows an example of one way to use multiple movies.

Loading Movies

You use the loadMovie action to load a movie. You must know the name of the Flash Player movie file you want to load (Flash Player files have a .SWF extension) and also its location. As with the getURL action, you can specify an absolute or relative path for the location.

You can load a new movie either in place of, or on top of, the current movie, or into a movie clip symbol. If you load a new movie into the current movie, the new movie will inherit the frame rate, dimensions, and background color of the current movie. The new movie will appear starting in the upper-left corner of the current movie, which may cause design issues if your movies are not the same size; make sure to test how the additional movies will load before publishing a site. Loading a new movie into a movie clip gives you more control over the size and placement of the movie. One useful technique is to create a blank movie clip symbol that you name, position it on the Stage where you want the new movie to appear, and then load the movie into the blank movie clip symbol. Figure 20 shows the ActionScript for loading movies.

Understanding Levels

The concept of levels becomes important when you add new movies to the current movie. Levels are similar to layers on the Timeline; they establish a hierarchy that determines what's displayed on the screen. The current movie, also called the base movie, is considered to be at Level 0. You can add the new movie at Level 0, in which case it replaces the current movie; or at Level 1, in which case it appears on top of the current movie. The movie originally at Level 0 continues to control the frame rate, dimensions, and background color of all other movies, even if you replace it.

For example, a new movie could appear on top of the current movie if loaded at Level 1. Parts of the current movie, such as the links or areas of a background image, could remain in view and active. Alternatively, you could load the new movie at Level 0, in which case none of the original movie would remain in view, but the frame rate, dimensions, and background color of the original movie would remain.

As you load additional movies, you can continue to add them in place of an existing movie, or at a higher level. Movies at higher levels appear on top of movies at lower levels. Each level can contain only one movie.

QUICKTIP

The loadMovie action becomes loadMovieNum when you specify a level at which to load a movie.

Unloading Movies

Flash also includes unloadMovie (for movies loaded into movie clips) and unloadMovieNum (for movies loaded at a level) actions to remove a movie from the Flash Player. Including this action when you no longer need a movie loaded can create smoother transitions between movies, ensure there's no visual residue between movies of different sizes, and reduce the memory required by the Flash Player. When a movie is unloaded, it is removed from the player but it is still available to be played again without having to download it again.

QUICKTIP

Loading a new movie into the same level as an existing movie automatically unloads the existing movie from the Flash Player.

FIGURE 19
A Flash site that takes advantage of using multiple movies

Each of the links on this page could open a separate .SWF file, saving the user download time

FIGURE 20
ActionScript for loading a movie

```
1  on (release) {
2      loadMovieNum("frog.swf", 2);
3  }
4
```

Load a movie

1. Open fl11_4.fla, then save it as **letterf**.

   This movie has three buttons and the letter F displayed on the Stage. All objects are on level 0 of the movie.

   TIP The steps use relative paths to load new movies. Make sure to copy the two movies you will load, fish.swf and frog.swf, to the same drive and folder where you save the letterf.fla file.

2. Click the **Selection tool** ▶ on the Tools panel, click the **fish button** to select it, then display the Actions panel.

3. Verify Script Assist is on and fish appears in the lower left of the Script pane.

   The following steps use Script Assist to create code to load a movie.

   TIP Alternately, you can turn Script Assist off and then type code directly in the Script pane.

4. Click the **Add a new item to the script button** ⊞, point to **Global Functions**, point to **Movie Clip Control**, then click **on**.

5. Click the **Add a new item to the script button** ⊞, point to **Global Functions**, point to **Browser/Network**, then click **loadMovie**.

   Note: Mac users will need to turn off Script Assist and type in the code.

6. Click inside the URL text box, type **fish.swf**, then compare your screen to Figure 21.

   The 0 indicates the level.

7. Test the movie, click the **fish button**, then compare your screen to Figure 22.

   (continued)

FIGURE 21
ActionScript to replace a movie with a new movie

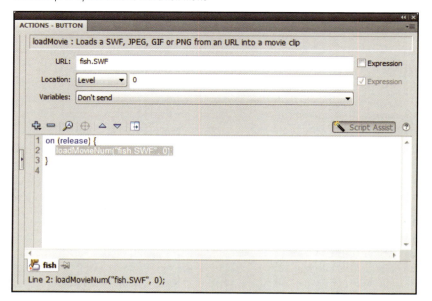

FIGURE 22
The fish movie loaded in place of the original movie

fish.swf replaces the original letterf.swf movie at level 0

Using Advanced ActionScript

FIGURE 23
Setting the movie to load at Level 1

FIGURE 24
The fish movie loaded on top of the original movie

The fish movie replaces the original movie
letterf.swf.

> TIP If an error occurs, make sure that
> fish.swf is in the same location as letterf.fla.

8. Close the Flash Player window.

*You specified that a new movie (fish.swf) replace
the currently playing movie (letterf.swf) in the
Flash Player when the user clicks a button.*

Set a level for a movie

1. Verify the fish button is still selected,
   double-click the **0** in the Location text box,
   then type **1**, as shown in Figure 23.

2. Test the movie, click the **fish button**, then
   compare your screen to Figure 24.

   The 1 causes the fish movie to appear on top
   of the original movie.

3. Close the Flash Player window.

You set a level for a movie.

Stack movies

1. Click the **frog button** to select it.

   Hint: The ActionScript code to stack movies (that is to have both movies playing with one appearing on top of the other) is the same as the code to load a movie.

2. Verify frog appears in the lower left of the Script pane, click the **Add a new item to the script button** ⊕ , point to **Global Functions**, point to **Movie Clip Control**, then click **on**.

3. Click the **Add a new item to the script button** ⊕ , point to **Global Functions**, point to **Browser/Network**, then click **loadMovie**.

   Note: Mac users will need to turn off Script Assist and type in the code.

4. Click inside the URL text box, type **frog.swf**, double-click the **0** in the Location text box, then type **2**.

5. Test the movie, click the **fish button**, click the **frog button**, then compare your screen to Figure 25.

   Each movie appears on top of the original movie. No matter the order in which you click the buttons, the frog movie will always appear on top.

6. Close the Flash Player window.

You loaded two movies at different levels, which allows the movies to be stacked.

FIGURE 25
The fish and frog movies are stacked because the fish movie loaded at Level 1 and the frog movie at Level 2

Referencing loaded movies in ActionScript

You can create a reference to the Timeline of a loaded movie by including the level number of the movie. For example, to add a goto action that goes to frame 10 of the movie loaded at Level 1 and stops the movie, type the following, including the semicolon: _level1.gotoAndStop(10);

Using Advanced ActionScript

FIGURE 26

ActionScript to unload movies at Levels 1 and 2

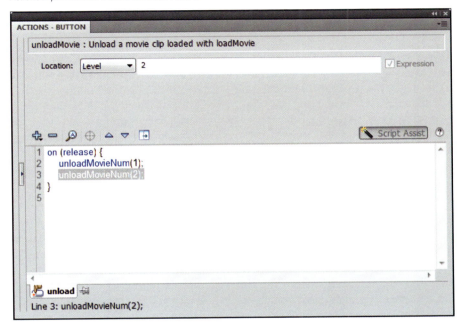

1. Click the **unload button** to select it.

2. Verify unload appears in the lower left of the Script pane, click the **Add a new item to the script button** ⊕ , point to **Global Functions**, point to **Movie Clip Control**, then click **on**.

3. Click the **Add a new item to the script button** ⊕ , point to **Global Functions**, point to **Browser/Network**, then click **unloadMovie**.

4. Double-click the **0** in the Location text box, then type **1**.

   This line of ActionScript removes the movie loaded at Level 1, which is fish.swf.

5. Click the **Add a new item to the script button** ⊕ , point to **Global Functions**, point to **Browser/Network**, then click **unloadMovie**.

6. Double-click the **0** in the Location text box, type **2**, then compare your Script pane to Figure 26.

   This line of ActionScript removes the movie loaded at Level 2, which is frog.swf.

7. Test the movie, clicking the **fish**, **frog**, and **unload buttons** in different sequences.

   If both the fish and the frog movies are loaded, then both the fish and frog movies will unload when you click the unload button. If only one movie is loaded, then that movie will unload when you click the unload button.

8. Close the Flash Player window, save your work, then close the file.

You added actions to unload movies.

WORK WITH
CONDITIONAL ACTIONS

What You'll Do

 In this lesson, you will work with conditional actions and use ActionScript to duplicate movie clip symbols.

Using the Else and Else If Actions

In Chapter 9, you used the *if* action to test for a condition. If the condition was true, the *if* action ran a series of actions enclosed in curly brackets. Otherwise, it skipped the actions in brackets and ran the next set of actions in the Script pane.

ActionScript also includes an *else* action you can use to create more sophisticated branching. An *else* action lets you specify one set of actions to run if a condition is true, and an alternate set to run if the condition is false. If a condition has more than two possible states, you can use *else if* to set up a series of possible branches. For example, if you are creating an online test, there might be four possible answers a student could provide, and you might want to create a different branch for each answer. Figure 27 shows ActionScript that uses *else if* to create multiple branches.

Creating Conditional Loops

A **loop** is an action or set of actions that repeat as long as a condition exists. Creating a loop can be as simple as taking a variable, assigning a value to it, executing a statement, and if the statement is false, adding one to the variable and trying again. You can often just use an *if* action to create a loop.

ActionScript includes other actions with which you can create more sophisticated conditional loops. The *for*, *while*, and *do while* loops all let you set up conditions for a loop and actions to run repeatedly. The *for* loop takes a series of arguments with which you set up a condition, a series of actions to take if the condition is true, and a counter that keeps track of the number of loops; this counter is often used in conjunction with the condition, for instance, to run the loop a user-specified number of times. The *while* and *do while* loops let you enter a series of actions to run while a condition is true. The difference is that *do while* runs the actions at least one time, then evaluates if the condition is true, where as *while* evaluates the condition and then runs the actions if the conditions are met. Figure 28 shows some examples of using ActionScript to create loops.

Duplicating Movie Clip Symbol Instances

An action frequently used with conditional loops is *duplicateMovieClip*. This action displays one of the more powerful abilities of ActionScript, which is to add and remove movie clip symbols as a movie is playing. The *duplicateMovieClip* creates a copy of a movie clip symbol instance; it includes arguments that let you specify a new instance name and a depth level at which to insert the new movie clip symbol (either in place of or on top of existing instances). You can then use the *setProperty* action or specific Properties actions (such as _x and _y) to change the location and appearance of the new instance of the movie clip symbol.

The *duplicateMovieClip* is often used in games to create multiple copies of an object based on a variable or user interaction—for example, a juggling game could ask a user how many balls they want to try to keep up in the air. Based on the answer, a looping action determines the number of times to run the duplicateMovieClip action.

FIGURE 27

ActionScript to create multiple branches

FIGURE 28

ActionScript to create loops

This **for** loop increments the variable n a number of times specified by a separate variable named counter

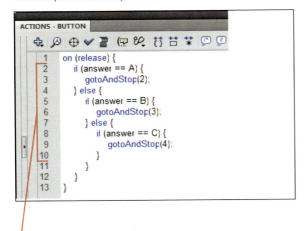

If the user types the answer A in an input text box, the movie jumps to frame 2; other answers jump to other frames

This **do while** loop also increments a variable n, but repeats based on the value of n

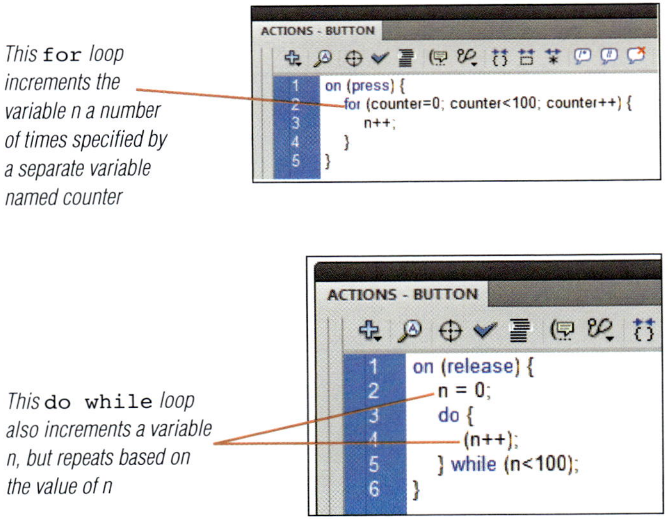

Create conditional branching using if and else actions

1. Open fl11_5.fla, save it as **branching**, drag the **playhead** to view the three screens, then return to frame 1.

2. Click the **Selection tool** ▸ on the Tools panel, click the **login button** on the Stage to select it, then display the Actions panel.

3. Verify Script Assist is on and that login is displayed in the lower left of the Script pane.

4. Click the **Add a new item to the script button** ⊕ , point to **Global Functions**, point to **Movie Clip Control**, then click **on**.

5. Click the **Add a new item to the script button** ⊕ , point to **Statements**, point to **Conditions/Loops**, then click **if**.

   The action appears in the Script pane, but the condition for the if statement has not been set yet.

6. Click inside the Condition text box, then type **pass == "letmein"**.

   "pass" is the variable for the input text field on the Super Secure Login page.

7. Click the **Add a new item to the script button** ⊕ , point to **Global Functions**, point to **Timeline Control**, then click **goto**.

8. Click the **Go to and stop option button** at the top of the Script pane, double-click the **1** in the Frame text box, type **2**, then compare your screen to Figure 29.

(continued)

FIGURE 29
Adding an `if` *action*

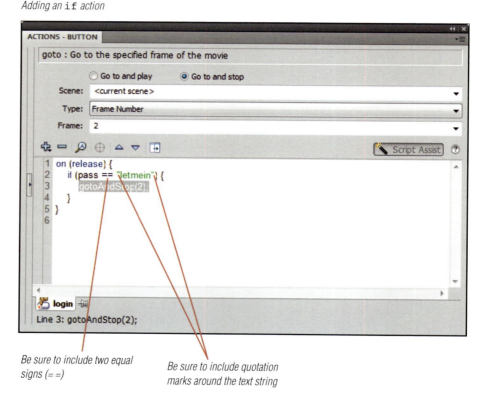

Be sure to include two equal signs (= =)

Be sure to include quotation marks around the text string

FIGURE 30

Adding an else *action*

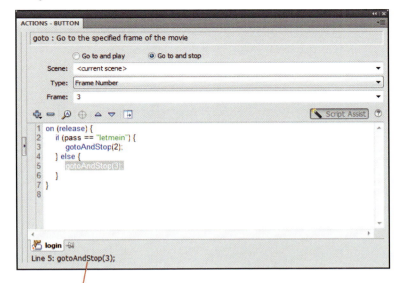

If the user supplies anything but the string "letmein" the movie jumps to frame 3

FIGURE 31

Entering the password to log in

9. Click the **Add a new item to the script button** ⊞, point to **Statements**, point to **Conditions/Loops**, then click **else**.

10. Click the **Add a new item to the script button** ⊞, point to **Global Functions**, point to **Timeline Control**, then click **goto**.

11. Click the **Go to and stop option button** at the top of the Script pane, double-click the **1** in the Frame text box, type **3**, then compare your Script pane to Figure 30.

12. Test the movie, type **xyz** for the password, then click the **login button**.

The movie jumps to the "Access Denied" screen.

13. Close the Flash Player window, test the movie again, type **letmein** for the password, as shown in Figure 31, then click the **login button**.

The movie jumps to the "Access Granted" screen.

14. Close the Flash Player window.

You used if and else actions to create a conditional branch that takes different actions based on user behavior (input of password).

Create a loop using if

1. Insert a **new layer** above the text layer, name it **loop**, then click **frame 1** on the loop layer.

2. Display the Actions panel, turn Script Assist off, then verify loop:1 is displayed in the lower left of the Script pane.

3. Click **Line 1** in the Script pane, type **n = 0;**, then press **[Enter]** (Win) or **[return]** (Mac) to move to the next line.

   This line of ActionScript creates a variable named "n" and sets the value of the variable to 0.

4. Type **stop();**, then compare your screen to Figure 32.

5. Click the **Pasteboard** to deselect all objects, click the **login button** to select it, click at the **end of Line 4** in the Script pane of the Actions panel, then press **[Enter]** (Win) or **[return]** (Mac) to create a blank Line 5.

6. Type **n++;** on Line 5 in the Script pane, then press **[Enter]** (Win) or **[return]** (Mac).

   This line of ActionScript increments the variable n by one each time the else statement is processed—that is, each time the user provides the wrong password.

   (continued)

FIGURE 32
Creating a variable and setting the value to 0

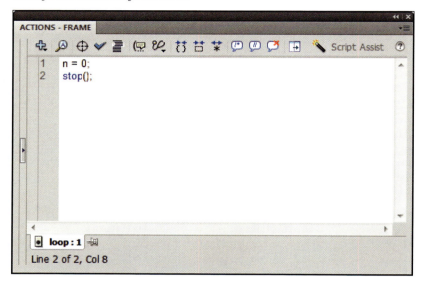

Using Advanced ActionScript

FIGURE 33

Using the **if** action to create a loop

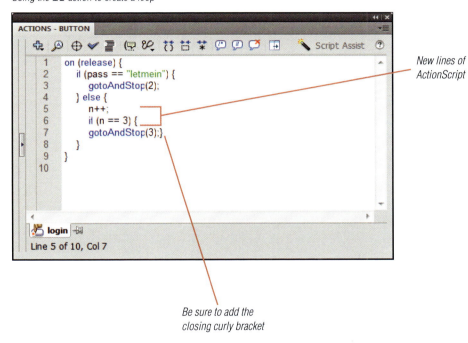

New lines of ActionScript

Be sure to add the closing curly bracket

---

7. Type **if (n == 3) {** on Line 6.

This line of ActionScript creates a condition: the statements that follow the if action will only be processed when the variable n is equal to 3.

8. Click at the **end of Line 7** in the Script pane, type **}**, then compare your Script pane to Figure 33.

The closing curly bracket is necessary to complete the new if action.

9. Test the movie, type **xyz** for the password, then click the **login button**.

Note that nothing seems to happen. This is because you set the counter to 3. The user has three tries to get the password correct.

10. Delete the text in the password text box, type **abc**, then click the **login button**.

11. Delete the text in the password text box, type **123**, then click the **login button**.

The movie jumps to the Access Denied screen only after the third attempt to log in.

12. Close the Flash Player window.

You used the if action to create a loop that, based on user behavior, repeats three times and then takes another action.

Add user feedback to the loop

1. Click **frame 1** on the text layer, then click the **Pasteboard** to deselect any selected objects.

2. Click the **Text tool** T on the Tools panel, then use the Properties panel to set the Family to **Arial**, the Style to **Bold**, and the Size to **14**.

3. Click the **Text type list arrow**, click **Dynamic Text**, click the **Show border around text button** to deselect it, unlock the text layer, then draw a **text box** below the words "Super Secure Login," as shown in Figure 34.

4. Click the **Variable text box** in the Properties panel, type **feedback**, then press **[Enter]** (Win) or **[return]** (Mac).

5. Display the Actions panel, click the **Selection tool** on the Tools panel, click the **login button** to select it, click at the **end of Line 5** in the Script pane, then press **[Enter]** (Win) or **[return]** (Mac) to create a blank Line 6.

6. Type **feedback = "Sorry. Tries left: " + (3-n);**, then press **[Enter]** (Win) or **[return]** (Mac).

   This line of ActionScript populates the dynamic text field named feedback with a text string and number. The number is calculated by subtracting the variable n, which is incrementally counting the number of attempts the user makes from 3 (the maximum number of tries).

   TIP Be sure to include a blank space after the colon and before the closing quotation mark.

   (continued)

FIGURE 34
Drawing the dynamic text box

Make sure the text box is this size; the text box is transparent when it is not selected

FIGURE 35

ActionScript to provide user feedback

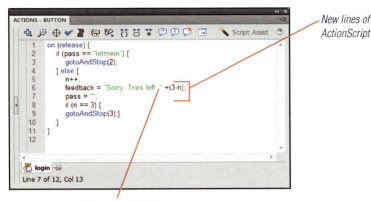

New lines of
ActionScript

Be sure to include a space
after the colon and before
the closing quotation mark

FIGURE 36

Logging in with an incorrect password with user feedback

The feedback = "Sorry. Tries
left: " + (3-n); ActionScript
statement populates the
dynamic text box

The pass = "" ; ActionScript
statement clears the input text
box of the incorrect password

7. Type **pass = "";** on Line 7 in the Script pane,
then compare your Script pane to Figure 35.

This line of ActionScript clears the incorrect
password the user has entered.

8. Test the movie, type **xyz** for the password,
click the **login button**, then notice the feedback text, as shown in Figure 36.

9. Repeat twice using different passwords.

The password screen provides feedback, and
the movie jumps to the "Access Denied"
screen only after the third attempt to enter
the password.

TIP If you don't see the number of tries left
in the text box, widen the text box to ensure
there is enough room to display the text and
the number.

10. Close the Flash Player window, then test the
movie again by typing **letmein** and clicking
the login button.

11. Save and close the movie.

*You added actions to provide user feedback as
part of a conditional loop.*

Using the Password line type in an input field

You may not want passwords to be visible onscreen as users enter them. For security,
you can set an input text field to display asterisks rather than the actual keystrokes
being typed by a user. To do this, display the Properties panel for the text field, click
the Line type list arrow, and then click Password.

Create a while loop to duplicate movie clip symbols

1. Open fl11_6.fla, then save it as **duplicator**.

   This file contains an input text field with the variable name "amount" and the face movie clip symbol.

2. Click the **Selection tool** on the Tools panel, click the **duplicate button** to select it, display the Actions panel, then verify Script Assist is off.

3. Click **Line 1**, type **on (release) {**, then press **[Enter]** (Win) or **[return]** (Mac).

   Figure 37 shows the ActionScript code you will create in the following steps. An explanation of the code follows each step.

4. Type **n = 0;** on Line 2, then press **[Enter]** (Win) or **[return]** (Mac).

   This line of ActionScript creates a variable, n, and sets its value to 0.

5. Type **while (n < amount) {** on Line 3, then press **[Enter]** (Win) or **[return]** (Mac).

   This line of ActionScript creates a `while` loop that takes the n variable and checks to see if it is less than the amount variable.

6. Type **duplicateMovieClip ("_root.face", "face_" + n, n);** on Line 4, then press **[Enter]** (Win) or **[return]** (Mac).

   This line of ActionScript runs as long as the while condition is true. It duplicates the face movie clip symbol instance, assigning it a text string name "face_" concatenated with the current value of the variable n, and putting it on a level determined by the current value of the variable n.

   (continued)

FIGURE 37
ActionScript to create a loop to duplicate a movie clip symbol

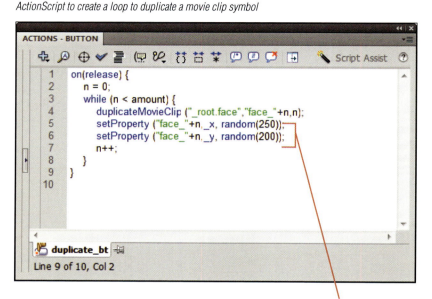

Be sure to include two parentheses—one to close the random *action, and one to close the* setProperty *action*

FIGURE 38

Ten duplicate instances of the movie clip symbol appear on the Stage

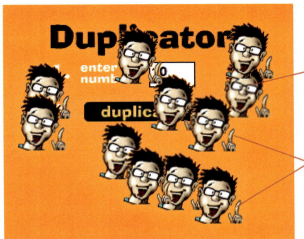

The eleventh face is the original one on the Stage

Placement of images as they are duplicated is random, so your images will appear in different places

Using the random action

The random action returns a random integer between 0 and one less than the value specified as an argument for the action. For example random(5) returns an integer between 0 and 4. Whereas, random(5)+1 returns an integer between 1 and 5. You can use random with setProperty to create unpredictable behavior for movie clip symbols or to generate random numbers for variables. When using random to position movie clip symbols, consider adding an offset value to keep the movie clip symbols from overlapping other objects on the screen. For example, setProperty("instance_" + n, _y, random(200)+130); adds 130 units to the random number generated for the Y coordinate of the new movie clip symbols.

7. Type **setProperty ("face_" + n, _x, random(250));** on Line 5, then press **[Enter]** (Win) or **[return]** (Mac).

   This line of ActionScript sets the x coordinate of the new instance to a random number between 0 and 249 (1 less than 250, which is the argument value for the random action).

8. Type **setProperty ("face_" + n, _y, random(200));** on Line 6, then press **[Enter]** (Win) or **[return]** (Mac).

   This line of ActionScript sets the y coordinate of the new instance to a random number between 0 and 199.

9. Type **n++;** on Line 7, then press **[Enter]** (Win) or **[return]** (Mac).

   This line of ActionScript increments the value of the n variable by 1.

10. Type **}** on Line 8, then press **[Enter]** (Win) or **[return]** (Mac).

11. Type **}** on Line 9, then compare your Script pane to Figure 37.

    Note: Click the Check syntax button to be sure your code is correct.

12. Test the movie, type **10** in the box next to the words "enter a number," click the **duplicate button**, then compare your screen to Figure 38.

    The ActionScript loops 10 times, creating 10 random instances of the movie clip symbol on the screen.

13. Close the Flash Player window, save and close the movie, then exit Flash.

You used a while action to create a loop that duplicates a movie clip symbol a number of times specified by a user.

Create complex interactivity.

(*Note:* It is good practice to use the Check syntax button and the Auto format button each time you complete the code for an action. This allows you to troubleshoot the code as you go.)

1. Start Flash, open fl11_7.fla, then save it as **skillsdemo11**.
2. Click frame 1 on the actions layer, open the Actions panel, verify Script Assist is off, then add a Mouse.hide (); action on Line 1 in the Script pane to hide the mouse cursor. (*Hint*: Don't forget to include a semicolon at the end of the action and move the other actions down one line.)
3. Select the cross-hairs symbol on the Stage, then display the Properties panel. (*Hint*: Click on the black lines to select the cross-hairs movie clip. Verify that cross_hairs is specified as the Instance of in the Properties panel.)
4. Assign the movie clip an instance name of **aim**.
5. Display the Actions panel, verify Script Assist is off and aim is in the lower left of the Script pane, then type **onClipEvent (enterFrame) {** on Line 1 in the Script pane to indicate that the next set of actions should happen as soon as the movie clip instance is displayed, then add a new line.
6. Type **_root.aim._x = _root. _xmouse;** on Line 2 in the Script pane to set the x coordinate of the aim movie clip instance equal to the x coordinate of the hidden mouse pointer, then add a new line. (*Hint*: If a code hint menu appears, continue typing to dismiss the menu.)
7. Type **_root.aim._y = _root. _ymouse;** on Line 3 in the Script pane to set the y coordinate of the aim movie clip instance equal to the y coordinate of the hidden mouse pointer, then add a new line.
8. Type **}** (a closing curly bracket) on Line 4 in the Script pane.
9. Test the movie. (*Hint*: The cross-hairs symbol becomes the pointer. The game ends when the value in the "shots" box falls below 0. The hits are not displayed because the code has not been written.)
10. Close the Flash Player window, then save your work.

Track user interactions with the increment and decrement operator.

1. Use the Selection tool to click frame 50 on the Timeline.
2. Click the Pasteboard, then click the black heart to select it.
3. Verify masked_target appears in the lower left of the Script pane.
4. Type **on (press) {** on Line 1 in the Script pane, then add a new line.
5. Type **if (_root.shots == 0) {** on Line 2, then add a new line. This checks to see if the variable shots is equal to 0.
6. Type **_root.gotoAndStop("gameOver");** on Line 3, then add a new line. If shots is equal to 0, the playhead jumps to the frame named gameOver.
7. Type **} else {** on Line 4, then add a new line.
8. Type **_root.hits++;** on Line 5, then add a new line. If shots is not equal to 0, then the variable hits is incremented by 1.
9. Type **_root.shots--;** on Line 6, then add a new line. If shots is not equal to 0, then the variable shots is decreased by 1.
10. Type **}** on Line 7, then add a new line.
11. Type **}** on Line 8.
12. Check the syntax, then save your work.

Use ActionScript to create external links.

1. Click frame 51 on the actions layer, select the More Games button, then verify Web_link appears in the lower left of the Script pane.
2. Type **on (release) {** on Line 1, then add a new line.
3. Type **getURL ("http://www.adobe.com", "_self");** on Line 2 for the URL address and the Window.
4. Add a line, then type **}** on Line 3.
5. Select the Comments? button on the Stage, then verify Email appears on the lower left of the Script pane.
6. Repeat steps 2 and 3, changing the getURL address to: **"mailto:webmaster@server.com", "_self"**.
7. Add a line, then type **}** on Line 3.
8. Save your work.

Load new movies.

1. Click frame 1 on the actions layer, select the Easy button on the Stage, then verify easy appears on the lower left of the Script pane.
2. Click at the end of Line 3 in the Script pane, press [Enter] (Win) or [return] (Mac), then type **loadMovieNum("easy_level.swf", 1);** on Line 4. This loads the movie easy_level.swf at level 1. (*Hint*: The two movies you will load, easy_level.swf and hard_level.swf, must be in the same file location where you saved skillsdemo11.fla.)
3. Click the Hard button to select it, then verify Hard appears on the lower left of the Script pane.
4. Click at the end of Line 3 in the Script pane, press [Enter] (Win) or [return] (Mac), then type **loadMovieNum("hard_level.swf", 1);** on Line 4. This loads the movie hard_level.swf at level 1.
5. Test the movie, then save your work.

Work with conditional actions.

1. Click frame 51 on the actions layer, then verify actions:51 appears on the lower left of the Script pane.
2. Click Line 1 in the Script pane, add a new line to move the stop (); action to Line 2, then click Line 1 again to begin adding actions.
3. Type **if (hits > 8) {** on Line 1 in the Script pane to set a condition, then press [Enter] (Win) or [return] (Mac).
4. Type **feedback = "You're a winner!";}** on Line 2 in the Script pane to specify the actions to perform if the condition is true, then press [Enter] (Win) or [return] (Mac). (*Hint*: "feedback" is the variable name of a dynamic text box on this screen.)
5. Type **else {** on Line 3 in the Script pane to perform different actions when the if condition is not true, then press [Enter] (Win) or [return] (Mac).
6. Type **feedback = "Better luck next time.";}** on Line 4 in the Script pane to specify the alternate actions, then press [Enter] (Win) or [return] (Mac).
7. Type **unloadMovieNum(1);** on Line 5 in the Script pane to unload the loaded movie.
8. Test the movie.
9. Compare your screen to Figure 39, save your work, then close the file.
10. Exit Flash.

FIGURE 39
Completed Skills Review

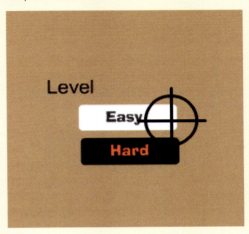

Ultimate Tours would like you to build a banner for their website which, when a button on the banner is clicked, will load a new movie containing their latest travel specials. By creating the banner in one SWF file and the specials in another, Ultimate Tours can update the specials at any time, just by replacing one file. As a way to encourage users to look at and interact with the banner, they would also like you to create an input text field in the banner which, when the user types the name of a city and clicks a button, displays a page from *www.weather.com* with the current weather for that location.

1. Open fl11_8.fla, then rename the file **ultimatetours11**.

2. Select the see specials button, then open the Actions panel.
3. Add actions which, upon a click of the button, load a new movie called **specials.swf** at Level 1. (*Hint*: Use the on (release) and loadMovieNum action to create this effect. The specials.swf movie must be in the same file location where you saved ultimatetours11.fla.)
4. Click frame 1 on the content layer, click the Text tool on the Tools panel, then draw an input text box beneath the text that reads, **Traveling? Type a city name to check the weather:** Use these settings: color of **black**, font of **Times New Roman**, font size of **14**, **Bold**, with a border displayed around the text. Assign the new input text box a variable name of **where**.

5. Select the get weather button, then in the Script pane of the Actions panel add a getURL action which, upon a click of the button, uses the GET method to send variables to a CGI script with a URL of **"http://www.weather.com/search/search"**. The new website should open in the current browser window.
6. Test the movie, click the see specials button to load the new movie, then type a city name and click the get weather button.
7. Save your work, then compare your image to Figure 40.

FIGURE 40
Sample completed Project Builder 1

You have volunteered to use Flash to create an interactive, educational counting game that will get first-graders comfortable with computers. The game will display a random number of cookies spilled from a cookie jar, ask students to count the cookies, type the number, and then give feedback on whether or not the answer is correct.

1. Open fl11_9.fla, then save it as **counting_game11**.
2. Click frame 1 on the content layer, then create an input text box with a variable named **check** above the go button that is big enough to accommodate a two-digit number. Settings: Arial, 16 pt, Regular style, black color, with a border displayed around the text.
3. Click frame 2 on the content layer, then create a dynamic text box with a variable named **score** that fills the area above the cookie jar image. Use these settings: Arial, 24 pt, Regular style, black color, Multiline line type.
4. Copy the dynamic text box named score from frame 2 on the content layer to the same location in frame 3 on the content layer.
5. Click frame 1 on the content layer, click the cookie to select an instance of the aCookie movie clip, display the Properties panel, then assign it an instance name of **cookie**.
6. Select the start button in frame 1 on the content layer, then add ActionScript which, upon a click of the button, does the following:
   - Creates a variable named **value** and sets it to a random number between 1 and 5

- Creates a variable named **n**, and sets its value to **0**
- Creates a loop using the while action, which says that while the variable named n is less than the variable named value, duplicate the cookie movie clip symbol, name the new instance with the word **cookie**, an underscore, and the value of the variable n, and set the new instance at a depth of the value of the variable n. The while loop should also use two SetProperty actions to set the location of the new movie clip instance: the X coordinate should be set to a random number between 1 and 200, with an offset of 10, and the Y coordinate should be set to a random number between 1 and 100, with an offset of 250.
- Increments the value of the variable n by 1
7. Select the go button in frame 1 on the content layer, then add ActionScript that, upon a click of the button, does the following:
   - Uses the if action to check if the number in the variable named check is equal to the number in the variable named value and, if so, jumps to frame 2 and populates the dynamic text box named score with the words **"Good job, the number of cookies that spilled is "** and then the variable named value. (*Hint*: Add a plus sign and a period in quotation marks +"." after the value variable in the ActionScript code.)

- Uses the else action to perform the following actions when the condition is not true: jump to frame 3 and populate the dynamic text box named score with the words **"No, that's not right. The number of cookies that spilled is "** and then the variable named value.
8. Test the movie, compare your image to Figure 41, then save your work.

FIGURE 41
Sample completed Project Builder 2

DESIGN PROJECT

Figure 42 shows a page from a website created using Flash. Study the figure and complete the following. For each question, indicate how you determined your answer.

1. Connect to the Internet, then go to this URL: *http://v4.2a-archive.com/flashindex.htm*.

2. Open a document in a word processor or open a new Flash document, save the file as **dpc11**, then answer the following questions. (*Hint*: Use the Text tool in Flash.)

   - What is the purpose of this site? Does the design of the site contribute to its purpose?

   - Move the mouse pointer around the screen and note the different effects as you pass over links and buttons. Do you think these effects were achieved with ActionScript or some other way?

   - Click the links in the main navigation bar. What changes occur on the screen? Do you think the links are jumping to a different frame in this movie or loading a new movie? What specific actions could be used to achieve this effect?

   - List some of the advantages of loading a new movie for links, in the context of this site.

   - Click the Portfolio link, then click the View button for the featured website. What happens? What specific actions

might be associated with the Launch button to achieve this effect?

   - Click the Contact button near the top of the screen, then click the Sales button to display a form. There is a field to enter your contact information, including an

e-mail address. Also, there is a Send button. What do you think happens when you press the Send button? What specific actions might be involved in the processing of the e-mail information?

FIGURE 42
Design Project

You have decided to create a portfolio with five screens, each in a separate frame and on a separate layer. One screen contains examples of the Flash work you have done throughout this book, and one creates a password-protected, clients-only area. You will create the links to your Flash movies by loading new SWF files. You can use your favorites from the files you have developed throughout this book, or any other SWF files you have created on your own.

1. Open a new Flash document, then save it as **portfolio11**.

2. Create a screen with a heading of **home** in frame 1 on a layer called Home Page. Add another layer named **Navigation-buttons** and create three buttons named **home**, **flash samples**, and **clients only**.

3. Create a screen in frame 2 on a layer called **Flash Samples**, using a format that fits in visually with the rest of your site. On this screen include a title and at least three buttons, each of which, when clicked, loads a new Flash movie at Level 1. (*Hint*: New movies appear starting in the upper-left corner of the current movie. You may need to reduce the size of your SWF files or change the location of your navigation buttons to achieve the effect you want. Be sure the SWF files are in the same folder as your movie.)

4. Create a screen in frame 3 on a layer called **Clients Only**. On this screen, create the text "Enter password" and an input text box with the variable name **password**.

5. Create another screen that says: **Welcome to the client's area.**

6. Create another screen that says: **Sorry, that is not correct. Please contact me to receive or verify your password.** Then, add a button to the page which, when clicked, opens the user's default e-mail program to a new mail message with your e-mail address filled in.

7. On the Clients Only screen that prompts for a password, create a button with the text **Submit**. Open the Actions panel, then set up a conditional action which, if the user types the word "password" in the input text box, jumps to the "welcome" screen, or, if the user types anything else, jumps to the "sorry" screen.

FIGURE 43
Sample completed Portfolio Project

8. Add actions to the buttons on the home screen which, when clicked, jump to the new Flash Samples and Clients Only screens, respectively.

9. Add an unloadMovieNum(1) action to each navigation button on the Home Page screen that jumps to a new screen. (*Hint*: If you don't add this action, the movies you load on the Flash Samples screen will remain loaded, even when you navigate away from the Flash Samples screen.)

10. Test the movie, then compare your movie to Figure 43.

11. Save your work.

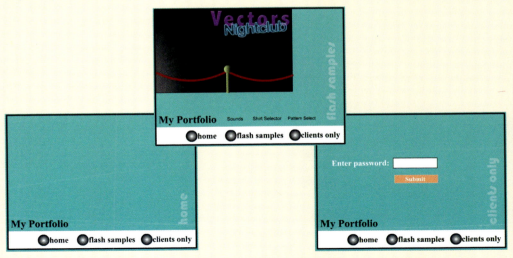

chapter

12

WORKING WITH BEHAVIORS
AND COMPONENTS

1. Work with Behaviors

2. Work with Components

12 WORKING WITH BEHAVIORS
AND COMPONENTS

Introduction

Completion of an effective Adobe Flash application depends on several factors, including the nature of the application (straightforward versus complex), the allotted development time, and the developer's expertise. Flash provides two features, Behaviors and Components, that enable developers to speed up the development process and create effective applications without writing ActionScript code.

Behaviors

In previous chapters, you learned how to use ActionScript to add control, interactivity, and multimedia to an application. Using Behaviors, you can quickly and easily incorporate these features into your application. **Behaviors** are blocks of prewritten ActionScript code that you can apply by using pop-up menus and dialog boxes without having to write the ActionScript code yourself. For example, you can create a button and then use a Behavior to apply a gotoAndPlay action to the button.

Tools You'll Use

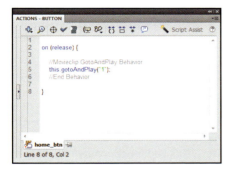

Behaviors (continued)

Flash has several built-in Behaviors that you can use as you develop an application. These built-in Behaviors are for the most common types of functions, such as jumping to a frame, playing a sound, or linking to a website. Other Behaviors are available from third-party companies and independent developers; some are free and others must be purchased. The Adobe website is one source for obtaining third-party Behaviors. In addition, you can create your own custom Behaviors by creating an XML file that contains the ActionScript 2.0 code to perform the desired Behavior. Custom Behaviors are stored in the Behaviors folder on your computer. While many of the more common functions can be incorporated using built-in Behaviors, more complex interactions require a knowledge of ActionScript. Behaviors are not available for Flash documents using ActionScript 3.0. Therefore, if you are using Behaviors, make sure ActionScript 2.0 is designated on the Flash tab of the Publish Settings dialog box.

Components

Components are another time-saving feature of Flash. There are four categories of Components:

- **User Interface (UI)**—Components (such as buttons and menus) that are used to create the visual interface for a Flash application
- **Media**—Components used to add streaming video to a Flash application
- **Data**—Components used to connect to a data source, download data to a Flash application, and update the data remotely
- **Video**—Components used to insert a flv video file into a Flash document and allow the user to control the playback of the video including start, stop, and mute controls.

Components are commonly used for creating check boxes, drop-down menus, and forms with boxes for entering user data, such as name and address. You can quickly add functionality to a movie by dragging and dropping Components (predeveloped movie clips) from the Components panel to the Stage.

As with Behaviors, you are not required to enter ActionScript code when using Components. When you select a Component to use, it is placed in the Library panel for reuse in another part of the movie.

In addition to the Components provided in Flash, you can obtain other Components from third-party companies and individuals. Often these are mini-applications, such as calendars, photo galleries, and preloaders, that add functionality to a Flash movie.

Behaviors and Components can work together. For example, you can add a button Component to the Stage and then apply a Behavior to the button that creates a link to an external website. Figure 1 shows several pages of a website. Each page has one or more Components and/or Behaviors.

FIGURE 1

Web pages with Components and Behaviors

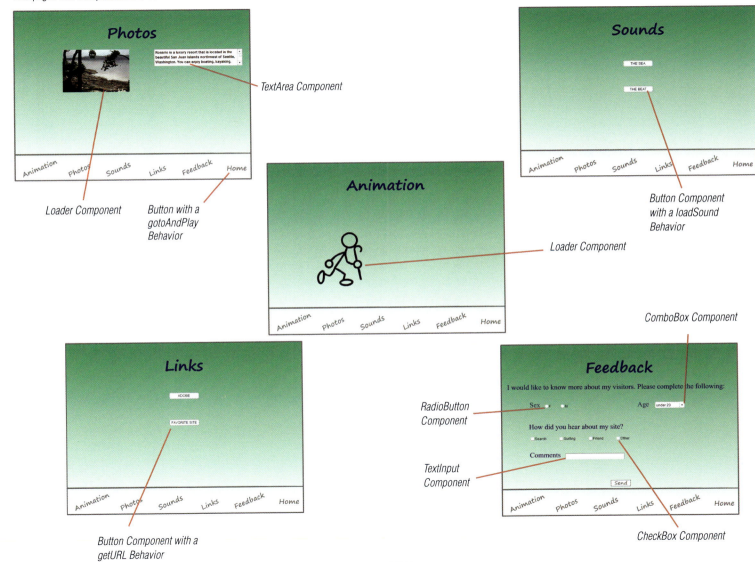

TextArea Component

Loader Component

Button with a
gotoAndPlay
Behavior

Button Component
with a loadSound
Behavior

Loader Component

ComboBox Component

RadioButton
Component

TextInput
Component

Button Component with a
getURL Behavior

CheckBox Component

WORK WITH
BEHAVIORS

What You'll Do

In this lesson, you will learn how to use Behaviors to create a button link.

Using Behaviors

A Behavior, like any ActionScript, can be placed on a frame or linked to an instance of an object, such as a button (which must be a movie clip). If the Behavior is placed on a frame, the ActionScript is run when the playhead gets to the frame. If the Behavior is linked to an object, the ActionScript is run when a particular event that triggers the Behavior occurs. For example, a Behavior assigned to a button could be triggered by a button click (event). When working with Behaviors assigned to an object, you must specify the event.

To use Behaviors, first you must select the frame or object instance to which the Behavior will be applied. Then you select the desired Behavior from the Behaviors panel and complete any dialog boxes that appear. For example, if you want to use the Behaviors feature to assign a gotoAndPlay script to a button, you would first select the button on the Stage and then open the Behaviors panel. Figure 2 shows the Behaviors panel with the drop-down menu listing the categories of Behaviors. The Movieclip category is selected and the "Goto and Play at frame or label" Behavior is selected in the sub-menu. After making a choice from the submenu, a dialog box appears allowing you to specify the movie clip and frame to begin playing when the event (click) occurs. The ActionScript, as shown in Figure 3, is automatically assigned to the button. In this case, when the user clicks the button ("release"), the playhead goes to frame 1 of the current Timeline ("this" indicates the current Timeline).

The default event that triggers the script is click; however you can specify a different event such as pressing a key. Behaviors can be edited or deleted using the Behaviors panel, and the ActionScript they create can be edited using the Actions panel.

FIGURE 2
The Behaviors panel with the category list and submenu displayed

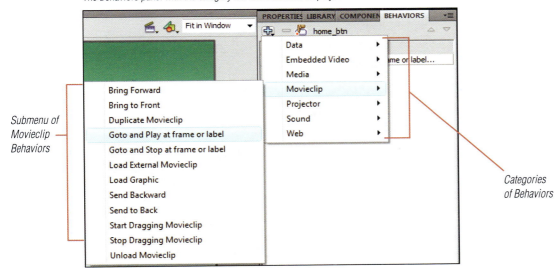

Submenu of
Movieclip
Behaviors

Categories
of Behaviors

FIGURE 3
ActionScript inserted for the gotoAndPlay Behavior

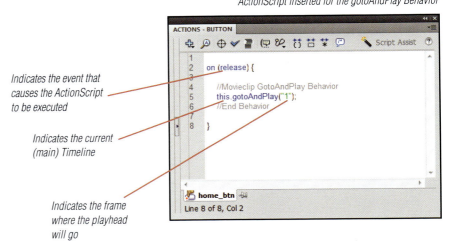

Indicates the event that
causes the ActionScript
to be executed

Indicates the current
(main) Timeline

Indicates the frame
where the playhead
will go

Set up the workspace

1. Start Flash.

2. Open fl12_1.fla from the drive and folder where your Data Files are stored, then save it as **mySamples**.

   Note: If a message opens stating that the font used in this file is not available on your computer, you can choose to use a default font or substitute another font.

   The Stage size is set to width: 800 px and height: 600 px.

3. Click **View** on the menu bar, point to **Magnification**, then click **Fit in Window**.

4. Click **File** on the menu bar, click **Publish Settings**, click the **Flash tab**, then verify ActionScript 2.0 is displayed.

5. Click **OK** to close the Publish Settings dialog box.

6. Click **Control** on the menu bar, then click **Test Movie**.

7. Click each of the **navigation text buttons** at the bottom of the screen.

   This is a basic website with simple screen headings. The Home button has not been completed. There is no content on the other screens except for the Feedback form, which has several text box labels, but the input boxes associated with the labels have not been created yet.

8. Close the Flash Player window.

9. Verify the navigation layer is displayed, as shown in Figure 4.

(continued)

FIGURE 4

The Timeline showing the navigation layer

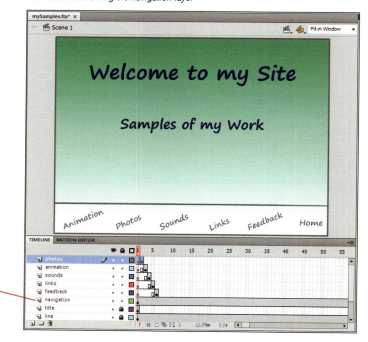

Navigation layer

FIGURE 5
The configured workspace

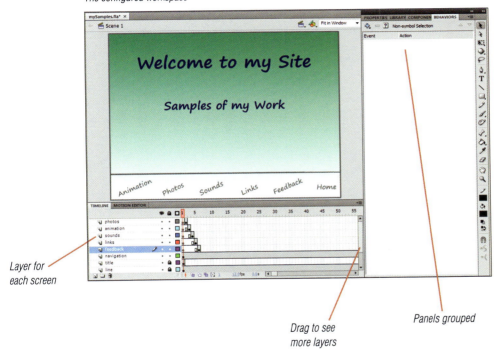

Layer for
each screen

Drag to see
more layers

Panels grouped

10. Open the Behaviors panel and the Components panel.

11. Dock the Components panel and the Behaviors panel with the Library panel and the Properties panel, as shown in Figure 5.

    Hint: Widen the panels area, drag the tab of a panel until it is on top of the tab of another panel and a blue rectangle appears, then release the panel to dock it.

12. Look at the Timeline and notice there is a layer for each screen associated with a link, such as animation, photos, and so on.

13. Drag the **playhead** to view each frame from frame 1 to 6 and notice how the objects on the Stage change.

14. Save the file to save the changes to your workspace.

You configured the workspace by displaying and arranging panels and setting the magnification. You then viewed each frame of the movie.

Use Behaviors to create a button link

1. Click **frame 1** on the Timeline, then click **Home** to select this text button.

2. Verify the Behaviors panel is displayed, then click the **Add Behavior button** to display the options.

3. Point to **Movieclip**, then click **Goto and Play at frame or label**.

   A dialog box appears, as shown in Figure 6, allowing you to specify the movie clip to begin playing when the event (click) occurs and to specify the frame number for the movie clip. In this case, the movie clip to be played is main (_root) Timeline. Frame 1 is the default; this is the frame you want displayed when the user clicks the Home button.

4. Click **OK**.

   Notice the Behaviors panel displays the Event: On Release and the Action: Goto and Play at frame or label.

5. Click **Control** on the menu bar, then click **Test Movie**.

6. Click **Photos**, then click **Home**.

(continued)

FIGURE 6
Specifying the movie clip and frame to play

Default frame

gotoAndPlay(1) and gotoAndStop(1)

Both of these actions direct the playhead to a frame in the movie, in this case frame 1. The difference is that gotoAndStop(1) stops the playhead at frame 1, while gotoAndPlay(1) moves to frame 1 and begins to play the movie. In the mySamples movie, there is a stop action assigned to frame 1. When there is a stop action assigned to frame 1, then the gotoAndPlay(1) action goes to frame 1 and stops.

FIGURE 7

The ActionScript code created using the Movieclip Behavior

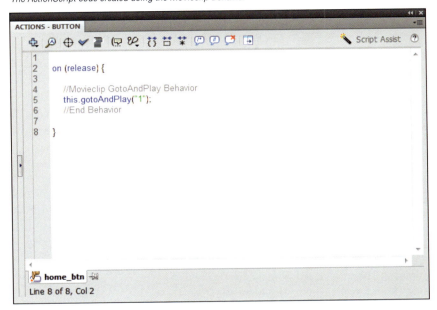

7. Close the Flash Player window.

8. Verify Home is selected, then open the Actions panel.

9. Study the ActionScript code shown in Figure 7 that was automatically created using the Movieclip Behavior.

   This ActionScript generated by the Behavior is saying: "When the home_btn is clicked (on release) the playhead jumps to and plays frame 1. Notice **home_btn** and the button symbol at the bottom left of the Script pane. The ActionScript is applied to this button. The // indicates a comment and is not part of the executable code. Comments can be used to explain code and thus help when editing code. The word "this" in the line of code that reads: this.gotoAndPlay ("1"): refers to the current Timeline.

10. Collapse the Actions panel.

11. Save your work.

You used Behaviors to create a link for the Home button.

WORK WITH
COMPONENTS

What You'll Do

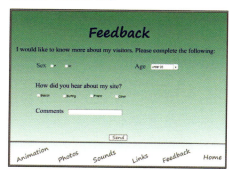

 In this lesson, you will learn how to use Components and Behaviors to load external graphics and animations, play sounds, link to external websites, and create forms.

Using Components

Figure 8 shows the Components panel expanded and the list of available User Interface Components displayed. Each Component name and icon provides a clue to its type, such as Button, CheckBox, and ScrollPane. Many of the User Interface Components are used as part of forms that can gather data from a user. Some, such as the Loader Component, are used to display content. The Loader Component can load external jpg graphic files and swf movie files. The files do not have to be in the Library panel or on the Stage in the original movie. They are loaded from a folder, using either a relative or an absolute path, when the movie is running. This can reduce the size of the movie and allow for easy updating of website content by simply changing the jpg or swf files on the external site.

Depending on the type of Component used, you will need to specify one or more of the following parameters:

- contentPath—This parameter is used to specify the location (server, directory, folder, etc.) for the content that is to be displayed using the Component. For example, when using the Loader component, if the jpg file is not located in the same folder as the movie file, a path to the jpg file needs to be specified.
- scaleContent—This parameter can be set to true or false. If it is set to true,

the content will automatically resize (reduce or enlarge but not crop) to the size of the Component. For example, a Loader Component has a default size of 100 px by 100 px. If a graphic with dimensions of 50 px by 50 px is loaded, and the scaleContent parameter is set to true, the graphic will expand to the larger size. If it is set to false, the Component will be scaled to the smaller graphic size.

■ autoLoad—This parameter can be set to true or false. If it is set to true, the Component will automatically display the specified contents. If it is set to false, the contents will not be displayed until some other action, such as a button click, occurs.

■ label—This parameter allows you to type a text label. For example, you could label a button Component Contact us. The text appears on the button graphic.

To use a Component, you first select the frame and layer where the Component will be placed, then drag the Component from the Component panel to the desired location on the Stage. To complete the process, you use the Component Inspector panel to set the Component parameters.

FIGURE 8
The Component panel with the User Interface Components displayed

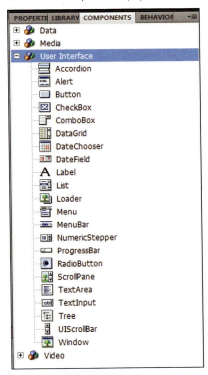

Use Behaviors and Components to create links to websites

1. Verify that the mySamples.fla file is open in Flash, click **frame 5** on the links layer, then click the **Pasteboard** to deselect the Links heading.

2. Display the Components panel, then click the **User Interface expand button** ⊞ (Win) or gray triangle (Mac) to display the UI Components.

   The User Interface is often referred to as UI.

3. Drag a **Button Component** to the Stage and position it below the Links heading.

4. Click **Window** on the menu bar, then click **Component Inspector**.

   The Component Inspector dialog box appears displaying the parameters used with Button Components.

5. Click **Button** in the Value column, type **ADOBE**, as shown in Figure 9, then press **[Enter]** (Win) or **[return]** (Mac).

6. Display the Behaviors panel, click the **Add Behavior button** ✛, point to **Web**, then click **Go to Web Page**.

7. Verify *http://www.adobe.com* is specified for the url, click the **arrow** next to the Open in list box, then click **"_blank"**.

   The Open in option allows you to specify the browser window where the web page will be displayed. The "_self" option displays the web page in the current browser window, replacing the Flash swf movie. The "_blank" option displays the web page in a new browser window, separate from the one displaying the Flash swf movie.

   (continued)

FIGURE 9
Setting the parameters for the button

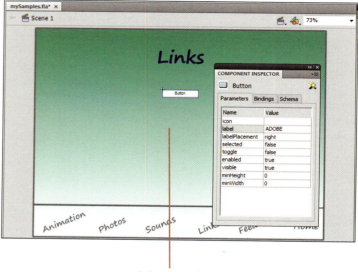

Button changed
to ADOBE

FIGURE 10

The completed dialog box for the Behavior settings to link to a web page

Open in arrow

8. Verify your Go to URL dialog box looks similar to Figure 10, then click **OK**.

9. Drag a second **Button Component** to the Stage and position it below the first button, repeat steps 5 through 7 changing the label to **FAVORITE SITE** in the Component Inspector and the URL to a site of your choice in the Go to URL dialog box, verify the Open in option is set to "_blank", then collapse the Component Inspector.

10. Click **File** on the menu bar, point to **Publish Preview**, then click **Default – (HTML)**.

   The web page appears in a browser window.

11. Click **Links**.

12. Click the **ADOBE button**.

   Note: If a security message appears, do the following: Click OK, close your browser, click File on the menu bar, click Publish Settings, click the Flash tab, click the Local playback security list arrow, click Access network only, click Publish, click OK, then repeat steps 10–12.

13. Close the tab or browser window displaying the Adobe website to return to the mySamples website.

14. Click **FAVORITE SITE**.

15. View the website, then close the tab or browser window to return to the mySamples website.

16. Close the browser window for the mySamples website.

17. Save your work.

You used Components and Behaviors to create buttons that link to external web pages.

Use Components to load graphics

1. Click **frame 2** on the photos layer.

2. Drag a **Loader Component** from the Components panel to the left side of the Stage, as shown in Figure 11.

3. Display the Component Inspector panel, click the **contentPath text box** (Win) in the Value column or click beneath the first occurrence of **true** (Mac) in the Value column, type **rosario.jpg**, then press **[Enter]** (Win) or **[return]** (Mac).

   The rosario.jpg file should be in the same folder as the mySamples.fla file. If it is not, the complete path to the rosario.jpg file needs to be specified.

4. Verify that autoLoad is set to true.

5. Click the word **true** to the right of the scaleContent label, click the **scaleContent list arrow**, then click **false**.

   The Component Inspector panel should resemble Figure 12.

You placed a Loader Component on the Stage and changed the parameters to have it scale to the size of the graphic. You also specified the graphic to be loaded.

FIGURE 11
Positioning the Loader Component on the Stage

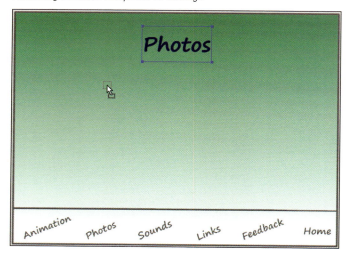

Photos

Animation   Photos   Sounds   Links   Feedback   Home

FIGURE 12
The completed parameters settings for the Loader Component

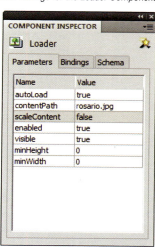

COMPONENT INSPECTOR

Loader

Parameters | Bindings | Schema

Name	Value
autoLoad	true
contentPath	rosario.jpg
scaleContent	false
enabled	true
visible	true
minHeight	0
minWidth	0

Working with Behaviors and Components

FIGURE 13

The rosario.txt in a text editor

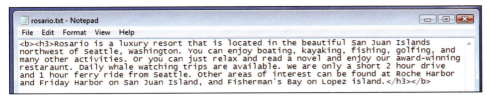

FIGURE 14

The text pasted into the text box in the Component Inspector panel

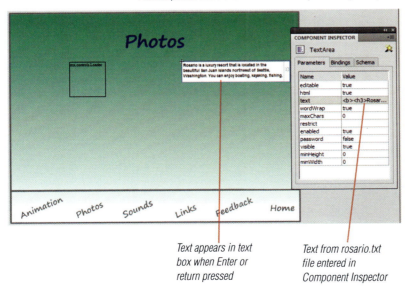

Text appears in text
box when Enter or
return pressed

Text from rosario.txt
file entered in
Component Inspector

Use Components to load text

1. Drag a **TextArea Component** from the Components panel to the Stage and position it to the right of the loader.

2. Using the Component Inspector panel, set editable, html, and wordWrap to true.

3. Display the Properties panel, then set the width to **300** and the height to **60**.

4. Use your file management program to navigate to the drive and folder where your Data Files are stored, then double-click **rosario.txt** to open the file in a text editor, as shown in Figure 13.

   TIP If the text appears on one long line in Notepad, click Format on the menu bar, then click Word Wrap.

   Notice there is some html coding <b> and <h3>, which is used to format the text.

5. Use the text editor menu commands to select all the text, repeat to copy all the text, then close the text editor window.

6. Return to the Flash document, click in the **text text box** in the Component Inspector panel, press and hold **[Ctrl]**, press **[v]** (Win) or [command] (Mac), then press **[Enter]** (Win) or **[return]** (Mac) to paste the text into the text box, as shown in Figure 14.

7. Click **Control** on the menu bar, then click **Test Movie**.

8. Click **Photos**, then drag the **scroll buttons** to read all the text in the text box.

   Note: If the text box overlaps the photo, you can adjust the position of either object when you return to the Flash workspace.

(continued)

9. When you are done, close the Flash Player window, then save your work.

You used the TextArea Component to display text by copying the text to the Component Inspector panel.

Use Components to load an animation (.swf file)

1. Click **frame 3** on the animation layer.

2. Drag a **Loader Component** from the Components panel to the Stage and position it at the left side of the Stage, below the heading Animation.

3. Verify that autoLoad is set to true in the Component Inspector.

4. Click in the **contentPath text box** (Win) or click beneath the first occurrence of **true**(Mac), type **animation.swf**, then press **[Enter]** (Win) or **[return]** (Mac).

   The animation.swf file should be in the same folder as the mySamples.fla file. If it is not, the complete path to the animation.swf file needs to be specified.

5. Set scaleContent to false, as shown in Figure 15.

6. Click **Control** on the menu bar, then click **Test Movie**.

7. Click **Animation**.

8. When you are done, close the Flash Player window, then save your work.

You used a Loader Component to display a .swf file by specifying the autoLoad, contentPath, and scaleContent parameters.

FIGURE 15
The Component Inspector panel with the completed parameter settings

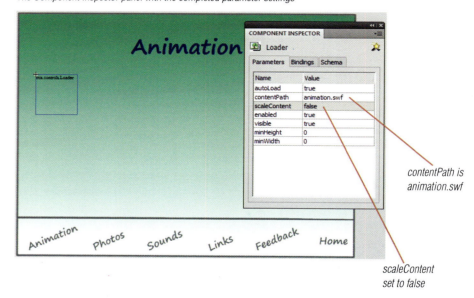

contentPath is animation.swf

scaleContent set to false

FIGURE 16

The completed Sound Properties dialog box

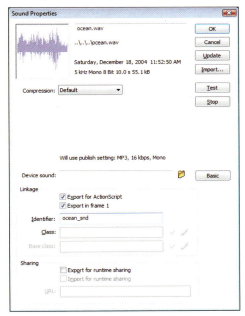

Will use publish setting: MP3, 16 kbps, Mono

FIGURE 17

The completed dialog box for playing a sound from the Library panel

Load Sound from Library

Type the linkage ID of the sound in the library to play:

`ocean_snd`

Type a name for this sound instance for later reference:

`ocean_snd`

☑ Play this sound when loaded

OK   Cancel

Use Components and Behaviors to load a sound from the Library panel

1. Click **frame 4** on the sounds layer.

2. Drag a **Button Component** from the Components panel to the Stage and position it below the heading.

3. Change the label to **THE SEA** in the Component Inspector.

4. Display the Library panel, then open the sounds folder.

5. Right-click (Win) or [control]-click (Mac) **ocean.wav**, then click **Properties**.

6. Click the **Export for ActionScript check box** in the Linkage area, then type **ocean_snd** as the identifier, as shown in Figure 16.

   As you learned in a previous chapter, in order for a sound to be loaded from the Library panel, it needs to be made available through a process called linkage. The sound is selected in the Library panel and, using the Sound Properties dialog box, an identifier is specified. The identifier is used in the ActionScript (which is created using the Load Sound from Library Behavior) to cause the sound to play when the button is clicked.

7. Click **OK**.

8. Display the Behaviors panel, click the **Add Behavior button** ⊕, point to **Sound**, then click **Load Sound from Library**.

9. Click in the first text box (if necessary), type **ocean_snd**, press **[Tab]**, type **ocean_snd**, as shown in Figure 17, then click **OK**.

You used a Button Component and a Behavior to set up a linkage to load a sound from the library.

Use Components and Behaviors to add a streaming sound

1. Drag a second **Button Component** to the Stage and position it below the first button.

2. In the Component Inspector panel, change the label to **THE BEAT**, then press **[Enter]** (Win) or **[return]** (Mac).

3. Click the **Add Behavior button** ⊕ on the Behaviors panel, point to **Sound**, then click **Load streaming MP3 file**.

4. Type **thebeat.mp3** as the URL, press **[Tab]**, then type **thebeat_snd** for the instance name, as shown in Figure 18.

   The file thebeat.mp3 should be in the same folder as the mySamples file. If it is not, the complete path to thebeat.mp3 file needs to be specified.

5. Click **OK**.

6. Click **Control** on the menu bar, click **Test Movie**, then click **Sounds**.

7. Click **THE SEA button** and listen to the sounds.

8. When you are done, click **THE BEAT button** and listen to the sounds.

9. When you are done, close the Flash Player window, then save your work.

You used a Button Component and a Behavior to add a streaming sound.

FIGURE 18
The completed dialog box for specifying an MP3 file to stream

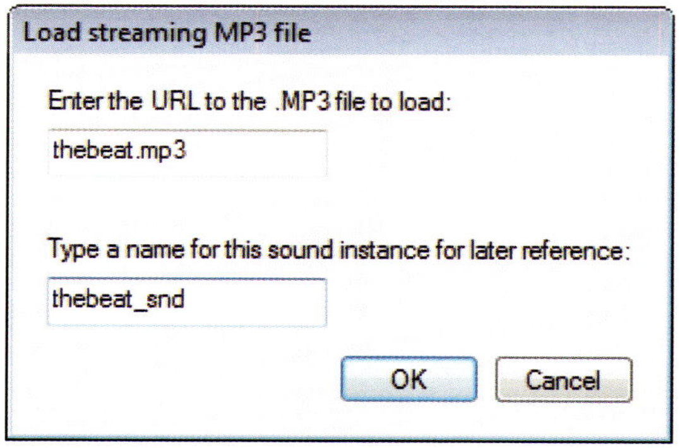

Add streaming sound to a Flash movie

MP3 sound files can be loaded dynamically into a flash movie as it is running—a process called streaming. The MP3 file does not have to be in the Library panel or on the Stage. The process is to select the object (such as a button) that will cause the sound to stream, and then use the Load streaming MP3 file Behavior to identify the file name (and path, if necessary), as well as specify an instance name. The instance name is used in the ActionScript that causes the sound to stream.

FIGURE 19

Changing a label in the Component Inspector panel

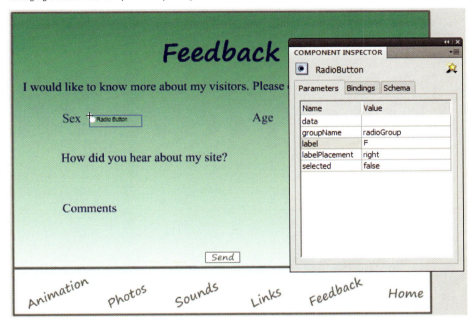

Use Components to create a form

1. Click **frame 6** on the feedback layer.

2. Drag a **RadioButton Component** from the Component panel and position it next to Sex.

3. Change the label in the Component Inspector panel to **F**, as shown in Figure 19.

4. Repeat steps 2 and 3 to add a second RadioButton with the label set to M.

5. Drag a **ComboBox Component** from the Component panel and position it next to Age.

6. In the Component Inspector panel, double-click ☐ in the Value column next to labels.

   The Values dialog box opens.

7. Click the **Add value button** ➕, click **defaultValue**, then type **under 20**.

8. Click the **Add value button** ➕, click **defaultValue**, then type **21 – 40**.

9. Click the **Add value button** ➕, click **defaultValue**, then type **41 – 60**.

(continued)

10. Click the **Add value button** ➕ , click **defaultValue**, then type **over 60**.

    Your screen should resemble Figure 20.

11. Click **OK**.

12. Drag a **CheckBox Component** from the Component panel and position it below How did you hear about my site?

13. Change the label in the Parameters tab of the Component Inspector panel to **Search**.

14. Repeat steps 12 and 13 to add three more check boxes for **Surfing**, **Friend**, and **Other**, as shown in Figure 21.

15. Drag a **TextInput Component** from the Component panel to the Stage and position it next to Comments.

16. Verify that editable is set to true in the Component Inspector panel.

17. Verify the TextInput Component is selected on the Stage, display the Properties panel, then change the width to **200**.

(continued)

FIGURE 20
The completed Combobox Values settings

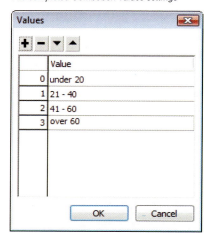

FIGURE 21
The completed check boxes

Radio buttons

Check boxes

Combo box

FIGURE 22
The completed form

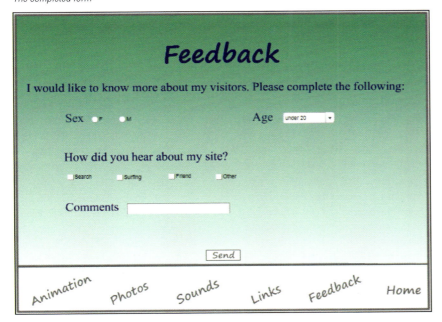

18. Use the arrow keys to adjust the placement of the Component as needed, then click the **Pasteboard** to deselect the Component.

   Your screen should resemble Figure 22.

19. Click **Control** on the menu bar, then click **Test Movie**.

20. Click **Feedback**, then fill in the form.

   Notice that you can only select one radio button, and you can only select one option from the list in the combo box. You can select as many check boxes as you want, and you can type freely in the comments text input box. As you type in the comments input box, the text scrolls horizontally to allow additional text.

21. When you are done, close the Flash Player window.

22. Save your work, then exit Flash.

You used Components to create a form.

Use Behaviors to create a button link.

1. Start Flash, open fl12_2.fla, then save it as **skillsdemo12**.
2. Click Home to select this text button.
3. Display the Behaviors panel.
4. Click the Add Behavior Button, point to Movieclip, then click Goto and Stop at frame or label.
5. Verify that the main (_root) Timeline is specified in the dialog box and 1 is specified for the frame number, then click OK.
6. Save your work.

Use Behaviors and Components to create a web link.

1. Select frame 2 on the web links layer.
2. Display the Components panel, expand the User Interface folder if it is not already open, then drag a Button Component to the middle of the Stage.
3. Display the Component Inspector panel, then change the label to **My School** (or My Company, if appropriate).
4. Click the Add Behavior button on the Behaviors panel, point to Web, then click Go to Web Page.
5. Type in the URL for your school (or company), change the Open in option to "_blank", then click OK to close the dialog box.
6. Click File on the menu bar, point to Publish Preview, then click Default–(HTML).
7. Click the button for the Links to Web sites option, then click the My School or My Company button.

(*Hint*: If a warning box opens, be sure the Local playback security setting on the Flash tab in the Publish Settings dialog box is set to Access network only.)

8. Close your browser and display the Flash document.
9. Save your work.

Use Components to load graphics.

1. Select frame 3 on the loading graphics and text layer.
2. Drag a Loader Component to the left side of the Stage.
3. Set the width to **200** and the height to **200**.
4. Click the contentPath text box on the Parameters tab of the Properties panel, type **kayaking.jpg**, then press [Enter] (Win) or [return] (Mac).
5. Verify that autoLoad and scaleContent are set to true.
6. Verify that the kayaking.jpg file is in the same folder as the skillsdemo12.fla file.
7. Save your work.

Use Components to load text.

1. Drag a TextArea Component to the Stage and position it to the right of the loader.
2. Using the Component Inspector panel, set editable, html, and wordWrap to true.
3. Change the width to **250** and the height to **100**.
4. Use your file management program to navigate to the drive and folder where your Data Files are stored, then open the file kayaking.txt in a text editor.

5. Select and copy the text in the kayaking.txt file, close the text editor, then paste the text into the text box in the Component Inspector panel and press [Enter] (Win) or [return] (Mac).
6. Test the movie, then click the arrow button for Loading graphics and text.
7. Use the scroll bar to read the text, as needed.
8. When done, close the Flash Player window, then save your work.

Use Components to load an animation.

1. Select frame 4 on the loading animations layer.
2. Drag a Loader Component to the left edge of the Stage beneath the heading.
3. Use the Component Inspector to verify that autoLoad is set to true, then set the scaleContent to false.
4. Type **kayaker.swf** for the contentPath, then press [Enter] (Win) or [return] (Mac).
5. Test the movie and click the Loading animations arrow button to view the animation.
6. When done, close the Flash Player window.
7. Save your work.

Use Components and Behaviors to load a sound from the Library panel.

1. Select frame 5 on the loading sound layer.
2. Drag a Button Component to the Stage below the heading.
3. Change the label parameter to **Background-1**.
4. Display the Library panel, right-click (Win) or [control]-click (Mac) accent1.mp3, then click Properties to open the Sound Properties dialog box.

Working with Behaviors and Components

5. Select the Export for ActionScript check box, then type **accent1_snd** as the identifier.

6. Click OK to close the dialog box.

7. Verify that the Background-1 button is selected on the Stage.

8. Click the Add Behavior button on the Behaviors panel, point to Sound, then click Load Sound from Library.

9. Type **accent1_snd** for the linkage ID and the sound instance, then click OK to close the dialog box.

10. Test the movie, click the Loading sounds button, then click the Background-1 button.

11. Close the Flash Player window, then save your work.

Use Components and Behaviors to add a streaming sound.

1. Drag a Button Component to the Stage beneath the Background-1 button.

2. Change the label to **Background-2**.

3. Click the Add Behavior button on the Behaviors panel, point to Sound, then click Load streaming MP3 file.

4. Type **accent2.mp3** as the URL and **accent2_snd** for the instance name, then click OK.

5. Verify that the accent2.mp3 file is located in the same folder as the skillsdemo12.fla file.

6. Test the movie, click the Loading sounds button, then click the Background-2 button. (*Note*: Increase volume on your speakers as needed.)

7. Close the Flash Player window, then save your work.

Use Components to create a form.

1. Select frame 6 on the "a form" layer.

2. Drag two radio Button Components to the right of the financial aid question and label them **yes** and **no**.

3. Drag four CheckBox Components to the right of the Areas of Interest question and label them: **Arts/Hum**; **Business**; **Science**; and **Soc Science**.

4. Drag a CheckBox Component to below the Art/Hum check box and label it: **Other (specify)**.

5. Drag a TextInput Component to the right of the Other (specify) check box.

FIGURE 23
Completed Skills Review

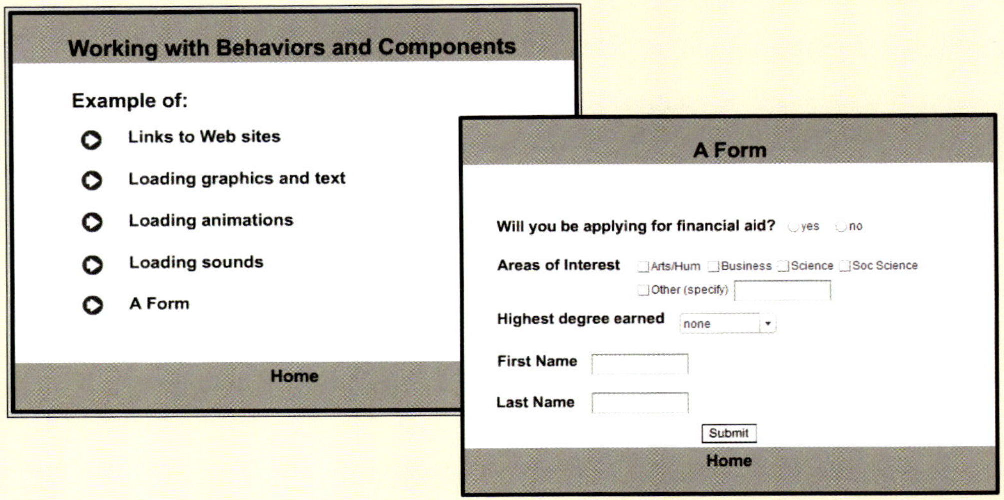

6. Drag a ComboBox to the right of Highest degree earned.

7. Double-click the brackets in the labels text box on the Parameters tab on the Component Inspector.

8. Use the Values dialog box to add the following labels: **none**; **High School**; **2-Year**; **4-Year**; **Masters**; **Doctorate**.

9. Drag Text Input Components to the right of First Name and Last Name.

10. Test the movie, test each Component, and compare your screens to Figure 23.

11. Close the Flash Player window.

12. Save your work.

13. Exit Flash.

The Ultimate Tours travel company wants to promote a special destination that changes periodically. They have asked you to design a page that will be called "Destination Revealed." The page is to contain an animated heading, photo of the site, short description, and sound, as appropriate. The page is to link to the home page. You decide to create the page using Components so that the company can easily update the photo, description, and sound. Figure 24 shows the link on the home page, which was created using a Button Component; the destination page Loader Components for the animated heading and photo, TextArea Component for the description, and a Button Component to play sound.

1. Open fl12_3.fla, then save it as **ultimate-tours12**.

    (*Hint*: If the font used in this file is not available on your computer, you can choose to use a default font or substitute another font.)

2. Select the button with the question mark (?) and use the Behaviors panel to add an action to go to and stop at frame 2 when the button is clicked.

3. Insert a new layer, name it **Destination page**, then add a keyframe to frame 2 on the layer. (*Hint*: You can rename a layer by right-clicking (Win) or [control]-clicking (Mac) the layer name, clicking Properties on the menu

that opens, and then typing the new layer name in the Name text box.)

4. Add a Loader Component to the top of the destination page and change the width to **550** pixels and the height to **50** pixels.

5. Have the Loader Component load the destination.swf file when the viewer enters the page.

6. Add a Loader Component to the middle of the destination page and change the height and width to **200** pixels.

7. Have the Loader Component load the kapalua.jpg file.

FIGURE 24
Sample completed Project Builder 1

8. Add a TextArea Component below the graphic Loader Component and change the width to **200** pixels and height to **60** pixels.

9. Open kapalua.txt in a text editor and copy the text to the text box in the Component Inspector.

10. Drag a Button Component to the right of the graphics loader, label the button **Sounds**, then have the seashore.wav sound play from the Library panel when the button is clicked. (*Hint*: Use seashore_snd as the linkage ID and as the instance name.)

11. Test the movie, then compare it to the sample images shown in Figure 24.

12. Close the Flash Player window, then save your work.

The International Student Association (ISA) is interested in obtaining information that could be used to determine the effectiveness of its website and improve the site contents. Management would like to add a page with a survey form to its website. Management has asked you to develop three sample forms. After reviewing the forms, management will select one to be linked to the ISA home page. The intent is to keep the survey short so that site visitors are encouraged to complete and submit it. Figure 25 shows a sample form. Using this as a guide, create three similar forms.

1. Create a new Flash document, then save it as **isa_survey1**.
2. Add a background color.
3. Place the following on separate layers:
   - a border
   - the ISA heading
   - the text for the form
   - radio buttons for the ratings with appropriate labels
   - comboBox for the times visited with appropriate choice
   - check boxes for the sections visited with appropriate labels
   - TextInput box for the comments
   Make sure the parameters of the Components have the appropriate settings, such as editable for the TextInput Component.

4. Test the movie, then close the Flash Player window.
5. Publish the movie and display it in a browser.
6. Close your browser, then save your work.
7. Create two more forms with similar content for ISA, then test each form.

FIGURE 25

Sample completed Project Builder 2

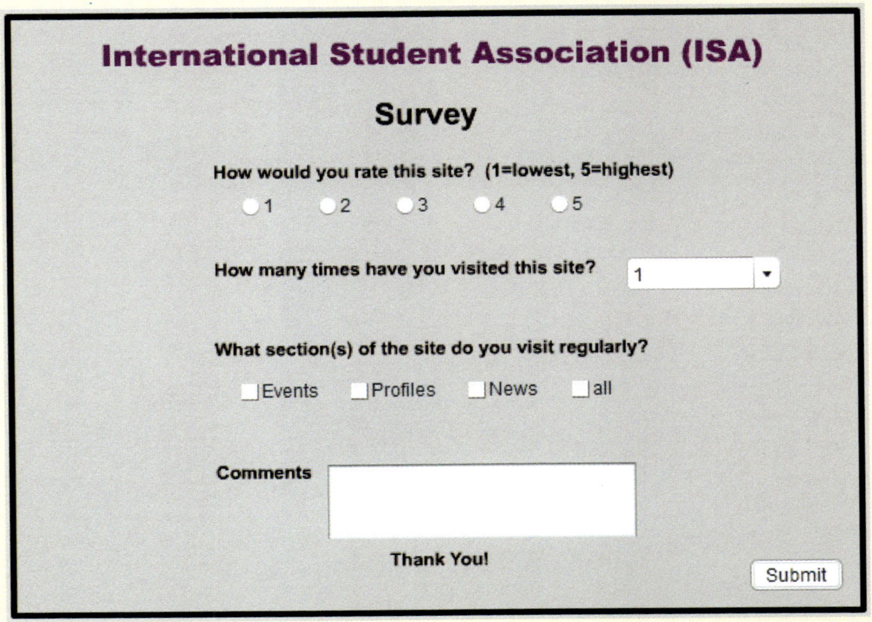

DESIGN PROJECT

Figure 26 shows the home page of a website. Study the figure and complete the following questions. For each question, indicate how you determined your answer.

1. Connect to the Internet, then go to *http://www.nlfoundation.org/SL_tissue_request.cfm.*

2. Open a document in a word processor or create a new document in Flash, save the file as **dpc12**, then answer the following questions.

- Whose website is this?
- What is the goal of the site? (*Note:* Click on the SightLife logo in the upper left of the screen to display the home page to answer this question.)
- Who is the target audience?
- How might Components and Behaviors be used in this site? (*Note:* Return to the Tissue Request Form page to answer this question.)
- What other types of forms might the site developers create?

FIGURE 26
Design Project

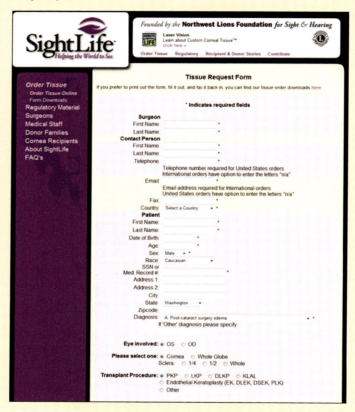

You have been asked by a local artist to help design the gallery page for her website. The page will include samples of her artwork and will be linked to her home page. The gallery page could be used to showcase her work as an online portfolio. Figure 27 shows the home page and a sample gallery page.

1. Open fl12_4.fla, then save it as **gallery**. (*Hint*: The Edwardian Script ITC font is used in this file. If this font is not available on your computer, you can choose to use a default font or substitute another font.)
2. Select the Gallery button and use the Behaviors panel to add an action that displays frame 2 when the button is clicked.
3. Use the steps to create the Gallery page. Add layers as indicated and name them appropriately. Use frame 2 for the Gallery page.
   - Add the Gallery heading in frame 2 on its own layer.
   - Insert a new layer, name it **paintings**, then use Loader Components to have the six paintings appear on the Gallery page. Set the scaleContent parameter so that the Loader scales to the size of the jpg file.
   - Insert a new layer, name it **captions**, then use TextArea Components to have the six painting captions appear on the Gallery page. Set the width of each TextArea Component to **150**.

- Insert a new layer, name it **home button**, then create a Home button in frame 2.
- Use the Behaviors panel to add an action that displays frame 1 when the Home text button is clicked.
4. Verify that all of the .jpg files are in the same folder as the gallery.fla file.
   (*Hint*: Use your file management program to navigate to the drive and folder where your data files are stored.)

5. Test the movie and test the Gallery and Home buttons.
6. Close the Flash Player window.
7. Publish the movie and display it in a browser.
8. Close the browser window, then save your work.

FIGURE 27
Sample completed Portfolio Project

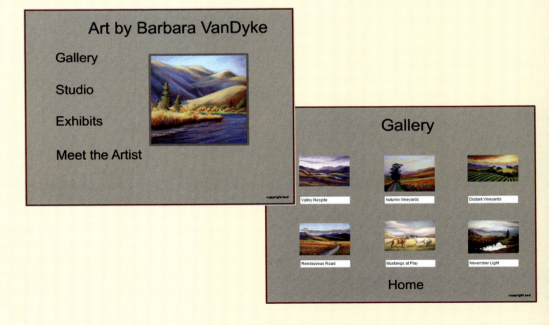

Read the following information carefully!

Find out from your instructor the location where you will store your files.

- To complete many of the chapters in this book, you need to use the Data Files provided on the CD at the back of the book.

- Your instructor will tell you whether you will be working from the CD or copying the files to a drive on your computer or on a server. Your instructor will also tell you where you will store the files you create and modify.

Copy and organize your Data Files.

- Use the Data Files List to organize your files to a USB storage device, network folder, hard drive, or other storage device if you won't be working from the CD.

- Create a subfolder for each chapter in the location where you are storing your files, and name it according to the chapter title (e.g., chapter_1).

- For each chapter you are assigned, copy the files listed in the **Data File Supplied** column into that chapter's folder. Note that you can also copy each folder and its contents to the storage location rather than creating the folders yourself.

- If you are working from the CD, you should still store the files you modify or create in each chapter in the chapter folder.

Find and keep track of your Data Files and completed files.

- Use the **Data File Supplied** column to make sure you have the files you need before starting the chapter or exercise indicated in the **Chapter** column.

- Use the **Student Creates File** column to find out the filename you use when saving your new file for the exercise.

- The **Used in** column tells you the lesson or end of chapter exercise where you will use the file.

Files Used in this Book

Adobe Flash CS4

Chapter	Data File Supplied	Student Creates New File	Used In
1		workspace.fla	Lesson 1
	fl1_1.fla		Lesson 2
		tween.fla	Lesson 3
		layers.fla	Lesson 4
	*layers.fla		Lesson 5
			Lesson 6
	fl1_2.fla		Skills Review
		demonstration.fla	Project Builder 1
	fl1_3.fla		Project Builder 2
		dpc1.fla	Design Project
			Portfolio Project
2	fl2_1.fla		Lessons 1-4
	fl2_2.fla		Lesson 5
	fl2_3.fla		Skills Review
		ultimatetours2.fla	Project Builder 1
		thejazzclub2.fla	Project Builder 2
		dpc2.fla	Design Project
		portfolio2.fla	Portfolio Project
3	fl3_1.fla		Lesson 1
	fl3_2.fla		Lessons 2-4
	islandview.jpg sailboat.ai	sailing.fla	Lesson 5
	fl3_3.fla BeachScene.jpg		Skills Review
	**ultimatetours2.fla UTLogo.jpg		Project Builder 1
		isa3.fla	Project Builder 2
		dpc3.fla	Design Project
	**portfolio2.fla		Portfolio Project

*Created in a previous Lesson or Skills Review in current chapter

**Created in a previous chapter

Chapter	Data File Supplied	Student Creates File	Used In
4	fl4_1.fla fl4_2.fla		Lesson 1
	fl4_3.fla		Lesson 2
	fl4_4.fla fl4_5.fla		Lesson 3
	fl4_6.fla fl4_7.fla fl4_8.fla		Lesson 4
	fl4_9.fla		Lesson 5
	fl4_10.fla		Lesson 6
	fl4_11.fla		Skills Review
	**ultimatetours3.fla ship.gif		Project Builder 1
		jumper4.fla	Project Builder 2
		dpc4.fla	Design Project
	**portfolio3.fla		Portfolio Project
5	fl5_1.fla		Lesson 1
	fl5_2.fla CarSnd.wav beep.wav		Lesson 2
	fl5_3.fla fireworks.mov		Lesson 3
	fl5_4.fla		Lesson 4
	fl5_5.fla fl5_6.fla		Lesson 5
	fl5_7.fla		Lesson 6
	fl5_8.fla fl5_9.fla tour-video.mov		Skills Review
	fl5_10.fla **ultimatetours.fla		Project Builder 1
	fl5_11.fla		Project Builder 2
		dpc5.fla	Design Project
	**portfolio4.fla		Portfolio Project

*Created in a previous Lesson or Skills Review in current chapter

**Created in a previous chapter

Chapter	Data File Supplied	Student Creates New File	Used In
6	fl6_1.fla	planeLoop.gif planeLoop.jpg	Lesson 1
	fl6_2.fla		Lesson 2
	fl6_3.fla		Lesson 3
	*planeFun.fla	planeFun-caption.html	Lesson 4
	fl6_4.fla	skillsdemo6.jpg skillsdemo6-caption.html	Skills Review
	**ultimatetours5.fla	ultimatetours6.fla ultimatetours6.gif ultimatetours6.jpg ultimatetours6-caption.html	Project Builder 1
		publish6.gif publish6.jpg publish6-caption.html	Project Builder 2
		dpc6.fla	Design Project
	**portfolio5.fla	portfolio6.jpg portfolio6-caption.html	Portfolio Project

*Created in a previous Lesson or Skills Review in current chapter

**Created in a previous chapter

Chapter	Data File Supplied	Student Creates New File	Used In
7	dragonfly.png tree.ai, background.psd		Lesson 1
	meadow.jpg		Lessons 2
	moon.jpg		Lesson 3
	fl7_1.fla rose.jpg		Lesson 4
	dayMoon.jpg logo.png nightsky.jpg mountain.jpg	skillsdemo7.fla	Skills Review
	gtravel1.jpg gtravel2.jpg gtravel3.jpg gtravel4.jpg gtravel5.jpg gtravel6.jpg	ultimatetours7.fla	Project Builder 1
	gantho1.jpg gantho2.jpg gantho3.jpg gantho4.jpg gantho5.jpg	anthoart7.fla	Project Builder 2
		dpc7.fla	Design Project
		portfolio7.fla	Portfolio Project
8	fl8_1.fla		Lesson 1
	fl8_2.fla		Lesson 2
	fl8_3.fla		Lessons 3-4
	fl8_4.fla		Skills Review
		ultimatetours8.fla	Project Builder 1
		ocean_life8.fla	Project Builder 2
		dpc8.fla	Design Project
	**portfolio7.fla		Portfolio Project

**Created in a previous chapter

Chapter	Data File Supplied	Student Creates New File	Used In
9	fl9_1.fla		Lesson 1
	fl9_2.fla		Lesson 2
	fl9_3.fla		Lesson 3
	fl9_4.fla		Lesson 4
	fl9_5.fla		Skills Review
	**ultimatetours8.fla		Project Builder 1
		test_question9.fla	Project Builder 2
		dpc9.fla	Design Project
	**portfolio8.fla		Portfolio Project
10	fl10_1.fla accent1.mp3 accent2.mp3 background.mp3		Lessons 1-2
	fl10_2.fla		Lesson 2
	*nightclub.fla		Lesson 3
	fl10_3.fla		Lesson 4
	fl10_4.fla		Skills Review
	fl10_5.fla		Project Builder 1
	fl10_6.fla		Project Builder 2
		dpc10.fla	Design Project
	**portfolio9.fla accent1.mp3 accent2.mp3 background.mp3 portfolio_voiceover.wav		Portfolio Project

**Created in a previous chapter

Chapter	Data File Supplied	Student Creates New File	Used In
11	fl11_1.fla		Lesson 1
	fl11_2.fla fl11_3.fla		Lesson 2
	fl11_4.fla frog.swf fish.swf		Lesson 3
	fl11_5.fla fl11_6.fla		Lesson 4
	fl11_7.fla easy_level.swf hard_level.swf		Skills Review
	fl11_8.fla specials.swf		Project Builder 1
	fl11_9.fla		Project Builder 2
		dpc11.fla	Design Project
	shirt.swf shirt2.swf sounds.swf	portfolio11.fla	Portfolio Project

Chapter	Data File Supplied	Student Creates New File	Used In
12	fl12_1.fla		Lesson 1
	rosario.jpg rosario.txt animation.swf thebeat.mp3		Lesson 2
	fl12_2.fla kayaking.jpg kayaking.txt kayaker.swf accent1.mp3 accent2.mp3		Skills Review
	fl12_3.fla destination.swf kapalua.jpg kapalua.txt		Project Builder 1
		isa_survey1.fla	Project Builder 2
		dpc12.fla	Design Project
	fl12_4.fla AutumnVineyrds.jpg DistantVineyards.jpg Mustangs.jpg Novlight.jpg Rendezvous.jpg ValleyRespite.jpg yakimariver.jpg		Portfolio Project

3D Effects
A process in Flash that animates 2D objects through 3D space with 3D Transformation tools.

Absolute path
A path containing an external link that references a link on a web page outside of the current website, and includes the protocol "http" and the URL, or address, of the web page.

ActionScript
The Adobe Flash scripting language used by developers to add interactivity to movies, control objects, exchange data, and create complex animations.

Actions panel
The panel where you create and edit Action Script code for an object or a frame.

Actions Toolbox pane
The section of the Actions panel displaying the categories of actions that can be selected to build ActionsScript code.

Adobe Flash CS4
A development tool that allows you to create compelling interactive experiences, often by using animation.

Animated graphic symbol
An animation stored as a single, reusable symbol in the Library panel.

Animation
The perception of motion caused by the rapid display of a series of still images.

Balance
In screen design, the distribution of optical weight in the layout. Optical weight is the ability of an object to attract the viewer's eye, as determined by the object's size, shape, color, and other factors.

Bandwidth Profiler
A feature used when testing a Flash movie that allows you to view a graphical representation of the size of each frame and the frame-by-frame download process.

Behaviors
Blocks of prewritten ActionScript code that you can apply by using pop-up menus and dialog boxes without having to write the ActionScript code.

Bitmap image
An image based on pixels, rather than mathematical formulas. Also referred to as a raster image.

Break apart
The process of breaking apart text to place each character in a separate text block. Also, the process of separating groups, instances, and bitmaps into ungrouped, editable elements.

Broadband
A type of data transmission, such as DSL and cable, in which a wide band of frequencies is available to transmit more information at the same time.

Button symbol
Object on the Stage that is used to provide interactivity, such as jumping to another frame on the Timeline.

Code hints
Hints appearing in a pop-up window that give the syntax or possible parameters for an action.

Components
Predeveloped movie clips that can quickly add functionality to a movie by dragging and dropping them from the Components panel to the Stage. Commonly used for creating forms with boxes for entering user data (name, address, and so on), check boxes, and drop-down menus.

Conditional action
ActionScript that tests whether or not certain conditions have been met and, if so, can perform other actions.

Controller
A window that provides the playback controls for a movie.

Coordinate
The position on the Stage of a pixel as measured across (X coordinate) and down (Y coordinate) the Stage.

Decrement action
An ActionScript operator, indicated by — (two minus signs), that subtracts 1 unit from a variable or expression.

Dock

A collection of panels or buttons surrounded by a dark gray bar. The arrows in the dock are used to maximize and minimize the panels.

Document

A Flash file which, by default, is given the .fla file extension.

Dot syntax

A way to refer to the hierarchical nature of the path to a movie clip symbol, variable, function, or other object, similar to the way slashes are used to create a path name to a file in some operating systems.

Drop Zone

A blue outline area that indicates where a panel can be moved.

DSL

A broadband Internet connection speed that is available through phone lines.

Dynamic text field

A field created on the Stage with the Text tool that takes information entered by a user and stores it as a variable.

Embedded video

A video file that has been imported into a Flash document and becomes part of the SWF file.

Event sound

A sound that plays independently of the Timeline. The sound starts in the keyframe to which it is added, but it can continue playing even after a movie ends. An event sound must download completely before it begins playing.

Expressions

Formulas for manipulating or evaluating the information in variables.

External links

Links from a Flash file or movie to another website, another file, or an e-mail program.

File Transfer Protocol (FTP)

A standard method for transferring files from a development site to a web server.

Filters

Special effects, such as drop shadows, that can be applied to text using options on the Filters area in the Properties panel.

Flash Player

A free program from Adobe that allows Flash movies (.swf and .exe formats) to be viewed on a computer.

Flowchart

A visual representation of how the contents in an application or a website are organized and how various screens are linked.

Frame-by-frame animation

An animation created by specifying the object that is to appear in each frame of a sequence of frames (also called a frame animation).

Frame label

A text name for a keyframe, which can be referenced within ActionScript code.

Frames

Individual cells that make up the Timeline in Flash.

GET

An option for sending variables from a Flash movie to another URL or file for processing. GET is best for small amounts of information, as it can only send a string of up to 1,024 characters.

Gradient

A color fill that makes a gradual transition from one color to another causing the colors to blend into one another.

Graphic Symbols

Objects, such as drawings, that are converted to symbols and stored in the Library panel. A graphic symbol is the original object. Instance (copy) of a symbol can be made by dragging the symbol from the Library to the Stage.

Graphics Interchange Format (GIF)

A graphics file format that creates compressed bitmap images. GIF graphics are viewable on the web.

Guide layers
Layers used to align objects on the Stage.

Increment action
An ActionScript operator, indicated by ++ (two plus signs), that adds 1 unit to a variable or expression.

Input text field
A field created on the Stage with the Text tool that displays information derived from variables.

Instances
Editable copies of symbols that are placed on the Stage.

Inverse Kinematics
A process using a bone structure that allows objects to be animated in natural ways, such as a character running, jumping or kicking.

Joint Photographic Experts Group (JPEG)
A graphics file format that is especially useful for photographic images. JPEG graphics are viewable on the web.

Keyframe
A frame that signifies a change in a movie, such as the end of an animation.

Layers
Rows on the Timeline that are used to organize objects and that allow the stacking of objects on the Stage.

Level
A hierarchical designation used when loading new movies into the current movie; similar to layers on the Timeline.

Library panel
The panel that contains the objects (graphics, buttons, sounds, movie clips, etc.) that are used in a Flash movie.

Linkage identifier string
The name used to identify a sound from the Library panel in an ActionScript statement. You assign a linkage identifier in the Linkage Properties dialog box.

Loader Component
A Component that can load external jpg graphic files and swf movie files.

Main Timeline
The primary Timeline for a Flash movie that is displayed when you start a new Flash document.

Mask layer
A layer used to cover up the objects on another layer(s) and, at the same time, create a window through which you can view various objects on the other layer.

Menu bar
A bar across the top of the program window that is located under the program title bar and lists the names of the menus that contain commands.

Merge Drawing Model
A drawing mode that causes overlapping drawings (objects) to merge so that a change in the top object, such as moving it, may affect the object beneath it.

Morphing
The animation process of changing one object into another, sometimes unrelated, object.

Motion guide
Feature that allows you to draw a path and attach motion-tweened animations to the path. A motion guide has its own layer.

Motion Tween Presets
Pre-built animations, such as a bouncing effect, that can be applied to objects in Flash.

Motion tweening
The process used in Flash to automatically fill in the frames between keyframes in an animation that changes the properties of an object such as the position, size, or color. Motion tweening works on groups and symbols.

Movement
In screen design, the way the viewer's eye moves through the objects on the screen.

Movie clip symbol
An animation stored as a single, reusable symbol in the Library panel. It has its own Timeline, independent of the main Timeline.

MP3 (MPEG-1 Audio Layer 3)
A sound compression option primarily used for music and longer streaming sounds, but which can also be applied to speech.

Nesting
Including another symbol within a symbol, such as nesting a graphic symbol, button, or another movie clip symbol within a movie clip symbol.

Number variable
In ActionScript, a variable type that contains a number with which you can use arithmetic operators, such as addition and subtraction.

Object Drawing Model
A drawing mode that allows you to overlap objects, which are then kept separate, so that changes in one object do not affect another object. You must break apart these objects before being able to select their stroke and fills.

Objects
Items, such as drawings and text, that are placed on the Stage and can be edited and manipulated.

Onion Skin
Feature that displays the outlines of an animated object so that the positions of the object in a series of frames can be viewed all at once.

Panels
Individual windows in Flash used to view, organize, and modify objects and features in a movie.

Parameters
Properties of Components, such as autoload, that can be changed using the Properties panel or the Component Inspector.

_parent
In creating target paths with dot syntax, the movie clip in which the current clip is nested.

Parent-child relationship
A description of the hierarchical relationship that develops between nested symbols, especially nested movie clip symbols. When you insert a movie clip inside another movie clip, the inserted clip is considered the child and the original clip is the parent.

Pasteboard
The gray area surrounding the Flash Stage where objects can be placed and manipulated. Neither the pasteboard nor objects placed on it appear in the movie unless the objects move onto the Stage during the playing of the movie.

Persistence of vision
The phenomenon of the eye capturing and holding an image for one-tenth of a second before processing another image.

Pixel
Each dot in a bitmap graphic. Pixels have an exact position on the screen and a precise color.

Playhead
An indicator specifying which frame is playing in the Timeline of a Flash movie.

Portable Network Graphics (PNG)
A graphics file format developed specifically for images that are to be used on the web.

POST
An option for sending variables from a Flash movie to another URL or file for processing. POST collects variables and sends them in a file. POST can accommodate more variable information and is more secure than the alternate method of sending variables, GET.

Preloader
An animation and ActionScript code (which could be a movie clip) that is played at the beginning of a movie to provide feedback to the viewer on the progress of downloading the movie frames.

Progressive download
The process of delivering an external Flash FLV video file at runtime.

Projector
A standalone executable movie, such as a Windows .exe file.

Properties panel (also called Property inspector)
In Flash, the panel that displays the properties of the selected object, such as size and

color, on the Stage or the selected frame. The Properties panel can be used to edit selected properties.

Property inspector
A panel that allows you to display and edit the properties of a selected object or frame.

Publish
The process used to generate the files necessary for delivering Flash movies on the web, such as swf and HTML files.

QuickTime
A file format used for movies and animations that requires a QuickTime Player.

Raster image
An image based on pixels, rather than mathematical formulas. Also referred to as a bitmap image.

Raw
A sound compression option that exports a sound with no compression. You can set stereo to mono conversion and a sampling rate.

Registration point
The point on an object that is used to position the object on the Stage using ActionScript code.

Relative path
A path to a file based on the current location of the Flash .swf file referencing the file.

Rulers
On screen markers that help you precisely measure and position an object. Rulers can be displayed using the View menu.

_root
Refers to the main Timeline when creating target paths with dot syntax.

Scene
A Timeline designated for a specific part of the movie. Scenes are a way to organize long movies by dividing the movie into sections.

Script Assist
A feature found in the Actions panel which can be used to generate ActionScript without having to write programming code.

Script Navigator pane
The section of the Actions panel that provides a list of elements (objects, movie clips, frames) that contain scripts. It can be used to quickly locate an object, such as a button, and display its code.

Script pane
The section of the Actions panel that displays the code and a toolbar for editing the code. Also, displays the Script Assist dialog box.

Shape hints
Indicators used to control the shape of a complex object as it changes appearance during an animation.

Shape tweening
The process of animating an object so that its shape changes. Shape tweening requires editable graphics.

Sound object
A built-in object that allows ActionScript to recognize and control a sound. To associate a specific sound with a sound object, use the new Sound action.

Speech compression
A sound compression option best used for voice-overs and other speech. You can set a sampling rate when you choose this option.

Stage
The area of the Flash workspace that contains the objects that are part of the movie and that will be seen by the viewers.

Stage-level object
A vector object that you draw directly on the Stage, unlike a symbol, which you place on the Stage from the Library panel.

Start synchronization option
A synchronization option that can be applied to sounds and that acts just like event sounds, but that will not begin again if an instance of the sound is already playing.

Stop synchronization option
A synchronization option that can be applied to sounds and lets you end an event sound at a specific keyframe.

Storyboard

A sketch showing the layout of the various screens. It describes the contents and illustrates how text, graphics, animation, and other screen elements will be positioned. It also indicates the navigation process, such as menus and buttons.

Streaming sound

A sound that is tied to the Timeline. No matter its length, a streaming sound stops at the end of the movie. Streaming sounds can start playing as they download.

Streaming video

The process of delivering video content using a constant connection established with a Flash Communication Server.

String variable

In ActionScript, a sequence of characters including letters, numbers, and punctuation. To indicate a string variable, enclose it in single or double quotation marks.

Symbols

The basic building blocks of a Flash application. There are three types: graphic, button, and movie clip.

T1

An extremely fast Internet connection that is widely used by businesses.

Target

A reference in an action to a movie clip symbol or other object that includes a path and name.

Time In control, Time Out control

Controls in the Edit Envelope dialog box that let you trim the length of a sound file.

Timeline

The component of Flash used to organize and control the movie's contents over time by specifying when each object appears on the Stage.

Tools panel

The component of Flash that contains a set of tools used to draw, select, and edit graphics and text. It is divided into four sections.

Trace

The process of turning a bitmap image into vector paths for animation and other purposes.

Transformation point

The point used to orient an object as it is being animated and the point of an object that snaps to a motion guide.

Tweening

The process of filling the in-between frames in an animation.

Unity

Intra-screen unity refers to how the various screen objects relate in screen design.

Inter-screen unity refers to the design that viewers encounter as they navigate from one screen to another.

Upload

The process of transferring files from a local drive to a web server.

Variable

A container that holds information and is used in ActionScript code.

Vector image

An image calculated and stored according to mathematical formulas rather than pixels, resulting in a smaller file size and the ability to resize the image without a loss in quality.

Web server

A computer dedicated to hosting web sites that is connected to the Internet and configured with software to handle requests from browsers.

Workspace

The area in the Flash program window where you work with documents, movies, tools, and panels.